KINANTHROPOMETRY AND EXERCISE PHYSIOLOGY LABORATORY MANUAL

Volume One: Anthropometry

D0082371

Kinanthropometry is the study of human body size, shape and form and how those characteristics relate to human movement and sporting performance. In this fully updated and revised edition of the classic guide to kinanthropometric theory and practice, leading international sport and exercise scientists offer a clear and comprehensive introduction to essential principles and techniques.

Each chapter guides the reader through the planning and conduct of practical and laboratory sessions and includes a survey of current theory and contemporary literature relating to that topic. The book is fully illustrated and includes worked examples, exercises, research data, chapter summaries and guides to further reading throughout.

Volume One – *Anthropometry* – covers key topics such as:

- Body composition, proportion and growth
- Evaluating posture, flexibility and range of motion
- Children's physiology, maturation and sport performance
- Field work
- Statistical methods for kinesiology and sport
- Accurate scaling of data for sport and exercise sciences.

The *Kinanthropometry and Exercise Physiology Laboratory Manual* is essential reading for all serious students and researchers working in sport and exercise science, kinesiology and human movement.

Roger Eston (ISAK Level 3 Anthropometrist) is a Professor of Human Physiology and Head of School of Sport and Health Sciences at Exeter University.

Thomas Reilly is Professor of Sports Science and Director of the Research Institute for Sport and Exercise Sciences at Liverpool John Moores University.

KINANTHROPOMETRY AND EXERCISE PHYSIOLOGY LABORATORY MANUAL

Tests, procedures and data
Third Edition

Volume One: Anthropometry

Edited by
Roger Eston

and

Thomas Reilly

Routledge
Taylor & Francis Group

LONDON AND NEW YORK

First edition published 1996
by E & FN Spon, an imprint of the Taylor & Francis Group

Second edition published 2001
by Routledge
2 Park Square, Milton Park, Abingdon, Oxon, OX14 4RN

Third edition published 2009
by Routledge
2 Park Square, Milton Park, Abingdon, Oxon, OX14 4RN

Simultaneously published in the USA and Canada
by Routledge
270 Madison Avenue, New York, NY 10016

Routledge is an imprint of the Taylor & Francis Group, an informa business

© 1996 E & FN Spon, 2001, 2009 Roger Eston and Thomas Reilly for selection and
editorial matter; individual contributors, their contribution

Typeset in Sabon by Pindar NZ, Auckland, New Zealand
Printed and bound in Great Britain by TJ International Ltd, Padstow, Cornwall

British Library Cataloguing in Publication Data
A catalogue record for this book is available from the British Library.

Library of Congress Cataloging-in-Publication Data
Kinanthropometry and exercise physiology laboratory manual : tests, procedures, and
data / edited by Roger Eston and Thomas Reilly.—3rd ed.
    p. ; cm.
    Includes bibliographical references and index.
    1. Anthropometry—Laboratory manuals. 2. Exercise—Physiological aspects—
Laboratory manuals. I. Eston, Roger G. II. Reilly, Thomas, 1941-
    [DNLM: 1. Biomechanics—Laboratory Manuals. 2. Anthropometry—methods—
Laboratory Manuals. 3. Exercise—physiology—Laboratory Manuals. 4. Kinesiology,
Applied—methods—Laboratory Manuals. WE 25 K51 2009]
    GV435.K56 2009
    599.94—dc22   2008018782

ISBN 13: 978-0-415-43720-2 pbk
ISBN 13: 978-0-415-43721-9 hbk

ISBN 10: 0-415-43721-0 hbk
ISBN 10: 0-415-43720-2 pbk

ISBN 978-0-415-46671-4 set

CONTENTS

11 Scaling: adjusting for differences in body size   300

EDWARD M. WINTER AND ALAN M. NEVILL

ILLUSTRATIONS

FIGURES

TABLES

LIST OF CONTRIBUTORS FOR
ANTHROPOMETRY

Greg Atkinson
Research Institute for Sport and Exercise
Sciences
Liverpool John Moores University, Henry
Cotton Building
Liverpool, UK

Alan Barker
School of Sport and Health Sciences
St Lukes Campus
University of Exeter
Exeter, UK

Gaston Beunen
Department of Biomedical Kinesiology
Faculty of Kinesiology and Rehabilitation
Sciences
Leuven (Heverlee), Belgium

Colin Boreham
Institute for Sport and Health
University College Dublin
Belfield, Ireland

Jan Borms
Human Biometry and Health Promotion
Vrije Universiteit Brussel
Brussels, Belgium

J. E. Lindsay Carter
School of Exercise and Nutritional Sciences
San Diego State University
San Diego, USA

Peter H. Dangerfield
School of Medical Education
The University of Liverpool
Liverpool, UK

William Duquet
Department of Human Biometry and
Biomechanics
Vrije Universiteit Brussel
Brussel, Belgium

Roger Eston
School of Sport and Health Sciences
St Lukes Campus
University of Exeter
Exeter, UK

Michael Hawes
Faculty of Kinesiology
University of Calgary
Calgary, Canada

Alan Martin
School of Human Kinetics
University of British Colombia
Vancouver, Canada

Alan M. Nevill
School of Sport, Performing Arts and
Leisure
University of Wolverhampton
Walsall, UK

Tim S. Olds
Centre for Applied Anthropometry
University of South Australia
Adelaide, Australia

Thomas Reilly
Research Institute for Sport and Exercise
Sciences
Liverpool John Moores University, Henry
Cotton Building
Liverpool, UK

Ann V. Rowlands
School of Sport and Health Sciences
St Lukes Campus
University of Exeter
Exeter, UK

Mark A. Scott
Research Institute for Sport and Exercise
Sciences
Liverpool John Moores University, Henry
Cotton Building
Liverpool, UK

Peter Van Roy
Department of Experimental Anatomy
Vrije Universiteit Brussel
Brussels, Belgium

Emmanuel van Praagh
Exercise Physiology
Université Blaise Pascal
Clermont-Ferrand, France

Edward M. Winter
The Centre for Sport and Exercise Science
Sheffield Hallam University
Collegiate Crescent Campus
Sheffield, UK

PREFACE

The subject area referred to as kinanthropometry has a rich history, although the subject itself was not formalised as a discipline until the International Society for Advancement of Kinanthropometry (ISAK) was established in Glasgow in 1986. The Society supports its own international conferences and publication of proceedings linked with these events. Until the publication of the first edition of *Kinanthropometry and Exercise Physiology Laboratory Manual: Tests, Procedures and Data* by the present editors in 1996, there was no laboratory manual that would serve as a compendium of practical activities for students in this field. Accordingly, the text was published under the aegis of ISAK in an attempt to make good the deficit.

Kinanthropometrists concern themselves with the relation of structure and function of the human body, particularly within the context of movement. Kinanthropometry has applications in a wide range of areas including, for example, biomechanics, ergonomics, growth and development, human sciences, medicine, nutrition, physical therapy, healthcare, physical education and sports science. Initially, the idea for the book was motivated by the need for a suitable laboratory resource that academic staff could use in

the planning and conduct of class practicals in these areas.

The content of the first edition in 1996 was designed to cover specific teaching modules in kinanthropometry and other academic programmes, mainly physiology, within which kinanthropometry is sometimes subsumed. It was intended also to include practical activities of relevance to clinicians, for example, measuring metabolic functions, muscle performance, physiological responses to exercise, posture and so on. In all cases the emphasis was placed on the anthropometric aspects of the topic. By the time of the second edition in 2001, all the original chapters were updated and seven new chapters were added, mainly concerned with physiological topics. Consequently, it was decided to separate the overall contents of the edition into two volumes, one focusing on anthropometry practicals whilst the other contained largely physiological topics.

It seems that 6–7 years is a reasonable life cycle for a laboratory-based text in a field that is expanding. In the third edition, the structure of the previous two volumes has been retained without the need for any additional new chapters. Nevertheless, all chapters in both volumes have been altered and updated – some more radically than others needed to be. New content is reflected in the literature trawled, the new illustrations included and changes in the detail of some of the practical laboratory exercises.

The content of both volumes is oriented towards laboratory practicals, but offers much more than a series of laboratory exercises. A comprehensive theoretical background is provided for each topic so that users of the text are not obliged to conduct extensive literature searches in order to place the topic in context. Each chapter contains an explanation of the appropriate methodology and, where possible, an outline of specific laboratory-based practicals. Across all the content is an emphasis on tests, protocol and procedures, data collection and handling and the correct interpretation of observations. The last two chapters in Volume 1 are concerned with basic statistical techniques and scaling procedures, which are designed to inform researchers and students about data analysis. The information should promote proper use of statistical techniques for treating data collected on human participants as well as avoid common abuses of basic statistical tools.

Many of the topics included within the two volumes called for unique individual approaches and so a rigid structure was not imposed on contributors. Nevertheless, in each chapter there is a clear set of aims for the practicals outlined and an extensive coverage of background theory. As each chapter is independent of the others, there is an inevitable reappearance of concepts across chapters, including those of efficiency, metabolism, maximal performance, measurement error and issues of scaling. Nevertheless, the two volumes represent a collective set of experimental sessions for academic programmes in kinanthropometry and exercise physiology.

It is hoped that this third edition in two volumes will stimulate improvements in teaching and instruction strategies in kinanthropometry and physiology. In this way, editors and authors will have made a contribution towards furthering the education of the next generation of specialists concerned with the relation between human structure and function.

Roger Eston
Thomas Reilly

INTRODUCTION

The third edition of this twin-volume text covers both anthropometry (Volume 1) and exercise physiology (Volume 2). These volumes are complementary in covering areas related to sport and exercise sciences, physical therapy and healthcare professionals. Across all the content is an emphasis on tests, protocol and procedures, data collection and analysis and the correct interpretation of observations.

The first edition of this book was published as a single volume in 1996. The book has been used widely as a laboratory manual in both undergraduate and post-graduate programmes and in the continuous education and development workshops of a number of professional bodies. The subject area referred to as kinanthropometry has a rich history although the subject itself was not formalised as a discipline until the International Society for Advancement of Kinanthropometry (ISAK) was established in Glasgow in 1986. The Society supports its own international conferences and publication of Proceedings linked with these events. Until the publication of the first edition of *Kinanthropometry and Exercise Physiology Laboratory Manual: Tests, Procedures and Data* by the present editors in 1996, there was no laboratory manual that would serve as a compendium of practical activities for students in this field. Accordingly, the text was published under the aegis of ISAK in an attempt to make good the deficit, later expanded into two volumes to reflect related areas and topics.

Kinanthropometrists are concerned about the relation between structure and function of the human body, particularly within the context of movement. Kinanthropometry has applications in a wide range of areas including, for example, biomechanics, ergonomics, growth and development, human sciences, medicine, nutrition, physical therapy, healthcare, physical education and sports science. Initially, the idea for the book was motivated by the need for a suitable laboratory resource that academic staff could use in the planning and conduct of class practicals in these areas.

The content of the first edition in 1996 was designed to cover specific teaching modules in kinanthropometry and other academic programmes, mainly physiology, within which kinanthropometry is sometimes subsumed. It was intended also to include practical activities of relevance to clinicians; for example, measuring metabolic functions, muscle performance, physiological responses to exercise, posture and so on. In all cases the emphasis was placed on the anthropometric aspects of the topic. By the time of the second edition in 2001, all the original chapters were updated and seven new chapters were added, mainly concerned with physiological topics. Consequently, it was decided to separate the overall contents of the edition into two volumes, one focusing on anthropometry practicals whilst the other contained largely physiological topics.

In the current revised edition, the ways in which anthropometry and physiology complement each other on academic programmes in the sport and exercise sciences are evident in the practical laboratory sessions across the two volumes. The structure of the previous two volumes has been retained, without the need for any additional new chapters. Nevertheless all chapters in both volumes have been altered and updated – some more radically than others needed to be. New content is reflected in the literature trawled, the new illustrations included and changes in the detail of some of the practical laboratory exercises. New authors are also included where appropriate. The most radical changes in Volume 1 have been introduced by the new authors in Chapters 1, 8 and 10. The initial chapter on body composition analysis has been re-vamped to acknowledge developments in this field and discard some of the field methods now deemed obsolete or discredited. Chapter 8 has been restructured and contains further information on growth and development and aerobic metabolism in children, in accordance with recent developments in the field. Chapter 10 has been re-worked so that the ubiquitous use of SPSS in data analysis is more directly recognised. In Volume 2, the new authors have also introduced substantial changes to Chapters 3, 9 and 10. The third chapter on lung function has been restructured and contains more recent population-specific regression equations for predicting lung function. Chapter 9 has been reworked and introduces new concepts and content, particularly in perceived exertion,

and Chapter 10 has been rewritten to reflect the considerable and significant advances in knowledge regarding oxygen uptake kinetics and critical power in the last eight years.

We regret, earlier in 2008, the death of William Duquet co-author of Chapter 2 with J. E. L. Carter. Completion of the chapter was his last professional contribution to the literature on kinanthropometry before his passing. Apart from his many likeable and personable characteristics – especially as a caring mentor and tutor – he will be remembered for the methodical manner in which he approached and conducted his professional work. This chapter should stand as a tribute by which we can remember him.

As with the very first edition, the content of both volumes is oriented towards laboratory practicals, but offers much more than a series of laboratory exercises. A comprehensive theoretical background is provided for each topic so that users of the text are not obliged to conduct extensive literature searches in order to place the topic in context. The book therefore serves as a 'one-stop shop' for writing up the assignments set on each topic. Each chapter contains an explanation of the appropriate methodology and, where possible, an outline of specific laboratory-based practicals. Across all the content is an emphasis on tests, protocol and procedures, data collection and handling and the correct interpretation of observations. The last two chapters in Volume 1 are concerned with basic statistical techniques and scaling procedures, which are designed to inform researchers and students about data analysis. The information should promote proper use of statistical techniques for treating data collected on human participants as well as avoid common abuses of basic statistical tools. Nevertheless, there is a common emphasis on rigour throughout all the chapters in each volume and guidance on the reduction of measurement error.

Many of the topics included within the two volumes called for unique individual approaches and so a rigid structure was not imposed on contributors. Nevertheless, in each chapter there is a clear set of aims for the practicals outlined and an extensive coverage of background theory. As each chapter is independent of the others, there is an inevitable reappearance of concepts across chapters, including those of efficiency, metabolism, maximal performance, measurement error and issues of scaling. Nevertheless, the two volumes represent a collective set of experimental sessions for academic programmes in kinanthropometry and exercise physiology.

It is hoped that this third edition in two volumes will stimulate improvements in teaching and instruction strategies in kinanthropometry and physiology. In this way, editors and authors will have made a contribution towards furthering the education of the next generation of specialists concerned with the relation between human structure and function.

Roger Eston
Thomas Reilly

PART ONE

BODY COMPOSITION, PROPORTION AND
GROWTH: IMPLICATIONS FOR HEALTH
AND PERFORMANCE

CHAPTER 1

HUMAN BODY COMPOSITION

Roger Eston, Michael Hawes, Alan Martin and Thomas Reilly

1.1 AIMS

The aims of this chapter are to develop understanding in:

- body composition models;
- chemical versus anatomical partitioning;
- levels of validity and the underlying assumptions of a variety of methods;
- the theory and practice of the best-known techniques: underwater weighing, plethysmography;
- dual-energy x-ray absorptiometry, skinfolds and bioelectric impedance;
- the importance of body fat distribution and how it is measured; and
- sample specificity and the need for caution in applying body composition equations.

1.2 INTRODUCTION

The assessment of body composition is common in fields as diverse as medicine, anthropology, ergonomics, sport performance and child growth. Much interest still centres on quantifying body fatness in relation to health status and sport performance,

but there are good reasons to measure the amounts of other constituents of the body. As a result, interest in techniques for assessing body composition has grown significantly in recent years as new technologies have been applied to compositional problems. The traditional method of densitometry is no longer regarded as the 'gold standard' for determining per cent body fat because of better appreciation of the frequent violation of one of its basic assumptions. Despite the increasing number of methods for assessing body composition, validation is still the most serious issue, and because of this there is confusion over whether one method is more accurate than another. In this chapter we examine the important methods, investigate their validation hierarchy, provide practical details for assessing many body constituents and suggest directions for future research.

It is common to explain human structure in terms of increasing organizational complexity ranging from atoms and molecules to the anatomical, described as a hierarchy of cell, tissue, organ, system and organism. Body composition can be viewed as a fundamental problem of quantitative anatomy, which may be approached at any organizational level, depending on the nature of the constituents

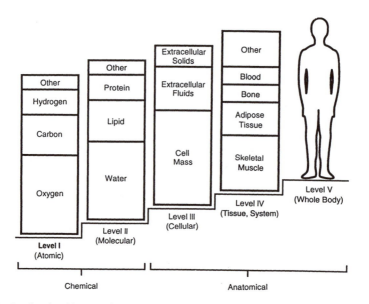

Figure 1.1 The five levels of human body composition (adapted from Wang *et al.* 1992).

of interest (Figure 1.1). Knowledge of the interrelationship of constituents within a given level or between levels is also important and may be useful for indirectly estimating the size of a particular compartment (Wang *et al.* 1992).

1.3 LEVELS OF APPROACH

At the first level of composition are the masses of approximately 50 elements that comprise the *atomic level*. Total body mass is 98% determined by the combination of oxygen, carbon, hydrogen, nitrogen, calcium and phosphorous, with the remaining 44 elements comprising less than 2% of total body mass (Keys and Brozek 1953). Technology is available for measurement *in vivo* of all of the major elements found in humans. Current methods usually involve exposure of the subject to ionising radiation, which places severe restrictions upon the utility of this approach. Examples of body composition analysis at this level are the use of whole-body potassium 40 (40K) counting to determine total body potassium, or the use of neutron activation to estimate the body's nitrogen

or calcium. The primary importance of the atomic level is the relationship of specific elements to other levels of organization, as in estimating total body protein stores from its nitrogen content, for example. The great scarcity of the required instrumentation makes this level inaccessible to all but a few researchers.

The *molecular level* of organization is made up of more than 100,000 chemical compounds, which may be reduced to five main chemical groupings: lipid, water, protein, carbohydrate (mainly glycogen) and mineral. Some confusion arises with the term lipid, which may be defined as those molecules that are insoluble in water but soluble in organic solvents such as ether. Though there are many forms of lipid found in the human body, by far the most common is triglyceride, the body's main caloric reservoir, with a relatively constant density of 0.900 g. ml^{-1}. Other forms of lipid typically comprise less than 10% of total body lipid and have varying densities, for example phospholipids (1.035 $g.ml^{-1}$) and cholesterol (1.067 $g.ml^{-1}$) (Keys and Brozek 1953). Lipid is often categorised as 'essential' or 'non essential' on the basis of function. Essential (or non-adipose) lipids are those without which other structures could not function, for example lipid found in cell membranes and nervous tissue. Though commonly taken to be about 3–5% of body mass, data from the only five cadavers in which non-adipose lipid has been measured suggest much greater variability (Martin and Drinkwater 1991). The term 'fat' is sometimes used to refer to adipose tissue. To avoid confusion, the term 'fat' will be used interchangeably with the term 'lipid' and will not refer to adipose tissue.

Any measure of total body fat (such as per cent fat by underwater weighing or skinfold calliper) gives a single value that amalgamates all body fat regardless of function or location. The remainder, after removal of all fat, is the fat-free mass (FFM), composed of fat-free muscle, fat-free bone, fat-free adipose tissue and so on. The lean body mass (LBM) is the FFM with the inclusion of the essential (non-adipose) lipids; however, LBM is sometimes erroneously used as a synonym for FFM. It should be clear that there is no means of direct *in vivo* measurement of the fat compartment, so fat must always be estimated indirectly, as for example, by measuring body density. Other molecular compartments may be estimated by isotope dilution (total body water), dual-energy x-ray absorptiometry (DXA, bone mineral content), neutron activation analysis of nitrogen (total body protein).

At the *cellular* level the body is divided into total cell mass, extra-cellular fluid (ECF) and extra-cellular solids (ECS). The total cell mass is comprised of all the different types of cells including adipocytes, myocytes and osteocytes. There is no direct method of measuring discrete cell masses or total cell mass.

The ECF includes intravascular plasma and extravascular plasma (interstitial fluid). This fluid compartment is predominantly water and acts as a medium for the exchange of gases, nutrients and waste products, and may be estimated by isotope dilution methods. The ECS includes organic substances such as collagen and elastin fibres

in connective tissue, and inorganic elements such as calcium and phosphorous, which are found predominantly in bone. The ECS compartment cannot be directly measured although several of its components may be estimated by neutron activation analysis.

The fourth level of organization includes *tissues, organs and systems*, which, although of differing levels of complexity, are functional arrangements of tissues. The four categories of tissue are connective, epithelial, muscular and nervous. Adipose and bone are forms of connective tissue, which, together with muscle tissue, account for about 75% of total body mass. Adipose tissue consists of adipocytes together with collagen and elastin fibres, which support the tissue. It is found predominantly in the subcutaneous region of the body, but is also found in smaller quantities surrounding organs, within tissue such as muscle (interstitial) and in the bone marrow (yellow marrow). The density of adipose tissue ranges from about 0.92 g.ml^{-1} to 0.96 g.ml^{-1} according to the proportions of its major constituents, lipid and water, and declines with increasing body fatness.

There is no direct method for the *in vivo* measurement of adipose tissue mass, but advances in medical imaging technology (ultrasound, magnetic resonance imaging, computed tomography) allow accurate estimation of the areas of adipose and other tissues from cross-sectional images of the body. Tissue areas from adjacent scans may be combined by geometric modelling to predict regional and even total volumes accurately, if the whole body is scanned. Although there is limited access and high cost associated with these techniques, they have the potential to serve as alternative criterion methods for the validation of more accessible and less costly methods for the assessment of body composition.

Bone is a specialised connective tissue with an elastic protein matrix, secreted by osteocytes, onto which is deposited a calcium phosphate-based mineral, hydroxyapatite, which provides strength and rigidity. The density of bone varies considerably according to such factors as age, gender and activity level. The range of fresh bone density in cadaveric subjects has been reported as 1.18–1.33 g.ml⁻¹ (Martin *et al.* 1986). The mass of bone mineral may be accurately estimated by dual energy x-ray absorptiometry (DXA), but DXA-derived bone densities are areal densities (i.e. $g.cm^{-2}$) and are therefore subject to bone size artifacts.

Muscle tissue is found in three forms, skeletal, visceral and cardiac. Its density is relatively constant at about 1.065 g.ml^{-1} (Mendez and Keys 1960; Forbes *et al.* 1953), although the quantity of interstitial adipose tissue within the tissue will introduce some variability. Surprisingly, there are few methods for quantifying the body's muscle mass; of these, the medical imaging techniques appear to be the most accurate, while anthropometry and urinary creatinine excretion have both been used.

The other tissues, nervous and epithelial, have been regarded as less significant tissues in body composition analysis. As a result, attempts have not been made to quantify these tissues; they are usually regarded as residual tissues.

The *whole body* or organismic level of organization considers the body as a single unit dealing with overall size, shape, surface area, density and external characteristics. Clearly these characteristics are the most readily measured and include stature, body mass and volume.

The five levels of organization of the body provide a useful framework within which the different approaches to body composition may be situated. It is evident that there must be inter-relationships between levels, which may provide quantitative associations facilitating estimates of previously unknown compartments. The understanding of inter-relationships between levels of complexity also helps guard against erroneous interpretation of data determined at different levels. As an example, body lipid is typically assessed at the molecular level while the quantity of muscle tissue, in a health and fitness setting, is addressed at the tissue or system level by means of circumference measurements and correction for skinfold thicknesses. The two methods are incompatible in the sense that they overlap by both including the interstitial lipid compartment.

Since the whole-body level is not strictly a compositional level and the atomic and cellular levels are of very limited interest to most people, the organizational system reduces to two levels: the molecular and tissue levels. This is then identical to the two-level system proposed by Martin and Drinkwater (1991), the *chemical* and *anatomical* levels – a system which will be used here.

1.4 VALIDITY

The validity of a method is the extent to which it accurately measures a quantity whose true value is known. Body composition analysis is unusual in that only cadaver dissection can give truly valid measures, but almost no validation had been carried out this way. In fact, there is not a single subject for whom body density and body fat (by dissection and ether extraction) have been measured. This has resulted in the acceptance of an indirect method, densitometry, as the criterion for fat estimation.

In addition to the five levels of organization, there are three levels of validation in body composition, as in the assessment of body fat, for example. At level I, total fat mass is measured directly by cadaver dissection, i.e. ether extraction of lipid is carried out for all tissues of the body. At level II, some quantity other than fat is measured (e.g. body density or the attenuation of an x-ray beam in DXA), and a quantitative relationship is established to enable fat mass to be estimated from the measured quantity. At level III, an indirect measure is again taken (e.g. skinfold thickness or bioelectrical impedance) and a regression equation against a level II method, typically densitometry, is derived. Thus level III methods are *doubly* indirect in that they incorporate all the assumptions of the level II method they are calibrated against, as well as having their own inherent limitations. The regression approach also means that methods, such as skinfold thickness measurement, are highly sample-specific, since the quantitative relationship between skinfold thickness and body density depends on many variables including body hydration, bone density, relative muscularity, skinfold compressibility and thickness, body fat patterning and the relative amount of intra-abdominal fat. This, along with the use of different subsets of skinfold sites, is why there are several hundred equations in the literature for estimating fat from skinfolds.

Calibration of level III methods against densitometry also precludes the possibility of *validating* any level III method against densitometry, as this is merely a circular argument. For example, the computed per cent body fat by bioelectrical impedance analysis (BIA) cannot be validated by underwater weighing, on the basis that both methods give similar values, because the BIA equations are based on regression against per cent fat by underwater weighing. To validate BIA against densitometric values, the actual impedance values derived from the BIA machine should be used. It should be clear that assessment of body composition is far from an exact science and all methods should be scrutinised for the validity of their underlying assumptions. For the purposes of this chapter, it is convenient to separate assessment methods by the type of constituent they measure: chemical or anatomical.

1.5 THE CHEMICAL MODEL

At the chemical level, the body is broken down into various molecular entities. A model may consist of any number of components, with the simple requirement that when added together they give total body mass. The simplest chemical model is the well-known two-component model consisting of the fat mass and the fat-free mass (FFM).

Since the great majority of body composition techniques have this partition as their aim, this will be covered in some detail here.

1.5.1 Densitometry: Underwater weighing and plethysmography

The 2-component chemical densitometric model: Densitometry is an approach to estimating body fatness based on the theory that the proportions of fat mass and FFM can be calculated from the known densities of the two compartments and the measured whole-body density (Keys and Brozek 1953). In essence, the theory is based on the following assumptions and procedures (for the complete derivation see Martin and Drinkwater 1991):

The body, of mass M, is divided into a fat component of mass (FM) and density (df) and a fat-free component of mass (FFM) and density (dffm). The masses of the two components must add up to the body's mass (M) and the volumes (mass/density) of the two components must add up to the body's volume. If D is the whole-body density, then combining these two equations and rearranging gives per cent fat, F:

$$F = \frac{100 d_f d_{ffm}}{d_{ffm} - d_f} \frac{1}{D} - \frac{100 d_f}{d_{ffm} - d_f} \quad (1)$$

This equation contains three unknowns; it is solved by assuming values for d_f and d_{ffm} and measuring D. The standard assumptions are $d_f = 0.900$ g.ml^{-1} and $d_{ffm} = 1.100$ g.ml^{-1}; although as explained in more detail later, the numeric value of d_{ffm} has been questioned recently as more accurate estimates have become availabe. Putting these respective values in to equation (1) results in *Siri's equation* for per cent fat:

$$F = \frac{495}{D} - 450$$

a) Hydrodensitometry: Whole-body density, D, is then determined, usually by measuring body volume by underwater weighing or similar technique (Figure 1.2a and b). Underwater, or hydrostatic, weighing is based on Archimedes' principle, which states that the upthrust on a body fully submerged in a fluid is equal to the weight of fluid that it displaces. Therefore the weight of water displaced by a submerged body is its weight in air minus its weight in water. Dividing this by the density of water gives the body's gross volume. This must be corrected for lung volume and gastrointestinal gas. If the underwater weight is obtained when the subject has completely exhaled (residual volume), then this value must be subtracted from the body's gross volume, along with a correction for gastrointestinal gas, usually taken to be 100 ml. Though some systems measure residual volume at the same time as the underwater weight, it is typically determined outside the underwater weighing tank, by the subject exhaling maximally and then breathing within a closed system that contains a known quantity of pure oxygen (Wilmore *et al.* 1980). Nitrogen is an inert gas; hence the quantity of N_2 inhaled and exhaled as part of air does not change in response to metabolic processes. Therefore the quantity of N_2 in the lungs after maximum exhalation is representative of the residual volume. This remaining N_2 is diluted by a known quantity of pure oxygen during several breaths of the closed circuit gas. Analysis of the resulting gas mixture from the closed circuit system yields the dilution factor of N_2 and since N_2 is present in a fixed proportion in air, the residual volume can be calculated. This procedure and the necessary calculations are described in section 1.9.3.

Density of the fat-free body: measurement and assumptions

If these procedures are carried out by an experienced technician, the determination of corrected whole body density is both accurate and precise. However, the two-compartment hydrodensitometric model assumes an FFM density of 1.1000 g.cm^3, which is invariant of age, gender, genetic endowment and training. These assumptions about the component densities must be scrutinised. The fat compartment of the body consists primarily of triglyceride, which has a constant density of nearly 0.900 g.ml^{-1}. There are small quantities of other forms of lipid in the body located in the nervous system and within the membrane of all cells. Though the density of

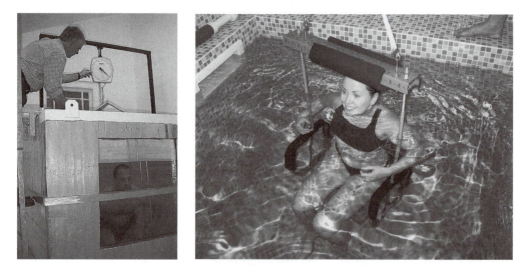

Figure 1.2a and 1.2b Examples of underwater weighing procedures for calculating whole-body density.

these lipids is greater than that of triglyceride, the relatively small quantity of each has little effect upon overall density of body lipid. Thus the density of body fat may be accepted as relatively constant at 0.900 g.ml^{-1}. However, the second assumption is much less tenable, since the density of the FFM has never been measured, and the value of 1.100 g.ml^{-1} assigned by Behnke more than 50 years ago was acknowledged to be only an estimate (Keys and Brozek 1953). This density is based on analyses of just three male cadavers, ages 25, 35 and 46 years (Brozek *et al.* 1963). In the absence of a direct measurement this value has remained in use, and it is only with the recent ability to measure bone mineral density and total body water, along with data from the Brussels Cadaver Study and elsewhere, that the extent of the variability of the fat-free density has been appreciated. On the basis of available evidence, the standard deviation of the fat-free density has been estimated at 0.02 g.ml^{-1} (Martin and Drinkwater 1991). This may not appear to be problematic, since it corresponds to a coefficient of variation of less than 2%. However, equation (1) is particularly sensitive to changes in fat-free density. An example will demonstrate this. If a lean male has a whole-body density, D = 1.070 g.ml^{-1}, then estimated body fat by the Siri equation is 12.6%. If his fat-free density is actually 1.12 g.ml^{-1} rather than the assumed value of 1.100 g.ml^{-1}, then from equation (1) his true fat is 19.1%. Conversely, if his fat-free density is 1.080 g.ml^{-1}, his true fat is 4.7% (Figure 1.3). In the former situation the Siri equation gives a 43% underestimate, in the latter a 168% overestimate. It is important to note therefore that *subjects with fat-free densities greater than 1.100 g.ml^{-1} will have their per cent fat underestimated by the Siri equation.* This can lead to anomalous values that are lower than the generally accepted lower limit for essential fat of about 3–4%. Some athletes who combine leanness with a high fat-free density may even yield a negative per cent fat, which occurs when the measured whole-body density is greater than

1.100 g.ml^{-1}. Ethnic factors also contribute to error. Schutte *et al.* (1984) have estimated that fat-free density in Black Americans is 1.113 g.ml^{-1}. If this is true, then there is an underestimate of about 5% fat in assuming a fat-free density of 1.100 g.ml^{-1} in a non-athletic Black population whose whole-body densities are in the range 1.06–1.10 g.ml^{-1}. The error will be greater in an athletic population, particularly in 'power athletes' whose bone density is high. Conversely, those with low fat-free densities will have their per cent fat overestimated. This applies particularly to older subjects, especially women. This is also true for lean female athletes with chronic amenorrhea, and its resultant bone loss. Densitometric evaluation of per cent fat in children requires a sliding value for fat-free density from the 1.063 g.ml^{-1} for newborns suggested by Lohman *et al.* (1984), to the adult value of 1.100 g.ml^{-1} at physical maturity, but it is difficult to attribute a particular value to a given child, without information on sexual maturation.

For these reasons, it is best to use a population-specific formula if the density of the fat-free body is known or can be assumed. Table 1.1 shows examples of how the equation varies according to differences in the density of the fat-free body. Examples of how variations in the density of the fat-free

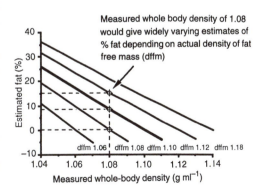

Figure 1.3 Siri's equation for estimation of per cent fat plotted for different values of assumed density of fat free mass (dffm) (adapted from Martin and Drinkwater 1991).

Table 1.1 Examples of the differences in density of the fat-free body and derived equations based on the two component densitometric model

Population	Age	Gender	Estimated density of FFB (g.cc)*	Derived equations from estimated density of FFB to predict % fat
Race				
African American	9–17	Female	1.088	(521 / Db) – 479
	18–32	Male	1.113	(470 / Db) – 422
	24–79	Female	1.106	(483 / Db) – 437
Caucasian	7–12	Male/Female	1.086	(525 / Db) – 484
	13–16	Male	1.094	(507 / Db) – 464
		Female	1.093	(510 / Db) – 466
	17–19	Male	1.098	(499 / Db) – 454
		Female	1.095	(505 / Db) – 462
	20–80	Male	1.100	(495 / Db) – 450
		Female	1.097	(501 / Db) – 457

* The FFB density values are largely taken from Heyward and Stolarzyk (1996) and Heyward and Wagner (2004). The formulae have been calculated independently by the authors from the assumed FFB density values.

body impacts on the calculation of per cent body when compared to the Siri equation is shown in Figure 1.3 and Table 1.5.

b) Air Displacement Plethysmography:

Though body volume for the determination of body density has primarily been assessed by underwater weighing and Archimedes' principle, a more direct approach is to measure the volume of a fluid that the body displaces. Simple water displacement, while in principle an excellent approach, is limited in practice by the difficulty of measuring accurately the change in water level before and after submersion of the body. Alternatively, body volume can be measured using air displacement plethysmography. Currently one commercial system is available, the Bod Pod (Life Measurement, Inc. Concord, CA). Compared with hydrodensitometry, the Bod Pod offers a much quicker assessment that is much less demanding on the subjects and can be safely used in virtually any adult subject population. This equipment consists of a test chamber large enough to hold an adult, separated by a diaphragm from a reference chamber. Vibration of the diaphragm induces pressure changes, which allow determination

of the test chamber volume, first with then without the subject, permitting the measurement of the subject's volume (Dempster and Aitkins 1995). A number of corrections are required for surface area, clothing and lung volume.

Several studies have tested the validity of air displacement plethysmography using established methods of body composition assessment with mixed results. Although some studies have suggested that the Bod Pod yields biased results (Demerath *et al.* 2002; Radley *et al.* 2003; Ball and Altena 2004), others have reported agreement between the Bod Pod and established methods (Levenhagen *et al.* 1999; McRory *et al.* 1995). Reliability appears to be excellent (Noreen and Lemon 2006) and although it is reported to detect changes in fat and fat-free mass (Secchiutti *et al.* 2007), a study to compare actual changes in body composition as a result of diet or training compared to a more established criterion has yet to be completed. Plethysmography is subject to the same errors as underwater weighing when using the Siri or similar equation to convert density into per cent fat.

Because of the uncertainty regarding the assumption of constancy of the FFM and the potentially large errors that result, it is not reasonable to rely on densitometry alone as a criterion method for per cent fat any more. This is of particular importance since, as will be detailed shortly, most indirect methods are, in effect, calibrated against densitometry. While there is no current replacement, many researchers agree that DXA, with some improvements, will fulfil that role in the future (Kohrt 1998).

1.5.2 Dual-energy x-ray absorptiometry

Bone densitometry instruments have evolved from single- to dual-photon to DXA over the last three decades and widespread availability of whole-body scanners has made their use for body composition far more feasible (Lohman 1996). The DXA unit consists of a bed on which the subject lies supine, while a collimated dual-energy x-ray beam from a source under the bed passes through the subject. The beam's attenuation is measured by detectors above the subject, and both source and detector move so that either the whole body or selected regions of the subject are scanned in a rectilinear fashion (Figure 1.4). Some systems use a pencil beam; others use an array of beams and detectors for faster scanning. The dual energy of the beam allows quantification of two components in each pixel. In boneless regions these are fat and a lean component. It should be noted that the lean component is actually all the fat-free, bone mineral-free constituents; this is not muscle, as some mistakenly believe. In bone mineral-containing pixels, the three component system must be reduced to two components, bone mineral and a soft tissue component, which contain an assumed fat-to-lean ratio. Strategies for estimating this ratio vary by manufacturer but consist in part of extrapolation of the measured fat-to-lean ratios of soft tissue pixels adjacent to bone. In this way, the fat, bone mineral and lean content of each pixel is determined (Kohrt 1995). Summing these for all pixels gives the

Figure 1.4 Dual energy x-ray absorptiometer procedure for assessing body density and body composition.

composition of the whole body (Figure 1.5). Thus DXA uses a three-component chemical model of the body, and can therefore be compared with underwater weighing. Comparison of per cent fat determined by underwater weighing and DXA show differences that are correlated with bone mineral density (BMD) probably reflecting the effect of BMD on the fat-free density.

DXA is accepted as one of the most valid methods of body composition analysis (Prior *et al.* 1997; Kohrt 1998). It has been validated against various multicompartment models in young (Prior *et al.* 1997; Clasey *et al.* 1999), old (Clasey *et al.* 1999) and a wide age range of healthy sedentary individuals (Gallagher *et al.* 2000). As a level II method the component values are calibrated against standards. The quality of the body composition assessment is therefore dependent only on the theoretical and practical aspects of the DXA technology. It does not rely on calibration against underwater weighing, unlike skinfold assessment.

A whole-body DXA scan can give regional composition as well as whole-body values, but precision values are considerably poorer than for the whole body. The default breakdown consists of six to seven regions: head, torso, pelvis and four limbs, but other segments can be defined by the operator. Since DXA does not suffer the basic weakness of densitometry, in that there is no requirement for constant density of the FFM, it has the potential to

University of Wales, Bangor

A12029902   Thu 02.Dec.1999 11:43
Name: A R
Comment:
I.D.: 22   Sex: F
S.S.#:   - -   Ethnic: W
ZIPCode: Height: 173.00 cm
Scan Code: SP   Weight: 59.2 kg
BirthDate: 02.Feb.74   Age: 25
Physician:
Image not for diagnostic use

TOTAL BMC and BMD CV is < 1.0%
C.F.   1.011   1.093   1.000
Region   Area   BMC   BMD
          (cm2)   (grams) (gms/cm2)

Region	Area (cm2)	BMC (grams)	BMD (gms/cm2)
L Arm	188.47	155.77	0.827
R Arm	186.45	154.98	0.831
L Ribs	156.12	123.41	0.790
R Ribs	140.75	112.04	0.796
T Spine	165.42	180.12	1.089
L Spine	68.35	89.93	1.316
Pelvis	298.48	418.71	1.403
L Leg	368.05	517.87	1.404
R Leg	361.57	515.29	1.425
SubTot	1934.46	2268.12	1.172
Head	228.92	512.44	2.239
TOTAL	2163.38	2780.56	1.285

HOLOGIC

·02.Dec.1999 12:11 [330 x 150]
Hologic QDR-1500 (S/N 1522)
Enhanced Whole Body V5.72

Region	BMC (grams)	Fat (grams)	Lean (grams)	Lean+BMC (grams)	Total (grams)	% Fat (%)
L Arm	155.8	694.1	1942.2	2097.9	2792.0	24.9
R Arm	155.0	679.7	2090.1	2245.1	2924.7	23.2
Trunk	924.2	4274.9	24083.9	25008.1	29283.0	14.6
L Leg	517.9	2596.8	6630.1	7148.0	9744.8	26.6
R Leg	515.3	2650.9	6766.1	7281.4	9932.3	26.7
SubTot	2268.1	10896.3	41512.4	43780.6	54676.9	19.9
~Head	512.4	654.8	3098.0	3610.4	4265.2	15.4
TOTAL	2780.6	11551.1	44610.4	47391.0	58942.1	19.6

~assumes 17.0% brain fat
LBM 73.2% water

HOLOGIC

Figure 1.5 Analysis of body composition of a female dual energy x-ray absorptiometry. Note that the sum of the individual predicted masses from the segments analyzed by the DXA equates very closely to the whole body mass of the subject – a factor which is essential for the validity of the technique.

become the criteria for fat estimation. It is also relatively independent of fluctuations in hydration, as water excess or deficit has been shown to affect only the lean component – as it should. It allows for a rapid, non-invasive estimation of body fat with minimal radiation exposure (van der Ploeg *et al.* 2003) and has the advantage of a three-compartment model of body composition that quantifies fat, soft lean tissue and bone mineral.

Nevertheless, the validity of the method has remained subject to question, particularly with regard to concerns over tissue thickness and hydration levels (Laskey *et al.* 1992; Jebb *et al.* 1995; Pietrobelli *et al.* 1998; Wang *et al.* 1998; van der Ploeg *et al.* 2003), which will vary between individuals and groups of subjects. Furthermore, the method is confounded by the different manufacturers' detection, calibration and analysis techniques, as well as type of beam and the specifics of the analysis software. Despite these difficulties, there is optimism among researchers that with continued improvement, DXA will at some point become the gold standard for body fat assessment.

1.5.3 Multi-component models for predicting body fat

Advances in *in vivo* measurement techniques has led to the development of multi-component models that estimate body fat by equations, which incorporate a number of measured variables (Heymsfield *et al.* 1996). This has allowed researchers to assess variations in hydration levels and bone mineral contents that are not possible to measure by hydrodensitometry alone. An example of a four-component chemical model might be fat, water, bone mineral and a residual component (i.e. all the fat-free, bone mineral-free, dry constituents). Adding measurements of total body water (by deuterium dilution), bone mineral density (by DXA), and whole-body density (by hydrodensitometry), allows the possibility to measure individual variances in mineral and water, and in theory, lead to more accurate measurement of per cent body fat (Peterson *et al.* 2003). The 4C model has been used as the criterion method in studies with children (Fields and Goran 2000), younger and middle-aged adults (Friedl *et al.* 1992; Withers *et al.* 1998), and the elderly (Baumgartner *et al.* 1991). Ryde *et al.* (1998) used a five compartment model of body composition comprising FFM, where FFM = water + protein + minerals + glycogen to calculate body fat changes in ten overweight women on a 10-week very low calorie diet. An example of using such a procedure is given in Practical 7, using the methods and data from the study by Withers *et al.* (1998).

1.5.4 Level III methods

The defining characteristic of a level III method is that it uses an equation that represents an empirically-derived mathematical relationship between its measured parameter and per cent fat by the level II method – almost always underwater weighing (though with the rise in acceptance of DXA, more DXA-based equations, e.g. Stewart *et al.* 2000, are likely to be published). This relationship is derived by regression analysis, and typically is a simple linear regression, linear regression of a logarithmic variable, or a quadratic curve fit. Thus all level II methods are *doubly indirect*, and as such, they are vulnerable to the errors and assumptions associated with underwater weighing, as well as those deriving from their own technique, whether this is skinfold callipers, bioelectrical impedance, infrared interactance or some other approach.

a) Skinfold thickness: There is good face validity to the idea that a representative measure of the greatest depot of body fat (i.e.

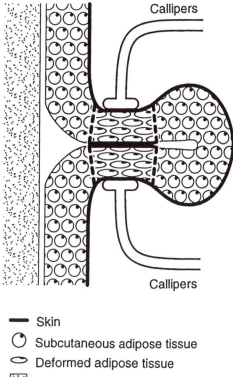

Callipers

Callipers

▬ Skin
◯ Subcutaneous adipose tissue
⬭ Deformed adipose tissue
▦ Underlying muscle

Figure 1.6 Schematic section through a skinfold at measurement site (adapted from Martin *et al.* 1985). The calliper jaws exert a constant pressure over a wide range of openings. The skinfold includes skin that varies in thickness from site to site and individual to individual; adipose tissue of variable compressibility and varying proportionate volume occupied by cell membranes, nuclei, organelles and lipid globules.

subcutaneous) might provide a reasonable estimate of total body fat. This notion becomes less tenable as a greater understanding emerges with respect to various patterns of subcutaneous fat depots and different proportions of fat in the four main storage areas. However, the fact that so many equations have been derived for estimating per cent body fat from skinfold thickness suggests the need for caution, and an examination of the assumptions underlying the use of skinfold callipers reinforces this.

The skinfold method measures a double fold of skin and subcutaneous adipose by means of callipers, which apply a constant pressure over a range of thicknesses (Figure 1.6). In converting this linear distance into a per cent fat value, various assumptions are required (Martin *et al*. 1985). Initially, one must accept that a compressed double layer of skin and subcutaneous adipose is representative of an uncompressed single layer of adipose tissue. This implies that the skin thickness is either negligible or constant and that adipose tissue compresses in a predictable manner. Clearly skin thickness will comprise a greater proportion of a thin skinfold compared to a thicker skinfold and its relationship cannot be regarded as constant. In addition it has been shown that skin thickness varies from individual to individual as well as from site to site, which suggests that it cannot be regarded as negligible (Martin *et al*. 1992). With respect to compressibility, the evidence suggests that adipose tissue compressibility varies with such factors as age, gender, site, tissue hydration and cell size. The dynamic nature of compressibility is readily observed when callipers are applied to a skinfold and a rapid decline in the needle gauge occurs. The lipid fraction of adipose tissue must also be constant if skinfold thickness is to be indicative of total body lipid. Adipose tissue includes structures other than fat molecules; these include cell membranes, nuclei and organelles. In a relatively empty adipocyte the proportion of fat to other structures may be quite low while a relatively full adipocyte

will occupy a proportionately greater volume. Orpin and Scott (1964) suggested that fat content of adipose tissue may range between 5.2% and 94.1% although Martin *et al*. (1994) suggested a general range of 60–85%.

The previous three assumptions relate to the measurement of a single skinfold. There remain two assumptions that must be considered with respect to the validity of skinfold thickness as a predictor of total body fat. The first deals with the assumption that a limited number of skinfold sites in some way represent the remaining subcutaneous adipose tissue; that is, the distribution of fat shows some regularity from one person to another. Despite the two general patterns of fat distribution, android (central predominance) and gynoid (gluteofemoral predominanc), fat patterns are quite individual. The final assumption is that a limited number of subcutaneous sites are representative of fat deposited non-subcutaneously (omentum, viscera, bone marrow and interstices). While there is some evidence that internal fat increases with subcutaneous fat, this relationship is affected by many variables, particularly age.

The procedure for generating per cent fat equations for level III methods can be illustrated by examining the classic approach of Durnin and Womersley (1974). They measured body density (D) by underwater weighing, as well as the sum of four skinfolds on 464 men and women, categorised by age and gender. The resulting plots showed a curvilinear shape, so they used the $\log_{10}$ of the sum of the four skinfolds to linearise the relationship and then carried out a linear regression to establish the constants of the equation. As an example, their equation for 20–29 year old men is:

$$D = 1.1631 - 0.0632 \times \log_{10}\Sigma 4SF$$

Siri's equation can then be used to calculate per cent fat.

It is important to note that the slopes and intercepts were different for all their gender and age groups, demonstrating that the relationship between body density and the sum of skinfolds differed. Put another way, people from different age and gender groups who have the same sum of skinfolds have different body densities. For a given sum of skinfolds, men have higher body density than women mainly because of higher bone density, greater muscularity and the women's tendency to have more subcutaneous fat in the gluteo-femoral region which is not assessed by the four skinfolds that they chose. Similarly, for a given sum of skinfolds, older men have lower body density than young men because of increasing internalisation of fat, as well as a decline in muscle mass and bone density. There are other factors, such as skin thickness and skinfold compressibility whose variability potentially affects the relationship between skinfolds and body density.

In view of the complexity of per cent fat prediction from skinfold thickness, some guidelines are helpful when choosing an equation to estimate per cent fat in a particular subject. It is important to select an equation that has been derived from a sample whose characteristics (ethnicity, age, gender, athletic status, health status and so on) are similar to those of the subject to be measured. Equations with few skinfolds cannot detect deviations in fat patterning, so it is better to use equations with skinfold sites that include arm, leg and trunk. Not all equations are based on the same type of skinfold calliper, and since these give different readings for a given skinfold, the choice of calliper becomes important. Proper site location and correct technique will help minimise error.

An alternative approach to the use of skinfold measurement is the sum of a number of skinfold thicknesses to form a simple indicator of fatness. Use of this measure avoids many of the untenable assumptions that are inherent in the calculation of per cent fat from skinfold thickness. This approach can be useful when normative values for the sum of skinfolds are available, as the sum can then be converted into a percentile, showing an individual's relative standing within a population.

Importance of including lower limb skinfold measures as indicators of total body fatness

Skinfolds or measures of adipose tissue thicknesses from the lower limb, both independently or in combination with selected upper-body skinfolds, explain significant variance in total body fat. This has been observed using several criterion methods; for example, hydrodensitometry (in adults (Jackson and Pollock 1978; Jackson *et al.* 1980; Eston *et al.* 1995); in children (Slaughter *et al.* 1988; Eston and Powell 2003); cadaver dissection (Martin *et al.* 1985; Clarys *et al.* 1987); ultrasound (Eston *et al.* 1994); DXA (Stewart and Hannan 2000; Eston *et al.* 2005) and a four-compartment model of body composition (van der Ploeg *et al.* 2003; Eston *et al.* 2005). The correlation between subcutaneous abdominal adipose tissue volume and thigh fat volume (assessed by magnetic resonance imaging) is also reported to be greater than the corresponding correlation for the sum of the biceps, triceps, subscapular and iliac crest (Eliakim *et al.* 1997). The importance of including the thigh and calf skinfolds to improve the estimation of body fat in adults has led to previous comment and discussion (Durnin 1997; Stewart and Eston 1997).

On the basis of the potential importance of the thigh skinfold as a predictor of total body fat, the steering group of the British Olympic Association (BOA) recommended that the anterior thigh skinfold should be added to the sum of the four skinfolds used in the equation of Durnin and Womersley (1974) to provide a more valid estimate of body fat in fit and healthy adults (Reilly *et al.* 1996). The value of adding the thigh skinfold to the sum of the four skinfolds has since been confirmed using DXA and a four compartment model as the criterion in young, healthy men and women (Eston *et al.* 2005). They also observed that the thigh and calf skinfolds explained the most variance in body fat. The lower limb skinfolds may be particularly useful predictors of running performance. In a longitudinal study on 37 top class runners, improvements in performance over 3 years

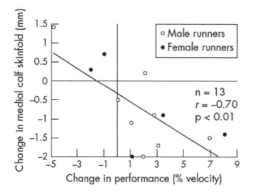

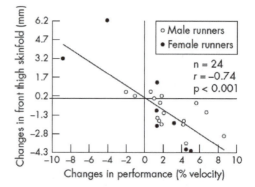

Figure 1.7a Relationship between the changes in medial calf skinfold (mm) and performance (percentage velocity) induced after three years of intense athletic conditioning in sprint trained runners.

Figure 1.7b Relationship between the changes in front thigh skinfold (mm) and performance (percentage velocity) induced after three years of intense athletic conditioning in endurance trained runners (from Legaz and Eston, 2005).

were consistently associated with a decrease in the lower limb skinfolds (Legaz and Eston 2005; Figure 1.7).

Validation of skinfold-thickness prediction equations with a four-compartment model

Three of the most widely used generalized skinfold thickness prediction equations are the equations developed by Durnin and Womersley (1974), Jackson and Pollock (1978) and Jackson *et al.* (1980). These equations were developed and validated by means of hydrodensitometry – a two-compartment model. As indicated above, the two-compartment model equation requires the assumption that the fat-free density (body hydration levels and bone mineral content) is stable. These assumptions are often violated because of significant variations in hydration levels and mineral content between groups of differing age, gender, race and training status. This will therefore lead to potentially large errors in estimates of per cent body fat. For these reasons, new equations have been developed from 681 healthy Caucasian adults using a four-compartment (4C) model as the criterion and compared against the above equations (Peterson *et al.* 2003). The final equations developed from this study included

the sum of the triceps, subscapular, suprailiac and mid-thigh skinfolds for men and women. These equations, which are shown in Practical 2 (Section 1.10.2), were significantly more accurate than the three skinfold thickness methods based on hydrodensitometry.

b) Bioelectrical Impedance Analysis: BIA is

a method of body composition analysis that has become increasingly popular for its ease, portability and moderate cost. The electrical properties, particularly impedance, of living tissue, have been used for more than 50 years to describe and measure certain tissue or organ functions. In recent years, bioelectrical impedance has been used to quantify the FFM allowing the proportion of body fat to be calculated. The method is based on the electrical properties of hydrous and anhydrous tissues and their electrolyte content. There have been a number of excellent reviews of BIA procedures and the various equations that have been derived from healthy subjects (Houtkooper *et al.* 1996; Kyle *et al.* 2004).

Nyboer *et al.* (1943) demonstrated that electrical impedance could be used to determine biological volume. On application of a low voltage to a biological structure, a small alternating current flows through it, using the intra- and extra-cellular fluids as a conductor and cell membranes as capacitors (condensers). The FFM, including the non-lipid components of adipose tissue, contain virtually all of the water and conducting electrolytes of the body and thus the FFM is almost totally responsible for conductance of an electrical current. Impedance to the flow of an electrical current is a function of the resistance and reactance of the conductor. The complex geometry and bioelectrical properties of the human body are confounding factors, but in principle, impedance may be used to estimate the bioelectrical volume of the FFM since it is related to the length and cross-sectional area of the conductor.

The impedance of biological structures can be measured with electrodes applied to the hands and feet, an excitation current of 800 µA at 50 kHz and a bioelectrical impedance analyzer that measures resistance and reactance. Some BIA instruments use other locations such as foot-to-foot (Jebb et al. 2000, Rowlands and Eston, 2001), or hand-to-hand electrodes. The resulting impedance value (though many systems use only the resistive component) is then entered into an appropriate equation.

Methods of bioelectrical impedance analysis include single frequency (SF-BIA), multi-frequency (MF-BIA), segmental BIA and localized BIA. Single frequency BIA is the most frequently applied method, which injects an excitation current of 800 µA at 50 kHz through surface electrodes, placed distally on the limbs. This technique estimates FFM and TBW, but it cannot determine differences in intra-cellular water (ICW). Multi-frequency BIA uses different frequencies (0, 1, 5, 50, 100, 200 to 500 kHz) to evaluate FFM, TBW, ICW and extra-cellular water (ECW). Segmental BIA, involving varied electrode placements on the limbs and trunk, has been used to determine fluid shifts and fluid distribution in some diseases. Although the trunk of the body represents as much as 50% of whole body mass, its large cross-sectional area contributes as little as 10% to whole-body impedance. Therefore, changes in whole-body impedance may be closely related to changes of the FFM (or muscle mass or body cell mass [BCM]) of the limbs and changes of the FFM of the trunk are probably not adequately described by whole body impedance measurements. Given that BIA measures various body segments and the validity of equations are therefore population-specific, localized BIA focuses on well defined body segments. For example, it has been used to determine local abdominal fat mass (Scharfetter et al. 2001).

Many equations have been published to predict the FFM from BIA for various healthy population subsets by age and gender. The most frequently occurring component in these equations is the resistive index, which is the square of stature, divided by resistance. Other variables that have been included in prediction equations include height, weight, gender, age, various limb circumferences, reactance, impedance, standing height, arm length and bone breadths. The reported R^2 values range between 0.80–0.988 with standard error of the estimate (SEE) ranging from 1.90 to 4.02 kg (approximately 2–3%). Slightly lower correlations ($R^2 = 0.76 – 0.92$) have been reported for the prediction of per cent fat with a prediction error (SEE) of 3–4%. Kyle et al. (2004) have provided a very useful summary of selected BIA equations published since 1990 for adults, which have been validated against a criterion measure for the variable of interest and which have involved at least 40 subjects. Given the vast array of equations available in the literature, Houtkooper et al. (1996) have suggested that the SEE of 2.0–2.5 kg and 1.5–1.8 kg in women and actual error of 0.0–1.8 kg is considered ideal. Prediction error of less than 3.0 kg for men and 2.3 kg for women would be considered to be very good. Three equations are presented in Practical 4 (Section 1.12.3) which satisfies these criteria.

Bioelectrical impedance is a safe, simple method of estimating the fat and fat-free masses, but some caution is needed. As "criterion" methods each have their limitations, these will be propagated into the BIA measurement. As with all level II methods, BIA equations tend to be population-specific with generally poor characteristics of fit for a large heterogeneous population. The measurement is influenced by electrode placement, dehydration, exercise, heat and cold exposure, and a conductive surface (Lukaski 1996), leading to the following recommendations for assessment procedures (Heyward 1991):

- no eating or drinking within 4 hours of the test
- no exercise within 12 hours of the test
- urinate within 30 minutes of the test
- no alcohol consumption within 48 hours of the test
- no diuretics within 7 days of the test.

Additionally,

- inaccuracies may be introduced during the pre-menstrual period for women (Gleichauf and Roe 1989);
- the changing pattern of water and mineral content of growing children suggests that a child-specific prediction equation should be used (Houtkooper *et al.* 1989; Eston *et al.* 1993; Bunc 2001; Rowlands and Eston 2001).

1.6 SIMPLE INDICES OF FATNESS, MUSCULARITY AND FAT DISTRIBUTION

1.6.1 Body mass index (BMI)

Body weight is often thought of as a measure of fatness, and this perception is reinforced by the use of height–weight tables as an indicator of health risk and life expectancy by the life insurance industry. Superficially it would appear that weight per unit of height is a convenient expression that reflects body build and body composition, and variations of this index have been a recurring theme in anthropometry for over 150 years following the pioneer work of Adolph Quetelet (1836). The simple ratio of weight to height may appear

to be the most informative expression, but it expresses a three-dimensional measure (weight) in relation to a one-dimensional measure. Since three-dimensional measures vary as the cube of a linear measure, dimensional consistency may be better served by the expression of mass to the cube of height, a ratio known as the *ponderal index*. Since the objective of the ratio is to examine weight in relative independence of height, several authors have concluded that w/h^2 – with weight in kg and height in m – is the most appropriate index, and this has been termed the *Body Mass Index* (BMI), the inverse of which was previously known as the *Quetelet Index*.

Although the BMI is not ideal, it does have significant practical advantages. It is based on common measures of height and weight and it is familiar to most practitioners. The use of BMI measures to define adult obesity (BMI > 30 kg.m^{-2}) and adult overweight (BMI 25–30 kg.m^{-2}) is commonly accepted. According to the Association for the Study of Obesity (www.aso.org.uk), the 'cut-offs' for adults in each classification have been formalized by the World Health Organization and are:

BMI (kg.m^{-2}) Classification

<18.5	Underweight, thin
18.5–24.9	Healthy weight, healthy
25.0–29.9	Grade 1 obesity, overweight
30.0–39.9	Grade 2 obesity, obesity
>40.0	Grade 3 obesity, morbid obesity

The above values are general guidelines. A female of average weight with the same height as an average-weight male, would normally have a lower BMI by one to two units. This is due to the greater proportion of fat-free mass in the male. Furthermore, these values apply to adults only as the cut-off values are significantly lower in children and vary significantly with age. The non-isometric changes in height, weight and shape occurring during growth are reflected in the huge variation in BMI in the growing years.

For example, at birth the median is as low as 13 kg.m^{-2}, increasing to 17 kg.m^{-2} at 1 year, decreasing to 15.5 kg.m^{-2} at 6 years, and then increasing to 21 kg.m^{-2} at 20 years (Cole *et al.* 2000).

In order to quantify body weight in relation to obesity, reference values for children using BMI values, which are defined to pass through 25 kg.m^{-2} and 30 kg.m^{-2} at age 18, have been calculated for male and female children at six-monthly intervals from age 2 years, using data from large-scale surveys of childhood BMI in six different countries across several continents (Cole *et al.* 2000). This approach has been recommended by the International Obesity TaskForce (IOTF) for the comparison of child populations (Dietz and Bellizzi 1999).

The premise of using such an index is that body weight corrected for stature is correlated with obesity and adiposity (Ross *et al.* 1986). Indeed, the BMI has gained acceptance because in many epidemiological studies it shows a moderate correlation with estimates of body fat. Nevertheless, the widespread and often unquestioned application of the BMI to represent adiposity has attracted strong criticism (e.g. Garn *et al.* 1986; Ross *et al.* 1988; Eston 2002; Nevill *et al.* 2006). For such a premise to be true, a number of properties and assumptions need to be satisfied: a) the index should be highly correlated with weight and minimally correlated with height; and b) the difference in weight for a given height between individuals should be largely attributable to differences in body fat. With few exceptions, such as in the case of 66 world champion body builders (Ross *et al.* 1986; *r* = 0.41), and 1,112 children between 5 and 10 years (Garn *et al.* 1986; *r* = 0.30), BMI tends to be largely independent of height (Keys *et al.* 1972). With regard to b), the BMI is accepted because in many epidemiological studies it shows a moderate correlation with estimates of body fat (e.g. Keys *et al.* 1972). These same studies also show similar correlations between BMI and estimates of lean body mass or body density.

As noted by others (Garn *et al.* 1986; Ross *et al.* 1986, 1987, 1988), the BMI reflects both the weight of lean tissue and the weight of fat tissue, and for some age groups, it may be a better measure of the amount of lean than of relative fatness (Garn *et al.* 1986). Unfortunately, the singular correlation values of BMI with body fat have been used to promote the use of the BMI for individual counselling with respect to health status, diet, weight loss and other fitness factors.

However, some of these studies also show very similar correlation values between BMI and estimates of lean body mass. In some populations the BMI is influenced to almost the same degree by the lean and fat compartments of the body, suggesting that it may be as much a measure of lean tissue as it is of fat. For example, in a study on 18,000 men and women aged 20–70 years to assess the predictive validity of the BMI as a means of estimating adiposity (Ross *et al.*1988), the highest correlation of the BMI was with muscularity (*r* = 0.58), as assessed by the corrected arm girth technique. The correlation of BMI and adiposity was *r* = 0.50.

The BMI may grossly underestimate the extent of lean tissue loss in certain diseases that are associated with sarcopenia (muscle wasting). For example, in a study on 97 rheumatoid arthritis patients in whom lean tissue loss exceeded fat loss, over half of the group were below the 10th percentile for muscularity, whereas only 13% were below the 5th percentile for BMI (Munro and Capell 1997). Similar observations are apparent in healthy men and women. In the large scale study by Ross *et al.* (1988) referred to above, 26% of those rated as extremely lean (BMI <20) had skinfolds above the 50th percentile and 16% of those rated as obese (BMI >27) had skinfolds below the 50th percentile.

Thus, for any individual, the use of BMI as a predictor of adiposity is seriously limited. On an individual basis, people of the same height will vary with respect to frame size, tissue densities and proportion of various tissues. A person may be heavy for his/her height because of a large, dense skeleton and large muscle mass while another may be as heavy for his/her height because of excess adipose tissue. The proportion and density of tissue is dependent on gender, age, ethnicity, lifestyle and training – among other factors.

The BMI is positively associated with indicators of frame size. Garn *et al.* (1986) reported correlations of 0.50 overall between BMI and bony chest breadth in over 2,000 children and adults. Ross *et al.* (1988) also reported an overall correlation of 0.51 for BMI and the sum of humerus and femur breadths in over 18,000 Canadian men and women. Given the sample sizes in these studies, these values represent highly significant correlations.

This is not the end of the discussion however, because a further complicating factor arises since body shape changes as height increases (Ross *et al.* 1987). Whatever exponent for height is selected, human beings are not geometrically proportional. Changes in weight, and to some extent the change in shape, are dependent on the nature of the weight change, i.e. whether it is due to an increase in lean or fat mass. The measure assumes geometric proportionality and similarity in humans, but this assumption does not hold true for all measures. For example, the ratio of sitting height to stature (relative length of the trunk) is positively correlated with BMI. Children, adolescents, or adults with short legs for their height have higher BMI values (Garn *et al.* 1986). These authors indicated that short-legged individuals may have BMI values that are higher by as much as five units! It is notable that male weightlifters, gymnasts, judo players and Olympic wrestlers tend to have relatively short legs for their height (Norton *et al.* 1996), so it is likely that their BMI will be partly attributed to their body shape.

On an individual basis it is therefore erroneous to consider relative weight as a measure of obesity or fatness – the scientific evidence is not nearly strong enough to suggest a basis for individual health decisions (Garn *et al.* 1986, Keys *et al.* 1972). In summary, BMI is a good indicator of fatness in populations whose overweight individuals are overweight because of fatness, a condition which may hold for certain populations, such as all American adults, but not for others, such as specific groups of athletes for whom it is completely inappropriate.

1.6.2 Fat-Free Mass Index (FFMI) and Fat Mass Index (FMI)

The major limitation of the BMI is that the actual composition of body weight is not taken into account. A high BMI may be due to excess adipose tissue or muscle hypertrophy, both of which will be judged as 'excess mass' (Schutz *et al.* 2002). A low BMI may be due to a deficit in FFM (sarcopenia). The original idea of calculating the FFMI and FMI in analogy to the BMI was proposed by Van Itallie *et al.* (1990) as a means of indicating nutritional status in patients. The potential advantage of this technique is that only one component of body mass, i.e. FFM or FM, is related to Ht^2. Consequently, a preliminary attempt to derive FFMI and FMI reference standards has been conducted by Schutz *et al.* (2002) for Caucasian men and women, varying in age from 24 to 98 years. They used BIA to assess FFM and FM. They concluded that reference intervals of FMI vs FFMI could be used as indicative values for the evaluation of nutritional status (overnutrition and undernutrition) of apparently healthy subjects and can provide complementary information to the classical expression of body composition reference values (Pichard *et al.* 2000). Schutz *et al.* (2002) inferred that with reference to such values the FFMI is able to identify individuals with elevated BMI but without excess FM. Conversely, FMI can identify subjects with 'normal' BMI but who are at potential risk because of elevated FM. The percentile values for the men and women aged 18–54 years from their study are presented in Table 1.2

A modification of the FFMI was suggested

Table 1.2 Percentile values for FFM and FM index in men and women aged 18–54 years. Values taken from Schutz *et al.* (2002)

	P5	P10	P25	P50	P75	P90	P95
FFMI							
Men*							
18–34 y	16.8	17.2	18.0	18.9	19.8	20.5	*21.1*
35–54 y	17.2	17.6	18.3	19.2	20.1	21.1	*21.7*
Women⁺							
18–34 y	13.8	14.1	14.7	15.4	16.2	17.1	*17.6*
35–54 y	14.4	14.7	15.3	15.9	16.7	17.5	*18.0*
FMI							
Men							
18–34 y	2.2	2.5	3.2	4.0	5.0	6.1	*7.0*
35–54 y	2.5	2.9	3.7	4.8	6.0	7.2	*7.9*
Women							
18–34 y	3.5	3.9	4.6	5.5	6.6	7.8	*8.7*
35–54 y	*3.4*	*3.9*	*4.8*	*5.9*	*7.3*	*8.8*	*9.9*

* (N = 1,088 and 1,323 for 18–34 years and 35–54 years, respectively) ⁺ (N = 1,019 and 1,033 for 18–34 years and 35–54 years, respectively).

by Kouri *et al.* (1995) in a study of 157 male athletes. It was designed to assess whether an athlete's muscularity was within the naturally attainable range or was beyond that which could reasonably be expected without pharmacological assistance. The formula is:

$$\text{FFMI} = \frac{\text{Mass (kg)} \times [(100 - \%\text{fat}/100)) + 6.1 \times (1.8 - \text{Height (m)}]}{\text{Height}^2}$$

The correctional factor ((6.1 × (1.8 – Height) is used only in calculations for males. According to Gruber *et al.* (2000) an FFMI of 18 kg.m² indicates a slight build with low musculature; 20 – average musculature; 22 – distinctly muscular; above 22 – not normally achieved without weighlifting or similar activity; 25 – the upper limit of muscularity that can be attained without use of pharmacological agents, whereby the FFMI could increase to 40! For women, a FFMI of 13 indicates low musculature; 15 – average; 17 – rather muscular; 22 – rarely achieved without using pharmacological agents (Gruber *et al.* 2000).

Similar FFMI techniques are applied in clinical populations to determine the extent of muscle wasting through disease.

1.6.3 Waist-to-hip ratio

The relationship between increasing body fat and health risk is generally accepted, even though two people with the same per cent fat may have very different risks for the cardiovascular-related diseases. This anomaly was addressed over 60 years ago by Vague (1947), who noted two general patterns of fat distribution on the body, which he designated as android and gynoid because of their predominance in males and females respectively. Greater health risk is associated with the android pattern of trunk deposition than the gynoid pattern of gluteofemoral deposition. The use of medical imaging techniques to quantify abdominal adiposity has demonstrated that it is the intra-abdominal adipose tissue that is associated with the highest health risk (Matsuzawa *et al.* 1995). Both magnetic resonance imaging (MRI) and computerised tomography (CT) have been used successfully to measure adipose compartments of the abdomen. The full procedure is to take a series of consecutive scans that cover the whole abdominal region. Areas of subcutaneous and internal adipose tissue are determined from each scan and the corresponding volumes are generated since the distance between scans is known. However, a single scan at the level of the umbilicus shows a very high correlation (r > 0.9) with intra-abdominal adipose tissue volume (Abate *et al.* 1997). These methods are very expensive and are more use in research than in screening or individual evaluation.

The simplest approach to quantifying fat distribution is the use of waist circumference and the ratio of waist circumference to hip circumference (WHR). A waist circumference value of approximately 95 cm in both men and women, and WHR values of 0.94 for men and 0.88 for women have been found to correspond to a critical accumulation of visceral adipose tissue (130 cm^2) (Lemieux *et al.* 1996). Waist circumference is variously taken at the waist narrowing, the umbilicus, or other skeletally-determined locations, while hip circumference is taken at the maximum gluteal girth. Bjorntorp (1984) suggested that a ratio of = 1.0 in men is indicative of a significant elevation in the risk of ischaemic heart and cerebro-vascular disease. The corresponding value representing increased risk for women is = 0.8. The robustness of the association of WHR with health risk factors in large-scale epidemiological studies has been underscored by a substantial body of research that demonstrates important metabolic differences between abdominal and gluteofemoral adipose tissue. A tentative explanation for why women of reproductive age have great difficulty in reducing gynoid fat deposits is that gluteofemoral adiposity is an evolutionary adaptation to store fat for the energy-demanding lactational phase of childbearing; studies show that lipolysis in this region is facilitated by the endocrine environment of lactation. Though

some women may want to reduce excess gluteofemoral fat, its presence is often more of an aesthetic issue than a health issue. As a general summary, this ratio appears to have some utility in the assessment of health risk although it should be used with caution.

1.7 THE ANATOMICAL MODEL

The anatomical model has been largely neglected since the rise of densitometry as the criterion method gave dominance to the chemical model. This is unfortunate since, for many applications, anatomical components are of major interest. Elite male athletes will show fat values that are typically in the range 6–12%, regardless of sport. However, measures of total and regional muscularity are considerably better at discriminating between athletes in different sports. Similarly, skeletal mass has been neglected and the chemical component, bone mineral content, has been the common measure of bone status. A strong argument can be made for the use of adipose tissue as a fatness measure since in lean people the amount of total body *fat* has almost no anatomical or physiological meaning. Despite the fact that, by their very nature, anatomical components have both anatomical and physiological significance, there are few proven techniques for estimating them.

1.7.1 Adipose Tissue

Surprisingly, there are no equations to estimate adipose tissue mass from skinfolds, BIA or any other level III method. The only current approach is the use of the medical imaging techniques such as CT, MRI or ultrasound. Though these methods depend on very different physical principles, from the viewpoint of body composition analysis, they are very similar. Each gives a cross-sectional view at a selected level of the body, from which areas of different tissues can be quantified. This quantification can be done with scan analysis software, or by scanning the resulting radiograph into a microcomputer for subsequent image analysis. A single scan is unable to yield adipose or any other tissue mass, however. It is at best an indicator of fatness in that region of the body. Adipose tissue volumes of a selected region, or of the whole body, can be calculated by geometric modelling of areas from a series of contiguous scans. A plot of adipose tissue area from each scan against the distance of the scan from one extremity of the body (foot) shows the distribution of adipose tissue along the body, and the area under this curve gives total adipose tissue volume; multiplying this by adipose tissue density gives adipose tissue mass. This approach has also used ultrasound imaging at measured points on the arm and thigh to estimate segmental fat and lean mass volumes (Eston *et al.* 1994). While medical imaging techniques could be used as a criterion measure against which level III methods may be calibrated – particularly skinfolds – this has yet to be done comprehensively as only a small number of subjects have been investigated in this manner. However, CT and MRI have proved very useful in the study of intra-abdominal adiposity, which is discussed in a later section.

1.7.2 Muscle

The quantity and proportion of body fat have remained a focal point in body composition analysis because of the perceived negative relationship of fatness to health, fitness and sport performance. It is evident to many working with high-performance athletes that knowledge of the changing total and regional masses of muscle in an athlete is an equal or perhaps more significant factor in sport performance. Estimation of total and regional skeletal muscle mass (SM) has not received the same attention as estimation of fat mass although it could be argued that there is more variability among athletes in muscle mass than in body fat, and therefore a greater need to know. Anatomical (tissue based) models for estimating total muscle mass have been proposed by Matiegka (1921),

Heymsfield *et al.* (1982), Drinkwater *et al.* (1986), and Martin *et al.* (1990). The early approach of Matiegka (1921) was based on the recognition that total muscle mass was in large part reflected by the size of muscles on the extremities. Thus, he proposed that muscle mass could be predicted by using skinfold-corrected diameters of muscle from the upper arm, forearm, thigh and calf multiplied by stature and an empirically derived constant. Drinkwater *et al.* (1986) attempted to validate Matiegka's formula using the evidence of the Brussels Cadaver Study and proposed modifications to the original mathematical constant. Martin *et al.* (1990) published equations for the estimation of muscle mass in men based on cadaver evidence. Data from six unembalmed cadavers were used to derive a regression equation to predict total muscle mass. The proposed equation was subsequently validated by predicting the known muscle masses from a separate cohort of five embalmed cadavers ($R^2 = 0.93$, SEE 1.58 kg, approximately 0.5%) and comparing the results to estimates derived from the equations of Matiegka (1921) and Heymsfield *et al.* (1982). The equation recommended by Martin *et al.* (1990) was much better able to predict muscle mass than the other two equations, which substantially underestimated the muscle mass of what must be regarded as a limited sample. Martin *et al.* (1990) attempted to minimise the specificity of their equation by ensuring that the upper and lower body were both represented in the three circumference terms.

Several of the above methods are based on the geometric model of extremity girths describing a circle and a single skinfold as representative of a constant subcutaneous layer overlying a circular muscle mass. A simple formula predicts the skinfold corrected geometric properties of the combined muscle and bone tissue (Figure 1.8).

$$\text{muscle and bone area} = \pi \left(\frac{c}{2\pi} - \frac{SF}{2} \right)^2$$

where *c* is girth measure (cm) and *SF* is skinfold (cm)

Further, the volume of the segments of the limb have been predicted by use of the formula for a cone. The anthropometric/geometric model has been found consistently to over-estimate muscle area when compared to areas measured from computed tomography and magnetic resonance images (de Koning *et al.* 1986; Baumgartner *et al.* 1992). Nevertheless, the correlation between anthropometrically derived areas and imaged areas has been shown to be very high $r > 0.9$.

More recently, the validity of the type of anthropometric procedures used in the above studies has been assessed *in vivo* on 244 non-obese adults ranging in age from 20 to 81 years (Lee *et al.* 2000). Using state-of-the-art whole-body multislice magnetic resonance imaging to measure skeletal mass, they assessed the predictive accuracy of the upper arm, calf and thigh circumferences (corrected for skinfold thickness), with height, race and gender as the other predictor variables. The final derived equation explained 91% of the variance in skeletal muscle mass with an SEE of 2.2 kg (refer to Practical 5, Section 1.13.2b). It is notable that of all the limb circumferences, corrected arm girth (CAG) had the highest correlation with total-body skeletal muscle mass ($R = 0.88$), which supports the frequent use of arm girth or arm muscle area as a measure of total-body SM and subject protein status.

The relationship of cross-sectional area of muscle to force output is well established (Ikai and Fukunaga 1968). Knowledge of the changing size of muscle resulting from particular training regimens is therefore important information for a coach evaluating the effect of the programme and for the motivation of the athlete (Hawes and Sovak, 1994). Size of muscle relative to body mass may provide information on a young athlete's stage of development and readiness for certain categories of skill development; changing size of muscle may reflect the effectiveness of a particular exercise or activity; diminished size may reflect a lack of recovery time (over-training) or in-season response to changing patterns of training. In all instances regular feedback of results to the coach may provide early information for adjustment or enhancement of the training regimens.

1.7.3 Bone

The skeleton is a dynamic tissue responding to environmental and endocrine changes by altering its shape and its density. Nevertheless it is less volatile than either muscle or adipose tissue and its influence upon human performance has been largely neglected. Matiegka (1921) proposed that skeletal mass could be estimated from an equation that included stature, the maximum diameter of the humerus, wrist, femur and ankle and a mathematical constant. Drinkwater *et al.* (1986) attempted to validate the proposed equation against recent cadaver data and found that an adjustment to Matiegka's constant produced a more accurate estimate in their sample of older, cadaveric persons. Drinkwater *et al.* (1986) commented that the true value of the coefficient probably lies between the original and their calculated

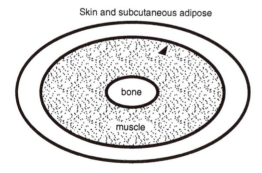

Figure 1.8 Schematic view of the derivation of estimated muscle and bone area from a measurement of external girth. There are inherent assumptions that the perimeters are circular and that a single skinfold measure is representative of the entire subcutaneous layer of the section. Muscle and bone area = $\pi ((c/2\pi) - (SF/2))^2$, where *c* = girth measure (cm), SF = skinfold (cm).

value. An estimation of bone mass within a prototypical model may provide insight into structural factors which contribute to athletic success. In a longitudinal study of high performance synchronized swimmers, Hawes and Sovak (1993) found that the world and Olympic champion had disproportionally narrow bony diameters compared with other synchronized swimmers competing at the international level. Since positive buoyancy contributes to the ease of performing exercises above water, a relatively small mass of the most dense body tissue might be construed as a morphological advantage in athletes of otherwise equal abilities.

1.8 OTHER CONSIDERATIONS

In this chapter, an overview of the issues surrounding the quantification of body composition *in vivo* has been presented. There are several issues in body composition that must be resolved before the field can advance to maturity. The most important is the absence of validation and the consequent lack of a true criterion method. While DXA is well placed to assume this role for per cent fat, some methodological improvements are needed before then. Considerable work has been

done in recent years on multi-component models that estimate body fat by equations incorporating a number of measured variables, such as body density, total body water, and bone mineral content. In this way it is hoped that the improvement in prediction is not offset by the increased error inherent in the measurement of many variables. The second problem is the traditional focus on the chemical model, specifically fat. This has meant that sport scientists and others have few proven tools for quantifying body constituents that have physiological and anatomical meaning, particularly skeletal muscle. The advances in medical imaging discussed here may help to address this issue, but these methods are expensive and difficult for many to access.

In summary, care must be taken in applying body composition methods because of their sample specificity and poor validation. Because of this the best use of body composition techniques is probably for repeated measures in the same individuals over a period of time to investigate change due to growth, ageing or some intervention. The following laboratory exercises are designed to provide an introduction to a variety of body composition assessment procedures.

1.9 PRACTICAL 1: DENSITOMETRY

1.9.1 Purpose

* To determine body composition by densitometry

1.9.2 Methods

1   The subject should report to the laboratory several hours postprandial. A form-fitting swim suit is the most appropriate attire.
2   Height, body mass and age should be recorded using the methods specified in Practical 3.
3   Determination of total body density.
    Facilities will vary from custom-built tanks to swimming pools. The following is an outline of the major procedures:

- Determine the tare weight of the suspended seat or platform together with weight belt
- Record the water temperature and barometric pressure.
- The subject should enter the tank and ensure that all air bubbles (clinging to hair or trapped in swim suit) are removed.
- Subjects who may have difficulty in maintaining full submersion should attach a weight belt of approximately 3 kg.
- The subject quietly submerses while sitting or squatting on the freely suspended platform and exhales to a maximum. Drawing the knees up to the chest will facilitate complete evacuation of the lungs. The subject remains as still as possible and the scale reading is recorded.
- This procedure is repeated 4–5 times with the most consistent highest value accepted as the underwater weight.

4   Determination of residual volume (RV)

- RV is the volume of air remaining in the lungs following a maximal exhalation.
- RV may be measured by the O_2 dilution method or estimated from age and height.
- If the RV is to be measured, there is evidence to suggest that the procedure should be completed with the subject submersed to the neck in order to approximate the pressure acting on the lungs in a fully submersed position.
- The equipment used to determine RV will vary from laboratory to laboratory. The fundamental procedure is as follows:
- The gas analyzer should be calibrated according to manufacturer's specifications.
- A three-way T valve is connected to a five-litre anaesthetic bag, a pure oxygen tank and a spirometer. The system (spirometer, bag, valve and tubing) should be flushed with oxygen three times. On the fourth occasion a measured quantity (approximately 5 l) of oxygen is introduced into the spirometer bell, the O_2 valve is closed and the T valve opened to permit the O_2 to pass into the anaesthetic bag. The bag is closed off with a spring clip and is removed from the system together with the T valve. A mouthpiece hose is attached to the T valve.
- The subject prepares by attaching a nose clip and immersing to the neck in the tank. The mouthpiece is inserted and the valve opened so that the subject is breathing room air. When comfortable the subject exhales maximally, drawing the knees to the chest in a similar posture to that adopted during underwater weighing, since RV is affected by posture (see Dangerfield, Chapter 4). At maximum exhalation the T valve is opened to the pure O_2 anaesthetic bag and the subject completes 5–6 regular inhalation-exhalation cycles. On the signal the subject again exhales maximally and the T valve to the anaesthetic bag is closed. The subject removes the mouthpiece and breathes normally. The anaesthetic bag is attached to the gas analyzers and values for the CO_2 and O_2 are recorded.

- Measurement of RV should be repeated several times to ensure consistent results.

1.9.3 Calculation of residual volume and density

(a) Measured residual volume (Wilmore et al. 1980)

$$RV = \frac{VO_2 \text{ (ml)} \times F_EN_2}{0.798 - F_EN_2} - DS \text{ (ml)} \times BTPS$$

where:

VO_2 is the volume of O_2 measured into the anaesthetic bag (~5 litres)

F_EN_2 is the fraction of N_2 at the point where equilibrium of the gas analyzer occurred calculated as:

$$[100\% - (\%O_2 + \%CO_2)]/100$$

DS is the dead space of mouthpiece and breathing valve (calculated from specific situation)

BTPS, the body temperature pressure saturated, is the correction factor which corrects the volume of measured gas to ambient conditions of the lung according to the following Table 1.3

Table 1.3 Correction factors for gas volumes at BTPS

Gas temp. (°C)	Correction Factor	Gas temp. (°C)	Correction Factor
20.0	1.102	24.0	1.079
20.5	1.099	24.5	1.077
21.0	1.096	25.0	1.074
21.5	1.093	25.5	1.071
22.0	1.091	26.0	1.069
22.5	1.089	26.5	1.065
23.0	1.085	27.0	1.062
23.5	1.082	27.5	1.060

b) Predicted residual volume

Using the equations of Quanjer et al. (1993).

Substitute 25 y in the equations for any adult under 25 y.

Men: RV = (1.31 × height (m)) − (0.022 × age (y)) − 1.23
Women: RV = (1.81 × height (m)) + (0.016 × age (y)) − 2.00

1.9.4 Body density calculations

Total body volume (l) = (Mass in air − mass in water)/Density of water corrected for water temperature

Total body density (kg l^{-1}) = (Mass in air)/(Total body volume (L) – trapped air)
where: trapped air = residual lung volume + tubing dead space + 100 ml
(100 ml is the conventional allowance for gastro-intestinal gases) and correction for
water temperature is according to Table 1.5:

Table 1.4 Water Temperature Correction

Water temp (°C)	Density of water
25.0	0.997
28.0	0.996
31.0	0.995
35.0	0.994
38.0	0.993

% Fat according to Siri (1956) = [(4.95 / body density) – 4.50] × 100
% Fat according to Brozek *et al.* (1963) = [(4.57/ body density) – 4.142] × 100

Effect of changes in assumed density of the fat-free body

You can compare the estimations of per cent body fat in the following hypothetical
pairs of individuals (who have identical hydrodensitometric values) when the %fat is
calculated by the Siri equation and when it is calculated from an equation which is
derived from respective assumed population-specific densities of the fat free body (FFB)
(see Table 1.5). Assume the temperature of the water is 35 degrees C.

It can be noted from these values, that when the density of the fat free body is *above*
the assumed value of 1.10 kg.l^{-1}, the per cent fat is underestimated when calculated using
the Siri equation. When the density of the fat free body is *below* the assumed value of
1.10 kg.l^{-1}, the per cent fat is overestimated when calculated using the Siri equation.

Table 1.5 Effects of changes in the assumed density of the fat-free body on per cent body fat

	Adult male A	Adult male B	Adult female A	Adult female B	Male child A	Female child A
Age (years)	30	30	30	30	15	15
Height (m)	1.80	1.80	1.70	1.70	1.70	1.60
Mass (kg)	90.0	90.0	63.0	63.0	70.0	55.0
RV (L)	1.80	1.80	1.10	1.10	1.10	1.05
Assumed GIG	0.10	0.10	0.10	0.10	0.08	0.06
Mass in water (kg)	4.4	4.4	2.3	2.3	3.0	2.0
Body volume (l)	86.1	86.1	59.9	59.9	65.8	51.9
Body density (kg.l^{-1})	1.0689	1.0689	1.0517	1.0517	1.0638	1.059
Density of FFB (kg.l^{-1})	1.100	1.113	1.097	1.106	1.094	1.093
% Fat (Siri)	13.1	13.1	20.6	20.6	15.3	17.4
% Fat from FFB density	13.1	17.7	19.4	22.2	12.6	15.6

1.10 PRACTICAL 2: MEASUREMENT OF SKINFOLDS

1.10.1 Purpose

- To develop the technique of measuring skinfolds.
- To compare various methods of computing estimates of proportionate fatness.

1.10.2 Methods

A well-organized and established set of procedures will ensure that test sessions go smoothly and that there can be no implication of impropriety when measuring subjects. The procedures should include:

- prior preparation of equipment and recording forms;
- arrangements for a suitable space which is clean, warm and quiet;
- securing the assistance of an individual who will record values;
- forewarning the subjects that testing will occur at a given time and place;
- ensuring that females bring a bikini-style swim suit to facilitate measurement in the abdominal region and that males wear loose-fitting shorts or speed swim suit;
- ensuring that the measurer's technique includes recognition and respect for the notion of personal space and sensitive areas;
- taking great care in the consistent location of measurement sites as defined in Figures 1.10–1.15 and section 1.10.3;
- recognition that the data are very powerful in both a positive and *negative* sense. Young adolescents in particular are very sensitive about their body image and making public specific or implied information on body composition values may have a negative effect on an individual.

(a) Skinfold measurements – general technique
- During measurement the subject should stand erect but relaxed through the shoulders and arms. A warm room and easy atmosphere will help the subject to relax, which will help the measurer to manipulate the skinfold.
- Ideally, but not essentially, the site should be marked with a washable felt pen.
- The objective is to raise a double fold of skin and subcutaneous adipose leaving the underlying muscle undisturbed.
- All skinfolds are measured on the right side of the body.

Measurements should be made in series – moving from one site to the next until the entire protocol is complete.

- The measurer takes the fold between thumb and forefinger of the left hand following the natural cleavage lines of the skin.
- The calliper is held in the right hand and the pressure plates of the calliper are applied perpendicular to the fold and 1 cm below or to the right of the fingers, depending on the direction of the raised skinfold. (see Figure 1.9 for examples at various sites).

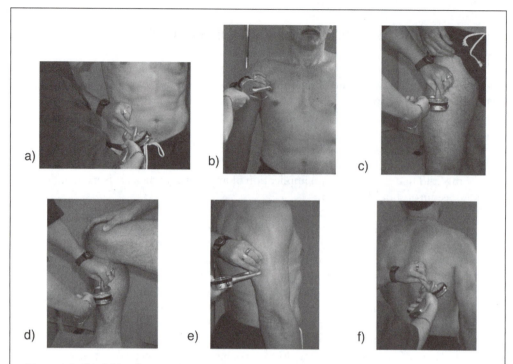

Figure 1.9 Skinfold calliper technique showing correct two-handed method and with calliper aligned to natural cleavage lines of the skin. Sites shown are supraspinale, pectoral, thigh, calf, triceps and subscapular.

- The calliper is held in position for 2 s prior to recording the measurement to the nearest 0.2 mm. The grasp is maintained throughout the measurement. In the case of large skinfolds, the needle is likely to be moving at this time, but the value is recorded nevertheless (Stewart and Eston 2006).
- The mean of duplicate or the median of triplicate measures (when the first two measures differ by more than 5%) is recommended.

(b) Secondary computation of fatness

There are over 100 equations for predicting fatness from skinfold measurements. The fact that these equations sometimes predict quite different values for the same individual leads to the conclusion that the equations are population-specific, i.e. the equation only accurately predicts the criterion value (usually densitometrically determined) for the specific population in the validation study. When applied to other populations the equation loses its validity. This diversity will be illustrated if estimates of per cent fat are computed from the following frequently used equations. It should be observed that while inter-individual comparisons of per cent fat may not be valid for many of the reasons previously discussed, intra-individual comparisons of repeated measurements may provide useful information. The summation of skinfold values will also provide comparative values avoiding some of the assumptions associated with estimates of proportionate fatness.

(c) Per cent fat equations (skinfold sites shown in Table 1.6)

Parizkova (1978) – ten sites

$$\%Fat = 39.572 \log \Sigma 10 - 61.25 \qquad \text{(females 17–45 y.)}$$
$$\%Fat = 22.320 \log \Sigma 10 - 29.00 \qquad \text{(males 17–45 y.)}$$

where $X = \Sigma 10$ skinfolds as specified (mm)

Durnin and Womersley (1974) – four sites

$$\text{body density} = 1.1610 - 0.0632 \, \text{Log}\Sigma 4 \quad \text{(men)}$$
$$\text{body density} = 1.1581 - 0.0720 \, \text{Log}\Sigma 4 \quad \text{(women)}$$
$$\text{body density} = 1.1533 - 0.0643 \, \text{Log}\Sigma 4 \quad \text{(boys)}$$
$$\text{body density} = 1.1369 - 0.0598 \, \text{Log}\Sigma 4 \quad \text{(girls)}$$

$$\%F \text{ (Siri, 1956)} = [(4.95 / \text{Body Density}) - 4.5] \times 100$$

where $\Sigma 4 = \Sigma 4$ skinfolds as specified (mm)

Jackson and Pollock (1978) – three sites (males)

$$\text{body density of males} = 1.1093800 - 0.0008267 \, (\Sigma 3_M) + 0.0000016 \, (\Sigma 3_M)^2$$
$$- 0.0002574 \, (\text{age y})$$

Jackson et al. (1980) – three sites (females)

$$\text{body density of females} = 1.099421 - 0.0009929 \, (\Sigma 3_F) + 0.0000023 \, (\Sigma 3_F)^2$$
$$- 0.0001392 \, (\text{age y})$$

$$\%F \text{ (Siri, 1956)} = [(4.95 / \text{Body Density}) - 4.5] \times 100$$

where $\Sigma 3_M = \Sigma 3$ skinfolds (mm) as specified for males
$\Sigma 3_F = \Sigma 3$ skinfolds (mm) as specified for females

Jackson and Pollock (1978) – seven sites

$$\text{body density of males} = 1.112 - 0.00043499 \, (\Sigma 7) + 0.00000055 \, (\Sigma 7)^2$$
$$- 0.00028826 \, (\text{age y})$$

Jackson et al. (1980) – seven sites

$$\text{body density of females} = 1.097 - 0.00046971 \, (\Sigma 7) + 0.00000056 \, (\Sigma 7)^2$$
$$- 0.00012828 \, (\text{age y})$$
$$\%F \text{ (Siri, 1956)} = [(4.95 / \text{Body Density}) - 4.5] \times 100$$

where $\Sigma 7 = \Sigma 7$ skinfolds as specified (mm)

Peterson et al. (2003) – four sites

For men:

$$\%\text{Fat} = 20.94878 + (\text{age} \times 0.1166) - (\text{Ht} \times 0.11666) + (\Sigma4 \times 0.42696) - (\Sigma4^2 \times 0.00159)$$

For women:

$$\%\text{Fat} = 22.18945 + (\text{age} \times 0.06368) + (\text{BMI} \times 0.60404) - (\text{Ht} \times 0.14520) + (\Sigma4 \times 0.30919) - (\Sigma4^2 \times 0.00099562)$$

Where Ht is in cm and $\Sigma4$ = the sum of skinfolds as specified

Table 1.6 Summary of skinfold sites used in selected equations for prediction of per cent fat

Reference	Parizkova (1978)	Jackson et al. (1980)	Jackson and Pollock (1978)	Jackson et al. (1980)	Jackson and Pollock (1978)	Durnin and Womersley (1974)	Peterson et al. (2003)	Peterson et al. (2003)
Sum of skinfolds	Σ10	Σ3	Σ3	Σ7	Σ7	Σ4	Σ4	Σ4
Population	M & F	female	male	female	male	M & F	male	female
BMI								*
Age (y)		*	*	*	*		*	*
Height (cm)							*	*
Skinfold Site								
Cheek	*							
Chin	*							
Pectoral (chest 1)	*		*	*	*			
Axilla (midaxillary)				*	*			
Chest 2	*							
Iliocristale	*							
Abdomen	*							
Abdominal			*	*	*			
Iliac Crest*						*	*	*
Suprailium		*		*	*			
Subscapular	*			*	*	*	*	*
Triceps	*	*		*	*	*	*	*
Biceps						*		
Patella	*							
Mid-thigh		*	*	*	*		*	*
Proximal calf	*							

*Referred to as 'suprailiac' by Durnin and Womersley (1974) and 'iliocristale' by Parizkova (1978).

1.10.3 Locations of skinfold sites

All measurements are taken on the right side of the body.

Cheek: *horizontal* skinfold raised at the midpoint of the line connecting the tragus (cartilaginous projection anterior to the external opening of the ear) and the nostrils (Figure 1.10).

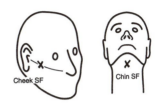

Figure 1.10 Location of the cheek and chin skinfold sites.

Chin: *vertical* skinfold raised above the hyoid bone: the head is slightly lifted but the skin of the neck must stay loose (Figure 1.10).

Pectoral (chest 1): *oblique* skinfold raised along the borderline of the m. pectoralis major between the anterior axillary fold and the nipple (Figure 1.9b and 1.11).

Females: measurement is taken at 1/3 of the distance between anterior axillary fold and nipple.

Males: measurement is taken at one-half of the distance between anterior axillary fold and nipple (Figure 1.9a and 1.11).

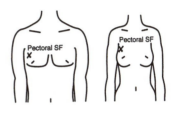

Figure 1.11 Location of the pectoral skinfold sites.

Axilla: *vertical* skinfold raised at the level of the xipho-sternal junction (midaxillary) on the mid-axillary line (Figure 1.12).

Chest 2: *horizontal* skinfold raised on the chest above the 10th rib at the point of intersection with the anterior axillary line – slight angle along the ribs (Figure 1.12).

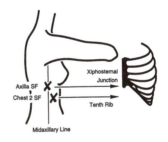

Figure 1.12 Location of the axilla and chest 2 skinfold sites.

Abdomen: *horizontal* fold raised 3 cm lateral and 1 cm inferior to the umbilicus (Figure 1.13).

Abdominal: *vertical* fold raised at a lateral distance of approximately 2 cm from the umbilicus (Figure 1.13).

Iliac crest: *diagonal* fold raised immediately above the crest of the ilium on a vertical line from the mid-axilla. This skinfold was

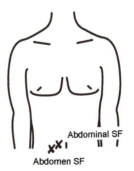

Figure 1.13 Location of the abdominal skinfold sites.

referred to as the 'suprailiac' by Durnin
and Womersley (1974) and 'iliocristale' by
Parizkova (1978) (Figure 1.14).

Supraspinale: *diagonal* fold raised immediately above the crest of the ilium on a
vertical line from the anterior axillary
fold.

Subscapular: *oblique* skinfold raised 1 cm
below the inferior angle of the scapula at
approximately 45° to the horizontal plane
following the natural cleavage lines of the
skin (Figure 1.9f and 1.15).

Triceps: *vertical* skinfold raised on the
posterior aspect of the m. triceps, exactly
halfway between the olecranon process
and the acromion process when the hand
is supinated (Figure 1.9e and 1.15).

Biceps: *vertical* skinfold raised on the
anterior aspect of the biceps, at the same
horizontal level as the triceps skinfold
(Figure 1.15).

Patella: *vertical* skinfold in the mid sagittal
plane raised 2 cm above the proximal edge
of the patella. The subject should bend the
knee slightly (Figure 1.16).

Mid-thigh: *vertical* skinfold raised on
the anterior aspect of the thigh midway
between the inguinal crease and the proximal border of the patella (Figure 1.9c and
1.16).

A preferred method is to flex the knee
slightly with the subject in the standing
position with the heel of the foot resting
on the other foot (as shown in Figure 1.8).
An alternative method is to flex the knee at
an angle of 90 degrees with the subject in a
seated position, or the subject could stand
with the foot placed on a box.

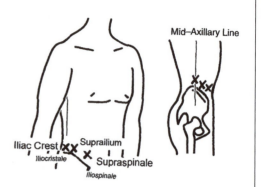

Figure 1.14 Location of the skinfold sites in the iliac crest region only.

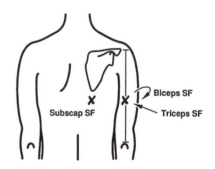

Figure 1.15 Location of the biceps, triceps and subscapular skinfold sites.

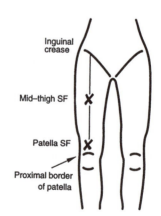

Figure 1.16 Location of the anterior thigh skinfold sites.

Proximal calf: *vertical* skinfold raised on the posterior aspect of the calf in the mid-saggital plane 5 cm inferior to the fossa poplitea (Figure 1.17).

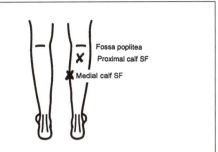

Medial calf: *vertical* skinfold raised on the medial aspect of the calf at the level of the maximal circumference. The subject may be sitting or have the foot placed on a box (Figure 1.9d and 1.17).

Figure 1.17 Location of the proximal and medial calf skinfold site.

1.11 PRACTICAL 3: SIMPLE INDICES OF BODY FAT DISTRIBUTION

1.11.1 Purpose

- to evaluate body mass index;
- to evaluate the fat-free mass index;
- to evaluate waist to hip ratio as a measure of fat patterning.

1.11.2 Method: body mass index (BMI)

- BMI = body mass (kg) / stature^2 (m);
- describes weight for height;
- often used in epidemiological studies as a measure of obesity;
- a high BMI means proportionately high weight for height.

(a) Stature
- As height is variable throughout the day the measurement should be performed at the same time for each test session. (Height may still vary due to activities causing compression of the intervertebral discs, i.e. running.)
- All stature measurements should be taken with the subject barefoot.
- The *Frankfort Plane* refers to the position of the head when the line joining the orbitale (lower margin of eye socket) to the tragion (notch above tragus of the ear) is horizontal.
- There are several techniques for measuring height which yield slightly different values.

The following technique is recommended:

(b) Stature against a wall
- The subject stands erect, feet together against a wall on a flat surface at a right angle to the wall mounted stadiometer.
- The stadiometer consists of a vertical board with an attached metric rule and a horizontal headboard that slides to contact the vertex.

- The heels, buttocks, upper back and (if possible) cranium should touch the wall.
- The subject's head should be in the Frankfort Plane; arms relaxed at sides.
- The subject is instructed to inhale and stretch up.
- The measurer slides the headboard of the stadiometer down to the vertex and records the measurement to the nearest 0.1 cm.

(c) Body mass
- Use a calibrated beam-type balance.
- The subject should be weighed without shoes and in minimal clothing.
- For best results, repeated measurements should be taken at the same time of day, in the same state of hydration and nourishment after voiding (preferably first thing in the morning – 12 hours after ingesting food).
- The measurement should be recorded to the nearest 0.1 kg.

(d) Interpretation
Values should be interpreted according to previous discussion (Section 1.6.1).

1.11.3 Method: fat free mass index (FFMI)

The FFMI has been used to assess whether an athlete's muscularity is within the naturally attainable range or is beyond that which could reasonably be expected without pharmacological assistance.

The correctional factor [6.1 x(1.8 – height (m)] is based on data from the study of Kouri *et al.* (1995) and is used only in calculations for males.

Insert the height, mass and per cent fat values into the following equation:

$$FFMI = \frac{\text{Mass (kg)} \times [(100 - \%\text{fat})/100)) + 6.1 \times (1.8 - \text{Height (m)}]}{\text{Height}^2}$$

Interpretation: Refer to Table 1.2 for percentile values.

MEN
18 = slight build low musculature; 20 = young man of average muscularity; 22 = distinctly muscular; 25 = upper limit that can be attained without use of anabolic steroids.

WOMEN
13 = low musculature; 15 = young woman of average muscularity; 17 = muscular woman; 22 = upper limit than can be used without use of anabolic steroids.

1.11.3 Method: waist-to-hip ratio (WHR)

- WHR = waist girth / hip girth.
- WHR may be used in conjunction with trunk skinfolds to determine whether excess fat is being carried in the trunk region.
- A high WHR combined with high trunk skinfolds has been shown to be associated

with increased morbidity; glucose intolerance, hyperinsulinaemia, blood lipid disorders and mortality.

- A high WHR with low skinfolds may be associated with high trunk muscle development.

(a) Tape technique (cross-handed technique)

- The metal case is held in the right hand and the stub end is controlled by the left hand.
- Girths are measured with the tape at right angles to the long axis of the bone.
- The tape is pulled out of its case and around the body segment by the left hand; the two hands are crossed intersecting the tape at the zero mark.
- The aim is to obtain the circumference of the part with the tape in contact with, but not depressing, the fleshy contour.

(b) Waist girth

- The subject stands erect with abdomen relaxed, arms at sides and feet together.
- The measurer stands facing subject and places a steel tape measure around the subject's natural waist (the obvious narrowing between the rib and the iliac crest).
- If there is no obvious waist, find the smallest horizontal circumference in this region.
- Measurement is taken at the end of a normal expiration to the nearest 0.1 cm.

(c) Hip girth

- The subject stands erect with buttocks relaxed, feet together and preferably wearing underwear or a swimsuit.
- The measurer stands to one side of the subject and places steel tape measure around the hips at the horizontal level of greatest gluteal protuberance (usually at the level of the symphysis pubis).
- Check that the tape is not compressing the skin and record to the nearest 0.1 cm.

(d) Interpretation

- Values of = 0.90 (males) and = 0.80 (females) are considered to place an individual in health risk zones according to morbidity and mortality data for males and females aged 20–70 years. These values should be considered within the context of the discussion presented previously.

1.12 PRACTICAL 4: BIOELECTRICAL IMPEDANCE ANALYSIS (BIA)

- BIA is based on the electrical conductance characteristics of hydrous (fat free) and anhydrous (fat component) tissues.
- The impedance to the flow of an electrical current is a function of resistance and reactance and is related to length and cross-sectional area of the conductor (the hydrous or fat free tissue).
- Electrical resistance (Ω) is most commonly used to represent impedance.

1.12.1 Test conditions

Prior to testing the subject should:

- not have had anything to eat or drink in the previous 4 hours;
- not have exercised within the previous 12 hours;
- not have consumed alcohol within the previous 48 hours;
- not have used diuretics within the previous 7 days;
- have urinated within the previous 30 minutes.

1.12.2 Anthropometric procedures

- as defined by the manufacturer (if using the pre-programmed function of the unit) or according to the equation of choice;
- subject should lie supine on a table with the legs slightly apart and the right hand and foot bare;
- four electrodes are prepared with electro-conducting gel and attached at the following sites (or as per manufacturer's instructions):
- just proximal to the dorsal surface of the 3rd metacarpal-phalangeal joint on the right hand
- on the dorsal surface of the right wrist adjacent to the head of the ulna
- on the dorsal surface of the right foot just proximal to the 2nd metatarsal-phalangeal joint
- on the anterior surface of the right ankle between the medial and lateral malleoli
- the subject should lie quietly while the analyzer is turned on and off;
- the subject should lie quietly for 5 minutes before repeating the procedure.

1.12.3 Calculations

- as per manufacturer instructions, or

For prediction of fat-free mass in adults:

i) **Kyle *et al.* (2001)** (derived from 343 healthy adults aged 18–94 years using DXA as the criterion)

FFM (kg) = $(0.518 \times Ht^2/R) + (0.231 \times$ body mass$) + (0.130 \times Xc) + (4.229 \times$ gender$) - 4.104$
$R^2 = 0.97$; SEE = 1.8 kg

ii) **Deurenburg *et al.* (1991)** (derived from 661 healthy adults using a multicomponent model and hydrodensitometry as the criterion)

FFM (kg) = $(0.34 \times Ht^2/R) + (0.1534 \times Ht) + (0.273 \times$ body mass$) - (0.127 \times$ age$) + (4.56 \times$ gender$) - 12.44$
$R^2 = 0.93$ SEE = 2.6 kg

where Ht = height (cm); R = resistance (Ω); Xc = Reactance, age = years, gender for males = 1, females = 0

For prediction of fat-free mass in children:
i) Houtkooper *et al.* (1989) (derived from 94 North American children aged 10–14 years using a multicomponent model using hydrodensitometry and TBW as the criterion)

FFM (kg) = 2.69 + (0.58 × Ht^2/R) + (0.24 × body mass)
R^2 = 0.96 SEE = 2.00 kg

ii) Eston *et al.* (1993) (derived from 94 Hong Kong Chinese children aged 11–17 years using a children's skinfold equation as the criterion)

FFM (kg) = 3.25 + (0.52 × Ht^2/R) + (0.28 × body mass)
R^2 = 0.93 SEE = 2.20 kg

For prediction of skeletal muscle (SM) mass in adults:

SM mass (kg) = (Ht^2/R × 0.401) + (gender × 3.825) + (age × 0.071) + 5.102
(Janssen *et al.* 2000)

where ht = height (cm); R = resistance (Ω); M = mass (kg); gender for males = 1, females = 0; age in years

1.13 PRACTICAL 5: ESTIMATION OF MUSCLE MASS AND REGIONAL MUSCULARITY USING *IN VITRO-* AND *IN VIVO-*DERIVED EQUATIONS

1.13.1 Purpose

• to develop the technique required to estimate total and regional muscularity

1.13.2 Methods

a) In vitro-derived equations
Matiegka (1921) – males and females

M (kg) = [(CDU + CDF + CDT + CDC)/8]^2 × ht (cm) × 6.5 × 0.001
M % = (M kg / body mass) × 100

where:

$$CDU = \frac{(\text{max upper arm girth})}{\pi} - \text{triceps SF (cm)}$$

$$CDF = \frac{\text{(max forearm girth)}}{\pi} - \frac{\text{forearm SF 1(cm)} + \text{forearm SF 2(cm)}}{2}$$

$$CDT = \frac{\text{(mid thigh girth)}}{\pi} - \text{mid thigh skinfold (cm)}$$

$$CDT = \frac{\text{(max calf girth)}}{\pi} - \text{mid calf skinfold (cm)}$$

- ht is stature in cm;
- variables for computing corrected diameters are defined on the following pages;
- CD is corrected diameter of U = upper arm, F = forearm, T = thigh, C = calf;
- note that skinfolds should be expressed in cm, i.e. caliper reading/10.

Martin et al. (1990) – males only

M (kg) = [ht × (0.0553CTG^2 + 0.0987FG^2 + 0.0331CCG^2) – 2445] × 0.001
M % = (M kg /body mass) × 100

where:

R^2 = 0.97, SEE = 1.53 kg
ht   is stature in cm
CTG   is corrected thigh girth = thigh girth – π (front thigh SF/10)
FG   is maximum forearm girth
CCG   is corrected calf girth = calf girth – π (medial calf SF/10)

b) In vivo-derived equations
Lee et al. (2000) males and females (derived from 244 men and women aged 20–81 years using MRI as the criterion)

i) Skinfold-circumference model

SM (kg) = Ht (cm) × (0.00744 × CAG^2) + (0.00088 × CTG^2)+ (0.00441 × CCG^2)
+ (2.4 × gender) × (0.048 × age) + race + 7.8,

where

R^2 = 0.91, P < 0.0001, and SEE = 2.2 kg;
CAG = corrected arm girth (cm) using the triceps skinfold
Corrected circumference = limb circumference – (π × skinfold)

CTG = corrected thigh girth (cm) using the mid-thigh skinfold
CCG = corrected calf girth (cm) using medial calf skinfold
gender = 0 for female and 1 for male,
race = –2.0 for Asian, 1.1 for African American, and 0 for white and Hispanic

ii) Body weight and height model

SM (kg) = (0.244 × body mass (kg)) + (7.80 × Ht (cm)) – (0.098 × age) + (6.6 × gender) + race – 3.3

where

R^2 = 0.86, P < 0.0001, and SEE = 2.8 kg;
gender = 0 for female and 1 for male,
race = –1.2 for Asian, 1.4 for African American, and 0 for white and Hispanic

1.13.3 Determination of variables related to estimation of muscle mass

Stature (ht) as before (Practical 3)

Maximum upper arm girth (cm)
- the girth measurement of the upper arm at the insertion of the deltoid muscle;
- subject stands erect with the arm abducted to the horizontal, measurer stands behind the arm of the subjects, marks the insertion of the deltoid muscle and measures the girth perpendicular to the long axis of the arm.

Maximum forearm girth (cm)
- the maximum circumference at the proximal part of the forearm (usually within 5 cm of the elbow);
- subject stands erect with the arm extended in the horizontal plane with the hand supinated; measurer stands behind the subject's arm and moves the tape up and down the forearm (perpendicular to the long axis) until the maximum circumference of the forearm is located.

Mid-thigh girth (cm)
- the girth taken at the midpoint between the trochanterion and the tibiale laterale;
- subject stands erect, feet 10 cm apart and weight evenly distributed, measurer crouches to the right side, palpates and marks the trochanterion and the tibiale laterale. The midpoint is found using a tape or anthropometer;
- the girth is taken at this level, perpendicular to the long axis of the thigh.

Maximum calf girth (cm)
- subject stands erect, feet 10 cm apart and weight evenly distributed; measurer crouches to the right side and moves the tape up and down the calf perpendicular to the long axis until the greatest circumference is located.

Triceps skinfold (cm)
- as before (Practical 2)

Mid-thigh skinfold (cm)
- as before (Practical 2)

Mid-calf skinfold (cm)
- as before (Practical 2)

Medial calf skinfold (cm)
- A vertical skinfold is taken on the medial aspect of the calf at the level of maximum calf girth; the subject stands with the right foot on a platform, flexing the knee and hip to 90°.

Forearm 1 (lateralis) (cm)
- A vertical skinfold is taken at the level of maximum forearm girth on the lateral aspect of the forearm with the hand supinated.

Forearm 2 (volaris) (cm)
- A vertical skinfold is taken at the level of maximum forearm girth taken on the anterior aspect of the forearm with the hand supinated.

1.14 PRACTICAL 6: ESTIMATION OF SKELETAL MASS

- an indication of skeletal robustness that correlates highly with bone breadths at the elbow, wrist, knee and ankle

1.14.1 Purpose

- to develop the technique required to estimate skeletal mass by anthropometry

1.14.2 Methods

Matiegka (1921) – males and females.

$$S \text{ (kg)} = [(HB + WB + FB + AB)/4]^2 \times ht \times 1.2 \text{ kg} \times 0.001$$
$$S \% = (S \text{ kg} / \text{ body mass}) \times 100$$

where: HB is biepicondylar humerus, WB is bistyloideus, FB is biepicondylar femur, AB is bimalleolar, ht is height in cm.

Drinkwater et al. (1986) – males and females

$$S \text{ (kg)} = [(HB + WB + FB + AB)/4]^2 \times ht \times 0.92 \text{ kg} \times 0.001$$
$$S \% = (\text{kg } S / \text{ body mass}) \times 100$$

where variables are as defined previously.

1.14.3 Determination of variables related to estimation of skeletal mass

- Landmarks for bone breadth measurements should be palpated with the fingers, and then the anthropometer is applied firmly to the bone, compressing soft tissue when necessary.

Stature (ht) as before (Practical 3)

Biepicondylar humerus breadth
- the distance between medial and lateral epicondyles of the humerus when the shoulder and elbow are flexed;
- the measurer palpates the epicondyles and applies the blades of an anthropometer or small spreading calliper at a slight upward angle while firmly pressing the blades to the bone.

Bistyloideus breadth
- the distance between the most prominent aspects of the styloid processes of the ulna and radius;
- the subject flexes the elbow and the hand is pronated so that the wrist is horizontal;
- the styloid processes are palpated and the anthropometer is applied firmly to the bone.

Biepicondylar femur breadth
- This is the distance between the most medial and lateral aspects of the femoral condyles (epicondyles).
- The subject stands with the weight on the left leg and the right knee flexed (the foot may rest on a raised surface or the subject may sit with the leg hanging).
- The measurer crouches in front of the subject, palpates the femoral condyles and applies the anthropometer at a slight downward angle while firmly pressing to the bone.

Bimalleolar breadth
- This is the maximum distance between the most medial and lateral extensions of the malleoli.
- The subject stands erect with the weight evenly distributed over both feet.
- The measurer palpates the malleoli and applies the anthropometer firmly to the bone.
- A horizontal distance is measured, but the plane between the malleoli is oblique.

1.15 PRACTICAL 7: EXAMPLE OF A MULTICOMPONENT (4C) MODEL OF BODY COMPOSITION ASSESSMENT USING THE MEAN DATA FROM WITHERS *ET AL.* (1998)

Withers *et al.* (1998) compared the accuracy of predicting per cent body fat from the two-component model of hydrodensitometry against a four-component model of body composition. The following practical uses the mean data from the group of 12 trained men in that study to exemplify how the prediction of per cent fat from hydrodensitometry tends to underestimate the true value when this is calculated from a model that can account for the various components of the fat-free body.

The mean values for the trained men in their study are:

Age = 22.3 ± 5.1 years, height = 175.2 ± 5.7, mass = 67.87 ± 5.30 kg, body density(D) = 1.0767 ± 0.0083 kg.l^{-1}, total body water (TBW) = 43.23 ± 3.59 L, total body bone mineral mass (BMM) = 3.40 ± 0.33 kg

The 4C Model used in the study was:

%fat = (251.3/D) − 73.9 (TBW/Mass) + 94.7 (BMM/mass) −179

Insertion of the average values into the above formula provides a close approximation of the reported mean %fat value for the trained group:

%fat = (251.3/1.0767) − 73.9 (43.23/67.87) + 94.7 (3.40/67.87) −179

The above 4C model prediction of %fat = 12.1%. The reported mean value was 12.1 ± 2.8 %fat.

The prediction of %fat using the Siri equation with the whole-body density value (1.0767) = 9.7% (*P*<0.01). Using these techniques, the density of the fat-free body was calculated to be greater (1.106360.005 (range 1.0974–1.1137) than the assumed value of 1.100 in the equation of Siri. When this value is used it underestimates %fat in the trained men.

1.16 ANTHROPOMETRIC LANDMARKS AND MEASUREMENT DEFINITIONS

These definitions are aligned with those of the International Society for the Advancement of Kinanthropometry, and are used here by permission of Turnpike Electronic Publications from whose CD-ROM, *Anthropometry Illustrated*, they are abridged.

1.16.1 Landmark definitions

Vertex (V): The vertex is the most superior point in the mid-sagittal plane on the skull when the head is held in the Frankfort Plane.

Gnathion (GN): The gnathion is the most inferior border of the mandible in the mid-sagittal plane.

Suprasternale (SST): The suprasternal notch is located at the superior border of the sternal notch (or incisura jugularis) in the mid-sagittal plane.

Mesosternale (MST): The mesosternale is the point located on the corpus sterni at the intersection of the mid-sagittal plane and the transverse plane at the mid-level of the 4th chondrosternal articulation.

Epigastrale (EG): The epigastrale is the point on the anterior surface of the trunk at the intersection of the mid-sagittal plane and the transverse plane through the most inferior point of the 10th rib.

Thelion (TH): The thelion is the breast nipple.

Omphalion (OM): The omphalion is the mid-point of the navel or umbilicus.

Symphysion (SY): The symphysion forms the superior border of the symphysis pubis at the mid-sagittal plane.

Acromiale (A): The acromiale is the point located at the superior and external border of the acromion process when the subject is standing erect with relaxed arms.

Radiale (R): The radiale is the point at the proximal and lateral border of the head of the radius.

Stylion (STY): The stylion is the most distal point on the styloid process of the radius. The stylion radiale is located in the so-called *anatomical snuffbox* (the triangular area formed when the thumb is extended at the 1st carpal-metacarpal joint, the area being defined by the raised tendons of the abductor pollicus longus, the external pollicus brevis and the extensor pollicus longus). It is the most distal point of the styloid process of the radius.

Dactylion (DA): The dactylion is the tip of the middle finger (3rd digit). It is the most distal point on the hand. The tips of the other digits are designated as the 1st, 2nd, 4th and 5th dactylions (the thumb being the 1st digit).

Metacarpale Radiale (MR): The metacarpale radiale is the most lateral point on the distal head of the 2nd metacarpal of the hand (located either on the outstretched hand or when gripping a dowel or pencil).

Metacarpale Ulnare (MU): The metacarpale ulnare is the most medial point on the distal head of the 5th metacarpal of the hand (located either on the outstretched hand or when gripping a dowel or pencil).

Iliocristale (IC): The iliocristale (or supracristale) is the most lateral point on the iliac crest. This is the site for locating the iliac crest skinfold that is immediately superior.

Iliospinale (IS): The iliospinale is the inferior aspect of the anterior superior iliac spine. The iliospinale is the undermost tip of the anterior superior iliac spine, not the most anterior curved aspect.

Spinale (SPI): The spinale is a less exact term for the iliospinale.

Trochanterion (TRO): The trochanterion is the most superior point on the greater trochanter of the femur, *not* the most lateral point.

Tibiale Mediale (TM): The tibiale mediale (or tibiale internum) is the most superior point on the margo glenoidalis of the medial border of the head of the tibia.

Tibiale Laterale (TL): The tibiale laterale (or tibiale externum) corresponds to the previously defined tibiale mediale, but is located on the lateral border of the head of the tibia (*not* to be confused with the more inferior capitum fibulare).

Sphyrion Laterale (SPH): The sphyrion laterale is on the malleolare mediale (or internum). It is the most distal tip of the malleolare mediale (or tibiale). It can be palpated most easily from beneath and dorsally (it is the distal tip, *not* the outermost point of the malleolare).

Sphyrion Fibulare (SPH F): The sphyrion fibulare is the most distal tip of the malleolare laterale (or externum) of the fibula. It is more distal than the sphyrion tibiale.

Pternion (PTE): The pternion is the most posterior point on the heel of the foot when the subject is standing.

Acropodion (AP): The acropodion is the most anterior, distal point on the longest phalange of the foot when the subject is standing. The subject's toenail may be clipped to locate this landmark when measuring.

Metatarsale Tibiale (MT T): The metatarsale tibiale is the most medial point on the head of the 1st metatarsal of the foot when the subject is standing.

Metatarsale Fibulare (MT F): The metatarsale fibulare is the most lateral point on the head of the 5th metatarsal of the foot when the subject is standing.

Cervicale (C): The cervicale is the most posterior point on the spinous process of the 7th cervical vertebra.

Gluteale (GA): The gluteale is the distal point in the mid-sagittal plane at the arch of the sacro-coccygeal fusion.

Measurement definitions

Stretch Stature: The maximum distance from the floor to the vertex of the head, when the head is held in the Frankfort Plane and a gentle traction force is applied.

Sitting Height: Stretch Sitting Height is the distance form the vertex of the head to the base of the sitting surface when the seated subject is instructed to sit tall and when gentle traction is applied to the mandible.

Body Weight: The force of gravity acting on the mass of the body.

Armspan: The distance from the left to the right dactylion of the hands when the palms are facing forward on the wall and the outstretched arms are abducted to the horizontal with the shoulders.

Lengths

Acromiale-Radiale Length (arm): The distance from the acromiale to the radiale.

Radiale-Stylion Length (forearm): The distance from the radiale to the stylion.

Mid-stylion-Dactylion Length (hand): The shortest distance from the mid-stylion line to the dactylion III.

Iliospinale Height (obtained height plus box height): Projected height from the box or tabletop to the iliospinale landmark.

Trochanterion Height (obtained height plus box height): Projected height from the box or tabletop to the trochanterion landmark.

Trochanterion-Tibiale Laterale Length (thigh): The distance from the trochanterion to the tibiale laterale.

Tibiale Laterale Height (leg): Distance from the box to the tibiale laterale landmark.

Tibiale Mediale-Sphyrion Tibiale (tibia length): Direct length from tibiale mediale to sphyrion tibiale.

Foot length: The distance between the acropodion and pternion (i.e. the most distal toe and posterior surface of the heel).

Breadths

Biacromial Breadth: The distance between the most lateral points on the acromion processes when the subject stands erect with the arms hanging loosely at the sides.

Biiliocristal Breadth: The distance between the most lateral points on the superior border of the iliac crest.

Transverse Chest Breadth: The distance between the most lateral aspects of the thorax at the mesosternale level.

Anterior-Posterior Chest Depth: The depth of the chest at the mesosternale level obtained with spreading calliper or anthropometer with recurved branches used as a sliding calliper.

Biepicondylar Humerus Breadth: Distance between medial and lateral epicondyles of the humerus when the arm is raised forward to the horizontal and the forearm is flexed to a right angle at the elbow.

Wrist Breadth: The bistyloid breadth when the right forearm is resting on a table or the subject's thigh and the hand flexed at the wrist to an angle of about 90°.

Hand Breadth: The distance between the metacarpale laterale and metacarpale mediale when the subject firmly grasps a pencil.

Biepicondylar Femur Breadth: The distance between medial and lateral epicondyles of the femur when the subject is seated and the leg is flexed at the knee to form a right angle with the thigh.

Ankle Breadth: The distance between maximum protrusions of the medial tibial malleolus and the lateral fibular malleolus.

Foot Breadth: The distance between metatarsale fibulare and the metatarsale tibiale.

Girths

Head Girth: The maximum perimeter of the

head when the tape is located immediately superior to the glabellar point (mid-point between brow ridges).

Neck Girth: The perimeter of the neck taken immediately superior to the larynx (Adam's apple).

Arm Girth (relaxed): The perimeter distance of the right arm parallel to the long axis of the humerus when the subject is standing erect and the relaxed arm is hanging by the sides.

Arm Girth (flexed and tensed): The maximum circumference of the flexed and tensed right arm raised to the horizontal position.

Forearm Girth: The maximal girth of the right forearm when the hand is held palm up and relaxed.

Wrist Girth: The perimeter of the right wrist taken distal to the styloid processes.

Chest Girth: The end-tidal perimeter of the chest at mesosternale level.

Waist Girth: The perimeter at the level of the noticeable waist narrowing located approximately half way between the costal border and iliac crest.

Omphalion Girth (abdominal): The perimeter distance at the level of the omphalion or mid-point of the umbilicus or navel.

Gluteal Girth (hip): The perimeter at the level of the greatest posterior protuberance and at approximately the symphysion pubis level anteriorly.

Thigh Girth (upper): The perimeter of the right thigh which is measured when the subject stands erect, weight equally distributed on both feet, and assisting by holding clothing out of the way.

Mid-Thigh Girth: The perimeter distance of the right thigh perpendicular to the long axis of the femur at the marked mid-trochanterion-tibiale level.

Calf Girth: The maximum perimeter of the calf when the subject stands with weight equally distributed on both feet.

Ankle Girth: The perimeter of the narrowest part of the lower leg superior to the sphyrion tibiale.

Skinfold Thicknesses
See descriptions in Practical 2.

ACKNOWLEDGEMENT

The authors acknowledge with thanks the contribution of Kate Plant and Daniela Sovak in the preparation of some of the laboratory activities; Steve Hudson in providing a graduate student perspective in the preparation of the text; Ann Rowlands for allowing us to use her results; and Dale Oldham for the preparation of computer-generated illustrations. We are also very grateful to Turnpike Electronics for permission to use excerpts from its CD-ROM.

FURTHER READING
Books/CD/DVD

Heymsfield S. B., Lohman T., Wang Z. and Going S. B. (2005) *Human body composition.* Human Kinetics; Champaign, IL.

Ross W. D., Carr R. V. and Carter J. E. L. (2000) *Anthropometry Illustrated*, Turnpike Electronic Publications (now Rosscraft), Canada.

Websites

http://www.nutrition.uvm.edu/bodycomp/
Department of Nutrition and Food Sciences, University of Vermont, USA. This website provides very useful interactive tutorials on hydrodensitometry, dual energy x-ray absorptiometry and bioelectrical impedance analysis techniques described in this chapter.

http://www.isakonline.com/
International Society for the Advancement of Kinanthropometry. This site contains a great deal of useful information and lots of useful links.

http://www.rosscraft.ca/
Rosscraft Incorporated (publishers of Anthropometry Illustrated) is a Canadian-based anthropometric instrument design, manufacturing and marketing company. This website contains a range of useful resources.

http://www.preventdisease.com/healthtools/
tools.html#roc

The health tools page of the Canadian-based *Preventdisease.com* is an excellent website, which includes dedicated programmes to calculate body fat from skinfolds, BMI, waist to hip ratios, etc.

REFERENCES

Abate N. A., Garg A., Coleman R. D., Grundy S. M. and Peshock R. M. (1997) Prediction of total subcutaneous abdominal, intraperitoneal and retroperitoneal adipose tissue masses in men by a single axial MRI scan. *American Journal of Clinical Nutrition*; **65**: 403–8.

Ball S. D. and Altena T. S. (2004). Comparison of the Bod Pod and dual x-ray absorptiometry in men. *Physiological Measurement*; **25**: 671–8.

Baumgartner R. N., Heymsfield S. B., Lichtman S., Wang J. and Pierson Jr. R. N. (1991) Body composition in elderly people: effect of criterion estimates on predictive equations. *American Journal of Clinical Nutrition*; **53**: 1345–53.

Baumgartner R. N., Rhyne R. L., Troup C., Wayne S., and Garry P. J. (1992). Appendicular skeletal muscle areas assessed by magnetic resonance imaging in older persons. *Journal of Gerontology*; **47**: M67–72.

Bjorntorp P. (1984). Hazards in subgroups of human obesity. *European Journal of Clinical Investigations*; **14**: 239–41.

Brozek J. Grande F. Anderson J. T. and Keys A. (1963). Densitometric analysis of body composition: revision of some quantitative assumptions. *Annals of the New York Academy of Sciences*; **110**: 113–40.

Bunc V. (2001) Prediction equations for the determination of body composition in children using bioimpedance analysis. In: (T. Jurimae and A. Hills, eds) *Medicine and Sports Science, Volume 44*; Karger Publishers; Basel, pp. 46–52.

Clarys J. P., Martin A. D., Drinkwater D. T. and Marfell-Jones M. J. (1987): The skinfold: myth and reality. *Journal of Sports Sciences*; **5**: 3–33.

Clasey J. L., Kanaley J. A., Wideman L., Heymsfield S. B., Teates C. D., Gutgeswell M. E., Thorner M. O., Hartman M. L. and Weltman A. (1999): Validity of methods of body composition assessment in young and older men and women. *Journal of Applied Physiology*; **86**: 1728–38.

Cole T. J,. Bellizzi M. C., Flegal K. M. and Dietz W. H. (2000) Establishing a standard definition for child overweight and obesity worldwide: international survey. *British Medical Journal*; **320**: 1240–3.

de Koning F. L,. Binkhorst R. A., Kauer J. M. G. and Thijssen H. O. M. (1986). Accuracy of an anthropometric estimate of the muscle and bone area in a transveral cross-section of the arm. *International Journal of Sports Medicine*; **7**: 246–9.

Demerath E. W., Guo S. S., Chumlea W. C., Towne B., Roche A. F. and Siervogel R. M. (2002) Comparison of percent body fat estimates using air displacement plethysmography and hydrodensitometry in adults and children. *International Journal of Obesity*; **26**: 389–97.

Dempster P. and Aitkins S. (1995). A new air displacement method for the determination of human body composition. *Medicine and Science in Sports and Exercise*; **27**: 1692–7.

Deurenberg P., van der Kooy K., Leenen R., Westrate J. A. and Seidell J. C. (1991) Sex- and age-specific prediction formulas for estimating body composition from bio-electrical impedance: a cross-validation study. *International Journal of Obesity*; **15**: 17–25.

Dietz W. H. and Bellizzi M. C. (1999) Assessment of childhood and adolescent obesity: results from an International Obesity TaskForce workshop, Dublin, 16 June 1997. *American Journal of Clinical Nutrition*; **70**: 117S–75S.

Drinkwater D. T., Martin A. D., Ross W. D. and Clarys J. P. (1986). Validation by cadaver dissection of Matiegka's equations for the anthropometric estimation of anatomical body composition in adult humans. In: (J. A. P. Day, ed) *The 1984 Olympic Scientific Congress Proceedings: Perspectives in Kinanthropometry*. Human Kinetics; Champaign, IL: pp. 221–7.

Durnin J. V. G. A. (1997): Skinfold thickness measurement. *British Journal of Nutrition*; **78**: 1042–3.

Durnin J. V. G. A. and Womersley J. (1974). Body fat assessed from total body density and its estimation from skinfold thickness: measurements on 481 men and women aged from 16 to 72 years. *British Journal of Nutrition*; **32**: 77–97.

Eliakim A., Burke G. S. and Cooper D. M. (1997) Fitness, fatness, and the effect of training assessed by magnetic resonance imaging and skinfold-thickness measurements in healthy adolescent females. *American Journal of Clinical Nutrition*; **66**: 223–31.

Eston R.G. (2002) Use of the body mass index (BMI) for individual counselling: the new section editor for Kinanthropometry is '*Grade 1 Obese, overweight*' (BMI 27.3), but dense and 'distinctly muscular' (FFMI 23.1)! *Journal of Sports Sciences*; **20**: 515–18.

Eston R. G., Cruz A., Fu F. and Fung, L. (1993) Fat-free mass estimation by bioelectrical impedance and anthropometric techniques in Chinese children. *Journal of Sports Sciences*; **11**: 241–7.

Eston R. G., Evans R. and Fu F. (1994) Estimation of body composition in Chinese and British males by ultrasonic assessment of segmental adipose tissue volume. *British Journal of Sports Medicine*; **28**: 9–13.

Eston R. G. Fu F. and Fung L. (1995) Validity of conventional anthropometric techniques for predicting body composition in healthy Chinese adults. *British Journal of Sports Medicine*; **29**: 52–6.

Eston R. G. and Powell C. (2003) Prediction of percent body fat in children using skinfolds from the upper and lower body. *Revista Portuguesa de Ciencias do Desporto*; **3**: 63 (abstract).

Eston R. G., Rowlands A. V., Charlesworth S., Davies A. and Hoppitt T. (2005) Prediction of DXA-determined whole body fat from skinfolds: importance of including skinfolds from the thigh and calf in young, healthy men and women. *European Journal of Clinical Nutrition*; **59**: 695–702.

Fields D. A. and Goran M. I. (2000) Body composition techniques and the four-compartment model in children. *Journal of Applied Physiology*; **89**: 613–20.

Friedl K. E., DeLuca J. P., Marchitelli L. J. and Vogel J. A. (1992) Reliability of body fat estimations from a four-compartment model by using density, water, and bone mineral measurements. *American Journal of Clinical Nutrition*; **55**: 764–70.

Forbes R. M., Cooper A. R. and Mitchell H. H. (1953) The composition of the adult human body as determined by chemical analysis. *Journal of Biological Chemistry*; **203**: 359–66.

Gallagher D., Heymsfield S. B., Heo M., Jebb S. A., Murgatroyd P. R. and Sakamato Y. (2000) Healthy percentage body fat ranges: an approach for developing guidelines based on body mass index. *American Journal of Clinical Nutrition*; **72**: 694–701.

Garn S. M., Leonard W. R. and Hawthorne V. M. (1986) Three limitations of the body mass index. *American Journal of Clinical Nutrition*; **44**: 996–7.

Gleichauf C. N. and Roe D. A. (1989) The menstrual cycle's effect on the reliability of bioimpedance measurements for assessing body composition. *American Journal of Clinical Nutrition*; **50**: 903–7.

Gruber A. J., Pope H. G., Borowiecki J. J. and Cohane G. (2000) The development of the somatomorphic matrix: a biaxial instrument for measuring body image in men and women. In: (K. Norton, T. Olds and J. Dollman, eds) *Kinanthropometry VI*. International Society for the Advancement of Kinanthropometry; Adelaide, Australia: pp. 217–31.

Hawes M. R. and Sovak D. (1993) Skeletal ruggedness as a factor in performance of Olympic and national calibre synchronized swimmers. In: (W. Duquet and J. A. P. Day, eds) *Kinanthropometry IV*. E. and F. N. Spon; London: pp. 107–13.

Hawes M. R. and D. Sovak (1994) Morphological prototypes, assessment and change in young athletes. *Journal of Sports Sciences*; **12**: 235–42.

Heymsfield S. B., McManus C., Smith J., Stevens V. and Nixon D. W. (1982) Anthropometric measurement of muscle mass: revised equations for calculating bone-free arm muscle area. *American Journal of Clinical Nutrition*; **36**: 680–90.

Heymsfield S. B., Wang Z. M., and Withers R. T. (1996) Multicomponent molecular level models of body composition. In: (A. F. Roche, S. B. Heymsfield and T. G. Lohman, eds) *Human Body Composition*, Human Kinetics; Champaign, IL: pp. 129–48.

Heyward V. H. (1991). *Advanced Fitness Assessment and Exercise Prescription*. Human Kinetics; Champaign, IL.

Heyward V. H. and Stolarczyk L. M. (1996) *Applied Body Composition Assessment.* Human Kinetics; Champaign, IL.

Heyward V. H. and Wagner D. R. (2004) *Applied Body Composition Assessment.* Human Kinetics; Champaign, IL.

Hodgdon J. A. and Fitzgerald P. I. (1987) Validity of impedance predictions at various levels of fatness. *Human Biology*; 59: 281–98.

Houtkooper L. B., Lohman T. G., Going S. B. and Hall M. C. (1989) Validity of bioelectrical impedance for body composition assessment in children. *Journal of Applied Physiology*; 66: 814–21.

Houtkooper L. B., Lohman T. G., Going S. B. and Howell W. H. (1996) Why bioelectrical impedance analysis should be used for estimating adiposity. *American Journal of Clinical Nutrition*; 64: 436S–48S.

Ikai M. and Fukunaga T. (1968). Calculation of muscle strength per unit cross-sectional area of human muscle by means of ultrasonic measurement. *Internationale Zeitscheift fur Angewandte Physiologie*; 26: 26–32.

Jackson A. S. and Pollock M. L. (1978). Generalized equations for predicting body density of men. *British Journal of Nutrition*; 40: 497–504.

Jackson A. S., Pollock M. L. and Ward A. (1980). Generalized equations for predicting body density of women. *Medicine and Science in Sports and Exercise*; 12: 175–82.

Janssen I., Heymsfield S. B., Baumgartner R. N. and Ross R. (2000) Estimation of skeletal muscle mass by bioelectrical impedance analysis. *Journal of Applied Physiology*; 89: 465–71.

Jebb S. A., Goldberg G. R., Jennings G. and Elia M. (1995): Dual energy x-ray absorptiometry measurements of body composition: effects of depth and tissue thickness, including comparisons with direct analysis. *Clinical Science* (London); 88: 319–24.

Jebb S. A., Cole T. J., Doman D., Murgatroyd P. R. and Prentice A. M. (2000) Evaluation of the novel Tanita body-fat analyser to measure body composition by comparison with a four-compartment model. *British Journal of Nutrition*; 83: 115–22.

Keys A. and Brozek J. (1953). Body fat in adult man. *Physiological Reviews*; 33: 245–345.

Keys A., Fidanza F,. Karvonen M. J., Kimura N. and Taylor H. L. (1972). Indices of relative weight and obesity. *Journal of Chronic Diseases*; 25: 329–43.

Kohrt W. M. (1995). Body composition by DXA: tried and true? *Medicine and Science in Sports and Exercise*; 27: 1349–53.

Kohrt W. M. (1998). Preliminary evidence that DXA provides an accurate assessment of body composition. *Journal of Applied Physiology*; 84: 372–7.

Kouri E. M., Pope H. G., Katz D. L. and Oliva P. (1995) Fat-free mass index in users and nonusers of anabolic-androgenic steroids. *Clinical Journal of Sports Medicine*; 5: 223–38.

Kyle U. G., Genton L., Karsegard L., Slosman D. O. and Pichard C. (2001) Single prediction equation for bioelectrical impedance analysis in adults aged 20–94 years. *Nutrition*; 17: 248–53.

Kyle U. G., Bosaeus I., De Lorenzo A. D., Deurenberg P., Elia M., Gómez J., Heitmann B., Kent-Smith L., Melchior J. and Pirlich M. (2004) Bioelectrical impedance analysis: part 1: review of principles and methods. *Clinical Nutrition*; 23: 1226–43.

Laskey M. A., Lyttle K. D., Flaxman M. E. and Barber R. W. (1992): The influence of tissue depth and composition on the performance of the Lunar dual energy x-ray absorptiometer whole body scanning mode. *European Journal of Clinical Nutrition*; 46: 39–45.

Lee R. C., Wang Z., Heo M., Ross R., Janssen I. and Heymsfield S.B. (2000) Total-body skeletal muscle mass: development and cross-validation of anthropometric prediction models. *American Journal of Clinical Nutrition*; 72: 796–803.

Legaz A. and Eston R.G. (2005) Changes in performance, skinfold thickness and fat patterning after three years of intense athletic conditioning in high-level runners. *British Journal of Sports Medicine*; 39: 851–6.

Lemieux S., Prud'homme D., Bouchard C., Tremblay A., Despres J. P. (1996) A single threshold value of waist girth identifies normal-weight and overweight subjects with excess visceral adipose tissue. *American Journal of Clinical Nutrition*; 64: 685–93.

Levenhagen D. K., Borel M. J. and Welch D. C., Piasecki J.H., Piasecki D.P., Chen K.Y. and Flakoll P.J. (1999) A comparison of air displacement plethysmography with three other techniques to determine body fat in healthy adults. *Journal of Parenteral and Enteral Nutrition*; 23: 293–9.

Lohman T. G., Slaughter M. H., Boileau R. A., Bunt J. and Lussier L. (1984). Bone mineral measurements and their relation to body density in children, youth and adults. *Human Biology*; 56: 667–79.

Lohman T. G. (1996) Dual-energy x-ray absorptiometry. In: (A. F. Roche, S. B. Heymsfield and T. G. Lohman, eds) *Human Body Composition* Human Kinetics; Champaign, IL: pp. 63–78.

Lukaski H. C. (1996). Biological indexes considered in the derivation of the bioelectrical impedance analysis. *American Journal of Clinical Nutrition*; 4 (Suppl.): 397S–404S.

McCrory M. A., Gomez T. D., Bernauer E. M. and Mole P. A. (1995). Evaluation of a new air displacement plethysmograph for measuring human body composition. *Medicine and Science in Sports and Exercise*; 19: 1686–91.

Martin A. D., Ross W. D., Drinkwater D. T. and Clarys J. P. (1985). Prediction of body fat by skinfold calliper: assumptions and cadaver evidence. *International Journal of Obesity*; 9: 31–39.

Martin A. D., Drinkwater D. T., Clarys J. P. and Ross W. D. (1986). The inconstancy of the fat-free mass: a reappraisal with applications for densitometry. In: (T. Reilly, J. Watkins and J. Borms, eds) *Kinanthropometry III. Proceedings of the VII Commonwealth and International Conference on Sport, Physical Education, Dance, Recreation and Health*. E & F Spon, London: pp. 92–7.

Martin A. D., Spenst L. F., Drinkwater D. T., and Clarys J. P. (1990). Anthropometric estimation of muscle mass in men. *Medicine and Science in Sports and Exercise*; 22: 729–33.

Martin A. D., Drinkwater D. T., Clarys J. P., Daniel M. and Ross W. D. (1992). Effects of skin thickness and skinfold compressibility on skinfold thickness measurement. *American Journal of Human Biology*; 6: 1–8.

Martin A. D., Daniel M., Drinkwater D. T., and Clarys J. P. (1994) Adipose tissue density, estimated adipose lipid fraction and whole-body adiposity in male cadavers. *International Journal of Obesity*; 18: 79–93.

Martin A. D. and Drinkwater D. T. (1991). Variability in the measures of body fat. *Sports Medicine*; 11: 277–88.

Matiegka J. (1921). The testing of physical efficiency. *American Journal of Physical Anthropology*; 4: 223–30.

Matsuzawa Y., Shimomura I., Nakamura T., Keon Y., Kotani K. and Tokunaga K. (1995) Pathophysiology and pathogenesis of visceral fat obesity. *Obesity Research*; 3 (Suppl.): 187S–94S.

Mendez J. and Keys A. (1960). Density and composition of mammalian muscle. *Metabolism*; 9: 184–7.

Munro R. and Capell H. (1997) Prevalence of low body mass in rheumatoid arthritis: association with the acute phase response. *Annals of Rheumatic Disease*; 56: 326–9.

Nevill A. M., Stewart A. D., Olds T. and Holder R. (2006) Relationship between adiposity and body size reveals limitations to BMI. *American Journal of Anthropology*; 129: 151–6.

Noreen E. E. and Lemon P. W. (2006). Reliability of air displacement plethysmoraphy in a large heterogeneous sample. *Medicine and Science in Sports and Exercise*; 38: 1505–9.

Norton K., Olds T., Olive S. and Craig N. (1996) Anthropometry and Sports Performance. In: (K. Norton and T. Olds, eds.) *Anthropometrica*. University of New South Wales; Sydney, Australia: pp. 287–364.

Nyboer J., Bagno S. and Nims L. F. (1943). The electrical impedance plethysmograph an electrical volume recorder. National Research Council, Washington DC. (Report No. 149).

Orpin M. J. and Scott P. J. (1964). Estimation of total body fat using skin fold calliper measurements. *New Zealand Medical Journal*; 63: 501–7.

Parizkova J. (1978). Lean body mass and depot fat during ontogenesis in humans. In: (J. Parizkova and V. A. Rogozkin, eds) *Nutrition, Physical Fitness and Health: International Series on Sport Sciences,* Vol. 7., University Park Press; Baltimore, MD: pp. 24–51.

Peterson M. J., Czerwinski S. A. and Siervogel R. M. (2003) Development and validation of skinfold-thickness prediction equations with a 4-compartment model. *American Journal of Clinical Nutrition*; 77: 1186–91.

Pichard C., Kyle U. G., Bracco D., Slosman D. O., Morabia A. and Schutz Y. (2000) Reference values of fat-free and fat masses by bioelectrical impedance analysis in 3393 healthy subjects. *Nutrition*; 16: 245–54.

Pietrobelli A., Wang Z., Formica C. and Heymsfield S. B. (1998): Dual energy x-ray absorptiometry: fat estimation errors due to variation in soft tissue hydration. *American Journal of Physiology*; **274**: E808–E16.

Prior B. M., Cureton K. J., Modlesky C. M., Evans E. M., Sloniger M. A., Saunders M. and Lewis R. D. (1997) *In vivo* validation of whole body composition estimates from dual-energy x-ray absorptiometry. *Journal of Applied Physiology*; **83**: 623–30.

Quanjer Ph. H., Tammeling G. J., Cotes J. E., Pedersen O. F., Peslin R., and Yernault J-C. (1993) Lung volumes and forced ventilatory flows. Report Working Party Standardization of Lung Function Tests, European Community for Steel and Coal. Official Statement of the European Respiratory Society. *European Respiratory Journal*; **S16**: 5–40.

Quetelet A. (1836) *Sur L'Homme et le Development des Facultes*; Brussels: Hauman.

Radley D., Gately P. J., Cooke C., Carroll S., Oldroyd B. and Truscott J. G. (2003) Estimates of percentage body fat in young adolescents: a comparison of dual-energy x-ray absorptiometry and air displacement plethysmography. *European Journal of Clinical Nutrition*; **57**: 1402–10.

Reilly T., Maughan R. J, and Hardy L. (1996): Body fat consensus statement of the steering groups of the British Olympic Association. *Sports Exercise and Injury*; **2**: 46–9.

Ross W. D., Eiben O. G., Ward R., Martin A. D., Drinkwater D. T. and Clarys J. P. (1986). Alternatives for conventional methods of human body composition and phsyique assessment. In: (J. A. P. Day, ed) *The 1984 Olympic Scientific Congress Proceedings: Perspectives in Kinanthropometry*. Human Kinetics; Champaign, IL: pp. 203–20.

Ross W. D., Martin A. D. and Ward R. (1987). Body composition and aging: theoretical and methodological implications. *Collegium Anthropologicum*; **11**: 15–44.

Ross W. D., Crawford S. M., Kerr D. A., Ward R., Bailey D. A. and Mirwald R. M. (1988) Relationship of the body mass index with skinfolds, girths, and bone breadths in Canadian men and women aged 20–70 years. *American Journal of Physical Anthropology*; **77**: 169–73.

Rowlands A. V. and Eston R. G. (2001) Assessment of body composition in children using two bioelectrical impedance analysis techniques and surface anthropometry. In: (T. Jurimae and A. Hills, eds) *Medicine and Sports Science, Volume 44.* Karger Publishers; Basel: pp. 14–24.

Ryde S. J. S., Eston R. G., Laskey M. A., Evans C. J. and Hancock D. A. (1998) Changes in body fat: measurements by neutron activation, densitometry and dual energy x-ray absorptiometry. *Applied Radiation and Isotopes*; **49**: 507–9.

Scharfetter H., Schlager T., Stollberger R., Felsberger R., Hutten H. and Hinghofer-Szalkay H. (2001) Assessing abdominal fatness with local bioimpedance analysis: basics and experimental findings. *International Journal of Obesity*; **25**: 502–11.

Schutte J. E., Townsend E. J., Huff J., Shoup R. F. and Malina R. M. (1984). Density of lean body mass is greater in Blacks than in Whites. *Journal of Applied Physiology*; **456**: 1647–49.

Schutz Y., Kyle U. U. G., and Pichard C. (2002) Fat-free mass index and fat mass index percentiles in Caucasians aged 18–98 y. *International Journal of Obesity*; **26**: 953–60.

Secchiutti A., Fagour C., Perlemoine C., Gin H., Durrieu J. and Rigalleau V. (2007) Air displacement plethysmography can detect moderate changes in body composition. *European Journal of Clinical Nutrition*; **61**: 25–9.

Segal K. R., van Loan M., Fitzgerald P. I., Hodgdon J. A. and Van Itallie T. B. (1988). Lean body mass estimation by bioelectrical impedance analysis: a four-site cross-validation study. *American Journal of Clinical Nutrition*; **47**: 7–14.

Siri W. E. (1956). Body composition from fluid spaces and density: analysis of methods. *University of California Radiation Laboratory Report* UCRL no. 3349.

Slaughter M. H., Lohman T. G., Boileau R. A., Horswill C. A., Stillman R. J., Van Loan M. D. and Bemben D. A. (1988): Skinfold equations for estimation of body fatness in children and youth. *Human Biology*; **60**: 709–23.

Stewart A. and Eston R. G. (1997): Skinfold thickness measurement. *British Journal of Nutrition*; **78**: 1040–2.

Stewart A. and Eston R. G. (2006). Surface Anthropometry. In: (E. M. Winter, A. M.

Jones, R.C.R. Davison, P. D. Bromley and T. H. Mercer, eds) *Sport and Exercise Physiology Testing Guidelines*. Routledge; Oxon: pp. 76–83.

Stewart A. D. and Hannan J. (2000) Prediction of fat and fat-free mass in male athletes using dual energy x-ray absorptiometry as the reference method. *Journal of Sports Sciences*; 18: 263–74.

Vague J. (1947) Sexual differentiation, a factor affecting the forms of obesity, *Presses Médicales*; 30: 339–40.

van der Ploeg G. E., Gunn S. M., Withers R. T. and Modra A. C. (2003): Use of anthropometric variables to predict relative body fat determined by a four-compartment body composition model. *European Journal of Clinical Nutrition*; 57: 1009–16.

Van Itallie T. B., Yang M-U, Heymsfield S. B., Funk R. C. and Boileau R. (1990) Height-normalized indices of the body's fat-free mass and fat mass: potentially useful indicators of nutritional status. *American Journal of Clinical Nutrition*; 52(6): 953–9.

Wang Z. M., Pierson Jr. R. N. and Heymsfield S. B. (1992). The five-level model: a new approach to organizing body-composition research. *American Journal of Clinical Nutrition*; 56: 19–28.

Wang Z. M., Deurenberg P., Guo S. S., Pietrobelli A., Wang J., Pierson R. N. and Heymsfield S. B. (1998): Six compartment body composition model: inter-method comparisons of total body fat measurement. *International Journal of Obesity*; 22: 329–37.

Wilmore J. H., Vodak P. A., Parr R. B., Girandola R. N. and Billing J. E. (1980) Further simplification of a method for determination of residual lung volume. *Medicine and Science in Sports and Exercise*; 12: 216–8.

Withers R. T., LaForgia J., Pillans R. K., Shipp N. J., Chatterton B.E., Schultz C.G. and Leaney F. (1998) Comparisons of two-, three-, and four-compartment models of body composition analysis in men and women. *Journal of Applied Physiology*; 85: 238–45.

CHAPTER 2

SOMATOTYPING

William Duquet* and J. E. Lindsay Carter

2.1 AIMS

The aims in this chapter are to:

- define the meaning of the terms 'endomorphy,' 'mesomorphy' and 'ectomorphy';
- provide an understanding of the somatotype rating so that the student can visualise the body type of a subject with a given somatotype;
- explain how to calculate an anthropometric somatotype;
- distinguish the dominance of a certain component within a person, and to relate this to a certain somatotype category;
- describe how to plot and interpret somatotypes on a somatochart;
- highlight possible stabilities or instabilities of the individual phenotypical appearance;
- compare global somatotypes between subjects and between samples;
- understand the specific advantages of using a somatotype method over single trait or index methods.

2.2 HISTORY

Somatotyping is a method for describing the human physique in terms of a number of traits that relate to body shape and composition. The definition of the traits, and the form of the scales that are used to describe the relative importance of the traits, vary from one body-type method to the other. Attempts to establish such methods date from Hippocrates, and continue to the present time. Excellent reviews of these early methods were published by Tucker and Lessa (1940a, 1940b) and by Albonico (1970).

A classic approach that led to today's commonly used method, was introduced by Sheldon *et al.* (1940). Their most important contribution to the field lies in the combination of the basic ideas of two other methods. The first was Kretschmer's (1921) classification, with three empirically determined and visually rated extremes of body build, with each subject being an amalgam of the three 'poles.' The second was the analytical, anthropometrically determined body-build

---

* Sadly, William Duquet died unexpectedly in Brussels on 4 February 2008. We will miss his presence and contributions to Kinanthropometry.

assessment of Viola (1933), in which the ratio of trunk and limb measures and thoracic and abdominal trunk values are expressed proportionate to a 'normotype.' In Sheldon's method an attempt is made to describe the genotypical morphological traits of a person in terms of three components, each on a 7-point scale. This genotypic approach, the rigidity of the closed 7-point ratings and a lack of objectivity of the ratings, made the method unattractive to most researchers, especially in the field of kinanthropometry.

From these three principal criticisms, and in addition those of Heath (1963), emerged a new method, created by Heath and Carter (1967). It was partly influenced by ideas from Parnell (1954, 1958). They proposed a phenotypic approach, with open rating scales for three components and ratings that can be estimated from objective anthropometric measurements. The Heath-Carter somatotype method is the most universally applied, and will be used in this laboratory manual. The most extensive description of the method, its development and applications, can be found in Carter and Heath (1990). Two other original methods were introduced by Lindegard (1953) and by Conrad (1963), but are used less often than the Heath-Carter method.

2.3 THE HEATH-CARTER SOMATOTYPE METHOD

2.3.1 Definitions

a) Somatotype
A somatotype is a quantified expression or description of the present morphological conformation of a person. It consists of a three-numeral rating, for example, 3.5-5-1. The three numerals are always recorded in the same order, each describing the value of a particular component of physique.

b) Anthropometric and photoscopic somatotypes
The principal rating of the component values is based on a visual inspection of the subject, or his or her photograph – preferably a front, a side and a back view – taken in minimal clothing. This rating is called the photoscopic (or anthroposcopic) somatotype rating. If the investigator cannot perform a photoscopic rating, the component values can be estimated from a combination of anthropometric measurements. The calculated three-numeral rating is then called the anthropometric somatotype. The recommended somatotyping procedure is a combination of an anthropometric followed by a photoscopic evaluation.

c) Components
A component is an empirically defined descriptor of a particular aspect or trait of the human body build. It is expressed as a numeral on a continuous scale, which theoretically starts at zero and has no upper limit. The ratings are rounded to the half-unit. In practice, no ratings lower than one-half are given (as a particular body build trait can never be absolutely absent), and a rating of more than seven is extremely high.

d) Endomorphy
The first component, called endomorphy, describes the relative degree of adiposity of the body, regardless of where or how it is distributed. It also describes corresponding physical aspects, such as roundness of the body, softness of the contours, relative volume of the abdominal trunk, and distally tapering of the limbs.

e) Mesomorphy
The second component, called mesomorphy, describes the relative musculo-skeletal development of the body. It also describes corresponding physical aspects, such as the apparent robustness of the body in terms of muscle or bone, the relative volume of the thoracic trunk and the possibly hidden muscle bulk.

The definitions of endomorphy and mesomorphy reflect the anatomical model of body composition.

f) Ectomorphy

The third component, called ectomorphy, describes the relative slenderness of the body. It also describes corresponding physical aspects, such as the relative 'stretched-out-ness,' the apparent linearity of the body or fragility of the limbs, in absence of any bulk, be it muscle, fat or other tissues.

g) Somatotype category

Category is the more qualitative description of the individual somatotype, in terms of the dominant component or components. For example, a subject with a high rating on mesomorphy and an equally low rating on endomorphy and ectomorphy, will be called a mesomorph or a balanced mesomorph. The complete list with possible categories and corresponding dominance variations is given in Practical 2 of this chapter.

2.3.2 Assessment

a) Anthropometric somatotype

The anthropometric somatotype can be calculated from a set of 10 measurements: height, weight, four skinfolds (triceps, sub-scapular, supraspinale and medial calf), two biepicondylar breadths (humerus and femur) and two girths (upper arm flexed and tensed and calf). Descriptions of measurement techniques are given later.

b) Photoscopic somatotype

The photoscopic somatotype can only be rated objectively by persons who have trained to attain the necessary skill, and whose rating validity and reliability is established against the evaluations of an experienced rater. This part of the procedure is therefore not included in the present text. It is, however, generally accepted that the anthropometric evaluation gives a fair estimate of the photoscopic procedure. Important deviations are only found in subjects with a high degree of dysplasia in fat or muscle tissue.

Many researchers, who do not use photographs or visual inspection, or who lack experience in rating photoscopically, report the anthropometric somatotype only. In reporting a somatotype, researchers should therefore always mention the method used.

2.3.3 Measurement techniques

The descriptions are essentially the same as in Carter and Heath (1990).

The following techniques ideally should be used for subsequent calculation of the Heath-Carter anthropometric somatotype. Where the choice is possible, measures should be taken both on left and right sides and the largest measure should be reported. In large-scale surveys, measuring on the right side is preferable.

The anthropometric equipment needed includes a weighing scale, a stadiometer (a height scale attached on a wall) and a Broca plane, or an anthropometer for measuring the height, a skinfold calliper, a small sliding calliper for the breadths and a flexible steel or fibreglass tape for the girths.

a) Weight

The subject, in minimal clothing, stands in the centre of the scale platform. Body mass should be recorded to the nearest tenth of a kilogram, if possible. A correction is made for clothing so that nude weight is used in subsequent calculations. Avoid measuring body mass shortly after a meal.

b) Height

The subject is standing straight, against an upright wall with a stadiometer or against an anthropometer, touching the wall or the anthropometer with back, buttocks and both heels. The head is oriented in the Frankfort Plane (i.e. the lower border of the eye socket and the upper border of the ear opening should be on a horizontal line). The subject is instructed to stretch upward and take and hold a full breath. The measurer should lower the Broca plane or the ruler until it touches the vertex firmly, but without exerting extreme pressure.

c) Skinfolds

Raise a fold of skin and subcutaneous tissue at the marked site firmly between thumb and forefinger of the left hand, and pull the fold gently away from the underlying muscle. Hold the calliper in the right hand and apply the edge of the plates on the calliper branches 1 cm below the fingers, and allow them to exert their full pressure before reading the thickness of the fold after about two seconds. The Harpenden or Holtain callipers are recommended. The four skinfold sites are illustrated in Chapter 1 (Eston *et al.* 2009).

i) Triceps skinfold

The subject stands relaxed, with the arm hanging loosely. Raise the triceps skinfold at the midline on the back of the arm at a level halfway between the acromion and the olecranon processes (Figure 1.9e and 1.15).

ii) Subscapular skinfold

The subject stands relaxed. Raise the subscapular skinfold adjacent to the inferior angle of the scapula in a direction which is obliquely downwards and outwards at 45 degrees (Figure 1.9f and 1.15).

iii) Supraspinale skinfold

The subject stands relaxed. Raise the fold 5–7 cm above the anterior superior iliac spine on a line to the anterior axillary border and in a direction downwards and inwards at 45 degrees (Figure 1.9a and 1.14). (This skinfold was called suprailiac in some former texts.)

iv) Medial calf skinfold

The subject is seated, with the legs slightly spread. The leg that is not being measured can be bent backwards to facilitate the measurement. Alternatively, the foot may be placed on a box with the knee flexed. Raise a vertical skinfold on the medial side (aspect) of the leg at the level of the maximum girth of the calf (Figure 1.9d and 1.17).

d) Breadths

i) Biepicondylar humerus breadth

The subject holds the shoulder and elbow flexed to 90 degrees. Measure the width between the medial and lateral epicondyles of the humerus. In this position, the medial epicondyle is always somewhat lower than the lateral. Apply the calliper at an angle approximately bisecting the angle of the elbow. Place firm pressure on the cross-branches of the calliper in order to compress the subcutaneous tissue.

ii) Biepicondylar femur breadth

The subject is seated, or standing upright with one foot on a pedestal, with knee bent at a right angle. Measure the greatest distance between the lateral and medial epicondyles of the femur. Place firm pressure on the cross-branches in order to compress the subcutaneous tissue.

f) Girths

i) Upper arm girth, flexed and tensed

The subject holds the upper arm horizontally and flexes the elbow 45 degrees, clenches the hand and maximally contracts the elbow flexors and extensors. Take the measurement at the greatest girth of the arm. The tape should not be too loose, but should not indent the soft tissue either.

ii) Standing calf girth

The subject stands with feet slightly apart. Place the tape horizontally around the calf and measure the maximum circumference. The tape should not be too loose, but should not indent the soft tissue either.

2.3.4 Further elaboration

The differences or similarities in somatotypes of subjects or groups of subjects can be visualised by plotting them on a somatochart (see Practical 1). A somatotype rating can be thought of as being a vector or a point in a three-coordinate system in which each axis carries a somatotype component scale. The somatochart is the orthogonal projection of this three-coordinate system, parallel to the bisector of the three axes, on a two-dimensional plane.

The somatotype is an entity and should be treated as such. One possible qualitative technique is the use of somatotype categories. A quantitative technique is the use of the Somatotype Attitudinal Distance (SAD), which is the difference in component units between two somatotypes, or in terms of the somatochart, the three-dimensional distance between two points.

In time series of somatotypes of the same subject, the ongoing changes in somatotype can be expressed by adding the consecutive SADs. This sum is called the Migratory Distance (MD).

These further elaborations will be covered in the Practicals.

2.4 RELEVANCE OF SOMATOTYPING

Why should you use somatotyping? Of what value is it in exercise and sports science? These are important questions that are often asked.

The somatotype gives an overall summary of the physique as a unified whole. Its utility is in the combination of three aspects of physique into a somatotype rating. It combines the appraisal of adiposity, musculo-skeletal robustness and linearity into the three-numbered rating and conjures up a visual image of the three aspects of the physique. The adiposity is related to the relative fatness or endomorphy; the relative muscle and bony robustness is related to the fat-free body or mesomorphy; and the linearity or ectomorphy gives an indication of the bulkiness or mass relative to stature in the physique. From a few simple

measurements, the somatotype gives a useful summary of a variety of possible measures or observations that can be made on the body.

The somatotype tells you what kind of physique you have and how it looks. It has been used to describe and compare the physiques of athletes at all levels of competition and in a variety of sports. Somatotypes of athletes in selected sports are quite different from each other, whereas somatotypes are similar in other sports. Somatotyping has also been used to describe changes in physique during growth, ageing and training, as well as in relation to physical performance. The somatotype is a general descriptor of physique. If more precise questions are asked, such as 'What is the growth rate in upper extremity bone segments?' then different and specific measures need to be taken.

Two examples illustrate how the somatotype gives more information than some typical measures of body composition. First, the somatotype indicates the difference between individuals with the same level of fatness. An elite male body-builder, gymnast and long distance runner may each have the same estimate of per cent body fat at 5%. All three are low in percentage body fat, but this fact alone does not tell you the important differences between the physiques of these athletes. They differ considerably in their muscle, bone and linearity. The body-builder may be a 1-9-1, the gymnast a 1-6-2, and the runner a 1-3-5 somatotype. They are all rated '1' in endomorphy, but they have completely different ratings on mesomorphy and ectomorphy. The somatotype describes these differences.

As a second example, two males with the same height and body mass, and therefore the same body mass index (BMI), can have physiques that look completely different. If they are both 175 cm tall and weigh 78 kg, they will have a BMI value of 25.5, and a somatotype height-weight ratio of 41.0. Their somatotypes are 6-3-1 and 3-6-1. They are completely different-looking physiques. Both have low linearity (1 in ectomorphy), but the BMI does not tell you anything about their specific differences in body composition as inferred from their opposite ratings of 6 (high) and 3 (low) in endomorphy or in mesomorphy.

In both the examples above, the potential performance characteristics for the subjects would be quite different because of the differences in mesomorphy and ectomorphy in the first example, and in endomorphy and mesomorphy in the second example.

For further details about and applications of somatotyping the following references are useful. History, methods and bibliographies are available in the website: www.somatype. org. A complete somatotype calculation and analysis program is available (Goulding 2002). For examples of studies on athletes in different sports refer to Amusa *et al.* (2003), Carter (2003), Carter and Ackland (2008), Carter *et al.* (2005), Claessens *et al.* (2001), and Underhay *et al.* (2005). The following are examples of studies on different populations: Buffa *et al.* (2005), Chaouachi (2005), Peeters *et al.* (2007), Stewart *et al.* (2003), and Vieira *et al.* (2003).

2.5 PRACTICAL 1: CALCULATION OF ANTHROPOMETRIC SOMATOTYPES

2.5.1 Introduction

The aim in this practical is to learn how to calculate anthropometric somatotypes, using the classical approach and using some fast calculation formulae, and to learn how to plot the results on a somatochart.

2.5.2 Methods

Endomorphy is estimated from the relation between the component value and the sum of three skinfold measures, relative to the subject's height.

Mesomorphy is estimated from the deviation of two girths and two breadths from their expected values, relative to the subject's height.

Ectomorphy is estimated from the relation between the component value and the reciprocal of the ponderal index, or height over cube root of weight ratio.

a) Steps for the manual calculation of the anthropometric somatotype

The following is a guide in 16 steps for calculating the anthropometric somatotype by means of the Heath-Carter somatotype rating form (Figures 2.1 and 2.2). Endomorphy is calculated in steps 2 to 5, mesomorphy in steps 6 to 10, and ectomorphy in steps 11 to 14. A worked example, in which these steps were followed, is given in Figure 2.1.

The measurements for subject B171 were: body mass: 59.5 kg; height: 165.6 cm; triceps skinfold: 11.3 mm; subscapular skinfold: 10.0 mm; supraspinale skinfold: 6.5 mm; calf skinfold: 12.0 mm; humerus breadth: 6.4 cm; femur breadth: 8.8 cm; biceps girth: 27.2 cm; calf girth: 37.1 cm.

Step 1: Record the identification data in the top section of the rating form.

Step 2: Record the values obtained from each of the four skinfold measurements.

Step 3: Sum the values of the triceps, subscapular and supraspinale skinfolds; record

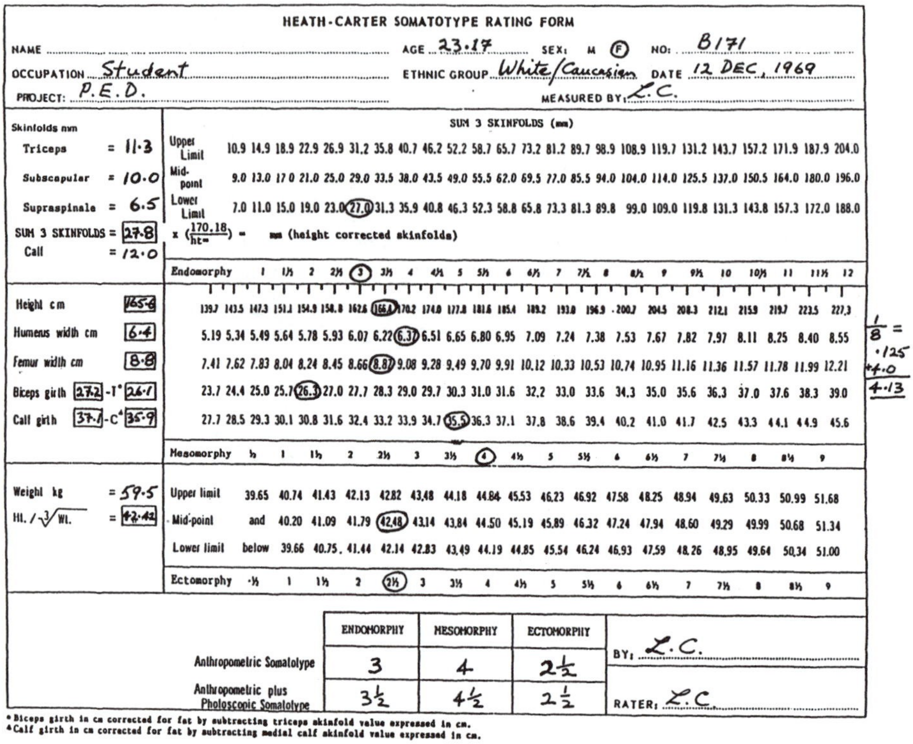
HEATH-CARTER SOMATOTYPE RATING FORM

NAME .... AGE 23.17 SEX: M (F) NO: B171

OCCUPATION Student ETHNIC GROUP White/Caucasian DATE 12 DEC, 1969

PROJECT: P.E.D. MEASURED BY: L.C.

Skinfolds mm

Triceps = 11.3

Subscapular = 10.0

Supraspinale = 6.5

SUM 3 SKINFOLDS = 27.8

Calf = 12.0

SUM 3 SKINFOLDS (mm)

Upper Limit 10.9 14.9 18.9 22.9 26.9 31.2 35.8 40.7 46.2 52.2 58.7 65.7 73.2 81.2 89.7 98.9 108.9 119.7 131.2 143.7 157.2 171.9 187.9 204.0

Mid-point 9.0 13.0 17.0 21.0 25.0 29.0 33.5 38.0 43.5 49.0 55.5 62.0 69.5 77.0 85.5 94.0 104.0 114.0 125.5 137.0 150.5 164.0 180.0 196.0

Lower Limit 7.0 11.0 15.0 19.0 23.0 (27.0) 31.3 35.9 40.8 46.3 52.3 58.8 65.8 73.3 81.3 89.8 99.0 109.0 119.8 131.3 143.8 157.3 172.0 188.0

x (170.18/ht=) = mm (height corrected skinfolds)

Endomorphy 1 1½ 2 2½ (3) 3½ 4 4½ 5 5½ 6 6½ 7 7½ 8 8½ 9 9½ 10 10½ 11 11½ 12

Height cm 165.6 | 139.7 143.5 147.3 151.1 154.9 158.8 162.6 (166.4) 170.2 174.0 177.8 181.6 185.4 189.2 193.0 196.9 200.7 204.5 208.3 212.1 215.9 219.7 223.5 227.3

Humerus width cm 6.4 | 5.19 5.34 5.49 5.64 5.78 5.93 6.07 6.22 (6.37) 6.51 6.65 6.80 6.95 7.09 7.24 7.38 7.53 7.67 7.82 7.97 8.11 8.25 8.40 8.55

Femur width cm 8.8 | 7.41 7.62 7.83 8.04 8.24 8.45 8.66 (8.87) 9.08 9.28 9.49 9.70 9.91 10.12 10.33 10.53 10.74 10.95 11.16 11.36 11.57 11.78 11.99 12.21

Biceps girth 27.2 - T* 26.1 | 23.7 24.4 25.0 25.7 (26.3) 27.0 27.7 28.3 29.0 29.7 30.3 31.0 31.6 32.2 33.0 33.6 34.3 35.0 35.6 36.3 37.0 37.6 38.3 39.0

Calf girth 37.1 - C^ 35.9 | 27.7 28.5 29.3 30.1 30.8 31.6 32.4 33.2 33.9 34.7 (35.5) 36.3 37.1 37.8 38.6 39.4 40.2 41.0 41.7 42.5 43.3 44.1 44.9 45.6

1/8 = .125 +4.0 = 4.13

Mesomorphy ½ 1 1½ 2 2½ 3 3½ (4) 4½ 5 5½ 6 6½ 7 7½ 8 8½ 9

Weight kg = 59.5

Ht./∛Wt. = 42.42

Upper limit 39.65 40.74 41.43 42.13 42.82 43.48 44.18 44.84 45.53 46.23 46.92 47.58 48.25 48.94 49.63 50.33 50.99 51.68

Mid-point and 40.20 41.09 41.79 (42.48) 43.14 43.84 44.50 45.19 45.89 46.32 47.24 47.94 48.60 49.29 49.99 50.68 51.34

Lower limit below 39.66 40.75 41.44 42.14 42.83 43.49 44.19 44.85 45.54 46.24 46.93 47.59 48.26 48.95 49.64 50.34 51.00

Ectomorphy ½ 1 1½ 2 (2½) 3 3½ 4 4½ 5 5½ 6 6½ 7 7½ 8 8½ 9

	ENDOMORPHY	MESOMORPHY	ECTOMORPHY	
Anthropometric Somatotype	3	4	2½	BY: L.C.
Anthropometric plus Photoscopic Somatotype	3½	4½	2½	RATER: L.C.

*Biceps girth in cm corrected for fat by subtracting triceps skinfold value expressed in cm.
^Calf girth in cm corrected for fat by subtracting medial calf skinfold value expressed in cm.

Figure 2.1 Example of a completed anthropometric somatotype rating.

this sum in the box opposite 'Sum 3 skinfolds.' Correct for height by multiplying this sum by 170.18/height(cm).

Step 4: Circle the closest value in the 'Sum 3 skinfolds' scale to the right. The scale reads vertically from low to high in columns and horizontally from left to right in rows. 'Lower limit' and 'upper limit' on the rows provide exact boundaries for each column. These values are circled if Sum 3 skinfolds is closer to the limit than to the midpoint.

Step 5: In the row 'Endomorphy' circle the value directly under the column circled in step 4.

Step 6: Record height and diameters of humerus and femur in the appropriate boxes. Make the corrections for skinfolds before recording girths of biceps and calf. (Skinfold corrections are as follows: convert triceps and calf skinfold to cm by dividing them by 10. Subtract converted triceps skinfold from the biceps girth. Subtract converted calf skinfold from calf girth.)

Step 7: On the height scale directly to the right, circle the height nearest to the measured height of the subject.

Step 8: For each bone diameter and girth, circle the figure nearest the measured value in the appropriate row. (If the measurement falls midway between the two values, circle

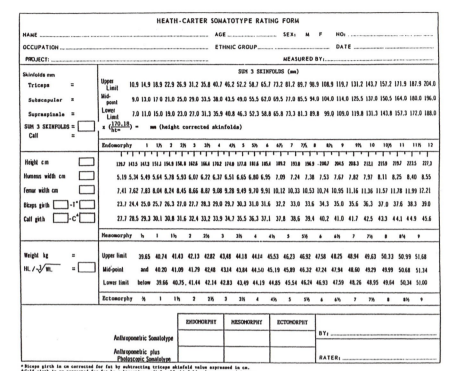

Figure 2.2 The Heath-Carter somatotype rating form.

the lower value. This conservative procedure is used because the largest girths and diameters are recorded.)

Step 9: In this step, deal only with columns as units, not with numerical values. Check the circled deviations of the values for diameters and girths from the circled value in the height column. Count the column deviations to the right of the height column as positive deviations, with columns as units. Deviations to the left are negative deviations. Calculate the algebraic sum of the deviations (D). Use this formula: Mesomorphy = (D/8) + 4. Round the obtained value of mesomorphy to the nearest one-half rating unit.

Step 10: In the row 'Mesomorphy,' circle the closest value for the mesomorphy calculated in step 9. (If the point is exactly midway between two rating points, circle the value closest to 4 on the scale. This conservative regression toward 4 guards against spuriously extreme ratings.)

Step 11: Record body mass (kg).

Step 12: Obtain height divided by cube root of weight (HWR) from a nomograph or by calculation. Record HWR in the appropriate box. Note: the HWR can be calculated easily with the help of a hand calculator. A calculator with a y to the x power (y^x) key is needed. To get the cube root, enter the base (y), press the 'y^x' key, enter 0.3333, and press the '=' key. If there is an 'INV y^x' function, or 'root of y' function ($^x\sqrt{y}$), either may be used by entering the base, then 3 and the '=' key for the cube root. A nomogram can be found in Carter and Heath (1990), p. 273.

Step 13: Circle the closest value in the HWR scale. Proceed with upper and lower limits as with endomorphy in step 4.

Step 14: In the row 'Ectomorphy' circle the ectomorphy value directly under the circled HWR.

Step 15: Record the circled values for each component in the row 'Anthropometric somatotype'. (If a photoscopic rating is available, the rater should record the final decision in the row 'Anthropometric and photoscopic somatotype'.)

Step 16: The investigator signs his/her name to the right of the recorded rating.

Note: If in step 7 the recorded height is closer to the midpoint than to the two adjacent column values, place a vertical arrow between the two values. Continue to work with this half column, calculating half units for the deviations in step 9.

b) Formulae for the calculation of the anthropometric somatotype by computer

The formulae in Table 2.1 were derived from the scales of the somatochart.

Table 2.1 Formulae for the calculation of the anthropometric Heath-Carter somatotype by calculator or computer

Endomorphy	$= -0.7182 + 0.1451X - 0.00068X^2 + 0.0000014X^3$	
Mesomorphy	$= 0.858HB + 0.601FB + 0.188AG + 0.161CG$	
	$- 0.131SH + 4.5$	
Ectomorphy	$= 0.732HWR - 28.58$	(if HWR > 40.74)
	$= 0.463HWR - 17.615$	(if $39.65 < HWR = 40.74$)
	$= 0.5$	(if HWR = 39.65)

Where: X = $\Sigma 3$ skinfolds, corrected for height; HB = humerus breadth; FB = femur breadth;

AG = corrected arm girth; CG = corrected calf girth; SH = standing height; HWR = height over cube root of mass.

c) Formulae for plotting somatotypes on the somatochart

The exact location of a somatotype on the somatochart (Figure 2.3) can be calculated using the formulae:

X = ectomorphy – endomorphy
Y = 2 × mesomorphy – (endomorphy + ectomorphy)

In our example, a subject with somatotype 3.0-4.0-2.5 is plotted with the following coordinates:

X = 2.5 – 3.0 = –0.5
Y = 2 × 4.0 – (3.0 + 2.5) = 2.5

2.5.3 Tasks

A group of six adult subjects was measured. The results are shown in 2.2.

Table 2.2 Anthropometric measurements of six adult male subjects

Subject:	1	2	3	4	5	6
Mass (kg):	82.0	67.7	60.5	64.4	82.4	80.8
Height (cm):	191.7	175.3	160.0	171.5	180.6	188.3
Triceps skinfold (mm):	7.0	5.0	3.0	4.2	11.2	17.1
Subscapular skinfold (mm):	6.0	7.0	5.0	5.7	8.8	12.1
Supraspinale skinfold (mm):	4.0	3.0	3.0	3.6	7.1	11.5
Medial calf skinfold (mm):	9.0	4.0	3.0	3.0	9.9	12.0
Humerus breadth (cm):	7.3	7.0	6.5	6.6	7.4	6.5
Femur breadth (cm):	10.1	9.4	8.9	9.7	9.2	9.1
Upper arm girth (cm): (Flexed and tensed)	33.2	35.7	34.4	29.5	36.1	36.5
Standing calf girth (cm):	36.0	34.4	36.4	34.5	40.6	38.6

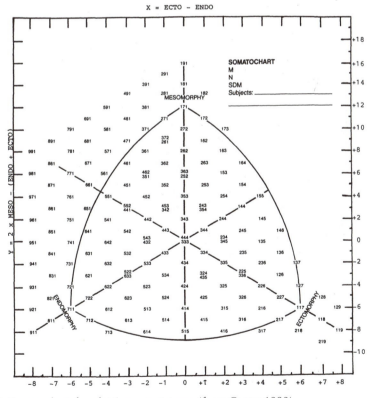

Figure 2.3 Somatochart for plotting somatotypes (from Carter 1980).

1   Calculate the anthropometric somatotype for each subject. Use copies of the somatotype rating form (Figure 2.2), and follow the example of Figure 2.1.
2   Calculate the anthropometric somatotype for each subject, using the formulae given in Table 2.1.
3   Check all calculations by rounding the second series of results to the half unit, and comparing the results with the first calculations.
4   Find the location of each subject on the somatochart, by calculating the XY-coordinates by means of the formulae above. Plot the somatotypes on a copy of the somatochart (Figure 2.2).

2.6 PRACTICAL 2: COMPARISON OF SOMATOTYPES OF DIFFERENT GROUPS

2.6.1 Introduction

The aim in this practical is to learn how to compare anthropometric somatotypes using the somatotype category approach and using SAD techniques.

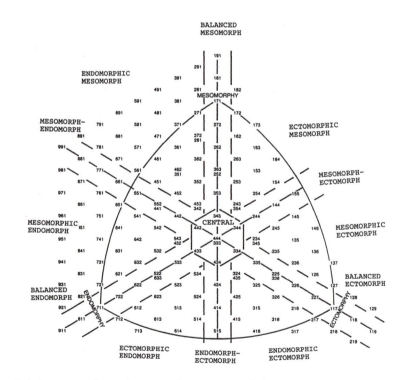

Figure 2.4 A somatochart showing the regions of the somatotype categories (from Carter.1980).

2.6.2 Methods

There are many ways to analyze somatotype data. The easiest way is to consider each component separately, and to treat it like any other biological variable, using descriptive and inferential statistics.

However, the somatotype is more than three separate component values. Two subjects with an identical value for one of the components can nevertheless have completely different physiques, depending on the values of the two other components. For example, a somatotype 2-6-2 is completely different from a somatotype 2-2-6, but they both have the same endomorphy value. It is precisely the combination of all three component values into one expression that is the strength of the somatotype concept. Hence, techniques were developed to analyze the somatotype as a whole, two of which are somatotype categories and SAD techniques (see Duquet and Hebbelink 1977; Duquet 1980; Carter *et al.* 1983)

a) Somatotype categories

Carter and Heath (1990) defined 13 somatotype categories, shown as areas in Figure 2.4.

The exact definitions are as follows:

Central type:	No component differs by more than one unit from the other two.
Balanced endomorph:	Endomorphy is dominant and mesomorphy and ectomorphy are equal (or do not differ by more than one-half unit).
Mesomorphic endomorph:	Endomorphy is dominant and mesomorphy is greater than ectomorphy.
Mesomorph-endomorph:	Endomorphy and mesomorphy are equal (or do not differ by more than one-half unit), and ectomorphy is smaller.
Endomorphic mesomorph:	Mesomorphy is dominant and endomorphy is greater than ectomorphy.
Balanced mesomorph:	Mesomorphy is dominant and endomorphy and ectomorphy are equal (or do not differ by more than one-half unit).
Ectomorphic mesomorph:	Mesomorphy is dominant and ectomorphy is greater than endomorphy.
Mesomorph-ectomorph:	Mesomorphy and ectomorphy are equal (or do not differ by more than one-half unit), and endomorphy is smaller.
Mesomorphic ectomorph:	Ectomorphy is dominant and mesomorphy is greater than endomorphy.
Balanced ectomorph:	Ectomorphy is dominant and endomorphy and mesomorphy are equal (or do not differ by more than one-half unit).
Endomorphic ectomorph:	Ectomorphy is dominant and endomorphy is greater than mesomorphy.
Endomorph-ectomorph:	Endomorphy and ectomorphy are equal (or do not differ by more than one-half unit), and mesomorphy is lower.
Ectomorphic endomorph:	Endomorphy is dominant and ectomorphy is greater than mesomorphy.

This classification can be simplified into seven larger groupings:

Central type: No component differs by more than one unit from the other two.

Endomorph: Endomorphy is dominant; mesomorphy and ectomorphy are more than one-half unit lower.

Endomorph-mesomorph: Endomorphy and mesomorphy are equal (or do not differ by more than one-half unit), and ectomorphy is smaller.

Mesomorph: Mesomorphy is dominant; endomorphy and ectomorphy are more than one-half unit lower.

Mesomorph-ectomorph: Mesomorphy and ectomorphy are equal (or do not differ by more than one-half unit), and endomorphy is smaller.

Ectomorph: Ectomorphy is dominant; endomorphy and mesomorphy are more than one-half unit lower.

Ectomorph-endomorph: Endomorphy and ectomorphy are equal (or do not differ by more than one-half unit), and mesomorphy is lower.

b) Somatotype attitudinal distance

The formulae for calculating the SAD are given in Table 2.3.

Table 2.3 Formulae for calculation of SAD parameters

$$SAD(A;B) = \sqrt{(end(A) - end(B))^2 + (mes(A) - mes(B))^2 + (ect(A) - ect(B))^2}$$

$$SAM(X) = \sum_i \frac{SAD(\bar{X} - X_i)}{N_X}$$

$$SAV(X) = \sum_i \frac{SAD(\bar{X} - X_i)^2}{N_X}$$

Where: SAD = Somatotype Attitudinal Distance; SAM = Somatotype Attitudinal Mean; SAV = Somatotype Attitudinal Variance; end = endomorpy rating; mes = mesomorpy rating; ect = ectomorpy rating; A = an individual or a group; B = an individual or a group; X = a group; X_i = an individual member of group X; $\bar{X}$ = somatotype mean of group X; N_X = number of subjects in group X.

The SAD is the exact difference, in component units, between two somatotypes (if A and B are subjects), or between two somatotype group means (if A and B are group means), or between the group mean and an individual somatotype (if A and B are a group mean and a subject, respectively).

Like other parametric statistics, the SAD can be used to calculate differences, hence mean deviations and variances. Table 2.3 also gives formulae for calculating the Somatotype Attitudinal Mean (SAM) and the Somatotype Attitudinal Variance (SAV). The SAM and the SAV describe the magnitude of the absolute scatter of a group of somatotypes around the group mean. The SAD can lead to relatively simple parametric statistical treatment for calculating differences and correlations of whole somatotypes. Multivariate techniques may be more appropriate, but are also more complicated (Cressie *et al.* 1986).

2.6.3 Tasks

Two groups of female middle distance runners were measured comprising international level runners and national level runners. The calculated somatotypes are shown in Table 2.4.

a) Separate component analysis

Calculate the means and standard deviations of each separate component for each group.

Calculate the significance of the differences between the two groups for each component separately. Use three t-tests for independent means.

Discuss the difference between the two groups in terms of their component differences.

Table 2.4 Somatotypes of 6 national level and 10 international level female middle distance runners (data from Day et al. 1977)

International	National
1.5-3.0-3.5	2.0-3.5-4.0
1.0-3.0-5.0	2.0-4.0-4.0
1.5-3.0-4.5	3.5-4.5-2.0
1.0-2.0-6.0	2.5-3.5-3.0
2.0-3.0-4.0	1.5-3.5-4.5
1.5-3.0-4.0	2.5-4.0-3.0
2.5-2.0-4.0	
1.0-4.0-3.0	
2.0-3.0-4.0	

b) Global somatotype analysis: location on the somatochart

Locate and plot each somatotype on a copy of Figure 2.3 by means of the XY-coordinates. Do the same for the two somatotype means.

Discuss this visual impression of the difference between the two samples. Is there a difference in location of the means? Is there a difference in dispersion of the individual somatotypes between the two groups?

c) Global somatotype analysis: somatotype categories

Determine the somatotype category for each subject of the two groups.

Construct a cross tabulation with the two groups as rows, and the different somatotype categories as columns. Discuss the difference in somatotype category frequencies between the two groups.

Use chi-square to calculate the significance of the difference between the two groups with regard to the somatotype categories. (Note that larger cell frequencies are necessary for a meaningful interpretation of chi square.)

d) Global somatotype analysis: SAD-techniques

Calculate the SAV for each group, using the formulae in Table 2.3.

Check the difference in scatter between the two groups by describing the SAM of each group, and by means of an F-test on their SAVs.

Calculate the difference in location between the two groups by means of the SAD between the mean somatotypes (use the formula in Table 2.3).

2.7 PRACTICAL 3: ANALYSIS OF LONGITUDINAL SOMATOTYPE SERIES

2.7.1 Introduction

The aim in this practical is to learn how to perform an analysis of a longitudinal series of somatotypes, using the somatochart approach and using SAD techniques.

2.7.2 Methods

Analysis of time series in biological sciences must take into account the specific fact that the measurement series are within-subject factors. This can be achieved for illustrative purposes by connecting the consecutive plots of a particular measurement with time for the same subject. The classic way would be the evolution with time of the separate component values. The somatotype entity can be preserved by connecting the consecutive plots on the somatochart. Quantitative analysis of the changes is possible with multivariate analysis of variance (MANOVA) techniques with a within-subject design.

A simple quantitative way to describe the total change in somatotype with time is the Migratory Distance (MD). The MD is the sum of the SAD values, calculated from each consecutive pair of somatotypes of the subject:

$$MD(a;z) = SAD(a;b) + SAD(b;c) + ... + SAD(y;z)$$

where: a = first observation; b = second observation; ...; z = last observation; SAD(p;q) = change from somatotype p to somatotype q.

2.7.3 Tasks

A group of 6-year-old children was measured annually until their 17th birthdays. The anthropometric somatotypes were calculated using the formulae in Table 2.1. The results are given in Table 2.5.

1   Plot the changes of each component with time. Construct diagrams with age on the horizontal axis, and the component value on the vertical axis. Prepare one complete line diagram per child, on which the evolution of each component is shown. Discuss the change in individual component values for each child with age, and also the dominance situations from age to age.

2   Calculate the XY-coordinates of each somatotype. Locate the consecutive somatotypes of each child on a copy of Figure 2.3, using the formulae given in Practical 1. Use

one somatochart per child. Discuss the change in global somatotype and the change in component dominances with age for each child.

3   Calculate the MD for each child using the formulae given above. Also calculate the mean MD per child. Discuss the differences in MD between the children, and compare with the somatochart profiles.

Table 2.5 Consecutive somatotypes of 6 children from their 6th to their 17th birthday (data from Duquet et al., 1993)

Subjects: age	1	2	3	4	5	6
6	2.7-5.3-2.5	2.0-5.7-1.6	3.2-3.9-3.5	2.7-4.8-2.2	1.7-3.6-3.3	2.9-4.7-2.1
7	3.4-5.2-2.0	2.4-4.7-2.1	2.6-3.4-4.3	1.6-4.4-3.1	1.7-3.2-4.4	3.6-4.5-2.3
8	4.2-5.2-1.6	2.3-4.5-2.3	2.3-2.3-5.3	1.6-4.1-3.5	1.6-3.2-4.2	4.6-4.7-1.8
9	4.8-5.6-1.3	2.3-4.6-2.4	2.1-2.0-5.3	1.8-3.8-4.3	1.3-2.9-4.2	6.2-5.1-1.0
10	5.3-5.8-1.2	2.2-4.7-2.6	2.1-2.1-5.5	1.5-3.4-4.3	1.6-2.8-4.4	6.9-5.1-0.7
11	6.0-6.0-1.3	2.0-4.7-2.4	1.8-1.8-5.6	1.6-3.3-4.5	1.8-2.5-4.8	7.7-5.4-0.7
12	7.2-5.7-1.3	1.9-5.0-2.4	1.5-1.1-6.1	1.3-3.0-4.8	2.2-2.7-4.1	8.3-5.6-0.5
13	7.5-5.9-0.5	1.5-5.2-2.8	2.4-1.2-5.5	1.1-2.8-5.0	2.9-2.8-3.4	8.4-5.8-0.5
14	6.3-5.9-0.8	1.1-5.2-3.1	2.2-1.1-6.0	1.2-2.5-5.1	3.5-2.9-3.5	8.6-5.9-0.5
15	3.8-5.3-1.7	1.3-5.3-2.8	2.0-1.2-5.5	1.6-2.5-4.9	3.7-3.0-2.9	8.0-5.9-0.5
16	3.0-5.4-1.6	1.8-5.5-2.6	2.4-1.0-5.4	1.7-2.3-4.6	3.8-3.2-2.7	7.9-6.2-0.5
17	2.9-5.5-1.6	1.5-5.4-2.7	1.8-0.8-6.0	1.9-2.6-4.5	2.8-2.9-3.5	8.3-6.4-0.5

2.8 PRACTICAL 4: VISUAL INSPECTION OF SOMATOTYPE PHOTOGRAPHS: AN INTRODUCTION TO PHOTOSCOPIC SOMATOTYPING

2.8.1 Introduction

The aim of this practical to demonstrate how to perform a visual evaluation of the degree of presence or absence of each component in an individual by means of a somatotype photograph, and to learn to evaluate the somatotype dominance situation within this individual.

2.8.2 Methods

A visual evaluation of the somatotype should be based on careful reading of the descriptions of the components in definitions 2.3.1 (c), (d), (e) and (f) or on the more detailed descriptions in Carter and Heath (1990). This practical should be seen as an introduction; a way to obtain a first impression of the technique. Expertise should be gained by comparing your own ratings with those of an experienced rater. The steps to follow in this first approach are given in the following tasks.

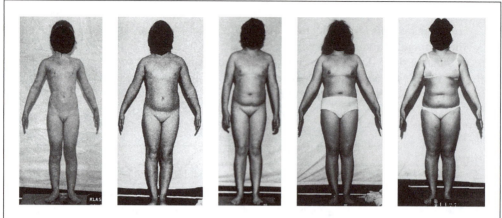

Figure 2.5 Somatotype photographs of the same child taken at ages 7.4, 10.0, 12.5, 14.5 and 17.0.

2.8.3 Tasks

Figure 2.5 shows somatotype photographs of the same child taken at ages 7.4, 10.0, 12.5, 14.5 and 17.0.

1   Read the definition of endomorphy, and try to decide through visual inspection at which age the child has the lowest level of endomorphy; at which age the second lowest level, degree, and so on.

  Next, draw an XY-coordinate graph, in which the horizontal axis represents the age points, and the vertical axis represents the level of endomorphy. Do not yet try to attach a scale to the ordinate. Try to draw a broken line that indicates, to your best impression, the way endomorphy eventually changes with age in the child.

2   Proceed in the same way with the component mesomorphy, and construct the polygon for mesomorphy on a separate page.

3   Proceed in the same way with the component ectomorphy, and construct the polygon for ectomorphy on a third page.

4   On the first photograph visually compare the level of each component at the lowest age, and try to decide if one or two components are less or more dominant than the other, or if they are of equal importance. Give your visual impression of the somatotype category at this age, using the definitions given in Practical 2.

  Now superimpose the three polygons. Shift one or more lines up or downwards if necessary, according to your photoscopic impression of the relative dominance of the components at this age.

  Continue in the same way for each age.

5   Compare the diagram obtained with the ones that resulted from task 1 of Practical 3. Try to find out which of the six subjects in Table 2.5 corresponds to the child in Figure 2.5.

6   Check if your visual impressions correspond to the anthropometric somatotype assessment at each age. Make the necessary corrections, and try to fit the scale of the vertical axis.

FURTHER READING

Book

Carter, J. E. L. and Heath B. H. (1990): *Somatotyping – Development and Applications*. Cambridge University Press; Cambridge.

Website

www.somatotype.org

REFERENCES

Albonico R. (1970) *Mensch-Menschen-Typen. Entwicklung und Stand der Typenforschung.* Birkhauser Verlag; Basel.

Amusa L. O., Toriola A. L. and Agbonjinmi A. P. (2003) Anthropometric profiles of top national track athletes. *African Journal for Physical, Health Education, Recreation and Dance;* **9** (1): 67–82.

Buffa R., Succa V., Garau D., Marini E. and Floris G. (2005). Variations of somatotype in elderly Sardinians. *American Journal of Human Biology,* **17**: 403–11.

Carter J. E. L. (1980) *The Heath-Carter Somatotype Method.* San Diego State University Syllabus Service; San Diego.

Carter J. E. L. (2003) Anthropometry of team sports. In: (T. Reilly and M. Marfell-Jones, eds) *Kinanthropometry VIII.* Routledge; London: pp. 117–30.

Carter J. E. L. and Ackland T. R. (2008) Somatotype in sport. In: (T. R. Ackland, B.C. Elliot and J. Bloomfield, eds) *Applied Anatomy and Biomechanics in Sport, 2nd Edition.* Human Kinetics; Champaign, IL.

Carter J. E. L. and Heath B. H. (1990): *Somatotyping – Development and Applications.* Cambridge University Press; Cambridge.

Carter J. E. L., Ross W. D., Duquet W. and Aubry S. P. (1983) Advances in somatotype methodology and analysis. *Yearbook of Physical Anthropology;* **26**: 193–213.

Carter J. E. L., Ackland T. A., Kerr D. A. and Stapff A.B. (2005). Somatotype and size of elite female basketball players. *Journal of Sports Sciences;* **23** (10): 1057–63.

Chaouachi M., Chaouachi A., Chamari K., Chtara M., Feki Y., Amri M. and Trudeau F. (2005). Effects of dominant somatotypes on aerobic capacity trainability. *British Journal of Sports Medicine;* **39**: 954–9.

Claessens A. L., Bourgois J., Lefevre B., Van Renterghem B., Philippaerts R., Loos R., Janssens M., Thomis M. and Vrijens, J. (2001). Body composition and somatotype characteristics of elite male junior rowers in relation to competition level, rowing style and boat type. *Journal of Sports Sciences;* **19** (8): 611 Abstract.

Conrad K. (1963) *Der Konstitutionstypus. Theoretische Grundlegung und praktischer Bestimmung.* Springer; Berlin.

Cressie N. A. C., Withers A. T. and Craig N. P. (1986) The statistical analysis of somatotype data. *Yearbook of Physical Anthropology;* **29**: 197–208.

Day J. A. P., Duquet W. and Meersseman G. (1977) Anthropometry and physique type of female middle and long distance runners, in relation to speciality and level of performance. In: (O. Eiben, ed) *Growth and Development; Physique.* Akademiai Kiado; Budapest: pp. 385–97.

Duquet W. (1980) Studie van de toepasbaarheid van de Heath & Carter – somatotypemethode op kinderen van 6 tot 13 jaar (Applicability of the Heath-Carter somatotype method to 6 to 13 year old children). PhD Dissertation. Vrije Universiteit Brussel; Belgium.

Duquet W. and Hebbelinck M. (1977) Application of the somatotype attitudinal distance to the study of group and individual somatotype status and relations. In: (O. Eiben, ed). *Growth and Development; Physique.* Akademiai Kiado; Budapest: pp. 377–84.

Duquet W., Borms J., Hebbelinck M., Day J. A. P. and Cordemans P. (1993): Longitudinal study of the stability of the somatotype in boys and girls. In: *Kinanthropometry IV* (W. Duquet and J. A. P. Day, eds). E. & F. N. Spon; London: pp. 54–67.

Eston R.G., Hawes M., Martin A.D. and Reilly T. (2009): Human body composition. In: (R. G. Eston and T. Reilly, eds) *Kinanthropometry Laboratory Manual (3rd Edition): Anthropometry (Chapter 1).* Routledge; Oxon: pp. 3–53.

Goulding M. (2002) *Somatotype – Calculation and Analysis – CD Rom.* Sweat Technologies; Mitchell Park, South Australia. [www.sweattechnologies.org]

Heath B. H. (1963) Need for modification of somatotype methodology. *American Journal of Physical Anthropology*; **21**: 227–33.

Heath B. H. and Carter J. E. L. (1967) A modified somatotype method. *American Journal of Physical Anthropology*; **27**: 57–74.

Kretschmer E. (1921) *Körperbau und Charakter.* Springer Verlag; Berlin.

Lindegård B. (1953) *Variations in human body build.* Munksgård; Copenhagen.

Parnell R. W. (1954) Somatotyping by physical anthropometry. *American Journal of Physical Anthropology*; **12**: 209–40.

Parnell R. W. (1958) *Behaviour and Physique.* E. Arnold; London.

Peeters M. W., Thomis M. A., Loos R. J. F., Derom C.A., Fagard R., Claessens A.L., Vlietinck R.F. and Beunen G.P. (2007). Heritability of somatotype components: a multivariate analysis. *International Journal of Obesity*; **31**: 1295–1301.

Sheldon W. H., Stevens S. S. and Tucker W. B. (1940) *The Varieties of Human Physique.* Harper and Brothers; New York.

Stewart A. D., Benson P. J., Michanikou E.G., Tsiota D.G. and Narli M.K. (2003). Body image perception, satisfaction and somatotype in male and female athletes and non-athletes: results using a novel morphing technique. *Journal of Sports Sciences*, **21** (10): 815–23.

Tucker W. B. and Lessa W. A. (1940a) Man: a constitutional investigation. *The Quarterly Review of Biolog*; **15**: 265–89.

Tucker W. B. and Lessa W. A. (1940b) Man: a constitutional investigation (cont'd). *The Quarterly Review of Biology*, **15**: 411–55.

Underhay C., De Ridder J.H., Amusa L.O., Toriola A.L., Agbonjinmi A.P. and Adeogun J.O. (2005). Physique characteristics of world-class African long distance runners. *African Journal for Physical, Health Education, Recreation and Dance*; **11** (1): 6–16.

Vieira F., Fragoso I., Silva L. and Canto e Castro L.C. (2003). Morphology and sports performance in children aged 10–13 years: identification of different levels of motor skills. In: (T. Reilly and M. Marfell-Jones, eds). *Kinanthropometry VIII*. Routledge; London: pp. 93–96.

Viola G. (1933) *La constituzione individuale.* Cappelli; Bologna.

CHAPTER 3

PHYSICAL GROWTH, MATURATION AND PERFORMANCE

Gaston Beunen

3.1 AIMS

This chapter aims to familiarize the students with growth evaluation, the assessment of sexual and skeletal maturation and the evaluation of physical performance as assessed with the Eurofit test battery. Some methodological considerations as well as practical applications are provided.

3.2 INTRODUCTION

Growth, maturation and development are three concepts that are often used together and sometimes considered as synonymous. Growth is a dominant biological activity during the first two decades of life. It starts at conception and continues until the late teens or even the early twenties for a number of individuals. Growth refers to the increase in size of the body as a whole or the size attained by the specific parts of the body. The changes in size are outcomes of: (a) an increase in cell number or hyperplasia; (b) an increase in cell size or cell hypertrophy; and (c) an increase in intercellular material, or accretion. These processes occur during growth, but the predominance of one or other process varies with age. For example, the number of muscle

cells (fibres), is already established shortly after birth. The growth of the whole body is traditionally assessed by the changes in stature measured in a standing position, or for infants, in supine position (recumbent length). To assess the growth of specific parts of the body, appropriate anthropometric techniques have been described (Weiner and Lourie 1969; Carter 1982; Cameron 1984; 2004a; Lohman *et al.* 1988; Norton and Olds 1996; Simons *et al.* 1990).

3.2.1 Definition of concepts

Maturation refers to the process of becoming fully mature. It gives an indication of the distance that is travelled along the road to adulthood. In other words, it refers to the tempo and timing in the progress towards the mature biological state. Biological maturation varies with the biological system that is considered. Most often the following biological systems are examined: sexual maturation, morphological maturation, dental maturation and skeletal maturation.

Sexual maturation refers to the process of becoming fully sexually mature, i.e. reaching functional reproductive capability. Morphological maturation can be estimated through the percentage of adult stature that is already attained at a given age, or by using the timing of the characteristics of the adolescent growth curve, namely age at onset and age at peak height velocity of the growth curve. Skeletal and dental maturation refers respectively to a fully ossified adult skeleton or dentition (Tanner 1962; 1989; Malina *et al.* 2004; Beunen *et al.* 2006). It should be noted that both the growth of somatic dimensions and the biological maturation are under the control of hormonal and biochemical axes and their interactions (Beunen *et al.* 2006).

Development is a broader concept, encompassing growth, maturation, learning, and experience (training). It relates to becoming competent in a variety of tasks. Thus one can speak of cognitive development, motor development and emotional development as the child's personality emerges within the context of the particular culture in which the child was born and reared. Motor development is the process by which the child acquires movement patterns and skills. It is characterized by continuous modification based upon neuromuscular maturation, growth and maturation of the body, residual effects of prior experience and new motor experiences *per se* (Malina *et al.* 2004).

Postnatal motor development is characterized by a shift from primitive reflex mechanisms towards postural reflexes and definite motor actions. It further refers to the acquisition of independent walking and competence in a variety of manipulative tasks and fundamental motor skills; such as running, skipping, throwing, catching, jumping, climbing and hopping (Keogh and Sugden 1985). From school age onwards, the focus shifts towards the development of physical performance capacities traditionally studied in the context of physical fitness or motor fitness projects. Motor fitness includes cardiorespiratory endurance, anaerobic power, muscular strength and power, local muscular endurance (sometimes called functional strength), speed, flexibility and balance (Pate and Shephard 1989; Simons *et al.* 1969, 1990).

3.2.2 Historical perspective

According to Tanner (1981) the earliest surviving statement about human growth appears in a Greek elegy of the sixth century BC. Solon the Athenian divided the growth period into hebdomads, that is, successive periods of seven years each. The infant (literally, while unable to speak) acquires deciduous teeth and sheds them before the age of seven. At the end of the next hebdomad the boy shows the signs of puberty (beginning of pubic hair), and in the last period the body enlarges and the skin becomes bearded (Tanner 1981).

Anthropometry was not born of medicine or science but of the arts. Painters and sculptors needed instructions about the relative proportions of legs and trunks, shoulders and hips, eyes and forehead and other parts of the body. The inventor of the term anthropometry was a German physician, Johann Sigismund Elsholtz (1623–1688). It is interesting to note that at this time there was not very much attention given to absolute size, but much more to proportions. Note also that the introduction of the 'mètre' occurred only in 1795 and even then other scales continued to be used.

The first published longitudinal growth study of which we have record was made by Count Philibert de Montbeillard (1720–1785) on request of his close friend Buffon (Tanner 1981). The growth and the growth velocity curves of Montbeillard's son are probably the best known curves in auxology (study of human growth). They describe growth and its velocity from birth to adulthood, which have been widely studied since then in various populations (see for example, Eveleth and Tanner 1990). Growth velocity refers to the growth over a period of time. Very often velocity is used to indicate changes in stature over a period of 1 year.

Another significant impetus in the study of growth was given by the Belgian mathematician Adolphe Quetelet (1796–1874). He was, in many ways, the founder of modern statistics and was instrumental in the foundation of the Statistical Society of London. Quetelet collected data on height and weight and fitted a curve to the succession of means. According to his mathematical function, the growth velocity declines from birth to maturity and shows no adolescent growth spurt. This confused a number of investigators until the 1940s (Tanner 1981). At the beginning of the nineteenth century there was an increased interest in the growing child, due to the appalling conditions of the poor and their children. A new direction was given by the anthropologist Franz Boas (1858–1942). He was the first to realize the individual variation in tempo of growth and was responsible for the introduction of the concept of physiological age or biological maturation. A number of longitudinal studies were then initiated in the 1920s in the USA and later in Europe. These studies served largely as the basis of our present knowledge on physical growth and maturation (Tanner 1981; Malina *et al.* 2004).

3.2.3 Fitness and performance

In several nations there is great interest in developing and maintaining the physical fitness levels of the citizens of all age levels, but special concern goes to the fitness of youth. Physical fitness has been defined in many ways. According to the American Academy of Physical Education, 'Physical fitness is the ability to carry out daily tasks with vigor and alertness, without undue fatigue and with ample energy to engage in leisure-time pursuits and to meet the above average physical stresses encountered in emergency situations' (Clarke 1979: 1).

Often the distinction is made between an organic component and a motor component. The organic component is defined as the capacity to adapt to and recover from strenuous exercise, and relates to energy production and work output. The motor component relates to the development and performance of gross motor abilities. Since the beginning of the eighties the distinction between health-

related and performance-related physical fitness has come into common use (Pate and Shephard 1989). Health-related fitness is then viewed as a state characterized by an ability to perform daily activities with vigour, and traits and capacities that are associated with low risk of premature development of the hypokinetic diseases (i.e. those associated with physical inactivity) (Pate and Shephard 1989). Health-related physical fitness includes cardiorespiratory endurance, body composition, muscular strength and flexibility. Performance-related fitness refers to the abilities associated with adequate athletic performance, and encompasses components such as isometric strength, power, speed-agility, balance and hand-eye coordination.

Since Sargent (1921) proposed the vertical jump as a physical performance test for men, considerable change has taken place both in the conceptualisation of physical performance and physical fitness and also about measurement. In the early days the expression 'general motor ability' was used to indicate one's 'general' skill. The term was similar to the general intelligence factor used at that time. Primarily under the influence of Brace (1927) and McCloy (1934) a fairly large number of studies were undertaken and a multiple motor ability concept replaced the general ability concept. There is now considerable agreement among authors and experts that the fitness concept is multi-dimensional and several abilities can be identified. Ability refers to a more general trait of the individual, which can be inferred from response consistencies on a number of related tasks, whereas skill refers to the level of proficiency on a specific task or limited group of tasks. A child possesses isometric strength since he or she performs well on a variety of isometric strength tests.

Considerable attention has been devoted to fitness testing and research in the USA and Canada. The President's Council on Youth Fitness; the American Alliance for Health, Physical Education, Recreation and Dance (AAHPER 1958, 1965; AAHPERD

1988); and the Canadian sister organization (CAHPER 1965) have done an outstanding job in constructing and promoting fitness testing in schools. Internationally, the fundamental works of Fleishman (1964) and the International Committee for the Standardization of Physical Fitness Tests (now the International Council for Physical Activity and Fitness Research) (Larson, 1974) have received considerable attention. These works served for example as the basis for nationwide studies in Belgium (Hebbelinck and Borms 1975; Ostyn *et al.* 1980; Simons *et al.* 1990). Furthermore, the fitness test battery constructed by Simons *et al.* (1969) served as the basis for studies in The Netherlands (Bovend'eerdt *et al.* 1980; Kemper *et al.* 1979) and for the construction of the Eurofit test battery (Adam *et al.* 1988).

In the following section, three laboratory practicals will be outlined focusing on standards of normal growth, biological maturity status and evaluation of physical fitness.

3.3 REFERENCE VALUES FOR NORMAL GROWTH

3.3.1 Methodological considerations

Growth data may be used in three distinct ways: (1) to serve as a screening device in order to identify individuals who might benefit from special medical or educational care; (2) to serve as control in the treatment of ill children (the paediatric use); and (3) as an index of the general health and nutritional status of the population or sub-population (Tanner 1989). A distinction must be made between growth standards and growth references. Standards refer to how growth, maturation and development should proceed under optimal environmental conditions for health. References are statistical indicators observed at a certain period in time for a certain population. A new International Growth Standard for infants and preschool children has been recently released by the WHO-Multicentre Growth Reference Group,

and planning is underway to complement these International Growth Standards with Growth Standards for preadolescents and adolescents (Butte *et al.* 2006).

Normal growth is usually considered in terms of attained stature or any other anthropometric dimension and, where available, also reference values for growth velocity. Reference values for attained stature are useful for assessing the present status to answer the question: 'Is the child's growth normal for his/her age and gender?' Growth velocity reference values are constructed to verify the growth process.

Reference charts of attained height, usually referred to as growth curves, are constructed on the basis of cross-sectional studies. In such studies, representative samples of girls and boys stemming from different birth cohorts and consequently different age groups are measured once.

It has to be remembered that the outer percentiles such as the 3rd and 97th are subject to considerably greater sample error than the mean or the 50th percentile (Goldstein 1986; Healy 1986). The precision of estimates of population parameters, such as the mean and median, depends on the sample size and the variability in the population. If Me is the sample mean, then the 95% confidence values, a and b, are two values such that the probability that the true population mean lies between them is 0.95. If the distribution of the measurement is Gaussian, then for a simple random sample a and b are given by:

a = Me +1.96SE mean
b = Me −1.96SE mean

in which SE mean = $\dfrac{SD}{\sqrt{n-1}}$

From these formulae it can be easily seen that for a given population variance the confidence intervals decrease when the sample size increases. Major standardizing studies use samples of about 1,000 subjects in each gender and age group, but 500 subjects normally produce useful percentiles (Eveleth and Tanner

1990). Recently, Cole (2006) argued, based on a simulation study, that a sample size of about 200 subjects for each gender group covering the age range between birth and 20 years should be sufficient. Representative samples can be obtained in several ways – the most commonly used being simple random samples and stratified samples. In a simple random sample each subject has an equal chance of being selected in the sample and each subject in the population must be identifiable. In a stratified sample, significant strata are identified and in each stratum a sample is selected. A stratification factor is one that serves for dividing the population into strata or subdivisions of the population, such as ethnic groups or degree of urbanization. The stratification factor is selected because there is evidence that this factor affects, or is related to, the growth process.

Growth velocity standards or reference values can be obtained only from longitudinal studies. In a longitudinal study a representative sample of boys and/or girls from one birth cohort is measured repeatedly at regular intervals. The frequency of the measurements depends on the growth velocity and also on the measurement error. During periods of rapid growth it is necessary to increase the frequency of the measurements. For stature, for example, it is recommended to carry out monthly measurements during the first year of life and to measure every three months during the adolescent growth spurt. Although some recent evidence (Lampl *et al.* 1992) suggests that there is much more variation in growth velocity, with periods of rapid change (stepwise or saltatory increase) followed by periods of no change (stasis) when growth is monitored over very short periods of time (days or weeks).

Cross-sectional references for growth are most often presented as growth charts. Such charts are constructed from the means and standard deviations or from the percentiles of the different gender and age groups. Conventionally, the 3rd, 10th, 25th, 50th, 75th, 90th and 97th are displayed. The 3rd and 97th percentiles delineate the outer borders of what is considered as 'normal' growth. This does not imply that on a single measurement one can decide about the 'abnormality' of the growth process. Children with statures outside the 3rd and 97th percentile need to be further examined.

Since growth is considered as a regular process over larger (years) time intervals, a smooth continuous curve is fitted to the sample statistics (means, means ± 1(2).SD, different percentiles P3, P10, P25, P50, P75, P90, P97). The series of sample statistics can be graphically smoothed by eye or a mathematical function can be fitted to the data. This mathematical function is selected so that it is simple and corresponds closely to the observations. In a common procedure a smooth curve is drawn through the medians (means). This can be done by fitting non-linear regressions to narrow age groups and estimate the centre of the group. The age groups are then shifted to the next age interval, resulting in a number of overlapping intervals in which corrected (estimated) medians are identified. The next step is to estimate the other percentiles taking into account the corrections that have been made to the medians in the first step. This can be done by using the residuals from the fitted 50th percentile curve within each age group to estimate the other percentiles. This procedure can be improved by setting up a general relationship between the percentiles we want to estimate and the 50th percentile (Goldstein 1984). The LMS-method (lambda-mu-sigma) developed by Cole and Green (1992) permits the construction of distance curves. This method estimates the age-changing distribution of the measurements in terms of their median, coefficient of variation and skewness.

3.3.2 Mathematical basis of velocity curves

Longitudinal growth velocity reference values are obtained from the analysis of individual growth data. Individual growth curves are fitted to the serial measurements of each child. For many purposes graphical fits (Tanner *et al.* 1966) are sufficient, but mathematical curves may also be employed (Goldstein 1979; Marubini and Milani 1986; Jolicoeur *et al.* 1992). Most mathematical curves or models presently in use are developed for growth in stature. Some models have also been applied for a few body dimensions, such as body mass and diameters. The mathematical functions can be divided into two classes: structural models and non-structural models.

3.3.3 Structural models

In the structural models the mathematical function, usually a family of functions or mathematical model, imposes a well-defined pre-selected shape to the growth curves that are fitted to the data. If the function reflects underlying processes, then the parameters of the function may have biological meaning (Bock and Thissen 1980). Jenss and Bayley (1937) proposed a model to describe the growth process from birth to 8 years. This model includes a linear and an exponential term in which the linear part describes the growth velocity and the exponential part describes growth deceleration. Several other functions have been used to describe the growth during the adolescent period (Deming 1957; Marubini *et al.* 1972; Hauspie *et al.* 1980). More recently, various models have also been proposed to describe the whole growth period from birth to adulthood (Preece and Baines 1978; Bock and Thissen 1980; Jolicoeur *et al.* 1992). Preece and Baines (1978) have derived a family of mathematical models to describe the human growth curve from the differential equation:

$$\frac{dh}{dt} = s(t)(h_1 - h) \qquad \text{(eq. 1)}$$

In which: h: height
h_1: is adult height
s(t): is a function of time

Model 1, in which s(t) was defined by

$$\frac{ds}{dt} = (s_1 - s)(s - s_0) \qquad \text{(eq. 2)}$$

was especially accurate and robust, containing only five parameters. The function is:

$$h = h_1 - \frac{2(h_1 - h_\theta)}{\exp[S_0(t-\theta)] + \exp[S_1(t-\theta)]} \qquad \text{(eq. 3)}$$

In which: $h\theta$ ($h\theta$ is height at t=θ) and h_1 (adult height) are two height parameters

θ is a time parameter
S_0 and S_1 are rate constants having dimensions inverse of time

From eq. 3 the velocity and acceleration function can be calculated. The position of the maximum and minimum growth velocity can be calculated from the acceleration curve and subsequently age at 'take-off,' age at 'peak height velocity' and height velocity at these points can be obtained. In Table 3.1 mean values are given for British adolescents.

This model proves to be reasonably accurate to describe the adolescent growth period (Hauspie *et al.* 1980). If, however, the whole growth period from birth to adulthood is considered, more complex models, using more than five parameters, are needed (Bock and Thissen 1980; Jolicoeur *et al.* 1992).

3.3.4 Non-structural models

For the non-structural approach, polynomials using various fitting techniques have been applied, such as spline functions and Kernel estimations (van't Hof *et al.* 1976; Largo *et al.* 1978; Gasser *et al.* 1984, 2004). Gasser *et al.* (2004) argued that most of the present parametric models are purely descriptive and often fail to capture the true shape of the regression function underlying the data. They demonstrate the applicability of the non-parametric Kernel estimation and shape-invariant modelling. As a rule they advise first to use Kernel estimations of the individual growth curves; if needed or desirable, shape-

Table 3.1 Mean values for parameters in model 1 (from Preece and Baines 1978)

| | Boys (n = 35) | | Girls (n = 23) | |
	Mean	SD	Mean	SD
h_1	174.6	6.0	163.4	5.1
$h\theta$	162.9	5.6	152.7	5.2
S_O	0.1124	0.0126	0.1320	0.0181
S_1	1.2397	0.1683	1.1785	0.1553
2	14.60	0.93	12.49	0.74

Key:

h_1: adult height

S_O: rate constant related to prepubertal velocity

S_1: rate constant related to peak height velocity

2: time parameter, near to age at peak height velocity

Exact values of the growth characteristics (take-off, peak velocity) can be mathematically derived.

invariant modelling could be applied in a later stage of the research project. The use of increments or difference scores between observations of adjacent intervals is often not indicated. The regularity of the growth process is overlooked; two measurement errors are involved in each increment; and successive increments are negatively related (van't Hof *et al.* 1976). The individual growth parameters obtained from the graphical or mathematical curve-fitting are then combined to form the so-called mean constant growth curve and by differentiation the mean constant growth velocity curve.

For most growth studies cross-sectional references have been published. Tanner (1989) has argued that 'tempo-conditional' standards, meaning standards that allow for differences in the tempo of growth between children, are much finer instruments to evaluate normality of growth. Such conditional standards combine information from longitudinal and cross-sectional studies. Other conditional standards can be used, such as standards for height that allow for height of parents (Tanner 1989).

3.3.5 Growth evaluation

Depending on the number of students in the class, 30–50 secondary school girls and/or boys from the local school can be measured.

Exact identification, including birth date and date of measurement, name and address and parents' heights should be asked in a small inquiry addressed to the parents. Informed consent to conduct the study can be obtained at the same time. Furthermore, consent has to be obtained from the school administration. It is also advisable to obtain approval for the project by the ethics committee of the institution.

Included here are reference data for British children (Figures 3.1 and 3.2) (Tanner 1989). If these standards are used for the evaluation of the school children, then height should be measured according to the procedures described by Tanner (1989, pp.182–6). Often reference data from USA are used (available at: http://www.cdc.gov/growthcharts/). When available, local and national reference data can also be used (for references see Eveleth and Tanner 1990, or more recently, Haas and Campirano 2006). When local references are used, it is obvious that the measurement techniques used in constructing these references should be adopted. The measuring techniques are all important and each student needs to get experienced with them, preferably by conducting a preliminary intra- and inter-observer study with an experienced anthropometrist.

Once the data are collected, each individual measurement is plotted against the reference

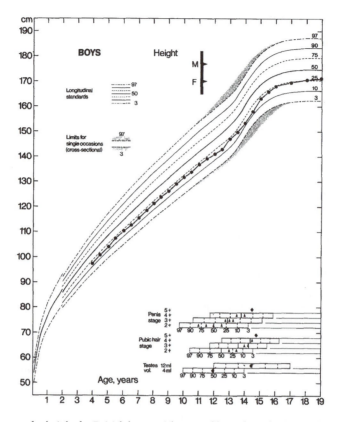

Figure 3.1 References for height for British boys, with normal boy plotted. (In North and South America, reprinted by permission of the publisher from *Fetus into Man: Physical Growth from Conception to Maturity* by J. M. Tanner, pp. 180–1, Cambridge, MA: Harvard University Press, Copyright © 1978, 1989 by J. M. Tanner. In the rest of the world reprinted by permission of the copyright holders, Castlemead publications.)

standards. Chronological age should be converted to decimal age expressed in years and tenths of a year. To calculate the decimal age, the year is divided into 10 not 12. Using Table 3.2, the child's birth date is recorded; e.g. a child born on June 26 1985 has the birthday 85.482. The date of the observation is, e.g. October 15, 1999, recorded as 99.786. Age at examination is obtained by simple subtraction, e.g.

$$99.786 - 85.482 = 14.304 \text{ rounded to}$$
14.30 years.

Table 3.3 presents data from two boys followed at annual intervals (data from the Leuven Longitudinal Study of Belgian Boys,

Beunen *et al.* 1992). To assess the growth process of these boys their data can be plotted against the British reference data (ignoring small differences between Belgian and British populations) (Figure 3.1).

3.3.6 Interpretation of the results

As expected the heights of the children are scattered over the growth chart. In order to evaluate the growth status, it is advisable to calculate the mid-parent percentile. This is the average of the percentile that corresponds to the height of the parents. (The gender specific growth charts are, of course, used to define these percentiles.) If one takes the mid-parent height percentile as the 'target' a

Table 3.2 Decimals of year

	1	2	3	4	5	6	7	8	9	10	11	12
	Jan	Feb	Mar	Apr	May	Jun	Jul	Aug	Sep	Oct	Nov	Dec
1	000	085	162	247	329	414	496	581	666	748	833	915
2	003	088	164	249	332	416	499	584	668	751	836	918
3	005	090	167	252	334	419	501	586	671	753	838	921
4	008	093	170	255	337	422	504	589	674	756	841	923
5	011	096	173	258	340	425	507	592	677	759	844	926
6	014	099	175	260	342	427	510	595	679	762	847	929
7	016	101	178	263	345	430	512	597	682	764	849	932
8	019	104	181	266	348	433	515	600	685	767	852	934
9	022	107	184	268	351	436	518	603	688	770	855	937
10	025	110	186	271	353	438	521	605	690	773	858	940
11	027	112	189	274	356	441	523	608	693	775	860	942
12	030	115	192	277	359	444	526	611	696	778	863	945
13	033	118	195	279	362	447	529	614	699	781	866	948
14	036	121	197	282	364	449	532	616	701	784	868	951
15	038	123	200	285	367	452	534	619	704	786	871	953
16	041	126	203	288	370	455	537	622	707	789	874	956
17	044	129	205	290	373	458	540	625	710	792	877	959
18	047	132	208	293	375	460	542	627	712	795	879	962
19	049	134	211	296	378	463	545	630	715	797	882	964
20	052	137	214	299	381	466	548	633	718	800	885	967
21	055	140	216	301	384	468	551	636	721	803	888	970
22	058	142	219	304	386	471	553	638	723	805	890	973
23	060	145	222	307	389	474	556	641	726	808	893	975
24	063	148	225	310	392	477	559	644	729	811	896	978
25	066	151	227	312	395	479	562	647	731	814	899	981
26	068	153	230	315	397	482	564	649	734	816	901	984
27	071	156	233	318	400	485	567	652	737	819	904	986
28	074	159	236	321	403	488	570	655	740	822	907	989
29	077		238	323	405	490	573	658	742	825	910	992
30	079		241	326	408	493	575	660	745	827	912	995
31	082		244		411		578	663		830		997

From Tanner and Whitehouse (1984). Reproduced with the permission of the copyright holders, Castlemead publications.

band of ± 10 cm for boys and ± 9 cm for girls can be plotted (use copies of the reference chart) for each child and the observed height should fall within this band. It is unlikely that a child with two small parents, at 25th percentile, will have a stature above the 75th percentile – the upper limit of the previously mentioned growth band. On the other hand it is to be expected that a child from two tall parents, at the 75th percentile, will have

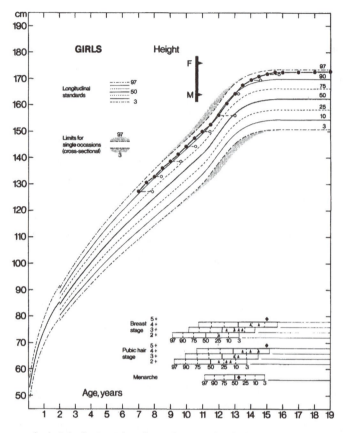

Figure 3.2 References for height for British girls, with normal girl plotted. (In North and South America, reprinted by permission of the publisher from *Fetus into Man: Physical Growth from Conception to Maturity* by J. M. Tanner, pp. 180–181, Cambridge, Mass.: Harvard University Press, Copyright © 1978, 1989 by J. M. Tanner. In the rest of the world reprinted by permission of the copyright holders, Castlemead publications.)

Table 3.3 Growth characteristics of two 'normal boys' (Beunen *et al.* 1992)

	Age (y)	Height (cm)	Body mass (kg)	Skinfolds subscapular (mm)	Triceps
CASE1	13	149.6	40.0	4.1	10.2
	14	154.2	43.0	5.1	9.6
	15	162.9	50.0	7.1	9.0
	16	169.8	55.0	5.6	8.4
	17	173.4	63.0	7.9	6.2
	18	175.3	65.0	7.3	7.2
CASE 2	13	158.5	48.5	7.6	10.8
	14	166.2	53.0	7.0	10.9
	15	172.3	57.5	6.2	8.6
	16	176.6	64.0	11.6	8.4
	17	177.8	67.0	10.2	8.0
	18	178.1	68.5	8.8	7.5

a stature at or even somewhat above the 75th percentile.

For the interpretation of the individual data it is important to know that the mean age at peak height velocity is about 14 years with a standard deviation of 1 year for boys in both the British and Belgian population.

The following questions can be considered: (1) Are these two boys small, average or tall for their age? (2) Are they early, average or late maturing children? (3) Do they have adequate body mass for their size? To answer these questions, reference data are needed for body mass, body mass index and/or skinfolds (for boys 14 years of age see Table 3.5).

3.3.7 Further recommendations

It should be remembered that the reported parents' heights are much more subject to error than when measured. In a growth clinic it is common practice that the parents' heights are measured.

If the height of only one parent is available, the height of the other parent can be estimated by adding (for the father's height) or subtracting (for the mother's height) 13 cm to or from the height reported by the mother or father, respectively.

If the British reference curves are used, it should be kept in mind that there are large interpopulation differences and that, even within a population, differences may occur due to ethnicity, social status or degree of urbanization to name a few (see, for example Eveleth and Tanner 1990; Haas and Campirano 2006).

3.4 BIOLOGICAL MATURATION: SEXUAL, MORPHOLOGICAL, DENTAL MATURATION AND SKELETAL AGE

3.4.1 Methodological considerations

It is well documented that somatic characteristics, biological maturation and physical performance are interrelated, and that young elite athletes exhibit specific maturity characteristics (Beunen 1989; Malina *et al.* 2004). Young elite male athletes are generally advanced in their maturity status, whereas young female athletes show late maturity status, especially in gymnastics, figure skating and ballet dancing. The assessment of biological maturity is thus a very important indicator of the growing child. It is therefore a valuable tool in the hands of experienced kinanthropometrists and all other professionals involved in the evaluation of the growth and development of children.

3.4.2 Assessment of sexual maturation

As mentioned already, several biological systems can be used to assess biological maturity status. In assessing sexual maturation the criteria described by Reynolds and Wines (1948, 1951) synthesized and popularized by Tanner (1962) are most often used. They should not be referred to as Tanner's stages since they were in use long before Tanner described them in *Growth at Adolescence*. Furthermore, there is considerable difference in the stages for breast, genital or pubic hair development. Five discrete stages for each area are described by Tanner (1962).

The breast development stages, which follow Reynolds and Wines (1948) are illustrated in Figure 3.3.

Stage 1: pre-adolescent: elevation of papilla only.

Stage 2: breast bud stage: elevation of breast and papilla as small mound, enlargement of the areola diameter.

Stage 3: further enlargement and elevation of breast and areola, with no separation of their contours.

Stage 4: projection of areola and papilla to form a secondary mound above the level of the breast.

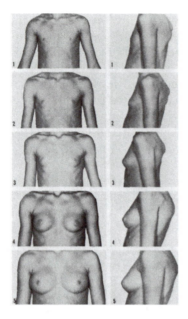

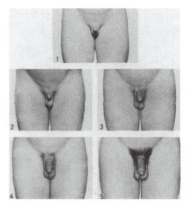

Figure 3.4 Genital stages (From Tanner, 1962, with permission).

Figure 3.3 Breast stages (From Tanner, 1962, with permission).

growth in breadth and development of glands. Further enlargement of testes and scrotum; increased darkening of scrotal skin.

Stage 5: genitalia adult in size and shape. No further enlargement takes place after stage 5 is reached; it seems, on the contrary, that the penis size decreases slightly from the immediately post-adolescent peak (Reynolds and Wines, 1951).

Stage 5: mature stage: projection of papilla only due to recession of the areola to the general contour of the breast.

(reprinted from Tanner 1962, with permission)

(reprinted from Tanner 1962, with permission)

The genital development stages are illustrated in Figure 3.4.

Stage 1: pre-adolescent. Testes, scrotum and penis are of about the same size and proportion as in early childhood.

Stage 2: enlargement of scrotum and of testes. The skin of the scrotum reddens and changes in texture. Little or no enlargement of the penis at this stage (which therefore comprises the time between points T1 and P1 of the Stolz's terminology).

Stage 3: enlargement of penis, which occurs at first mainly in length. Further growth of the testes and scrotum.

Stage 4: increased size of penis with

The pubic hair stages are illustrated in Figure 3.5 for boys and girls.

Stage 1: pre-adolescent. The vellus over the pubes is not further developed than that over the abdominal wall, i.e. no pubic hair.

Stage 2: sparse growth of long, slightly pigmented downy hair, straight or only slightly curled, appearing chiefly at the base of the penis or along the labia.

Stage 3: considerably darker, coarser and more curled. The hair spreads sparsely over the junction of the pubes. It is at this stage that pubic hair is first seen in the

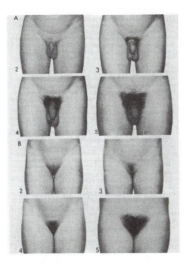

Figure 3.5 Pubic hair stages: (a) boys; (b) girls (from Tanner, 1962, with permission).

usual type of black and white photograph of the entire body; special arrangements are necessary to photograph stage 3 hair.

Stage 4: hair now resembles adult in type, but the area covered by it is still considerably smaller than in the adult. No spread to the medial surface of the thighs.

Stage 5: adult in quantity and type with distribution of the horizontal (or classically 'feminine') pattern. Spread to medial surface of thighs but not up to linea alba or elsewhere above the base of the inverse triangle.

(reprinted from Tanner 1962, with permission)

These stages must be assigned by visual inspection of the nude subject or from somatotype photographs from which the specific areas are enlarged. Given the invasiveness of the technique, self-inspection has been proposed as an alternative. The results of the validation studies of self-reported sexual maturity vary considerably depending on the age of the participants, gender, ethnicity, group

characteristics (e.g. socially disadvantaged children), and the settings in which the assessments were made (Cameron 2004b). Younger children tend to overestimate and older children underestimate. Boys overestimate and girls are more consistent with experts (Cameron 2004b).

Age at menarche, defined as the first menstrual flow, can be obtained retrospectively by interrogating a representative sample of sexually mature women. Note, however, that the error of recall has an influence on the reported age at menarche. Considerable errors have been documented for the individual age at menarche, but the recall data are reasonably accurate for group comparisons (Beunen 1989; Malina *et al.* 2004). The information obtained in longitudinal or prospective studies is of course much more accurate, but here other problems inherent to longitudinal studies interfere. In the status quo technique, representative samples of girls expected to experience menarche are interrogated. The investigator records whether or not menstrual periods have started at the time of investigation. References can be constructed using probits or logits for which the percentage of menstruating girls at each age level is plotted against chronological age, where after a probit or logit is fitted through the observed data. Note that the retrospective and prospective methods provide ages at menarche for individuals, whereas the status quo method provides an estimated age at menarche for a sample and does not apply for an individual.

3.4.3 Morphological maturation: Prediction of adult height and maturity offset.

When percentage of predicted adult height is used as an indicator of morphological maturity, the actual measured height is expressed as a percentage of predicted adult height. The problem here is to estimate or predict adult height. Several prediction techniques have been developed, and those by Bayley (1946), Roche *et al.* (1975a) and Tanner *et al.* (1983, 2001) seem to be the most accurate and most commonly used. The predictors in these techniques are actual height, chronological age, skeletal age and, in some techniques, parental height and/or age at menarche for girls. Based on data of the Fels Longitudinal Study, Wainer *et al.* (1978) demonstrated that in American white children reasonable accuracy can be obtained in predicting adult stature when skeletal age is replaced by chronological age. Khamis and Roche (1994) also showed that when current stature, current weight, and mid-parent stature are used as predictors, the errors of prediction are only slightly larger then those for the Roche-Wainer-Thissen method (1975a) which requires skeletal age. More recently, based on data of the Leuven Longitudinal Study on Belgian Boys, Beunen *et al.* (1997) proposed the Beunen-Malina method for predicting adult stature. In this method adult stature is predicted from four somatic dimensions: current stature, sitting height, subscapular skinfold, triceps skinfold, and chronological age. In the age range of 13–16 years, the accuracy of the Beunen-Malina method compares favourably with the original Tanner-Whitehouse-II method (Tanner *et al.* 1983). For boys 12.5–13.5 years, for example, adult stature can be predicted using the following regression equation (Beunen *et al.* 1997)

> adult stature = 147.99 cm + 0.87 stature (cm) − 0.77 sitting height (cm) + 0.54 triceps skinfold (mm) − 0.64 subscapular skinfold (mm) − 3.39 chronological age (years)

The main advantage of the Beunen-Malina method is that it is non-invasive and does not require the assessment of skeletal age based on radiographs. However, it is clear that the original Tanner-Whitehouse-II or the more recent Tanner-Whitehouse-III method (Tanner *et al.* 1983, 2001) is to be preferred when radiographs of the hand and wrist are available. It should also be noted that the Beunen-Malina method is only for boys.

In this respect it is of interest to note that at 2 years of age, boys attain nearly 50% of their adult stature, whereas girls reach this landmark already at 1.5 years. Boys reach 75% of adult stature at about 9 years and girls at 7.5 years. Finally, 90% is reached at about 13.5 years in boys and at 11.5 years in girls (Tanner, 1989). This clearly demonstrates that already at 2 years of age girls are biologically more mature than boys and that this advancement increases with age to reach a difference of about 2 years at adolescence.

Another non-invasive estimate of morphological or somatic maturity utilizes time before or after peak height velocity (PHV), labelled as maturity offset, as a maturity indicator (Mirwald *et al.* 2002). The protocol requires age, height, weight, sitting height and estimated leg length in gender-specific equations. The method has been validated in a sample of elite female gymnasts. Mean predicted age at PHV deviated linearly from the criterion age at PHV. There also was a systematic bias between the prediction and criterion; correlations between the two varied between −0.13 and +0.76. Care is therefore warranted in utilizing maturity offset *per se* and predicted age at PHV based on maturity offset as an indicator of biological maturity timing in female gymnasts and probably also in short, late-maturing females in general (Malina *et al.* 2006). Until now, no practical useful technique has been developed to assess 'shape age' as another indicator of morphological maturity.

3.4.4 Dental and skeletal techniques

Dental maturity can be estimated from the age of eruption of deciduous or permanent teeth or from the number of teeth present at a certain age (Demirjian 1978). However, eruption is only one event in the calcification process and has no real biological meaning. For this reason, Demirjian *et al.* (1973)

constructed scales for the assessment of dental maturity, based on the principles that Tanner *et al.* (1983) developed for the estimation of skeletal age.

Skeletal maturity is the most commonly used indicator of biological maturation. It is widely recognized as the best single biological maturity indicator (Tanner 1962). Three main techniques are presently in use: the atlas technique, first introduced by Todd (1937) and later revised by Greulich and Pyle (1950, 1959), the bone-specific approach developed by Tanner *et al.* (1983, 2001), the bone-specific approach developed by Roche *et al.* for the knee (1975b), and for the hand (1988).

3.4.5 Skeletal age assessment: TWIII system

In this section the assessment of skeletal age according to the Tanner-Whitehouse method (TWIII, Tanner *et al.* 2001) will be introduced. The TWIII method is a further adaptation to the TWII method (Tanner *et al.* 1983). The differences between TWII and TWIII are the 20-bone score (radius, ulna, short bones of the first, third and fifth fingers, and round bones) and corresponding skeletal age have been abolished in the TWIII method; the TWIII-reference charts have been updated using more recent samples from Argentina, Belgium, Italy, Japan, Spain, UK, and USA (Texas); and the other two modifications relate to the height prediction rather than the assessment of skeletal maturity *per se*. However, it is of importance to note that the stages and description of the stages of the bones have not been changed. They remain the same so that the ratings and calculations of the bone maturity scores in TWII are still valid for TWIII.

The TWIII is a bone-specific approach, which means that all the bones of a region of the body are graded on a scale and then combined to give an estimate of the skeletal maturation status of that area. The TWIII system is developed for the hand and wrist.

In this area, 28 ossification centres of long, short and round bones are found, including primary ossification centres (round bones) and secondary ossification centres (epiphyses of the short and long bones). The primary ossification centres of the short and long bones develop before birth and form the diaphyses. The secondary centres of the short and long bones generally develop after birth and form the epiphyses. For each centre a sequence of developmental milestones is defined. Such a milestone indicates the distance that has been travelled along the road to full maturity, meaning the adult shape and fusion between epiphysis and diaphysis for short and long bones. Such a sequence of milestones is invariant, meaning that the second milestone occurs after the first, but before the third. Based on careful examination of longitudinal series of normal boys and girls, stages of skeletal maturity were defined for all the bones in the hand and wrist. The stages are described in a handbook for the assessment of skeletal age (Tanner *et al.* 2001). Each stage is indicated by a letter and stages are converted to weighted maturity scores. These scores are defined in such a way as to minimize the overall disagreement between the scores assigned to the different bones over the total standardizing sample. Furthermore, a biological weight was assigned to the scores so that, for example, the distal epiphysis of the radius and ulna are given four times more weight than the metacarpals or phalanges of the third and fifth finger. Two scales are available in the TWIII method: one for the 13 short and long bones (RUS scale, Radius, Ulna and Short bones), and one for the carpal bones (CARP scale). Although 28 bone centres develop postnatally in the hand and wrist, only 20 bones are assessed in the total TWIII system. Since the metacarpals and phalanges, considered row-wise, show considerable agreement in their maturity status, only the first, third, and fifth fingers are estimated. Once the maturity stages are assigned to the bones, the stages are converted to maturity scores using one of the two scales. The scores are then simply added to form the overall maturity score for the long and short bones (RUS scale) or the carpals (CARP scale). For these overall maturity scores reference data are then constructed for a population (see, for example, Tanner *et al.* 2001; Beunen *et al.* 1990). Very often the maturity score is converted into skeletal age, which is the corresponding chronological age at which, on the average, an overall maturity score is reached.

3.4.6 Practical exercise

In assessing skeletal age, radiographs have to be taken in a standard position and with standard equipment (for instructions see Tanner *et al.* 2001). The descriptions and directions of the authors should also be carefully followed. This implies that the written criteria for the stages should be carefully studied and followed. The illustrations are only a guide for the identification of the stages. They represent the upper and lower limit of a given stage. For the assignment of stages the first criterion of the previous stage must be clearly visible and in the case of only one criterion this must be present; if there are two criteria one of the two must be present; and when three criteria are described two of the three must be visible. Depending on the scale (RUS, CARP) the corresponding scores for each gender must be given, then summed and compared to references for the population.

In order to familiarize students with the system, three radiographs (Figures 3.6, 3.7 and 3.8) are included for which the three maturity scores can be obtained. A scoring sheet is shown in Figure 3.9. As described above, the instructions in the handbook (Tanner *et al.* 2001) should be carefully followed and the bones are rated in the same order as indicated on the scoring sheet.

The scores obtained should then be compared with those of an experienced observer. In this case the ratings can be compared with those of the author (see Appendix). His ratings show considerable agreement

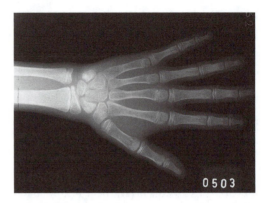

Figure 3.6 Radiograph of the hand and wrist of a Belgian boy (I).

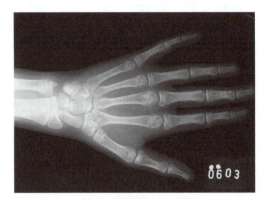

Figure 3.7 Radiograph of the hand and wrist of a Belgian boy (II).

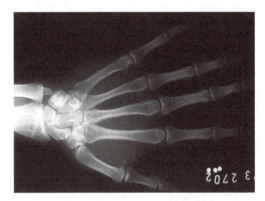

Figure 3.8 Radiograph of the hand and wrist of a Belgian boy (III).

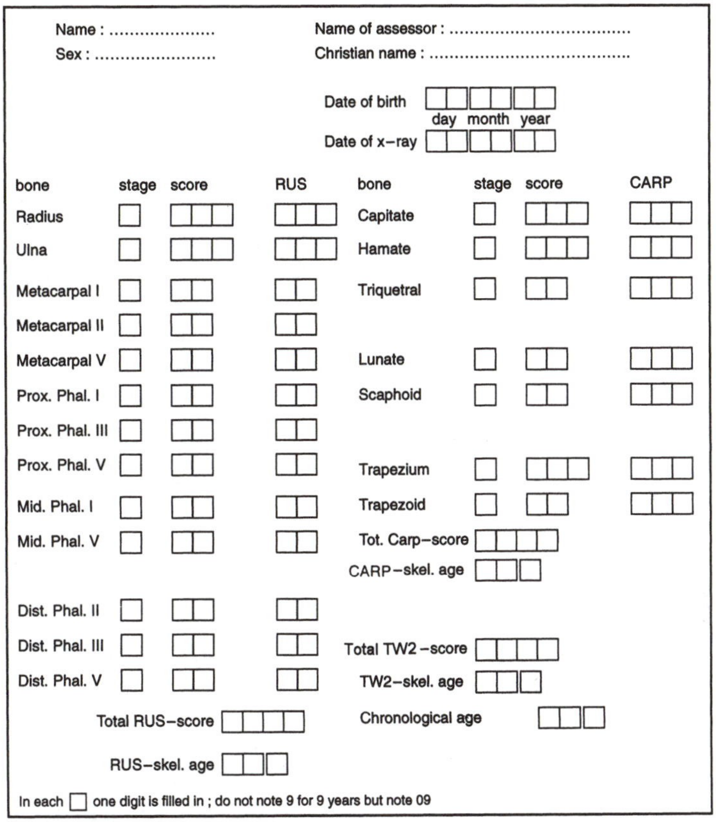

Name : .... Name of assessor : ....
Sex : .... Christian name : ....

Date of birth (day month year)
Date of x–ray

bone	stage	score	RUS	bone	stage	score	CARP
Radius				Capitate			
Ulna				Hamate			
Metacarpal I				Triquetral			
Metacarpal II							
Metacarpal V				Lunate			
Prox. Phal. I				Scaphoid			
Prox. Phal. III							
Prox. Phal. V				Trapezium			
Mid. Phal. I				Trapezoid			
Mid. Phal. V				Tot. Carp–score			
				CARP–skel. age			
Dist. Phal. II							
Dist. Phal. III				Total TW2 –score			
Dist. Phal. V				TW2–skel. age			

Total RUS–score

Chronological age

RUS–skel. age

In each ☐ one digit is filled in ; do not note 9 for 9 years but note 09

Figure 3.9 Scoring sheet for skeletal age assessment.

with those of the originators of the method (Beunen and Cameron 1980). The differences between the students' ratings and those of the expert need to be discussed and, if time permits, a second rating can be done with a minimum one-week interval.

In most cases the student will experience that he/she is able to obtain fairly close agreement between his/her ratings and those of the expert. This does not at all imply that the student is now experienced. From intra- and inter-observer studies conducted in our laboratory, it appears that before one becomes experienced, about 500 radiographs have to be assessed. The assessor also needs to verify his/her own intra-observer reliability and has to compare his/her ratings with those of an expert.

As previously mentioned, skeletal age is an important variable in the regression equations for predicting adult height. Given the characteristic physical structure of athletes and the role of stature in this respect it can be easily understood that the estimation of adult stature can be a useful factor in an efficient guidance of young athletes.

Finally, it should be mentioned that skeletal age correlates moderately to highly with other indicators of biological maturity, such as sexual maturity and morphological maturity. The association with dental maturity is considerably lower. However, the associations are never strong enough to allow individual prediction, but they are strong enough to indicate the maturation status of a group of children or populations. This means that when a group of female gymnasts is markedly delayed in sexual maturity, the group is also likely to be delayed in skeletal maturity (Beunen 1989; Malina *et al.* 2004).

3.5 PHYSICAL FITNESS

3.5.1 Methodological considerations

As mentioned earlier the physical fitness concept and its measurement have evolved over time and recently the distinction between health- and performance-related fitness has been introduced. Furthermore, Bouchard and Shephard (1994) broadened the concept to include: (1) a morphological component (body mass for height, body composition, subcutaneous fat distribution, abdominal visceral fat, bone density, flexibility); (2) a muscular component (power, strength, endurance); (3) a motor component (agility, balance, coordination, speed of movement); (4) a cardiorespiratory component (submaximal exercise capacity, maximal aerobic power, heart functions, lung functions, blood pressure); and (5) a metabolic component (glucose tolerance, insulin sensitivity, lipid and lipoprotein metabolism, substrate oxidation characteristics). Table 3.4 gives an overview of test batteries that have been used and, more importantly, for which reference values have been constructed. For the test batteries included in Table 3.4, attempts were made to obtain tests that are objective, standardized, reliable and valid. (For more information about test construction see Safrit 1973 and Anastasi 1988). For most of the batteries nationwide reference values were constructed. Attempts have also been made to construct criterion-referenced norms or standards (Blair *et al.* 1989). Within the context of the health-related fitness concept, standards of required fitness levels were created by expert panels, for example 42 ml.kg^{-1}.min^{-1} for $\dot{V}O_2$max in young men and 35 ml.kg^{-1}.min^{-1} for young women. Very little empirical evidence is available to create such criterion-related standards for the other health-related fitness items.

From Table 3.4 it is clear that, in most batteries, the same components are included and that quite often the same tests are proposed. Note, of course, that test batteries that are intended to evaluate health-related fitness do not incorporate performance-related items. With increasing awareness about safety and risks involved in testing, some testing procedures have been adapted; for example, sit ups were originally tested with straight legs and hands crossed behind the neck whereas in more recent procedures the arms are crossed over the chest, the knees are bent and the subject curls to a position in which the elbows touch the knees or thighs. In the latter procedure there is less risk of causing low-back pain.

In order to construct reference values for a population, large representative samples of boys and girls from different age levels must be examined. The same principles apply as for the construction of growth standards discussed previously. The data obtained must be transferred into reference scales so that the individual scores can be evaluated and test results can be compared. Most often reference values are reported in percentile scales, but raw scores can also be transformed into standard scales (z-scores), normalized standard scales (transformed into a normalized distribution) or age norms (motor age and motor coefficient as in the original Oseretstky motor development scale, Oseretsky, 1931). Probably none of these scales can be considered as best, and much depends on the needs of the test constructor and the needs of those that intend to use the test.

3.5.2 Physical fitness testing

Similarly to what has been explained in the growth evaluation section (Section 3.3.5), a number of secondary school children can be examined on a physical fitness test battery. In selecting a test battery, it should be kept in mind that appropriate and recent reference values need to be available, and that the battery selected has been constructed accord-

Table 3.4 Fitness components and test items in selected physical fitness test batteries

FITNESS COMPONENT	TEST BATTERIES				
	AAHPER youth fitness test (1958)	Fleishman (1964)	AAHPER youth fitness test (1965)	CAPHER (1965)	Simons et al. (1969)
Health-related components					
cardiorespiratory endurance	660-yard run-walk	660-yard run-walk	660-yard run-walk	300-yard run-walk	step test
body composition	—	—	—	—	triceps-subscapular-suprailiac-calf skinfolds
flexibility	—	turn and twist bend, twist and touch	—	—	sit and reach
upper body muscular endurance & strength	pull-ups	pull-ups	pulls-ups (boys) flexed arm hang (girls)	flexed arm hang	flexed arm hang
abdominal muscular endurance & strength	sit-ups	leg lifts	sit-ups	sit-ups	leg lifts
Performance-related components					
static (isometric) strength	—	handgrip	—	—	arm pull
explosive strength anaerobic power	standing long jump softball throw	softball throw	standing long jump softball throw	standing long jump	vertical jump
running speed	50-yard dash shuttle run	100-yard shuttle run	50-yard dash shuttle run	50-yard dash 40-yard shuttle run	50-m shuttle run
speed of limb movement	—	—	—	—	plate tapping
balance	—	one foot balance	—	—	need established
coordination	—	—	—	—	stick balance

cont.

FITNESS COMPONENT	TEST BATTERIES				
	ICPFT Larson (1974)	Fitnessgram (1987)	NCYFS II Ross & Pate (1987)	AAHPERD Physical Best (1988)	EUROFIT Adam et al. (1988)
Health related components					
cardiorespiratory endurance	600–800–1,000–1,500–2,000-m run	1 min walk-run for time	0.5 min run-walk 1 min run-walk	1 min run	endurance shuttle run (Léger & Lambert 1982) cycle ergometer test
body composition	–	triceps-calf skinfolds	triceps-subscapular calf skinfold	triceps-calf-skinfolds	triceps-biceps-subscap.-suprailiac-calf skinfold
flexibility	forward trunk flexion or sit and reach	sit and reach	sit and reach	sit and reach	sit-and-reach
upper body muscular endurance & strength	pull-ups (boys), flexed arm hang (girls and children)	pull-ups	modified pull-ups	pull-ups	flexed arm hang
abdominal muscular endurance & strength	sit-ups (bent knees)	sit-ups (bent knees)	sit-ups (bent knees)	sit-ups (curl to sitting position)	sit-ups (bent knees)
Performance related components					
static (isometric) strenght	handgrip	–	–	–	handgrip
explosive strength anaerobic power	standing long jump	–	–	–	standing long jump
running speed	50-m dash 40-m shuttle run	shuttle run (optional)	–	–	50-m shuttle run
speed of limb movement	–	–	–	–	plate tapping
balance	–	–	–	–	flamingo balance
coordination	–	–	–	–	–

Table 3.5 Profile chart of the Eurofit test for 14-year-old boys

ANTHROPOMETRY

	P3	P10	P25	P50	P75	P90	P97
Height (cm)	153.2	157.7	162.3	167.4	172.5	176.9	181.0
Mass (kg)	38.6	42.5	47.0	52.9	60.1	68.0	77.5
Triceps skinfold (mm)		5.9	6.9	8.4	11.4	16.0	
Biceps skinfold (mm)		3.2	3.6	4.3	5.1	9.5	
Subscapular skinfold (mm)		5.1	5.7	6.3	7.9	10.9	
Suprailiac skinfold (mm		3.8	4.2	4.8	6.9	11.2	
Calf skinfold (mm)		5.9	7.2	8.9	12.1	17.2	
Sum skinfolds (mm)		25.5	28.7	32.7	43.6	65.9	

PHYSICAL PERFORMANCE

	P10	P25	P50	P75	P90
Flamingo balance (n)	24.9	19.5	14.8	11.0	7.8
Plate tapping (s)	14.2	13.0	11.8	10.8	10.1
Sit-and-reach (cm)	11.2	16.0	21.0	25.7	29.5
Standing broad jump (cm)	164.5	179.6	194.2	208.0	221.0
Handgrip (N)	25.3	29.0	33.4	38.0	42.6
Sit-ups (n)	20.0	22.8	25.4	27.8	29.9
Flexed arm hang (cm)	5.1	13.6	23.2	34.0	45.8
Shuttle run (s)	23.3	22.2	21.2	20.4	19.7
Endurance shuttle run (n)	4.9	6.3	7.8	9.3	10.6

ing to well-established scientific procedures (see above). Furthermore, all the equipment necessary for adequate testing must be available.

The Eurofit test battery (Adam *et al.* 1988) was selected for this purpose. Reference values of the Belgian population are available (Lefevre *et al.* 1993). Table 3.4 shows that this battery includes health- and performance-related fitness items. If the Eurofit tests are examined and the reference values of 14-year-old Belgian children (Table 3.5 and 3.6) are used, then only 14-year-old children should be tested. In the reference tables, 14 years includes 14.00 to 14.99-year-old children. It should be noted that we prefer to use the 1993 reference values instead of the values collected in later fitness studies because it has been demonstrated that in several fitness components a decline is observed (Matton *et al.* 2007). The 1993 references present values of more fit adolescents.

Before the test session in the secondary school all students should be familiarized with the test procedure. It is advisable first to study the test instructions and descriptions (Adam *et al.* 1988), then to organize a demonstration session during which the tests are correctly demonstrated and then to practise the test with peers of the same class as subjects. Once the training period has finished, the session of testing in the school can be planned. As for the evaluation of growth, informed consent is needed from the parents and school, and for older children from the adolescents themselves. Care should be taken that children at risk are identified. The recommendations of the American College of Sports Medicine should be followed to identify individuals at risk (American College of Sports Medicine

Table 3.6 Profile chart of the Eurofit test for 14-year-old girls

ANTHROPOMETRY

	P3	P10	P25	P50	P75	P90	P97
Height (cm)	149.2	153.5	157.6	162.2	166.6	170.6	174.4
Mass (kg)	39.7	43.5	47.6	52.9	59.4	66.7	75.4
Triceps skinfold (mm)		9.0	11.0	14.2	18.7	24.4	
Biceps skinfold (mm)		4.6	5.9	8.1	11.7	16.9	
Subscapular skinfold (mm)		7.0	8.2	10.0	13.7	19.7	
Suprailiac skinfold (mm		5.5	7.1	9.4	13.6	19.7	
Calf skinfold (mm)		9.7	12.4	16.4	22.0	29.0	
Sum skinfolds (mm)		38.3	46.4	59.1	79.4	107.2	

PHYSICAL PERFORMANCE

	P10	P25	P50	P75	P90
Flamingo balance (n)	27.6	20.7	15.4	11.3	7.5
Plate tapping (s)	14.2	13.1	12.1	11.2	10.6
Sit-and-reach (cm)	16.9	21.9	26.9	31.4	34.8
Standing broad jump (cm)	140.0	152.5	166.0	179.4	191.6
Handgrip (N)	20.2	22.9	25.8	28.9	31.7
Sit-ups (n)	15.9	18.6	21.0	23.4	25.8
Flexed arm hang (cm)	0.0	2.8	7.5	14.4	23.1
Shuttle run (s)	24.2	23.3	22.3	21.4	20.7
Endurance shuttle run (n)	2.9	3.7	4.8	6.1	7.2

2006). Generally children that are allowed to participate in physical education classes can be tested, taking into account that some are only allowed to participate in certain exercise sessions.

Obviously the general recommendations for administering the Eurofit tests should be carefully followed. The individual scores are recorded on a special sheet (Figure 3.10). Once the tests are administered, the individual scores are converted to reference scales. For this purpose, reference scales of the Eurofit test battery for 14-year-old boys and girls are provided (Table 3.5 and 3.6 after Lefevre *et al.* 1993).

3.5.3 Interpretation and discussion

Each individual test score is plotted against the profiles given in Table 3.5 for boys and Table 3.6 for girls. From this profile the fitness level can be evaluated. As a guideline, the test results of a Belgian 14-year-old boy (Jan) will be discussed (Table 3.7).

Jan seems to perform above average in two of the five health-related fitness items (endurance and flexibility). His skinfolds are quite high, and he performs below the median for muscular endurance and strength of the upper body and abdomen (bent arm hang and sit-ups). For his health-related condition it can be concluded that his cardiorespiratory endurance is above average for his gender and age, but that given the rather high skinfolds his performance can probably be improved. To do this, Jan needs to be sufficiently active (endurance type activities) and control his energy intake (most probably excessive amounts of fat, or carbohydrates from soft drinks, sweets,

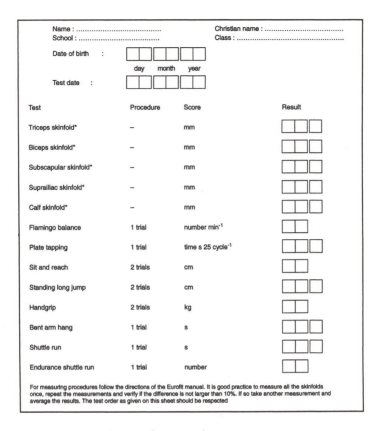

Figure 3.10 Proforma for recording the Eurofit test results.

snacks and so on). Furthermore, his muscular endurance and strength are weak and need to be improved. Note the negative influence of fatness (adiposity) on these items. For the performance-related items, quite large variability among tests is observed. Balance is excellent, and static strength is average. Note the positive influence of fatness on static strength. Jan scores poorly on tests that require explosive actions and speed (standing long jump, shuttle run and plate tapping). Undoubtedly, these poor performance levels will have an effect on Jan's sport specific skills. He will thus profit largely from an improvement in these capacities. In conclusion, Jan needs a general conditioning programme in which the weak performance capacities are trained.

In interpreting the results, one should bear in mind that all tests and measurements are affected by measurement error. Therefore small differences in test results should be ignored. Furthermore, the selection of the Eurofit tests were based on the factor analytic studies of Simons *et al.* (1969, 1990). In these studies it was shown that when fitness factors are rotated to an oblique configuration the factors showed only small inter-correlations; consequently the interrelationship between fitness items is low. This implies that it is very unlikely that a boy or girl would perform well on all items; generally there is some variation between tests. Note, however, that outstanding athletes perform above the median for most or all items. Note also that the tests correlate with somatic dimensions and biological maturity status. Static strength (handgrip) is positively correlated with height and body mass. Tests in which the subject performs against his own body mass or part

Table 3.7 Individual profile of a 14-year-old Belgian boy (Jan)

ANTHROPOMETRY

	P3	P10	P25	P50	P75	P90	P97
Height (cm)	153.2	157.7	162.3	167.4	172.5	176.9	181.0
Mass (kg)	38.6	42.5	47.0	52.9	60.1	68.0	77.5
Triceps skinfold (mm)	5.9	6.9	8.4	11.4	16.0		
Biceps skinfold (mm)	3.2	3.6	4.3	5.1	9.5		
Subscapular skinfold (mm)	5.1	5.7	6.3	7.9	10.9		
Suprailiac skinfold (mm	3.8	4.2	4.8	6.9	11.2		
Calf skinfold (mm)	5.9	7.2	8.9	12.1	17.2		
Sum skinfolds (mm)	25.5	28.7	32.7	43.6	65.9		

PHYSICAL PERFORMANCE

	P10	P25	P50	P75	P90
Flamingo balance (n)	24.9	19.5	14.8	11.0	7.8
Plate tapping (s)	14.2	13.0	11.8	10.8	10.1
Sit-and-reach (cm)	11.2	16.0	21.0	25.7	29.5
Standing broad jump (cm)	164.5	179.6	194.2	208.0	221.0
Handgrip (N)	25.3	29.0	33.4	38.0	42.6
Sit-ups (n)	20.0	22.8	25.4	27.8	29.9
Flexed arm hang (cm)	5.1	13.6	23.2	34.0	45.8
Shuttle run (s)	23.3	22.2	21.2	20.4	19.7
Endurance shuttle run (n)	4.9	6.3	7.8	9.3	10.6

of it, for example, tests of muscular endurance and power, are negatively correlated with height and weight. From the above it is also clear that in assessing the performance capacities and especially in guiding and prescribing exercise programmes, the assessment of habitual physical activity and of nutritional status add significantly to the advice and guidance.

3.6 SUMMARY AND CONCLUSIONS

- After a few historical notes this chapter considers growth evaluation, assessment of biological maturation and physical fitness evaluation.
- For each of the three sections, the concept, assessment and evaluation techniques are explained and a detailed description is given of a practical.

- For the growth and physical fitness evaluation, a small project is described in which data are collected and afterwards evaluated.
- For skeletal age assessment, x-rays are assessed according to the Tanner-Whitehouse technique.
- Each section ends with a number of recommendations and a short discussion of the evaluation and techniques that have been used.
- Additional details concerning the assessment of growth, maturation and performance are given by Barker, Boreham, Van Praagh and Rowlands in Chapter 8.

APPENDIX

Estimation according to the author of this chapter (for his intra- and inter-observer reliability see Beunen and Cameron 1980):

Estimations radiograph figure 3.6: Boy (I)
Radius: G, Ulna: E, MCI: F, MCIII: F, MCV: E

PPI: F, PPIII: F, PPV: F, MPIII: F, MPV: F, DPI: E, DPIII: F; DPV: F

Capitate: G, Hamate: G, Triquetral: G, Lunate: G, Schaphoid: G, Trapezium: G, Trapezoid: H

Estimations radiograph figure 3.7: Boy (II)
Radius: H, Ulna: G, MCI: G, MCIII: G, MCV: G

PPI: G, PPIII: G, PPV: G, MPIII: G, MPV: F, DPI: G, DPIII: G; DPV: F

Capitate: H, Hamate: H, Triquetral: H, Lunate: H, Schaphoid: H, Trapezium: H, Trapezoid: H

Estimations radiograph figure 3.8: Boy (III)
All bones reached the adult stage
RUS-age: adult, CARP-age: adult.

FURTHER READING

Beunen G. and Malina R. M. (1996) Growth and biological maturation: relevance to athletic performance. In: (O. Bar-Or, ed) *The Child and Adolescent Athlete, Vol. VI. Encyclopedia of Sports Medicine: an IOC Medical Commission Publication.* Blackwell; Oxford: pp. 3–24.

Beunen G. P., Rogol A. D. and Malina R. M. (2006) Indicators of biological maturation and secular changes in biological maturation. *Food and Nutrition Bulletin.* 27: S244–S256.

British Growth Charts. Castlemead Publications, 4a Crane Mead, Ware, Herts, SG12 9PY, UK.

Malina R. M. and Beunen G. (1996) Monitoring of growth and maturation. In: (O. Bar-Or, ed) *The Child and Adolescent Athlete, Vol. VI. Encyclopedia of Sports Medicine: an IOC Medical Commission Publication.* Blackwell; Oxford: pp. 647–72.

Malina R. M., Bouchard C. and Bar-Or O. (2004) *Growth, Maturation and Physical Activity.* Human Kinetics, Champaign, IL.

Tanner J. M. (1989) *Fetus into Man. Physical Growth from Conception to Maturity.* Harvard University Press; Cambridge, MA.

REFERENCES

AAHPER (1958) *Youth Fitness Test Manual,* AAHPER, Washington, DC.

AAHPER (1965) *Youth Fitness Test Manual,* revised edition. AAHPER, Washington, DC.

AAHPERD (1988) *The AAHPERD Physical Best Program.* AAHPERD, Reston, VA.

Adam C., Klissouras V., Ravassolo M. *et al.* (1988) *Eurofit: Handbook for the Eurofit Test of Physical Fitness.* Council of Europe. Committee for the Development of Sport, Rome.

American College of Sports Medicine (2006) *ACSM's Guidelines for Exercise Testing and Prescription.* Lippincott, Williams & Wilkins; Baltimore, MD.

Anastasi A. (1988) *Psychological Testing.* McMillan; New York.

Bayley N. (1946) Tables for predicting adult height from skeletal age and present height. *Journal of Pediatrics*; 28: 49–64.

Beunen G. (1989) Biological age in pediatric exercise research, in *Advances in Pediatric Sport Sciences*, vol. 3. In: (O. Bar-Or, ed.) *Biological Issues.* Human Kinetics; Champaign, IL: pp. 1–39.

Beunen G. and Cameron N. (1980) The reproducibility of TW2 skeletal age assessment by a self-taught assessor. *Annals of Human Biology*; 7: 155–62.

Beunen G., Lefevre J., Ostyn M., Renson R., Simons J. and Van Gerven D. (1990) Skeletal maturity in Belgian youths assessed by the Tanner-Whitehouse method (TW2. *Annals of Human Biology*; 17: 355–76.

Beunen G.P., Malina R. M., Renson, R., Simons, J., Ostyn M. and Lefevre J. (1992) Physical activity and growth, maturation and performance: a longitudinal study. *Medicine and Science in Sports and Exercise*; 24: 576–585.

Beunen G., Malina R. M., Lefevre J., Claessens A.L., Renson R. and Simons J. (1997) Prediction of adult stature and noninvasive assessment of biological maturation. *Medicine and Science in Sports and Exercise*; 29: 225–30.

Beunen G. P., Rogol A. D. and Malina R. M. (2006) Indicators of biological maturation and secular changes in biological maturation. *Food and Nutrition Bulletin*; 27: S244–S256.

Blair N., Clarke D. G., Cureton K. J. and Powell K. E. (1989) Exercise and fitness in childhood: implications for a lifetime of health. In: (C.

V. Gisolfi and D. R. Lamb, eds) *Perspectives in Exercise and Sports Medicine: Youth and Exercise and Sports*, vol. 2. Benchmark Press; Indianapolis, IN: pp. 401–30.

Bock R. D. and Thissen D. (1980) Statistical problems of fitting individual growth curves. In: (F. E. Johnston, A. F. Roche and C. Susanne, eds) *Human Physical Growth and Maturation: Methodologies and Factors*. Plenum Press; New York: pp. 265–90.

Bouchard C and Shephard R. J. (1994) Physical activity, fitness and health: The model and key concepts. In: (C. Bouchard, R. J. Shephard and T. Stevens, eds) *Physical Activity, Fitness, and Health*. International Proceedings and Consensus Statement Human Kinetics; Champaign, IL: pp. 77–88.

Bovend'eerdt J. H. F., Bernink M. J. E., van Hijfte T. (1980) *De MOPER Fitness Test*. De Vrieseborch; Haarlem, The Netherlands.

Butte N., Garza C. and de Onis M. (2006) Evaluation of the feasibility of international growth standards for school-aged children and adolescents. *Food and Nutrition Bulletin*; 27: S169–S174.

Brace D. K. (1927) *Measuring Motor Ability*. Barnes; New York.

CAHPER (1965) *Fitness Performance Test Manual for Boys*. CAHPER; Toronto, ON.

Cameron N. (1984) *The Measurement of Human Growth*. Croom Helm; London.

Cameron N. (2004a) Measuring growth. In: (R. C. Hauspie, N. Cameron and L. Molinari, eds) *Methods in Human Growth Research*. Cambridge University Press; Cambridge: pp. 68–107.

Cameron N. (2004b) Measuring maturity. In: (R. C. Hauspie, N. Cameron and L. Molinari, eds) *Methods in Human Growth Research*. Cambridge University Press; Cambridge: pp. 108–40.

Carter J. E. L. (ed) (1982) *Physical Structure of Olympic Athletes. Part I. The Montreal Olympic Games Anthropological Project. Medicine and Sport 16*. Karger; Basel.

Clarke H. H. (1979) Academy approves physical fitness definition. *Physical Fitness News Letter*; 25: 1P.

Cole T. J. (2006) The international growth standard for preadolescent and adolescent children: statistical considerations. *Food and Nutrition Bulletin*; 27: S237–S243.

Cole T. J. and Green P. J. (1992) Smoothing reference centile curves: the LMS method and penalized likelihood. *Statistics in Medicine*; 11: 1305–19.

Deming J. (1957) Application of the Gompertz curve to the observed pattern of growth in length of 48 individual boys and girls during the adolescent cyclus of growth. *Human Biology*; 29: 83–122.

Demirjian A. (1978) Dentition. In: (F. Falkner and J. M. Tanner, eds) *Human Growth: Postnatal Growth*, vol. 2. Plenum Press; New York: pp. 413–44.

Demirjian A., Goldstein H. and Tanner J. M. (1973) A new system for dental age assessment. *Human Biology*; 45: 211–27.

Eveleth P. B. and Tanner J. M. (1990) *Worldwide Variation in Human Growth*. Cambridge University Press; Cambridge.

Fitnessgram User's Manual (1987) Institute for Aerobics Research; Dallas, TX.

Fleishman E. A. (1964) *The Structure and Measurement of Physical Fitness*. Prentice Hall; Englewood Cliffs, NJ.

Gasser T., Gervine D. and Molinari L. (2004) Kernel estimation, shape invariant modelling and structural analysis. In: (R. C. Hauspie, N. Cameron and L. Molinari, eds) *Methods in Human Growth Research*. Cambridge University Press; Cambridge: pp. 179–204.

Gasser T., Köhler W., Müller H-G., Kneip A. Largo R., Molinari L. and Prader A. (1984) Velocity and acceleration of height growth using kernel estimation. *Annals of Human Biology*; 11: 397–411.

Goldstein H. (1979) *The Design and Analysis of Longitudinal Studies: Their Role in the Measurement of Change*. Academic Press; London.

Goldstein H. (1984) Current developments in the design and analysis of growth studies. In: (J. Borms, R. Hauspie, A. Sand, Susanne C, Hebbelinck M, eds) *Human Growth and Development*. Plenum Press; New York: pp. 733–52.

Goldstein H. (1986) Sampling for growth studies. In: (F. Falkner and J. M. Tanner, eds) *Human Growth: A Comprehensive Treatise*, 2nd edition, vol. 3. Plenum Press: New York: pp. 59–78.

Greulich, W. W. and Pyle, I. (1950) *Radiographic Atlas of Skeletal Development of the Hand*

and Wrist, Stanford University Press, Stanford.

Greulich, W. W. and Pyle, I. (1959, 2nd ed.) *Radiographic Atlas of Skeletal Development of the Hand and Wrist*, Stanford University Press, Stanford.

Haas J. D. and Campirano F. (2006) Interpopulation variation in height among children 7 to 18 years of age. *Food and Nutrition Bulletin*; 27: S212–S223.

Hauspie R. C., Wachholder A., Baron G., Cantraine F., Susanne C. and Graffar M. (1980) A comparative study of the fit of four different functions to longitudinal data for growth in height of Belgian boys. *Annals of Human Biology*; 7: 347–58.

Healy M. J. R. (1986) Statistics of growth standards. In: (F. Falkner and J. M. Tanner, eds) *Human Growth: a Comprehensive Treatise*, 2nd edition, vol. 3. Plenum Press; New York: pp. 47–58.

Hebbelinck M. and Borms J. (1975) *Biometrische Studie van een Reeks Lichaamskenmerken en Lichamelijke Prestatietests van Belgische Kinderen uit het Lager Onderwijs*, Centrum voor Bevolkings- en Gezinsstudiën (C.B.G.S.), Brussels.

Jenss R. M. and Bayley M. (1937) A mathematical method for studying the growth of a child. *Human Biology*; 9: 556–63.

Jolicoeur P., Pontier J. and Abidi H. (1992) Asymptotic models for the longitudinal growth of human stature. *American Journal of Human Biology*; 4: 461–8.

Kemper H. C. G., Verschuur R. and Bovend'eerdt J. (1979) The MOPER Fitness Test. I. A practical approach to motor performance tests in physical education in The Netherlands. *South African Journal for Research in Sport, Physical Education and Recreation*. 2 **nr.** 2: 81–93.

Keogh J. and Sugden D. (1985) *Movement Skill Development*. MacMillan; New York.

Khamis H. J. and Roche A. F. (1994) Predicting adult stature without using skeletal age: the Khamis-Roche method. *Pediatrics*; 94: 504–7.

Lampl M., Veldhuis J. D. and Johnson M. L. (1992) Saltation and stasis: a model of human growth. *Science*; 258: 801–3.

Largo R. H., Gasser T., Prader A., Stuetzle W. and Huber P. J. (1978) Analysis of the adolescent growth spurt using smoothing spline functions. *Annals of Human Biology*; 5: 421–34.

Larson L. A. (ed.) (1974) *Fitness, Health, and Work Capacity: International Standards for Assessment*. MacMillan; New York.

Lefevre J., Beunen G., Borms J., Renson R., Vrijens J., Claessens A. L. and Van der Aerschot H. (1993) *Eurofit Testbatterij. Leiddraad bij Testafneming en Referentie research*. BLOSO-Jeugdsportcampagne; Brussels.

Léger L. A. and Lambert J. (1982) A maximal multistage 20-m shuttle run test to predict $\dot{V}O_2$max. *European Journal of Applied Physiology*; 49: 1–12.

Lohman T. G., Roche A. F. and Martorell R. (eds.) (1988) *Anthropometric Standardization Reference Manual*. Human Kinetics; Champaign, IL.

McCloy C. H. (1934) The measurement of general motor capacity and general motor ability. *Research Quarterly 5*; Suppl. 1: 46–61.

Malina R. M., Bouchard C. and Bar-Or O. (2004) *Growth, Maturation, and Physical Activity*. Human Kinetics; Champaign, IL.

Malina R. M., Claessens A. L., Van Aken K., Thomis M., Lefevre J., Philippaerts R. and Beunen G. P. (2006) Maturity offset in gymnasts: application of a prediction equation. *Medicine and Science in Sports and Exercise*; 38: 1342–7.

Marubini E., Resele L. F., Tanner J. M. and Whitehouse R. H. (1972) The fit of the Gompertz and logistic curves to longitudinal data during adolescence on height, sitting height, and biacromial diameter in boys and girls of the Harpenden Growth Study. *Human Biology*; 44: 511–24.

Marubini E. and Milani S. (1986) Approaches to the analysis of longitudinal data. In: (F. Falkner and J. M. Tanner, eds) *Human Growth: A Comprehensive Treatise*, 2nd edition, vol. 3. Plenum Press; New York: pp. 33–79.

Matton L., Duvigneaud N., Wijndaele K., Philippaerts R., Duquet W., Beunen G., Claessens A. L., Thomis M. and Lefevre J. (2007) Secular trends in anthropometric characteristics, physical fitness, physical activity and biological maturation in Flemish adolescents between 1969 and 2005. *American Journal of Human Biology*; 19: 345–57.

Mirwald R. L., Baxter-Jones A. D. G., Bailey D.

A. and Beunen G. P. (2002)An assessment of maturity from anthropometric measurements. *Medicine and Science in Sports and Exercise*; **34**: 689–94.

Norton K. and Olds T. (eds) (1996). *Antropometrica*. University of New South Wales; Sydney.

Oseretsky, N. (1931) Psychomotorik Methoden zur untersuchung der Motorik. (Evaluation of Psychomotor Performance). Zeitschrft angewandte Psychologie; **17**: 1–58.

Ostyn M., Simons J., Beunen G., Renson R. and Van Gerven D. (1980) *Somatic and Motor Development of Belgian Secondary School Boys. Norms and Standards*. Leuven University Press; Leuven.

Pate R. and Shephard R. (1989) Characteristics of physical fitness in youth. In: (C. V. Gisolfi and D. R. Lamb, eds) *Perspectives in Exercise Science and Sports Medicine. Youth, Exercise and Sport*, vol. 2. Benchmark Press: Indianapolis, IN: pp. 1–45.

Preece M. A. and Baines M. J. (1978) A new family of mathematical models describing the human growth curve. *Annals of Human Biology*; **5**: 1–24.

Reynolds E. L. and Wines J. V. (1948) Individual differences in physical changes associated with adolescence in girls. *American Journal of Diseases of Children*; **75**: 329–50.

Reynolds E. L. and Wines J. V. (1951) Physical changes associated with adolescence in boys. *American Journal of Diseases of Children*; **82**: 529–47.

Roche A. F., Wainer H. and Thissen D. (1975a) Predicting adult stature for individuals. *Monographs in Pediatrics*; **3**: 1–114.

Roche A. F., Wainer H. and Thissen D. (1975b) *Skeletal Maturity: Knee Joint as a Biological Indicator*. Plenum Press; New York.

Roche A. F., Chumlea W. C. and Thissen D. (1988) *Assessing the Skeletal Maturity of the Hand-Wrist: Fels Method*. Thomas; Springfield, MA.

Ross J. G. and Pate R. R. (1987) The national children and youth fitness study II: a summary of findings. *Journal of Physical Education, Recreation and Dance*; **56**: 45–50.

Safrit M. J. (1973) *Evaluation in Physical Education: Assessing Motor Behavior*. Prentice-Hall; Englewood Cliffs, NJ.

Sargent D. A. (1921) The physical test of a man. *American Physical Education Review*; **26**: 188–94.

Simons J., Beunen G. and Ostyn M. (1969) Construction d'une batterie de tests d'aptitude motrice pour garçons de 12 à 19 ans par le méthode de l'analyse factorielle. *Kinanthropologie*; **1**: 323–62.

Simons J., Beunen G. P. and Renson R (eds) (1990) *Growth and Fitness of Flemish Girls. The Leuven Growth Study. HKP Sport Science Monograph Series 3*. Human Kinetics, Champaign, IL.

Tanner J. M. (1962) *Growth at Adolescence*. Blackwell Scientific Publications; Oxford.

Tanner J. M. (1981) *A History of the Study of Human Growth*. Cambridge University Press; Cambridge.

Tanner J. M. (1989) *Fetus into Man. Physical Growth from Conception to Maturity*, Harvard University Press; Cambridge, MA.

Tanner J. M., Whitehouse R. H. and Takaiski M. (1966) Standards from birth to maturity for height, weight, height velocity and weight velocity. *Archives of Diseases of Childhood*; **41**: 454–71, 613–35.

Tanner J. M., Whitehouse R. H., Cameron, N. Marshall W. A., Healy M. J. R. and Goldstein H. (1983) *Assessment of Skeletal Maturity and Prediction of Adult Height (TW2 method)*. Academic Press; London.

Tanner J. M., Healy M. J. R., Goldstein H. and Cameron N. (2001) *Assessment of Skeletal Maturity and Prediction of Adult Height (TW2 method)*. W.B. Saunders; London.

Todd J. W. (1937) *Atlas of Skeletal Maturation: Part 1. Hand*. Mosby; London.

van't Hof, M. A., Roede M. J. and Kowalski C. J. (1976) Estimation of growth velocities from individual longitudinal data. *Growth*; **40**: 217–40.

Wainer H., Roche A. F. and Bell S. (1978) Predicting adult stature without skeletal age and without parental data. *Pediatrics*; **61**: 569–72.

Weiner J. S. and Lourie J. A. (1969) *Human Biology*. F. A. Davis; Philadelphia, PA.

PART TWO

GONIOMETRIC ASPECTS OF MOVEMENT

CHAPTER 4

ASSESSMENT OF POSTURE

Peter H. Dangerfield

4.1 AIMS

The aims of this chapter are to:

- review the nature and definition of posture;
- examine various techniques of assessing the upright position and normal status;
- consider abnormalities in posture and their effects on performance with particular reference to the consequences for sporting activities.

4.2 INTRODUCTION

Maintenance of the upright posture by humans is unique among mammals and primates. During human evolution, complex control mechanisms in the brain were generally recognised as being in the lateral occipital cortex. A close link between balance and spatial cognition developed in the cerebral cortex leading to the accurate perception of all body parts.

Alignment of the body in an upright position is itself the key to human bipedalism and has been associated in evolution with decoupling of head and trunk movements. This has allowed us to develop the capability for endurance running. As the hindlimbs progressively assumed the role of locomotion, the vertebral column adapted from a horizontal compressed structure to a vertical weight-bearing rod and axial rotations and counter-rotations of the trunk developed to permit a wide range of activities unique to man to evolve. The relationship between the spine and the pelvic girdle distally and the skull proximally also changed, and changes occurred in the shape of the pelvis and sacrum. The centre of gravity also evolved, shifting backwards towards the hindlimbs as their length and musculature increased. At the same time, to reduce energy expenditure in countering needless body rotation about the centre of gravity, forces for forward propulsion passed through the centre of gravity. Early changes in body form also allowed the adoption of sitting positions, allowing the forelimb to be freed for manipulative functions. Further changes in the angulations of the lumbar vertebral column in females also enabled them to carry babies, an evolutionary trend that gave humans an advantage over potential predators (Whitcombe *et al.* 2007). Additionally, associated increases in flexibility of the vertebral column were accompanied by changes in size of the vertebrae in the lumbar region, which became more massive in order to cope with increased compression forces resulting from the upright stance. Further changes in the role of the sternum and abdominal muscles occurred which allowed less truncal stiffness, resulting in the wider shallow chest and reduced angulation of the ribs of humans.

Posture is maintained by a number of functions including an antigravity function, balance, body segment orientation and the adaptation of appropriate antigravity positions for ongoing movement. These functions also adapt as they develop sequentially during postnatal growth and development.

Adopting an upright posture and acquiring freedom to use the upper limb independently of the legs has increased the dynamic demands on the vertebral column. It developed the capability to produce and accumulate moments of force while transmitting and concentrating forces from other parts of the body. These forces include dynamic compressive forces, in which the intervertebral disc acts as a flexible link, lowering the resonant frequency of the spine. This then allows the spinal musculature and ligaments to dissipate energy. As a consequence, changing to an upright posture has resulted not only in specific human functional abilities, but also unique functional disabilities, which can have implications in sporting and physical activities. Such conditions might include spinal curvatures of an acquired type, or the problems sometimes developed by sports participants and professional musicians due to degenerative disease of the lumbar spine and other joints or as a consequence of repetitive injury or sprains. These may be accompanied by body asymmetry, which itself might adversely affect the normal posture and inertial properties of the body. This is a large subject in its own right and more fully discussed elsewhere (Dangerfield 1994; McManus 2002).

The study and definition of posture are possible from a number of different aspects. These include the evolution of bipedalism and the upright position, changes during development in infancy and childhood, mechanisms of physiological control and its role in health and its importance in sport, exercise and ergonomics. Thus, it is important to understand the concept of posture and to examine some of the methods that have been developed to assess it, allowing investigation of the factors that influence it in different states, such as rest and movement. Furthermore, since human posture is a complex control system, with constant correctional movements taking place to enable standing upright, it will inevitably change as the individual ages.

Posture may be defined in simple terms as a particular position of the body. In the context of the upright stance of the human, it is generally accepted that it is possible to define both static and dynamic posture. Static posture is a consequence of a state of muscular and skeletal balance within the body and this creates stability by an orientation of the constituent parts of the body in space at any moment in time. The least energy will be used by the body to achieve this stable state and any departure from it will lead to imbalance and the development of bad posture. This situation may be encountered in a range of health-related circumstances and can also be a problem for sports coaches and their trainees.

It is very rare for a normal individual to remain in a static position since the daily routines of life are essentially dynamic and involve movement. Dynamic posture is the state the segments of the body adopt when undertaking movement. Posture is always the relative orientation of the constituent parts of the body in space at any moment in time. Thus, maintaining an upright position requires constant dynamic adjustment by muscles in the trunk and limbs, under the automatic and conscious control of the central nervous system to counter the effects of gravity. Posture should therefore be regarded as a position assumed by the body before it makes its next move and relies on the brain's perceptions of position (Roaf 1977). This perception is closely related to the visual processing of information within the occipital cortex (Astafiev *et al.* 2004).

Assessment of posture requires consideration of the human body in an upright stance, in readiness for the next movement. This is easiest to measure using simple standard anthropometric equipment and methodologies. For example, if the working day includes sitting, sitting height should be measured. Good posture has been developed in cultures where sitting cross-legged leads to strong back muscles (Roaf 1977).

4.3 CURVATURES AND MOVEMENT OF THE VERTEBRAL COLUMN

The normal vertebral column possesses well marked curvatures in the sagittal plane in the cervical, thoracic, lumbar and pelvic regions. Three million years of evolution have caused rounding of the thorax and pelvis as an adaptation to bipedal gait. In infancy, functional muscle development and growth exert a major influence on the way the curvatures in the column take shape and also on changes in the proportional size of individual vertebrae, in particular in the lumbar region. The lumbar curvature becomes important for maintaining the centre of gravity of the trunk over the legs when walking commences. In addition, changes in body proportions exert a major influence on the subsequent shape of the curvatures in the column.

The cervical curvature is lordotic (Greek, meaning 'I bend'); that is, the curvature is convex in the anterior direction. It is the least marked vertebral curvature and extends from the atlas to the second thoracic vertebra. The thoracic curve is kyphotic (Greek, meaning 'bent forwards'). In other words the curvature is concave in the anterior direction (Figure 4.1). It extends from the second to the twelfth thoracic vertebrae. This curvature is caused by the increased posterior depth of the thoracic vertebral bodies. It appears to be at its minimum during the pubertal growth spurt (Willner and Johnson 1983). It is not

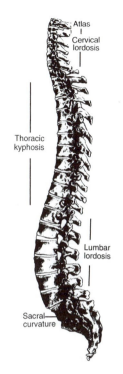

Figure 4.1 The curvatures of the vertebral column.

clear, however, whether it is greater or less in growing females (Fon *et al.* 1980; Mellin and Poussa 1992). The lumbar curve is naturally lordotic and has a greater magnitude in the female. It extends from the twelfth thoracic vertebra to the lumbo-sacral angle, with an increased convexity of the last three segments due to greater anterior depth of intervertebral discs and some anterior wedging of the vertebral bodies. The curvature develops in response to gravitational forces, which arise as the child assumes the upright position during sitting and standing; and to the forces exerted betweeen the psoas major and abdominal muscles and the erector spinae muscle. Lordosis also increases steadily during growth (Willner and Johnson, 1983). Comparing the thoracic spine to the lumbar spine, kyphosis in relationship to lordosis decreases with age (Leroux *et al.* 2000). Within the pelvis, the curve is concave antero-inferior and involves the sacrum and coccygeal vertebrae, extending from the lumbosacral joint to the apex of the coccyx.

The cervical and lumbar regions of the vertebral column are the most mobile regions; although, with the exception of the atlanto-occipital and atlanto-axial joints, little movement is possible between each adjacent vertebra. It is a summation of movement throughout the vertebral column that permits the human to enjoy a wide range of mobility. Anatomically, the movements are flexion and extension; lateral flexion to the left or right; and rotation. Anatomical circumduction occurs only in the mid-thoracic region as elsewhere any lateral flexion is always accompanied by some rotation.

When physical tasks are undertaken, the body should normally be in a relaxed position which evokes the least postural stress. This is particularly important in adopting a relaxed sitting position when working at a computer. If forces are imposed on the body which create stress, the risk of damage to biological structures increases. This is referred to as postural strain (Weiner 1982). Postural strain causes prolonged static loading in affected muscles.

The loading of the spine is localized in the erector spinae muscles and prolonged loading eventually leads to pain; for example, pain is a common result of sitting uncomfortably in a badly designed chair. The eventual result of excessive strain will be an injury. In the context of the spine, the more inappropriate the strain on the vertebral column, the greater the likelihood of back injury. For example, there is evidence to suggest that carriage of back-packs by children may lead to spinal damage, since pain can develop and immediate changes in the sagittal spinal curvatures have also been found (Korovessis et al. 2005; Chow et al. 2007). The lumbar region of the spine is the most susceptible to injury and low back pain is probably the largest cause of sickness among the working population, affecting three out of four adults (Alexander 1985). Such injury is often the result of arthritic changes affecting the lumbar facet joints (Eubanks 2007). Athletic injuries are usually of a minor nature (Vinas 2006) although there is a real risk of increased degeneration of the intervetebral discs and back pain (Baranto 2005). The reasons for the high risk of injury are due to the fundamental weakness of the vertebral structures; loading forces encountered in everyday living such as body weight; obesity; muscle contractions and external loading such as lifting; and recreational and sporting activities, particularly if the individual is unfit. These all contribute to the development of postural strain and injury.

Injury itself is caused by activities that increase weight loading, rotational stresses or back arching. The result is damage to the intervertebral disc, ligaments or muscles, and secondary consequences that affect the facet joints, sciatic and other nerves. Severe trauma might result in a fracture to the vertebral column. Symptoms of damage will include pain, stiffness and numbness or paraesthesia. It is also important to identify whether the pain was sudden in onset, such as after lifting an object or more gradual without any obvious antecedent. As such, back pain is often difficult to quantify or even prove to be a physical problem, rather than one which is psychosomatic in nature. Objective quantification still remains difficult although it can be assessed using motion analysis (D'Orazio 1993; Marras et al. 1999). Therefore, as the medical problems of diagnosis, treatment and rehabilitation as well as the extensive range of biomechanical and other investigations possible in this field are beyond the scope of this chapter, the reader should consult the appropriate orthopaedic and other literature.

4.4 DEFINING AND QUANTIFICATION OF POSTURE

4.4.1 Inertial characteristics

When maintaining an erect and well-balanced position, with little muscle activity, the line of

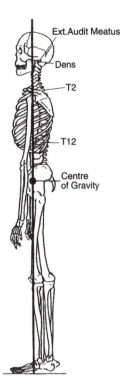

Figure 4.2 The line of centre of gravity of the body.

Figure 4.3 MRI image of the lumbar spine.

gravity of the body extends in a line from the level of the external auditory meatus, anterior to the dens of the axis, anterior to the body of the second thoracic vertebra and the body of the twelfth thoracic vertebra and the fifth lumber vertebra to lie anterior to the sacrum (Klausen 1965) (Figure 4.2). As a result, the vertebral bodies and intervertebral discs act as a weight-bearing pillar from the base of the skull to the sacrum. Furthermore, there is a cephalo-caudal increase in the cross-sectional surface area of the discs and vertebral bodies (Pal and Routal 1986). There is also a sexual dimorphism, with females having a lower width-to-depth ratio than males, due to the heavier body build of the male (Taylor and Twomey 1984).

4.4.2 Anthropometry and posture

A number of different methods for the measurement of a three-dimensional object such as the human body have been developed. All methods have their advantages and disadvantages. Extensive literature is available which details anthropometric techniques, applied to the field of biology, medicine and ergonomics (Weiner and Lourie 1969; Hrdlicka 1972; Pheasant 1986; Burwell and Dangerfield 2000; Cameron 2004). Such anthropometric methods at their simplest use a tape measure to acquire three-dimensional information about the body, but this can often be viewed as inefficient (Seitz *et al.* 2000).

Anthropometric techniques are similar in spite of their inefficiency, but may vary in the definition of the measured dimension. Direct surface measurements employ devices for measuring length, height and mass, such as the stadiometer for height and sitting height and the anthropometer for limb segment and pelvic or shoulder width. In the context of posture, anthropometry has been extensively employed in medicine in the study of scoliosis (spinal curvature) (See Burwell and Dangerfield 2000; Cole *et al.* 2000). Indirect methods include ultrasound, x-rays (conventional radiographs and computerised tomography [CT]), magnetic resonance imaging (MRI) (Figure 4.3) or light sources. Structured light projection is highly effective and low cost, but suffers from errors arising from subject movement. Laser-scanners have the advantage of speed in acquisition of data and are less affected by subject movement but are of much higher cost for researchers to use. All these indirect methods acquire data in different places in different planes and thus reconstruction of three-dimensional descriptions of body shape is possible.

Biostereometrics refers to the spatial and spatiotemporal analysis of form and function based on analytical geometry. It deals with three-dimensional measurements of biological subjects, which vary with time due to factors such as growth and movement. Adapted to sport and movement science, biostereometrics enables dynamic movement and technical performance in any particular sport to be studied. Problems do arise due to the complexity of human movement, and data collection still requires computer power. However, recent advances in gait analysis methods and other scanning processes have allowed considerable development in this field. It still needs to be remembered that traditional assessment of body shape, particularly in biomechanics and medicine, was governed by the need to examine the body in the anatomical position, standing still and maintaining this position like a shop dummy. This is an unrealistic position and contemporary analysis of movement has overcome many of the shortcomings of earlier investigations.

It still remains difficult, without a clear definition of the term *posture*, to offer precise and clear methods for measuring and thus quantifying it. As a result, methods used to quantify body shape and movement can by inference be applied to the understanding of posture.

4.5 ASSESSMENT OF POSTURE AND BODY SHAPE

Assessment of body shape can be considered as two groups:

i   Measurements in a static phase of posture;
ii Measurements in dynamic and changing posture.

4.5.1 Measurements in a static phase of posture

These measurements involve quantification of the normal physiological curves of the vertebral column, usually in the erect position. By the adoption of a standardized position (usually an erect position), the measurement can then tested for reproducibility (Ulijaszek and Lourie 1994).

4.5.2 Subjective measurement of static posture.

Static posture is usually assessed subjectively using a rating chart (Bloomfield *et al.* 2003). The subject stands in the upright position and is observed against the chart.

4.5.3 Objective measurement of spinal length, curvature and spinal shrinkage

Clinical and biological measurement of spinal length, curvature and shrinkage is needed to understand fully the effect of posture on the human body. This applies in both sport and medical contexts.

Various techniques are available to assess posture. Simple and low-cost manual techniques of assessing posture may be employed in clinical or field environments. Other methods can be more accurate, but costly. These range from invasive criterion techniques such as radiography or CT and MRI, which either involve potential exposure to radiation or to magnetic fields. Other techniques involve light-based systems using structured light beams or lasers which negate the risks of radiation exposure. These techniques are summarised below.

4.5.4 Non-invasive manual techniques of assessing posture

Accurate measurement of height and length can be achieved using anthropometric equipment such as goniometers or the range of Harpenden Portable Stadiometers and Anthropometers (Holtain Ltd, Crosswell, Crymych, Pembs., SA41 3UF www.anthropometer.com). Such equipment is essentially portable allowing it to be carried to field conditions. Lengths such as height, biacromial diameter, tibial length, or other parameters may be measured accurately (Figure 4.4). These instruments incorporate a manual counter recorder for ease of reading, which reduces the likelihood of recording error.

Profile measurements, which can be used to assess body angles, such as that between the spine and the vertical plan, may be recorded digitally with a camera. Such records are permanent; they can be computerised and analyzed and allow the recording of changes in posture and position over time, such as before and after athletic events or surgical interventions. Digital cameras are becoming more accurate with increasing pixel counts, commonly 10 million or more, permitting a highly accurate record to be collected, downloaded into a computer and examined and analyzed as required using appropriate software.

The most commonly assessed passive movement is spinal flexion. This is frequently done by visual inspection in the medical clinical situation, and thus is often undertaken inaccurately. Alternatively, it is feasible to measure spinal flexion using a simple tape to measure the increase in spinal length, in different positions of flexion or extension, between skin markings made over the spinous processes, although this can be time-consuming in a busy clinical environment.

In order to achieve accuracy in measure-

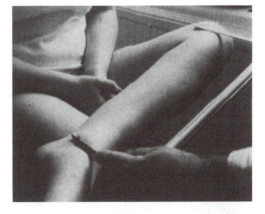

Figure 4.4 Holtain anthopometer used to measure tibial length. A counter recorder is employed, which gives an instant and accurate read-out of length.

ments in spinal flexion, goniometers and inclinometers are used. These simple instruments can measure a wide range of spinal and pelvic angles and positions to a high degree of accuracy and reproducibility.

Such instruments may include pantographic devices such as the kyphometer and simple plastic goniometers.

a) The kyphometer

The kyphometer is a device which was developed to measure the angles of kyphosis and lordosis within the vertebral column (Figures 4.5 and 4.6) (Protek AG, Bern, Switzerland). A dial indicates the angle between the feet placed on the spine. The angle of thoracic kyphosis is estimated by placing the feet over the T1 and T12 vertebra. This measurement is both accurate and reproducible. The angle decreases with inspiration and increases again with expiration and so care should be taken to standardize the measurement technique with the appropriate stage of the respiratory cycle. Lumbar lordosis is measured between T12 and L1 vertebrae and is also affected by the respiration cycle. It is likewise affected by sexual dimorphism between the male and female subject, being larger in post-pubertal females. However, experience has found that lumbar kyphosis is less easy to measure accurately than thoracic

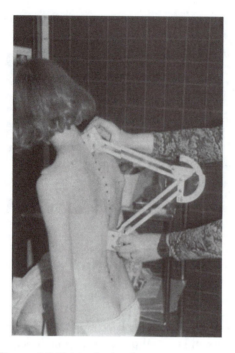

Figure 4.5 Using the kyphometer to measure thoracic kyphosis on a subject. The angle is read off the dial on the instrument.

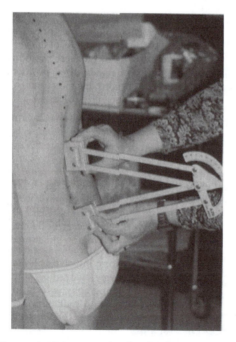

Figure 4.6 Measuring lumbar lordosis using the kyphometer.

kyphosis (Dangerfield *et al.* 1987; Korovessis *et al.* 2001). Both these measurements have been experimentally correlated with the same measurements undertaken on erect spinal radiographs (Dangerfield *et al.* 1987; Kado *et al.* 2006). Research employing this instrument reports its application to cross country skiers, scoliosis, back pain and other problems.

b) The goniometer

The goniometer is a device for measuring the range of movement of a joint and is widely used in clinical situations; for example, by orthopaedic surgeons and physiotherapists as well as in research programmes. The range of such instruments includes plastic scale devices and complex devices, all of which allow movement measurement about a fixed rotation point and all finding applications in fields such as biology, physics and surface science. Essentially simple tools, they can measure limb and trunk joint angles and also flexions within the spine. The goniometer offers a rapid and low-cost method of quantifying posture and spinal mobility by the measurement of angles in the spine, such as the proclive and declive angles (Figures 4.7, 4.8 and 4.9). These angles can be expanded to measurements at each level of the vertebral column and can thus give accurate indications of the shape of the entire vertebral column. Ranges of spinal mobility may be useful in studying athletic performance but again due allowance should be made for age and gender.

The same instrument may be used to assess the lateral flexibility of the spine by placing the dial over T1 vertebra and then asking the subject to flex to the right and to the left. This measurement is useful in assessing spinal movement in patients with deformity or arthritic diseases. Techniques for skin marking may also facilitate simple but accurate measurement of spinal flexion, and offer a useful measure of physical movement, although care must be taken to avoid inevitable movement of the skin over underlying bony landmarks.

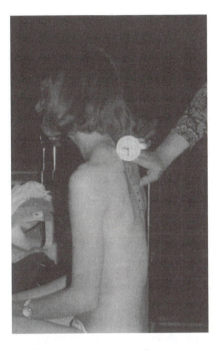

Figure 4.7 A goniometer used to measure the proclive angle, the angle between the spine and vertical at the level of the 7th cervical vertebra.

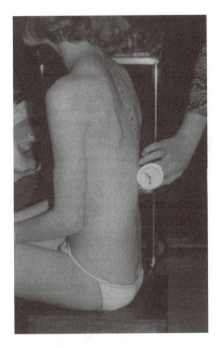

Figure 4.8 Measuring the angle at the thoraco-lumbar junction.

c) The scoliometer

Other specialist goniometers have been devised for studying the spine in scoliosis clinics. Scoliosis is an abnormal curvature of the spine, in which the vertebrae are rotated and laterally deflected, creating severe structural deformity and an associated rib-hump (Figure 4.10). Scoliotic curvatures may be due to primary pathological conditions, but can also result from leg length inequality or muscle imbalance encountered in sports such as tennis, or discus and javelin throwing (Burwell and Dangerfield 2000; Stokes *et al.* 2006). For example, the OSI scoliometer is used to quantify the hump deformity of scoliosis in the coronal plane (Orthopaedic Systems Inc, Hayward, CA, USA). A ball-bearing in a glass tube aligns itself to the lowest point of the tube when placed across the hump-deformity, permitting a reading of the angle of trunk inclination (ATI) from a scale on the instrument (Figure 4.11). This angle is a measure of the magnitude of the

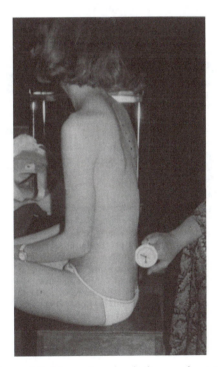

Figure 4.9 Measuring the declive angle at the lumbar-sacral junction.

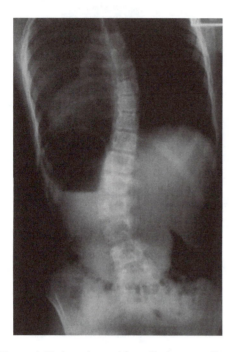

Figure 4.10 A patient with scoliosis: a condition in which the vertical column develops a lateral curvature and vertebral rotation, frequently leading to severe physical deformity.

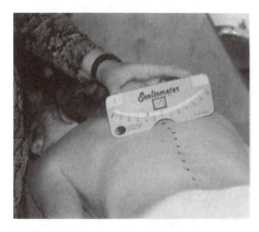

Figure 4.11 The OSI scoliometer used to measure the ATI in the spine of a scoliosis subject lying prone.

rib-cage or lumbar deformity, associated with the lateral curvature of the spine.

d) Other methods

Another method for quantifying body shape is to reproduce the outline of the structure under consideration using a rod-matrix device or a flexicurve. Contour outlines of the trunk and spine, both in the horizontal and vertical plane, can be measured using rod-matrix devices (Dangerfield and Denton 1986) (Figure 4.12) or a flexicurve (Tillotson and Burton, 1991; Harrison *et al.* 2005). Both these methods give a permanent record of shape by tracing the outline obtained onto paper but suffer from the tedium of use if more than one tracing is required. They are used in recording rib-cage shape and thoracic and lumbar lordosis and, in athletes, may be applied to assessment of lumbar movements following exercise.

These techniques are simple to employ but can be time-consuming and laborious in practical use. Accuracy depends on experience of the observer and careful use of the instrument. Furthermore, reproducibility of data collection is essential. Unfortunately, in assessing movement and posture related to the spine, the technique used is often flawed, due to practical difficulties in separating one movement from another within a complex anatomical structure.

4.6 OTHER CLINICAL METHODS OF POSTURE ASSESSMENT

4.6.1 Photographic methods

Using the moiré effect to measure deformation and shape is a mature field in experimental mechanics and optical metrology. Moiré photography employs optical interference patterns to record the three-dimensional shape of a surface. In biological fields, it was used to evaluate pelvic and trunk rotation and also trunk deformity (Willner 1979; Suzuki *et al.* 1981; Asazuma *et al.* 1986).

Stereophotogrammetry, originally developed for cartography, has been adopted in the

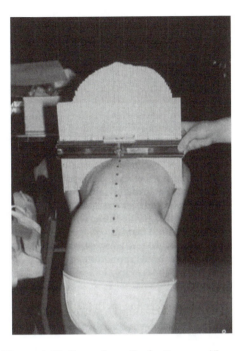

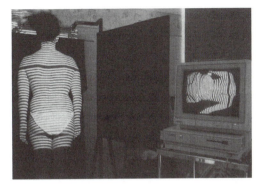

Figure 4.13 Grating projection system (SIPS: Spinal Image Processing System) used for clinical evaluation of trunk shape and scoliosis.

Figure 4.12 Formulator Body Contour Tracer used to record cross-sectional shape of the thorax in a patient with scoliosis (a lateral curvature of the spine causing a rib-hump deformity and asymmetry of the thorax).

evaluation of facial shape, structural deformity of the trunk and for posture measurement. Two cameras are used to take overlapping pairs of photographs. These can be analyzed to produce a three-dimensional contour map of the subject and can be described as points in terms of x, y and z co-ordinates (Sarasate and Ostman 1986, Enciso *et al.* 2004). This technique has also found limited application in the study of scoliosis.

Overlapping procedures use simultaneously acquired photographs taken from different angles and reconstruct the body in three-dimensions from predefined specific points on each image, with a fixed scale as the reference. With conventional digital cameras providing images, a computer program will allow rapid analysis of the images and provide the three-dimensional data required at relative low cost and speed (Seitz 2000).

An extension of this technique is stereo-radiography where two x-ray images are used instead of photographs, but this technique is invasive and potentially hazardous due to the use of ionising radiation. Consequently, it has found only limited application.

Non-invasive methods of postural assessment can employ the projection of structured light patterns, scanning laser beams, or infrared projection techniques. All these techniques are highly accurate and combined with a computer and suitable program can output results in real time. Such techniques have been applied to the study of trunk shape, for example, in scoliosis, in the clothing industry, and to the movement of joints such as the knee and shoulder.

4.6.2 3-D grating projection methods

Three-dimensional (3-D) image sensing has rapidly developed over the last 20 years opening up a very wide variety of applications, particularly those involving a need to know the precise 3-D shape of the human body, for example, e-commerce (clothing), medicine (assessment, audit, diagnosis and planning), anthropometry (vehicle design), postproduction (virtual actors) and industrial design (workspace design). In short, 3-D assessment has been applied when it is necessary to get the 3-D shape of a person into the computer.

Simple grating projection techniques are well suited to research into posture, applied anatomy and body movement and can allow outputting of three-dimensional reconstructions of the trunk (Dangerfield *et al.* 1992). The technique also allows automatic calculation of parameters of posture similar to those gathered using goniometers or flexicurves.

'Phase measuring profilometry' also uses grating projection. This method employs algorithms for the phase function, which are defined by the geometry of the system and the shape of the object (Halioua and Liu 1989; Halioua *et al.* 1990; Merolli *et al.* 1999). The object's shape is converted into a phase distribution as in interferometry and is analyzed by digital phase measuring techniques: accuracy to less than 1 mm is possible without the need for reference plane images. This technique has been used to measure the three-dimensional shape of the trunk, face and breasts and has obvious applications in plastic surgery. It is presently expensive for routine practical use as it employs precision optical components and high-speed computer image processing.

The BioPrint® system employs a calibrated wall grid and uses three digital photographs for postural analysis. The three photographs are a right lateral, an antero-posterior, and a posterior–anterior view of the subject. A complete postural profile of the subject is defined by 37 dependent variables that are primarily related to translations and rotations of the head, thorax and pelvis in the frontal and sagittal planes (BIOTONIX, Boucherville, QC, Canada). This system has found widespread commercial adoption by health professionals in fitness evaluation and research (Lafond *et al.* 2007)

The considerable advances in computer power over the last couple of decades has allowed considerable development in methods for scanning of the human body, driven in part by the clothing industry requiring accurate and up-to-date size measurements of populations. The Exyma whole-body scanner series from Giscan precisely scans the entire body in as little as 3 seconds (http://eng.exyma.com/product/whole.htm). These imaging systems have the advantage of very accurate rapid mapping of the entire torso, which is important if there is any indication of anatomical deviations from normal that may occur because of disease or injury.

Laser 3-D whole-body scanners have also been developed, which use a range of landmarks, allowing for feature recognition and data acquisition. It is possible to employ surface colour information as well as geometric relationships in this process, resulting in an algorithm that can achieve over 98% accuracy (Wang *et al.* 2007).

The future of static measurements lies with further developments of these light-based systems, whereby more and more detailed and accurate recording of the three-dimensional shape of the trunk and legs is routine.

4.6.3 Radiographic and magnetic resonance images

In order to understand the interaction of the underlying internal components of skeletal anatomy, invasive criterion techniques must be employed. These include conventional radiography, CT scans, MRI or other developing technologies. These methods are normally employed for the medical investigation of posture, especially if it is associated with injuries or deformities.

The radiographic approach has its attractions; it is widely employed in medical diagnostic investigations as it is relatively easy to interpret. Digitally-based systems have reduced the radiation dosage by a factor of up to 10 times, with the images being analyzed digitally on computers. However, it must be remembered that for the purposes of any research, the risks from ionising radiation remain, raising major ethical issues for anyone employing such methods as part of their protocols.

With the employment of the latest generation of spiral CT scanners, MRI scanners and other technologies, such as positron emission tomography (PET) scanners, it is relatively easy to create 3-D reconstructions of the skeletal, vascular and other soft-tissue structures of the body and limbs. There have been important applications in medicine and the study of sports-related injuries. However, while the presence of ionising radiation excludes the use of CT in research rather than purely clinical medical investigations, other techniques have been adopted.

MRI still offers a far wider range of possibilities as it can be used to obtain highly detailed images of soft tissue such as muscles, nerves and blood vessels (Figure 4.3), although it is less useful for bony tissue. The MRI method exploits the property of certain atoms, particularly hydrogen, to perform a precessing movement in a magnetic field when they are disturbed from a stationary state by application of a powerful magnetic field.

While they remain expensive tools for use in research, CT and MRI scanners are widely available in hospitals for routine diagnostic purposes. Scans are used in the investigation of sports-related injury, studies on body composition (see Chapter 1 by Eston *et al.*) as well as medical conditions ranging from soft tissue injury to cardiovascular problems. Changes in the shape and working of the scanners themselves hold promise for their wider availability within the research community; thus their use as research tools will increase. MRI can today image vascular structures, and the development of open 'walk-in' MRI scanners now allow the procuring of static and dynamic images, particularly of limb joints, which is important in sporting environments. The development of advanced image processing methods has led to the routine use of 3-D reconstruction of tissues in high detail. The water and other ionic contents of such tissue can be quantified using the decay times of molecular movement activated by the magnetic field (T1 and T2 images) and these processes are now applied to many different fields of application. This includes the acquisition of geometric joint data from the spine in functional motion studies.

4.6.4 Ultrasound

Ultrasound has been applied to imaging sub-surface bony and soft tissue structures. This technique employs sound waves, which are produced by a transducer and are reflected back from tissues within the body. Most widespread application has been in pregnancy, but applications have been developed using real-time equipment, which can reveal details of the body structures of the vertebral column. The images are often difficult to interpret, but are constantly improving. The recent introduction of 3-D ultrasound now enables clear 3-D images of organs, particularly developing foetuses, to be viewed. The advantage of ultrasound is that it uses non-invasive sound waves and has therefore negligible risk to the subject. Ultrasound is used for routine screening for spinal bifida during pregnancy and has been applied to spinal assessments in research into scoliosis.

4.7 MOVEMENT ANALYSIS: MEASUREMENTS IN A DYNAMIC PHASE OF POSTURE

In order to describe dynamic movement, considerations of qualitative and quantitative methods of biomechanical analysis are required. The former requires a careful, subjective description of movement, while the latter requires detailed measurement and evaluation of the collected data. The guidelines of the British Association of Sport and Exercise Sciences still remain a useful resource for the conduct of biomechanical analysis of performance in sport (Bartlett 1992).

Since the human body rarely assumes static posture for more than a few seconds, analysis of dynamic posture will involve study of the range of motion of the joints of the spine. The relative position of the spine constantly varies throughout any movement, such as during gait or in a sporting activity. With the rapid development of the PC over the last decade, real-time recording of moving images of sporting activities and other movements permits routine measurement of changes in posture. Qualitative analysis of a movement, or athletic technique within a sport, is undertaken with high-speed video with no disturbance to the subject performing their movements. It is relatively easy with appropriate software to quantify the captured images and assess movements, such as spinal displacement or stride length. Problems should be recognised when it comes to accurate determination of body landmarks, which still need to be marked on the subject for placement of sensors or reflective devices. It is well known that skin movements over underlying bony or muscular structures can affect surface markers. Skin landmarks are located and a special marker locator, which is sensitive to infra-red light, is placed in the appropriate place. Such locators are used in many movement analysis systems found in standard gait laboratories (see section 4.7.1).

It is not easy to adapt such laboratories to the investigation of posture, but there is a growing literature on the subject that should be relatively easy to find on standard scientific databases. Since the introduction of a time dimension, longitudinal studies on movement analysis can now be applied to assess the efficacy of training regimens and performance parameters. They also enable the sports biomechanist and physiologist the opportunity to identify events within a movement, which can be compared between individuals. While the results have been traditionally presented as outline and stick 'persons' developments, as a spin off from the cinema animation field, they are allowing infilling and realistic images to be presented. These are likely to develop rapidly in the next few years.

Application of these techniques of quantification of movement in the lumbar spine is important when examining patients with low-back pain, a symptom frequently associated with sporting pastimes. Ranges of spinal mobility may be useful in studying athletic performance, but allowance for age and gender should be made in interpreting observations.

Simple techniques can be employed that are frequently of low cost. Goniometers may be used to assess spinal range of motion (refer to the laboratory practical at the end of this chapter and also Chapter 5, Van Roy and Borms). These measurements are useful in assessing spinal movement in patients with deformity or arthritic diseases. Techniques for marking the skin may also facilitate simple but accurate measurement of spinal flexion. However, it is important to recognise the problems of skin movement as already mentioned in this chapter. These do offer a useful measure of physical movement, such as assessing the contribution of lumbar flexion to body posture, even when the technique requires only the use of a tape measure (MacRae and Wright 1969; Rae et al. 1984).

4.7.1 Movement analysis

Movement analysis is a complex specialist area that is increasingly available to clinicians, sports physiologists and other researchers within a number of specialist gait and movement laboratories. While setting up the laboratory and required equipment (such as force plates and multiple cameras), remains expensive, the potential for collecting information relating to posture and axial skeletal movement is great. Multiple channels of data input and real time analysis is possible with the powerful generation of PCs available today. Undoubtedly developments in this field will continue at rapid pace in the future. The most common form of dynamic research involves gait and movement analysis. This applies to a wide range of sports and medical problems, which can be related to posture. The tracking and analysis of human movement commenced with the early application of still photography. With the advent of inexpensive video cameras in the 1980s, video capture has been used in the analysis of performance of occupational and sports skills. Early models representing the human body as a mechanism consisting of segments or links and joints are still valid today and remain worth consulting (Kippers and Parker 1989; Vogelbach 1990). These have evolved into a wide range of systems; ranging from eye-tracking software to record actual movements of a subject, to movement analysis systems that record body segment position changes in gait and other position change cycles. There is also considerable choice in the range of analysis software available to researchers, ranging from 2-D tracking to sophisticated 3-D real-time biomechanical analysis, all of which can be adapted to examine the trunk (e.g. Quintic Consultancy Ltd – http://www.quintic.com/).

The application of this approach to the vertebral column remains a major challenge due to its multi-unit component structure, with each vertebra and disc acting almost as an independent unit. Consequently, the column and pelvis exhibit many varied movement patterns. The vertebral column has 25 mobile segments corresponding to each intervertebral joint from the base of the skull to the lumbar-sacral junction, each with its own unique movement potential. This is the concept of spinal coupling first described by Lovett in 1905 (reviewed by Panjabi et al. 1989). Posture affects the range of these coupled motions. In contrast, the pelvis moves about an axis through the hip joints. Rotational movements are generated during walking and these pass upwards from the lower limbs into the pelvis and upwards into the spine. By separating these individual units, any overall appreciation of the complex movements of the trunk and muscle involvement is highly complex and remains a challenge to modellers of the spine. This complexity is a key issue for anyone considering research in this area when investigating movements in the context of posture and applications either in biological, clinical or athletic terms.

The 3-D measurement of movement remains important in advancing our understanding of athletic performance. In all applications, the reproducibility and accuracy of the method must be established.

Early methods for the three-dimensional analysis of motion included a system called CODA, which was accurate, fast and non-invasive (Mitchelson 1988). It consisted of three rapidly rotating scanning mirrors used to view fan-shaped beams of light that sweep rapidly across the region of the subject under study. The signals detected by the scanners permitted triangulation and spatial measurement of markers placed on the subject and was used to record movement of the subject in three dimensions. This system found application in clinical studies of Parkinsonian tremor, scoliosis and gait analysis programmes associated with fitting a prosthesis. Selspot optoelectronics and similar systems have also been used for movement analysis in locomotion (Blanksby et al. 2005), in addition to electrogoniometers, which are used employed to monitor dynamic and precision measurement of joint movements (e.g. Biometrics Ltd – www.biometricsltd.com) including movements of the lumbar spine (Paquet et al. 1991). They have also been used to investigate position sense in the spine (Dolan and Green 2006). These tools offer a high degree of reliability and accuracy.

Contemporary biomechanical laboratory methods employ systems using reflective markers to record movement at a set frame rate. Examples of such systems include VICON (www.vicon.com) or the ProReflex System (www.qualisys.com). The use of the small reflective polystyrene markers permits these systems to locate the position of markers in 3-D 500 times per second with millimetre accuracy. The speed of recording the images is known as the sampling rate or frequency and the data acquired are then normally automatically digitised to generate results. These systems automatically track markers in real time with multiple cameras (as many as seven or eight). If combined with a force-plate to record dynamic changes in lower-limb forces during walking or other movements, researchers have the opportunity to examine highly complex relationships between the body and locomotion, revealing much about the dynamics of the spine and upper body. The whole field of gait and movement analysis is large and growing, and the reader is encouraged to investigate developments in the field in specialist journals.

Dynamic work is performed when any muscle changes its length. If the movement involves a constant angular velocity, it is called isokinetic, whereas if the muscle acts on a constant interial mass, it is isoinertial exertion. Isotonic exertion involves maintaining constant muscle tension throughout the range of motion (Rogers and Cavanagh 1984). These terminologies are imprecise and refer to movements which are artificial. Attempts have been made to quantify such movements using muscle testers or dynamometers (see www.jtechmedical.com/products/tracker/freedom_muscletesting.cfm) which act to control the range of motion and/or the resistance of muscles and can quantify strength loss due to injury or disease. These devices have been found to produce reliable results and can applied to measuring trunk movement and thus used in posture assessment. There are many different types of this equipment available for investigations, including cable tensiometers and strain-gauge dynamometers for the measurement of isometric forces and isokinetic devices for dynamic movements.

The Isostation B200 lumbar dynamometer (Isotechnologies, Carrboro, NC, USA) and Kin-Com physical therapy Isokinetic equipment (www.kincom.com/) have been applied to the measurement of limb and trunk motion, strength and velocity. Investigations have included the study of low-back pain and also normal lumbar spinal function (Lee and Kuo 2000).

While 3-D analysis of movement using opto-electronic methods produces sophisticated data on the dynamics of athletic performance, including the effects of an individual's posture on his or her athletic performance, future developments will link these data with information collected from other technologies. Thus, physiological investi-gations of metabolic functions of the body will develop further, increasing understanding of the dynamics of the body and lead to further optimizing of performance matching it to prevailing conditions in order to produce the best athletic performance from an individual.

Electromyography (EMG) employs surface electrodes applied to suitably prepared skin over appropriate muscle groups on the body's surface. Electrical activity generated by the underlying muscles can then be recorded using appropriate amplifiers and filters to process the signals. Muscle activity can be quantified using EMG, allowing investigation of the relationship between posture or body position and exercise response. Within EMG, a widely followed sub-speciality has developed called kinesiological EMG. This technique is used to analyze the function and co-ordination of muscles in different movements and postures, combining these with biomechanical analysis.

The application of EMG to the study of sports was reviewed in depth in the 1990s by Clarys and Cabri (1993) who set down standards for the methodology and the limitations of the method due to its partly descriptive nature. Subsequently, the field has developed greatly. A useful booklet about EMG by Konrad (2008) can be downloaded from Noraxon (www.noraxon.com/emg/index.php3). The EMG technique is also described in more detail by Gleeson (2009).

Electromyographic techniques have been applied to study the effect of posture and lifting on trunk musculature and, by inference spinal loading (Hinz and Seidel 1989; Mouton et al. 1991; Dolan et al. 2001). There are large individual variations in spinal and trunk muscle activity in relation to load. Furthermore, inertial moments differ between standing and sitting positions.

Accelerometers are devices that measure total external forces on a sensor and can be found incorporated into personal electronic devices, such as media players, mobile phones and gaming consoles such as the Wii. They may be used to measure the transmission of vibrations and forces acting on the body. Within the last several years, several companies (Nike, Polar, Nokia, etc.) have produced sports watches for athletes that include footpods incorporating accelerometers, which can determine the speed and distance covered by an individual wearing the unit. The Nokia 5500 can be used for counting stepping.

The study of human movement is developing rapidly as computing costs continue to fall. Overall, such research will increasingly widen our understanding of the problems of human posture and movement in sports and other occupations.

4.8 SPINAL LENGTH AND DIURNAL VARIATION

In anthropometry and ergonomics, stature is a fundamental variable. The vertebral column comprises about 40% of the total body length as measured in stature and has within it about 30% of its length occupied by the intervetebral discs. Spinal length and height vary throughout a 24-hour period. There is shrinking during daytime when the individual is normally active and walking about, but lengthening at night when the individual is sleeping in bed. This change is due to compressive forces acting on the intervertebral discs, eliminating fluid from the nucleus pulposus. The degree of shrinkage is related to the magnitude of the compressive load on the spine and has been used as an index of spinal loading (Corlett et al. 1987). Accurate measurement of spinal shrinkage has been applied in evaluating sports such as weight-training, running and jumping and also in assessing procedures used to prevent back injury (Reilly et al. 1991).

De Puky (1935), a pioneer investigator of spinal shrinkage, measured the change and found a daily oscillation of approximately 1% of total body height. This figure has subsequently been confirmed (Reilly et al. 1991). Wing et al. (1992) demonstrated that 40% of the change occurred in the lumbar spine, without any change in the lordosis depth and angle, and a further 40% occurred in the thoracic spine, associated with a reduction in the kyphotic angle. Most of the shrinkage appears to occur within an hour of assuming an upright posture, while this loss in height is regained rapidly in the prone position. Monitoring creep over 24 hours has demonstrated that 71% of height gained during the night is achieved within the first half of the night and 80% is lost again within 3 hours of arising (Reilly et al. 1984). The mechanism for these changes is that fluid dynamics within the intervertebral disc and vertebral body under compression forces fluid out of the disc, leading to the length variation in the spine observed in the diurnal cycle. Intradiscal pressure varies with load and position. While early studies used cadaveric material (Nachemson and Morris 1964; McNally and Adam 1992) more recent research has combined probe techniques with MRI (Sato et al. 1999). Applying MRI allows the dynamics of the lumbar spine to be studied, confirming that the intervetebral disc fluid has a dynamic mechanism and that the greatest amount of fluid is lost from the nucleus pulposus (Paajanen et al. 1994; Dangerfield et al. 1995; Roberts et al. 1998; Violas et al. 2007) These fluid dynamics are clearly important in sport. Disc damage is more likely if it has a high water content (Adams et al. 1987). The lumbar vertebrae have the highest fluid content. Furthermore, the degree of lumbar flexion increases in the late afternoon, due to disc shrinkage. The clear message from these observations is that time of day is relevant in strategies to avoid straining and overloading the vertebral column. Weight training and lifting are influenced not only by the size of the forces involved, but also in relation to the sleep pattern of the athlete. Avoiding such activities within the first few hours of rising reduces the risk of axial compression leading to disk damage through disc herniation and the subsequent onset of back pain.

4.9 DEVIATION FROM NORMAL POSTURE AND INJURY

Deviation from normal posture is common. While the human has evolved to adopt bipedalism, the underlying skeleton remains one which originally evolved for quadrapedal gait and several anatomical weaknesses remain which can give rise to problems. Sport and other stress-related activity can thus magnify problems affecting the feet, knees, spine and abdominal wall. The careful study of human anatomy is important to allow its application to the sporting and clinical fields and by implication the early detection of deviations from normality.

Low-back pain is probably the most common deviation from normal stability in humans and receives continuing attention from researchers, particularly as it is a major cause of loss of capacity for working. Attention must always be paid to the design, type of equipment and environment used for any activity, with risk assessment being undertaken if appropriate. For example, review of the causative mechanisms of specific soccer injuries has demonstrated that some soccer injuries may be attributable to the equipment used or the type of surface the sport is played on. The effects on the individual of injury are therefore of considerable importance and need consideration in the context of effects on posture and performance.

Thus, posture is compromised by a range of problems that affect the normal anatomy of bipedalism. Injury to a bone, ligament or muscle will alter the normal anatomical framework and so interfere with the maintenance of the normal posture. Bad habits such as slouching in a chair can lead to changes in both muscle and bone, which may develop into a permanent postural abnormality. The unequal loading of the spine can result in excessive strain and may eventually lead to an injury or pain. Asymmetries and skeletal imbalances are common, especially when they affect the lower limbs. A longer limb on one side of the body can lead to a pelvic

tilt and consequently affect the hip joint and lumbar spine. Untreated, this may result in the development of scoliosis (lateral deviation of the spine). Nerve root compression or stretching of the sciatic nerve can also lead to the subject adopting an abnormal stance or posture (White and Panjabi 1990). It also should be recognised that curvatures of the spine as a result of asymmetrical muscle function can also lead to postural and inertial abnormalities and may develop into acquired scoliosis.

Abnormal anatomical relationships, such as *pes cavus* (flat feet) and leg length asymmetry can rapidly result in injuries in sports, such as running. Early recognition of the defect by screening athletes is very important if the development of permanent anatomical deformity and eventual debilitation are to be avoided.

Traumatic injury to the body during any sporting activity can result in a wide range of pathological outcomes. They depend on the posture adopted, the anatomical spinal position, the fitness of the individual and the degree of force sustained. It should be noted that these may be trivial in many cases, but it still remains important to recognize them and initiate medical treatment as soon as possible to avoid potential permanent damage.

4.10 ERRORS AND REPRODUCIBILITY

In any scientific experiment, the methodology applied must be reproducible and accurate. In posture measurement, the actual technique adopted becomes irrelevant if the method is itself prone to errors in reproducibility. If a single person undertakes the measurement, then it is vital that the intra-observer accuracy is estimated by repeated measurement of the same subject. If a team is employed, then the inter-observer error is critical to establish in addition to the intra-observer error. There are numerous reports in the literature relating to this subject, including reviews (Ulijaszek and Lourie 1994; Kouchi *et al.* 1996; Wilmore *et al.* 1997) or subject specific reports such as in gait measurement or studies of nutrition (Moreno *et al.* 2003, Schwartz *et al.* 2004). Random errors can arise from the individual making a mistake using the equipment through to misinterpretation of numbers and data while all the time error is present in anthropometry since the body is not a rigid unmoving object. A recent study highlighted the reliability of visual inspection (Fedora *et al.* 2003). Error measurement is a large field and fuller details are clearly beyond the scope of a short chapter, but its consideration must always be a core component of any activity undertaken when measuring human body parameters.

4.11 CONCLUSION

This chapter provides a brief overview of a range of techniques that can be employed to study posture. It is recognised that it is a field in which rapid advances in all aspects of the technologies involved can lead to the development of totally new methods to study and define posture and movement. The reader should be prepared to consult the appropriate scientific journals for these developments. However, it still remains important to remember the dynamic nature of the living human body and that, at present, the study of movement is both complex and potentially expensive, and a great deal still needs to be discovered.

4.12 PRACTICAL 1: MEASUREMENT OF POSTURE AND BODY SHAPE

4.12.1 Sagittal plane

Erect spinal curvature is the basis of acceptable static posture. Expert opinion differs as to what constitutes 'good' posture, a term relating to energy economy and cosmetic acceptability. Large variations can be seen in groups of healthy subjects. Significant individual variation can be seen between slumped/erect states and deep inhalation/exhalation and it is important to standardize the position for each subject as described in the method. Both 'flat back' and excessive curvatures are considered problematic, having an association with subsequent back pain. Kyphosis of 20–45° and lordosis of 40–60° have been considered to indicate normal ranges (Roaf 1960). Fon *et al.* (1980) suggested that these figures are inappropriate for children and teenagers since spinal curvature changes with age. This change is due to the reduction in elasticity of the spinal ligaments and alterations in bone mineral content.

The two practicals detailed here are regularly used in back clinics and are called kyphometry and goniometry. These experiments will yield a range of values which describe back shape.

4.12.2 Equipment

i)   Debrunner's kyphometer. (Protek AG, Bern, Switzerland)
ii)   Goniometer (for example, MIE hygrometer (see Figure 5.2 Medical Research Ltd) or Myrin Goniometer (LIC Rehab., Solna, Sweden).

The subject is instructed to stand barefoot, with the heels together, in an upright and relaxed position, looking straight ahead and breathing normally with the arms hanging loosely by the body. The shoulders should be relaxed.

Debrunner's kyphometer consists of two long arms where the angle between these arms is transmitted through parallel struts to a protractor (Figures 4.5 and 4.6). Spinal curvature with the kyphometer should be assessed both with the subject exhaling and inhaling maximally. In order to measure thoracic kyphosis, one foot of the kyphometer should be located over T1 and T2 and the other over the T11 and T12. The kyphosis angle is read directly from the protractor.

Lumbar curvature is measured between the T11 and T12 and S1 and S2. The angle read directly from the protractor is lumbar lordosis.

A goniometer consists of a small dial that can be held to the patient's back (Figures 4.8, 4.9 and 4.10). The difference between the back angle and the vertical is measured with a pointer which responds to gravity. The difference between the measurements at T1 and T12 indicates the degree of kyphosis and the deviation between the angles at T12 and S1 indicates the degree of lumbar lordosis. Other angles such as the proclive and declive angles can also be measured (Figure 4.7).

Use of the kyphometer or goniometer allows the quantification of the normal curvatures of the vertebral column. The angle of thoracic kyphosis and lumbar lordosis will yield useful information on individual and group posture.

4.13 PRACTICAL 2: ASSESSMENT OF SITTING POSTURE

Sitting posture may be assessed by first sitting the subject on a high stool. The knees should be flexed to 90° and the thighs 90° relative to the trunk. Most of the weight is taken by the ischial tuberosities, acting as a fulcrum within the buttocks. If the hip angle exceeds 60°, hamstring tension increases and the spine compensates by losing the lordosis concavity of the lumbar spine. A comfortable position therefore requires consideration of the lengths of the tibia and femur, and the angles of the femur relative to the pelvis, and the lordosis angle of the lumbar spine (maintaining lumbar lordosis is important in avoiding lumbar postural strain). To ascertain the appropriateness of a chair for an individual, an investigation of this question usually can be easily undertaken using an anthropometer and goniometer.

The lateral flexibility of the spine can be assessed by placing the goniometer dial over T1 vertebra and then asking the subject to flex to the right and to the left. Sagittal flexibility can be measured by goniometry. It is more often quantified in field testing by the sit-and-reach test.

4.14 PRACTICAL 3: LATERAL DEVIATIONS

4.14.1 Equipment

Scoliometer; for example, Orthopedic Systems, Inc., Hayward, CA, USA.

4.14.2 Method

The scoliometer is employed to quantify lateral deviations of the spine expressed as an asymmetrical trunk deformity. Used in both the thoracic and lumbar regions, it has been found to be less sensitive for the identification of lumbar scoliosis. The reason for this is unclear since lateral spinal curvature and axial trunk rotation also occur in this region. Lateral deviations are found most commonly in scoliosis. Non-structural scoliosis may be formed by disparity in leg length and is usually non-progressive. Structural scoliosis is a serious condition with likelihood of progression throughout the growth period. If found, such cases should be referred for an urgent orthopaedic opinion.

The standing subject assumes a forward-bending posture with the trunk approximately parallel with the floor and feet together. The subject's hands are placed palms together and held between the knees. This position offers the most consistently reproducible results in clinical studies. The examiner places the scoliometer on the subject's back, with the centre of the device corresponding to the centre contour of the trunk, along the spinal column.

Starting where the neck joins the trunk, the scoliometer is moved down the spine to the sacrum, the maximum values for thoracic and lumbar areas being recorded.

Scoliometer readings in excess of 5–8° are taken to indicate significant scoliosis. The subject should be referred to a general practitioner or scoliosis specialist for radiography examination.

4.15 PRACTICAL 4: LEG-LENGTH DISCREPANCY

The subject lies on the floor (or suitable firm surface) with the feet approximately shoulder-width apart. A steel tape-measure is used to measure the distance between the medial malleolus and the anterior superior iliac spine (this is an orthopaedic measurement of leg-length discrepancy). Although differences in leg length are found in many normal subjects, a difference greater than 10 mm may result in postural or adaptive scoliosis.

The subject should then stand bare-footed in a normal, relaxed stance. The vertical distance between the anterior superior iliac spine and the floor immediately next to the subject's heel is measured. Any difference in the left and right side measurements may indicate that the hip is at an angle to the horizontal, indicating the presence of pelvic obliquity. If present, pelvic obliquity can also result in compensatory scoliosis. Pelvic obliquity can also be confirmed by placing the thumbs on each anterior superior iliac spines and eye-balling their heights to check for horizontal alignment.

A specimen data collection form which could be adapted for use in a laboratory or field situation is shown in Table 4.1.

Table 4.1 A sample of a data collection form

Subject Name	M		Date	9.6.95
Date of birth	1.1.80		Gender	Male
Height	1823.0 mm			
Body mass	73.6 kg			
	Test 1		Test 2	
Kyphometer				
Kyphosis Angle T1–T12	34.0 degrees		32.4 degrees	
Lordosis Angle T12–S1	23.5 degrees		24.5 degrees	
Goniometer				
Upper Proclive Angle	37.0 degrees		35.0 degrees	
Declive Angle	–11.0 degrees		–14.0 degrees	
Lower Proclive Angle	–7.0 degrees		–10.0 degrees	
Lordosis	– 30.0 degrees		35.0 degrees	
Kyphosis	20.0 degrees		24.0 degrees	
Flexibility				
Sit-and-Reach score	20.0 cm		20.5 cm	
Scoliometer				
ATI	3.0 degrees		5.0 degrees	
Lateral flexibility				
Right Side	25.0 degrees		23.0 degrees	
Left Side	20.0 degrees		20.0 degrees	
Leg length				
Supine				
Right leg	980.0 mm		980.0 mm	
Left leg	970.0 mm		975.0 mm	
Discrepancy	10.0 mm		5.0 mm	
Standing				
Right leg	950.0 mm		955.0 mm	
Left leg	945.0 mm		950.0 mm	
Discrepancy	5.0 mm		5.0 mm	

Data taken from P. H. Dangerfield (1995, unpublished data: Liverpool School Survey).

FURTHER READING

Books

Bloomfield J., Fricker P. A. and Fitch K. D. (1995). *Science and Medicine in Sport.* 2nd Edition. Blackwell Scientific Publications; Australia (new edition due in 2009).

Kent M. (2006) *Oxford Dictionary of Sports Science and Medicine.* Third Edition. Oxford University Press; Oxford, UK.

MacAuley D. (2006) (ed) *Oxford Handbook of Sports and Exercise Medicine.* Oxford University Press; Oxford, UK.

Palastanga N., Soames R. and Field D. (2006).

Anatomy And Human Movement. 5th Edition. Butterworth Heinemann.

White A. A. and Panjabi M. M. (1990). *Clinical biomechanics of the spine.* 2nd Edition. Lippincott–Raven; Philadelphia, PA.

REFERENCES

Adams M. A., Dolan P. and Hutton W. C. (1987) Diurnal variations in the stresses on the lumbar spine. *Spine*; **12**: 130–7.

Alexander M. J. (1985) Biomechanical aspects of lumbar spine injuries in athletes: a review. *Canadian Journal of Applied Sports Science*; **10**: 1–5.

Astafiev S. V., Stanley C. M., Shulman G. L., Corbetta M (2004) Extrastriate body area in human occipital cortex responds to the performance of motor actions. *Nature Neuroscience*; **7**: 542–548.

Asazuma T., Suzuki N. and Hirabayashi K. (1986) Analysis of human dynamic posture in normal and scoliotic patients. In: (J. D. Harris and A. R. Turner-Smith, eds) *Surface Topography and Spinal Deformity* III. Gustav-Fischer Verlag; Stuttgart: pp. 223–34.

Baranto A. (2005) Traumatic high-load injuries in the adolescent spine. Thesis. Sahlgrenska Academy at Göteborg University, Göteborg, Sweden www.bjdonline.org/ViewDocument. aspx?ContId=1176 (Accessed October 2007)

Bartlett R. (ed) (1992) Guidelines for the Biomechanical Analysis of Performance in Sport. British Association of Sport and Exercise Sciences; Leeds, UK.

Blanksby B. A., Wood G. A., Freedman L. (2005) Human kinesiology. *A J Phys Anthrop*; **24**: (S2) 75–100.

Bloomfield, J., Ackland, T.R. and Elliott, B.C. (2003) *Applied Anatomy and Biomechanics in Sport*, Western Australia, Blackwell Publishing Asia Pty Ltd (2003): p. 251.

Burwell R. G. and Dangerfield P. H. (2000) Adolescent idiopathic scoliosis: hypothesis of causation. *Spine: state of the art reviews*; **14** (2): 319–32.

Cameron N. (2004) Measuring growth. In: (R. Hauspie, N. Cameron and L. Molinari, eds) *Methods in Human Growth Research.* Cambridge University Press; Cambridge, UK: pp. 68–107.

Chow D. H., Leung K. T. and Holmes A. D. (2007). Changes in spinal curvature and proprioception of schoolboys carrying different weights of backpack. *Ergonomics*. **19**: 1–9.

Clarys J. P. and Cabri J. (1993) Electromyography and the study of sports movements: a review. *Journal of Sports Sciences*; **11**: 379–448.

Cole A. A., Burwell R. G. and Dangerfield P. H. (2000). Anthropometry. In: (R. G. Burwell, P. H. Dangerfield, T. G. Lowe and J. Y. Margulies, eds) *STAR volume 'Etiology of Idiopathic Scoliosis.'* Hanley and Belfus; Philadelphia, PA.

Corlett E. N., Eklund J. A. E., Reilly T. and Troup J. D. G. (1987) Assessment of work load from measurements of stature. *Applied Ergonomics*; **18**: 65–71.

Dangerfield P. H. (1994) Asymmetry and growth. In: (S. J. Ulijaszek and C. G. N. Mascie-Taylor, eds) *Anthropometry: The Individual and The Population.* Cambridge University Press; Cambridge, UK: pp. 7–29.

Dangerfield P. H. and Denton J. C. (1986) A longitudinal examination of the relationship between the rib-hump, spinal angle and vertebral rotation in idiopathic scoliosis. In: (J. D. Harris and A. R. Turner-Smith, eds) *Proceedings of the 3rd International Symposium on Moiré Fringe Topography and Spinal Deformity.* Oxford. Gustav Fischer Verlag; Stuttgart: pp. 213–21.

Dangerfield P. H., Denton J. C., Barnes S. B. and Drake N. D. (1987) The assessment of the rib-cage and spinal deformity in scoliosis. In: (I. A. F. Stokes, J. R. Pekelsky and M. S. Moreland, eds) *Proceedings of the 4th International Symposium on Moiré Fringe Topography and Spinal Deformity*, Oxford. Gustav Fischer Verlag; Stuttgart: pp. 53–66.

Dangerfield P. H., Pearson J. D., Atkinson J. T., Gomm J. B., Hobson C. A., Dorgan J. C. and Harvey D. (1992) Measurement of back surface topography using an automated imaging system. *Acta Orthopaedica Belgica*; **58**: 73–9.

Dangerfield P. H., Walker J., Roberts N., Betal D. and Edwards R. H. T. (1995) Investigation of the diurnal variation in the water content of the intervertebral disc using MRI. In: (M. D'Amico, A. Merolli and G. C. Santambrogio, eds) *Proceedings of a 2nd Symposium on 3-D Deformity and Scoliosis*, Pescara, Italy.

IOS Press; Amsterdam, The Netherlands: pp. 447–51.

De Puky P. (1935) The physiological oscillation of the length of the body. *Acta Orthopaedica Scandanavica*; **6**: 338–47.

Dolan P., Kingma I., De Looze M. P., van Dieen J. H., Toussaint H. M., Baten C. T. M. and Adams M. A. (2001) An EMG technique for measuring spinal loading during asymmetric lifting. *Clinical Biomechanics*; **16** (S1): S17–S24.

Dolan K. J. and Green A. (2006) Lumbar spine reposition sense: the effect of a 'slouched' posture. *Manual Therapy*; **11** (3): 202–7.

D'Orazio B. (ed.) (1993) *Back Pain Rehabilitation*. Andover Medical Publications; Oxford.

Enciso R. Alexandroni E. S., Benyamein K., Keim R. A., Mah J. (2004) Precision, repeatability and validation of indirect 3-D anthropometric measurements with light-based imaging techniques *Biomedical Imaging: Nano to Macro. IEEE International Symposium*; **2**: 1119–22.

Eston R., Hawes M., Martin A. and Reilly T. and Eston R. G. (2009) Human Body Composition. In: (R. G. Eston and T. Reilly, eds.) *Kinanthropometry Laboratory Manual: Anthropometry*. Routledge; Oxon.

Eubanks J. D., Lee M. J., Cassinelli E. and Ahn N. U. (2007) Prevalence of lumbar facet arthrosis and its relationship to age, sex, and race: an anatomic study of cadaveric specimens. *Spine*; **32** (19): 2058–62.

Fedora C., Ashworth N., Marshall J. and Paull H. (2003) Reliability of the Visual Assessment of Cervical and Lumbar Lordosis: How Good Are We? *Spine*; **28** (16): 1857–9.

Fon G. T., Pitt M. J. and Thies A. C. (1980) Thoracic kyphosis, range in normal subjects. *American Journal of Roentgenology*; **124**: 979–83.

Gleeson N. P. (2009) Assessment of neuromuscular performance using electromyography. In: (R. G. Eston and T. Reilly, eds.) *Kinanthropometry Laboratory Manual: Exercise Physiology*. Routledge; Oxon.

Harrison D. E., Haas J. W., Cailliet R., Harrison D. D., Holland B. and Janik T. J. (2005) Concurrent validity of flexicurve instrument measurements: sagittal skin contour of the cervical spine compared with lateral cervical radiographic measurements. *Journal of Manipulative and Physiological Therapeutics*; **28** (8): 597–603.

Halioua M. and Liu H.-C. (1989) Optical three-dimensional sensing by phase measuring profilometry. *Optics and Lasers in Engineering*; **11**: 185–215.

Halioua M., Liu H.-C., Chin A. and Bowings T. S. (1990) Automated topography of the human form by phase-measuring profilometry and model analysis. In: (H. Neugerbauer and G. Windischbauer, eds) *Proceedings of the Fifth International Symposium on Surface Topography and Body Deformity*. Gustav Fischer Verlag; Stuttgart: pp. 91–100.

Hinz B. and Seidel H. (1989) On time relation between erector spinae muscle activity and force development during initial isometric stage of back lifts. *Clinical Biomechanics*; **4**: 5–10.

Hrdlicka A. (1972) *Practical Anthropometry*. (Reprint). AMS Press; New York.

Kado D., Christianson L., Palemo L., Smith-Bindman R., Cummings S. and Greendale G. A. (2006) Comparing a supine radiologic versus standing clinical measurement of kyphosis in older women: the fracture intervention trial. *Spine*; **31** (4): 463–7.

Kippers V. and Parker A. W. (1989) Validation of single-segment and three segment spinal models used to represent lumbar flexion. *Journal of Biomechanics*; **22**: 67–75.

Klausen K. (1965) The form and function of the loaded human spine. *Acta Physiologica Scandinavica*; **65**: 176–90.

Konrad P. (2008) The ABC of EMG: a practical introduction to kinesiological electromyography www.noraxon.com/emg/index.php3 (Accessed October 2007)

Korovessis P., Petsinis G., Papazisis Z. and Baikousis A. (2001) Prediction of thoracic kyphosis using the Debrunner kyphometer. *Journal of Spinal Disorders*; **14**: 67–72.

Korovessis P., Koureas G., Zacharatos S. and Papazisis Z (2005). Backpacks, back pain, sagittal spinal curves and trunk alignment in adolescents: a logistic and multinomial logistic analysis. *Spine*; **30** (2): 247–55.

Kouchi M., Mochimaru M., Tsuzuki K., and Yokoi T. (1996) Random errors in anthropometry. *Journal of Human Ergology (Tokyo)*; **25** (2): 155–66.

Lafond D., Descarreaux M., Normand M. C. and

Harrison D. E. (2007) Postural development in school children: a cross-sectional study. Chiropractic & Osteopathy, 15: 1 (Accessed June 2008)

Lee Y.-H. and Kuo C.-L (2000) Factor structure of trunk performance data for healthy subjects Clinical Biomechanics; 15: 221–7.

Leroux M., Zabjek K., Simard G., Badeaux J., Coillard C., and Rivard C. H. (2000) A noninvasive anthropometric technique for measuring kyphosis and lordosis: an application for idiopathic scoliosis. Spine; 25 (13): 1689–94.

McManus, I. C. (2002) Right Hand, Left Hand: The Origins of Asymmetry in Brains, Bodies, Atoms and Cultures. London/Cambridge: Harvard University Press/Cambridge, MA.

McNally D. S. and Adams M. A. (1992) Internal intervertebral disc mechanics as revealed by stress profilometry. Spine; 17: pp. 66–73.

MacRae J. F. and Wright V. (1969) Measurement of back movements. Annals of Rheumatic Diseases; 28: 584–9.

Marras W. S., Ferguson S.A., Gupta P., Bose S., Parnianpour M., Kim, J-Y. and Crowell R. (1999) The quantification of low back disorder using motion measures: methodology and validation. Spine; 24: 2091–100.

Mellin G. and Poussa M. (1992) Spinal mobility and posture in 8- to 16-year-old children. J Orthop Res; 10: 211–16.

Merolli A., Guidi P., Kozlowski J., Serra G., Aulisa L. and Tranquillileali P. (1999). Clinical trial of CPT (Complex Phase Tracing) profilometry in scoliosis. In: (I. A. F. Stokes, ed). Research into Spinal Deformities 2, IOS Press; Amsterdam, Netherlands: pp. 57–60.

Mitchelson D. L. (1988) Automated three-dimensional movement analysis using the CODA-3 system. Biomedical Technik; 33: 179–82.

Moreno L. A., Joyanes M., Mesana M. I., González-Gross M., Gil C. M., Sarr'a A., Gutierrez A., Garaulet M., Perez-Prieto R., Bueno M. and Marcos A. (2003) Harmonization of anthropometric measurements for a multi-center nutrition survey in Spanish adolescents. Nutrition; 19 (6): 481–6.

Mouton L. J., Hof A. L., de Jongh H. J. and Eisma W. H. (1991) Influence of posture on the relation between surfae electromyogram amplitude and back muscle moment: consequences for the use of surface electromyogram to measure back load. Clinical Biomechanics; 6: 245–51.

Nachemson A. and Morris J. M. (1964) In vivo measurements of intradiscal pressure. Journal of Bone and Joint Surgery; 46: 1077–81.

Paajanen H., Lehto I., Alanen A., Erkintalo M. and Komu M. (1994) Diurnal fluid changes of lumbar discs measured indirectly by magnetic resonance imaging. Journal of Orthopaedic Research; 12: 509–14.

Pal G. P. and Routal R. V. (1986) A study of weight transmission through the cervical and upper thoracic regions of the vertebral column in man. Journal of Anatomy; 148: 245–61.

Panjabi M., Yamamoto I., Oxland T. and Crisco J. (1989) How does posture affect coupling in the lumbar spine? Spine; 14: 1002–11.

Paquet N., Malouin F., Richards C. L., Dionne J. P. and Comeau F. (1991) Validity and reliability of a new electrogoniometer for the measurement of sagittal dorso-lumbar movements. Spine; 16: 516–19.

Pheasant S. (1986) Bodyspace: Anthropometry, Ergonomics and Design. Taylor and Francis; London.

Rae P. S., Waddell G. and Venner R. M. (1984) A simple technique for measuring lumbar spinal flexion. Journal of the Royal College of Surgeons of Edinburgh; 29: 281–4.

Reilly T., Tyrrell A. and Troup J. D. G. (1984) Circadian variation in human stature. Chronobiology International; 1: 121–6.

Reilly T., Boocock M. G., Garbutt G., Troup J. D. and Linge K. (1991) Changes in stature during exercise and sports training. Applied Ergonomics; 22; 308–11.

Roaf R. (1960) The basic anatomy of scoliosis. Journal of Bone and Joint Surgery; 488: 40–59.

Roaf R. (1977) Posture. Academic Press; London.

Roberts N., Hogg D., Whitehouse G. H. and Dangerfield, P. (1998). Quantitative analysis of diurnal variation in volume and water content of lumbar intervertebral discs. Clinical Anatomy; 11: 1–8.

Rogers M. M. and Cavanagh P. R. (1984) A glossary of biomechanical terms, concepts and units. Physical Therapy; 64: 1886–902.

Sarasate H. and Ostman A. (1986) Stereophotogrammetry in the evaluation of the treatment of scoliosis. International Orthopaedics; 10: 63–7.

Sato K., Kikuchi S., Yonezawa T. (1999) *In vivo* intradiscal pressure measurement in healthy individuals and in patients with ongoing back problems. *Spine*; 24 (23): 2468–74.

Seitz T., Balzulat J. and Bubb H. (2000) Anthropometry and measurement of posture and motion. *International Journal of Industrial Ergonomics*; 25 (4): 447–53.

Schwartz M. H., Trosta J. P. and Wervey R. A. (2004). Measurement and management of errors in quantitative gait data. *Gait and Posture*; 20 (2): 196–203.

Stokes I. A. F., Burwell R. G., Dangerfield P.H. (2006) Biomechanical spinal growth modulation and progressive adolescent scoliosis – a test of the 'vicious cycle' pathogenetic hypothesis: Summary of an electronic focus group debate of the IBSE Scoliosis; 1: 16.

Suzuki N., Yamaguchi Y. and Armstrong G. W. D. (1981) Measurement of posture using Moiré topography. In: (M. S. Moreland, M. H. Pope and G. W. D. Armstrong, eds) *Moiré Fringe Topography and Spinal Deformity*. Pergamon Press; New York: pp. 122–31.

Taylor J. R. and Twomey L. (1984) Sexual dimorphism in human vertebral body shape. *Journal of Anatomy*; 138: 281–6.

Tillotson K. M. and Burton A. K. (1991) Noninvasive measurement of lumbar sagittal mobility. An assessment of the flexicurve technique. *Spine*; 16: 29–33.

Ulijaszek S. J. and Lourie J. A. (1994) Intra- and inter-observer error in anthropometric measurement. In: (S. J. Ulijaszek and C. G. N. Mascie-Taylor, eds) *Anthropometry: The Individual and The Population*. Cambridge University Press; Cambridge: pp. 30–55.

Van Roy P. and Borms J. (2009) Flexibility. In: (R. G. Eston and T. Reilly, eds.) *Kinanthropometry Laboratory Manual: Anthropometry*. Routledge; Oxon.

Vinas F. C. (2006) Lumbosacral Spine Acute Bony Injuries *WebMD eMedicine* http://www.emedicine.com/sports/topic67.htm (Accessed October 2007)

Violas P., Estivalezes E., Briot J., Gauzy J. S. and Swider P. (2007) Objective quantification of intervertebral disc volume properties using MRI in idiopathic scoliosis surgery. *Mag Reson Imag*; 25: 386–91.

Vogelbach S. K. (1990) *Functional Kinetics*. Springer Verlag; Stuttgart.

Wang M. JJ. Wu W. Y., Lin K. C., Yang S. N. and Lu J.M. (2007) Automated anthropometric data collection from three-dimensional digital human models. *The International Journal of Advanced Manufacturing Technology*; 32: 1–2, 109–115.

Weiner J. S. (1982) The measurement of human workload. *Ergonomics*; 25: 953–66.

Weiner J. S. and Lourie J. A. (1969) Anthropometry. In: *Human Biology: A Guide to Field Methods*. International Biological Programme Handbook no 9. Blackwell Scientific Publications; Oxford: pp. 3–42.

Whitcombe K. K., Shapiro L. J., Lieberman D. E. (2007) Fetal load and the evolution of lumbar lordosis in bipedal hominins. *Nature*; 450: 1075–8.

White A. A. and Panjabi M. M. (1990). *Clinical Biomechanics of the Spine*. (2nd Edition) Lippincott– Raven; Philadelphia, PA.

Willner S. (1979) Moiré topography for the diagnosis and documentation of scoliosis. *Acta Orthopaedica Scandinavica*; 50: 295–302.

Willner S. and Johnson B. (1983) Thoracic kyphosis and lumbar lordosis during the growth period in children. *Acta Pediatrica Scandinavica*; 72: 873–8.

Wilmore H. Stanforth P. R., Domenick M. A., Gagnon J., Daw E. W., Leon A. S., Rao D. C., Skinner J. S. and Bouchard C. (1997). Reproducibility of anthropometric and body composition measurements: the HERITAGE Family Study. *International Journal of Obesity*; 21: 297–303.

Wing P., Tsang L., Gagnon F., Susak L. and Gagnon R. (1992) Diurnal changes in the profile, shape and range of motion of the back. *Spine*; 17: 761–5.

CHAPTER 5

FLEXIBILITY

Peter Van Roy and Jan Borms

5.1 AIMS

The aims of this chapter are to:

- gain insight into the complexity of goniometric measurements of flexibility;
- gain insight into the need for test standardization;
- become acquainted with new measurement instruments, in particular goniometers;
- learn to mark certain anthropometric reference points;
- learn how to take several goniometric measurements of flexibility at both sides of the body;
- know how to interpret, compare and evaluate the results of goniometric measurements of flexibility;
- situate goniometry in a larger field of joint kinematics.

5.2 INTRODUCTION AND HISTORICAL OVERVIEW

5.2.1 Introduction

Flexibility may be defined as the range of motion (ROM) at a single joint (e.g. the hip joint) or a series of joints (e.g. the cervical spine). The ROM reflects the kinematic possibilities of the joint(s) considered, which – in normal healthy conditions – depend on:

- the degrees of freedom allowed by the architecture of the articular surfaces;
- the steering action of the capsuloligamentous system;
- the interaction between adjacent synovial joints and other types of bony junctions;
- the ability of muscles and connective tissue surrounding the joint(s) to be elongated within their structural limitations.

Whereas in engineering, the term 'flexibility' refers to deformation characteristics of (bio)materials resulting from external loading, in kinanthropometry, 'flexibility' basically refers to the ability of being supple, and generally focuses on the range of motion of a particular joint or joint unit. However, reaching a particular range of motion is dependent not only on the degrees of freedom provided by synovial joints, but also the mechanical properties of a number of involved tissues. Spinal motion is determined not only by the architecture of the facet joints and the directly involved capsuloligamentous system, but also by the properties of the adjacent intervertebral discs, representing cartilaginous joints of the symphysis type, and by the long ligaments, representing fibrous junctions of the syndesmosis type between the vertebrae. In the spine, synovial joints, symphyses and syndesmoses are arranged in parallel within one single motion segment while acting in a serial arrangement throughout the entire spinal region. In this way, muscular action continuously trims the complex osteofibrous tunnels of the central spinal canal and the intervertebral foramina, allowing for movement and deformation of the spine, without loss of the main configuration of these neurovascular tunnels (Van Roy *et al.* 2000). Thus, range of motion is often provided by the interaction of several joints or junctions. On the other hand, the limits of motion in a particular joint or joint unit are determined by the mechanical properties of a number of surrounding tissues.

Measurements of flexibility are widely used in medicine, sports and physical fitness. In the clinical practice, the improvement of the patient's flexibility is followed up by simple goniometric readings. Besides anthropometric databases, normative data concerning ROM also provide useful information for ergonomic design processes and improving the work area (Hsiao and Keyserling 1990).

5.2.2 Kinanthropometric background: flexibility as a component of physical fitness

There is little doubt that good flexibility is needed particularly in sports where maximum amplitude of movement is required for an optimal execution of technique. Testing this component has therefore been common practice in training situations as a means of evaluating progress in physical conditioning and of identifying problem areas associated with poor performance or possible injury (e.g. Cureton 1941). Ever since this quality has been considered as a component of physical

fitness, a test to express and evaluate it has been included in physical fitness test batteries (e.g. Larson 1974; AAHPERD 1984). These so-called field tests have been widely used to measure flexibility, specifically in trunk, hip and back flexion, such as Scott and French's (1950) Bobbing Test, Kraus and Hirschland's (1954) Floor Touch Test and the Sit-and-Reach Test of Wells and Dillon (1952). The latter test has been used worldwide in practice and is incorporated in the Eurofit test battery for European member states (Council of Europe, 1988).

In the 'sit-and-reach test,' the individual sits on the floor with the legs extended forward and feet pressed flat against a box that supports the measuring device. With the back of the knees pressed flat against the floor, the individual leans forward and extends the fingertips as far as possible. The distance reached is recorded and serves as an assessment of either the subject's flexibility at the hips, back muscle or hamstrings, or of the subject's general flexibility. It remains questionable which joints and muscles are being assessed because of the complexity of the movement. The test is used so widely perhaps because the bending movement is so popular as a synonym for being supple and probably because many health problems associated with poor flexibility are related to the lower back.

In spite of the popularity the test enjoys, its simple instructions, its low cost, its high reproducibility, its high loading on the flexibility factor in factor analysis studies, the test has been subjected to criticism, as were other tests where linear instead of angular measurements were applied. The individual with long arms and short legs will tend to be advantaged compared with an individual who shows the opposite anthropometric characteristics (Broer and Galles 1958; Borms 1984). Because the question of bias persisted for some individual extreme proportional arm/leg length differences, Hopkins and Hoeger (1986) proposed the modified sit-and-reach test to negate the effects of shoulder girdle mobility and proportional differences between arms and leg.

Another criticism relates to the specificity of the test, which purports to assess the individual's general flexibility, whereas it is now generally considered as a specific trait. In non-performance oriented testing, however, the indirect methods involving linear measurements can be suitable approximations of flexibility.

5.2.3 Historical background of clinical goniometry

(a) History of the development of equipment

The term 'goniometry' means 'measurement of angles.' In a clinical context, *protractor goniometers* were first introduced in the Grand Palais Hospital in Paris by Camus and Amar in 1915 (Fox 1917). Medical care of a large number of wounded limbs during the First World War called for a simple technique to evaluate the range of motion of injured joints. The first clinical goniometer for the knee joint provided armour-like cases for thigh and shin, with a protractor scale around the axis of the goniometer.

In that time the use of protractor charts, held along the considered joint, represented an alternative solution for evaluating the range of motion. Protractor charts were first described by Cleveland (1918) and later on by Clark (1920), Looser (1934) and Schlaaff (1937, 1938). Schlaaff called for standardization in measuring the range of motion by means of protractor charts. A year before, Cave and Roberts (1936) published a standardization proposal for the determination of the range of motion by means of protractor goniometers.

In the following decades, protractor goniometers became more popular than protractor charts and several types of metal protractor goniometers were designed. Plexiglas and plastic protractor goniometers became available in the second half of the twentieth century. With three different graduation scales and a precision of 1 degree, the international standard goniometer (Russe *et al.* 1972) was prepared for applying the standardization proposed by the American Academy of Orthopaedic surgeons (cfr. infra).

Many modified protractor goniometers were developed for particular joints or particular measuring conditions. An encyclopedic overview would be out of the scope of the present chapter.

Inclinometers represent another category of simple goniometric measuring tools. The range of inclination obtained by the goniometer, following the range of motion of a particular movement, is compared with an initial zero value, determined by the gravity vector. This category includes pendulum goniometers and hydrogoniometers (cfr. infra). According to Fox and van Bremen (1937), the first *pendulum goniometer* was developed by Falconer in 1918, later followed by other types developed by Hand (1938), Brown and Stevenson (1953), Leighton (1955, 1966), von Richter (1974), Zinovieff and Harborow (1975) and Labrique (1977). In particular, the Leigthon-flexometer received attention in kinanthropometric research. The principles of a traditional protractor goniometer and a pendulum goniometer were combined in the Labrique goniometer. Some pendulum goniometers were designed for particular movements or particular joint units. Claeys and Gomes (1968) presented a pendulum goniometer to evaluate inclination differences of the sacrum. Combining two pendulum goniometers and a compass needle-based inclinometer, the C-Rom is a popular contemporary instrument for the evaluation of cervical spine motion (Tousignant *et al.* 2000, 2006). The combination between an anthropometer and an inclinometer was realized in the Monus-goniometer.

Measuring an angle with respect of the gravity vector is also used in *hydrogoniometers*, based on the principle that the gravity force keeps the level of a liquid in a container horizontally, independently from the inclination of that container. To our knowledge, the first hydrogoniometers were presented by Buck *et al.* (1959) and by Schenker (1961, cit. in Moore, 1965). Later versions were presented by Loebl (1967) and Rippstein (1977). The first generation of hydrogoniometers could be characterized as air bubble hydrogoniometers, because of the use of an air bubble as a reference, such as in a level. In the 1980s, Ellis (1984) designed a hydrogoniometer with a half-filled circular liquid container, in which the inclination of the goniometer changes the position of the liquid meniscus with respect to the graduation scale, which has to be zeroed before starting the measuring procedure (Figure 5.2).

Karpovich and Karpovich (1959) introduced the *electrogoniometer*. The first types of electrogoniometers were potentiometric. One arm of the goniometer is attached to the body of a linear potentiometer, and the second arm is attached to its axis. Moving the latter arm relative to the other varies the resistance of the potentiometer. According to Ohm's law, this proportionally modifies the current intensity in the electric circuit to which the potentiometer is integrated. Following a calibration procedure, moving the arms of the electrogoniometer can be used for goniometric recordings. Initially, the electrogoniometer output was displayed on an oscilloscope or recorded by means of a plotter. Several prototypes were fundamentally used for clinically oriented research. Nowadays, several computerized systems are commercially available. Beside potentiometric goniometers or strain gauge electrogoniometers or flexible electrogoniometeres are also currently in use. In these the comparison between current intensity changes in two electric circuits provides the goniometric results. This system also requires calibration.

Other two-dimensional clinical goniometric measurements include the determination of joint angles from arthrographs, photographs and radiographic images (Kottke and Mundale 1959; Wright and Johns 1960, Backer and Kofoed 1989).

(b) Standardization efforts

Unfortunately, for a long time, the area of flexibility measurement has been characterized by confusion in terminology and lack of standardization (e.g. units, warming-up or not, starting position, active or passive motion, detailed description of procedures). Articles and handbooks about clinical goniometry, issued in the middle of the twentieth century, often revealed contradictory guidelines, clearly illustrating the lack of standardization in clinical goniometry. Depending on the manual, the maximally abducted arm, the arm hanging alongside the trunk or the anatomical position could be considered being the zero position in measuring abduction-elevation. Moore (1949) attacked this confusion. An important initiative to standardize goniometric techniques was presented by the American Academy of Orthopaedic Surgeons (1965), proposing a generalized use of the 'Neutral Zero Method' of Cave and Roberts (1936). The ROM is measured with respect to a specific reference position, which for every joint is defined as the *zero starting position*. Thus, the range of motion may not be confused with the angle, obtained between the bony segments at the end of motion. An increasing ROM is always characterized by increasing angular values.

Instead of the anatomical position, an upright position with the feet together and the arms hanging alongside the body with the thumbs forwards, serves as the reference position for goniometric measurements. The results obtained are compared with results at the opposite side, when possible; if not, they are compared with provided normative data.

Distinction is made between extension and hyperextension: the term 'extension' is used for anteroposterior angular movement, as long as the normal anatomy of the joint allows a distinct extension range, starting from the neutral zero position, for example, extension at the glenohumeral joint. However, when an extension from the neutral zero position represents the exception rather than the norm, the term 'hyperextension' is used. Typical examples are hyperextension in the elbow and knee joints.

The standardization proposed by the American Academy of Orthopaedic Surgeons largely received dissemination during the 1970s and is nowadays generally accepted on a world-wide basis. In 1979, the neutral zero method was subjected to a critical evaluation at the occasion of an international conference, initiated by the Evaluation and Research Advisory Committee of the British Association for Rheumatology and Rehabilitation. In 1982, an entire issue of *Clinics in Rheumatic Diseases* focused on the reliability, objectivity and validity of clinical goniometry (Wright, 1982). In summary, high reliability and objectivity scores were repeatedly reported, provided the goniometric measurements were taken in a standardized way. However, critical remarks were expressed concerning the content validity of clinical goniometry, and the demand for more normative data was put forward.

5.3 THEORY AND APPLICATION OF CLINICAL GONIOMETRY

5.3.1 Measurement instruments

Numerous research reports are illustrative of the wide range of measuring equipment that can be adopted for the study of joint movement, differing from simple two-dimensional measuring tools to several computerized systems for three-dimensional motion analysis.

The success of simple angular (two-dimensional goniometry) tests for evaluating flexibility is given by the combination of simplicity, low cost and standardization.

The *protractor goniometer* (Figure 5.1) is a simple but useful device consisting of two articulating arms, one of which contains a protractor made of plexiglas or metal, constructed around the fulcrum of the apparatus, around which the second arm rotates. The arm with the protractor scale is

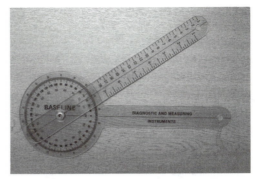

Figure 5.1 A protractor goniometer.

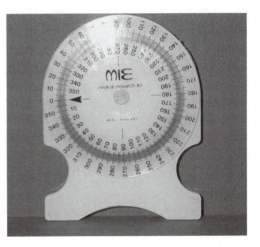

Figure 5.2 The MIE Hygrometer.

named the stationary arm; the second arm is called the moving arm.

The *inclinometer* is based on the principle that a joint movement is recorded as an angular change against the vector of the gravity force: this is the case in hydrogoniometers and pendulum goniometers.

In *hydrogoniometers*, angular values are recorded by moving a bubble of air or a fluid level relative to an initial zero position, using the fact that the bubble will always seek the highest position within a small fluid container, or using the principle that a fluid level will always tend to remain in a horizontal position (Figure 5.2).

The *pendulum goniometer* uses the effect of the force of gravity on the pointer (needle) of the goniometer, which is positioned in the centre of a protractor scale. The *Leighton Flexometer* (Leighton, 1966) contains a rotating circular dial marked off in degrees and a pointer counterbalanced to ensure it always points vertically. It is strapped on the appropriate body segment and the range of motion is determined relative to the perpendicular. The length of limbs or segment does not influence this assessment; neither is the axis of the bone lever a disturbing factor. On the other hand, special attention should be given to avoid bias due to compensatory movements (e.g. compensatory shoulder extension in elbow flexion).

In the *potentiometric electrogoniometer* the protractor has been replaced by a potentiometer; movement of the goniometer arm, attached to the axis of the potentiometer proportionally changes the resistance of the potentiometer, and, according to Ohm's law, also the current intensity in the electric circuit in which it is incorporated. Following calibration of the system, increasing movement of the electrogoniometer arms allows for the recording of an increasing range of motion. This measuring system has been adopted in many configurations, from simple two-dimensional applications to computerized triaxial electrogoniometers and spatial linkages allowing registrations up to six degrees of freedom.

The *strain gauge electrogoniometer* or *flexible goniometer* represents a valuable and easily applicable contemporary computerized alternative to the potentiometric electrogoniometer (Nicol 1987; Tesio *et al.* 1995). The intensity of the current in two electric circuits changes proportionally to the degree of movement. This system also requires calibration.

The success of these simple angular (two-dimensional goniometry) tests for evaluating flexibility results from the combination of simplicity, low cost and standardization. With this form, goniometry is constrained within a mechanistic approach where the articulating surfaces are seen as 'solids of revolution', rotating around a fixed axis that coincides with the axis of the goniometer.

5.3.2 Mechanistic approach versus functional anatomical realism

In anatomical books, the articular surfaces are often compared with 'solids of revolution', resulting in expressions like 'hinge joint', 'pivot joint', 'saddle joint', 'ellipsoid joint' or 'ball and socket joint.' Herein, every type is associated with a number of degrees of freedom. This mechanistic description evokes the idea that the articular surfaces resemble regular solids of revolution, moving around fixed joint axes. However, articular surfaces very often have particular characteristics, calling for a more detailed description. Although the humero-ulnar joint is very often characterized as a hinge joint, the trochlea humeri is not a perfect cylinder because the groove of the humeral trochlea has a functional role in elbow flexion and extension and leads to the typology of a 'modified hinge joint.' Radii of curvature may vary substantially depending on the considered part of the articular surfaces. Remarkable differences in radii of curvatures are found in different parts of the femoral condyles. Moreover the degree of congruence between the articular surfaces may substantially change during joint motion. Motion capacities depend not only on the architecture of the articular surfaces, but also on capsular and ligamentous steering and muscular control. The (maximally) close packed position represents the locked position of a joint and is characterized by maximal congruence between the articular surfaces and maximal tension in the capsuloligamentous system. This is in contrast with loose-packed positions, characterized by less congruence and less tension in the capsuloligamentous system.

Placement of the goniometer axis along the so-called fixed movement axis of the joint, as often described in manuals of goniometry, has been encouraged by the mechanistic approach, comparing articular surfaces with solids of revolution. A more realistic functional anatomical approach recognizes the presence of different radii of curvature in articular surfaces, as well as different degrees of articular congruence and tension of the capsuloligamentous system. This explains why, in two-dimensional motion analysis, centrodes (polodes) appear instead of one fixed centre of rotation.

5.3.3 Two-dimensional goniometry versus three-dimensional joint kinematics

Several joints reveal three-dimensional (3-D) motion characteristics. For example, the end range of knee extension is characterized by the screw home movement, bringing the joint in its close-packed position. Axial rotation and lateral bending of the spine reveal reciprocal coupling.

Dorsiflexion and plantarflexion of the ankle introduce small tibiofibular three-dimensional movement components (Lundberg 1989).

Depending on the nature of movements, two-dimensional or three-dimensional analysis is appropriate. Depending on the required level of accuracy and precision, several three-dimensional motion analysis systems may be adopted for *in vivo* registration of human joint movements. A number of these are commercially available and allow real-time recordings, such as computerized electro-goniometers, electromagnetic tracking devices and ultra-sound-based tracking devices. Depending on the time required for digitizing and analysis, several opto-electronic systems (e.g. video-based systems) can be used for research goals or for clinical evaluations. Cappozzo and colleagues (Cappozzo *et al.* 1995, 1996 and 2005; Chiari *et al.* 2005; Della Croce *et al.* 2005; Leardini *et al.* 2005) reported substantial efforts to improve the methodology of working with clusters of markers or landmarks when using opto-electronic systems. With modern medical imaging techniques, three-dimensional characteristics can be derived from the changes in orientation and position of helical joint axes, simultaneously with the analysis of contact area analysis displacements (Baeyens *et al.* 2001).

In performance-oriented investigations of flexibility (sports, dance), complex three-dimensional motion patterns are often analyzed in a broad field of view. Velocity, acceleration, coordination and muscle function may be important parameters. In clinically oriented investigations of flexibility, however, joint kinematics are more focused on diagnostic purposes and on treatment of impairments, reduction of disabilities and increase in the patient's participation. Gross motion of body segments (main motion) and particular intra-articular movement mechanisms such as 'coupled motion' in the spine, and 'locking and unlocking mechanisms' in the joints of the extremities are important issues in orthopaedics and rehabilitation. The field of view is rather reduced and particular attention may be given to joint-related features of intra-articular motion. The development of equipment and methodology for three-dimensional motion analysis has led to a remarkable evolution during the last decades (Allard *et al.* 1995, Cappozzo *et al.* 1995, Cappozzo *et al.* 1996; Bull and Amis 1998).

Standardization proposals concerning different aspects of three-dimensional methodology (reference frames, bony landmarks, Euler rotation sequences) reflect the need for communication and exchange about three-dimensional outcomes in a multidisciplinary context (Grood and Suntay 1983; Benedetti *et al.* 1994; Cappozzo and Della Croce 1994; Wu *et al.* 2002, 2005). Different aims and circumstances of investigation, but also time and cost factors indicate the choice of an appropriate measuring tool, varying from a simple measuring device providing real-time readings in the daily practice to a more complicated experimental set-up, for expert use or research purposes.

Broadening the field of application of three-dimensional joint kinematics will call for new developments, meeting the particular needs of different disciplines. Bringing three-dimensional movement analysis closer to the daily practice of health science workers and sports medicine requires a willingness to learn and to accept some biomechanical principles and expressions with regard to the methodology of joint motion. The possibilities and accuracies obtained in industrial robotics continue to contrast with those of the three-dimensional motion capture of human joints.

5.3.4 The effect of temperature and warm-up on flexibility

Although Wright (1973) demonstrated that stiffness increases with decreased temperature and vice-versa, and thus found a means of explaining the circadian variation in joint stiffness with lowest levels in the morning and late evening, others (Grobaker and Stull 1975 and Lakie *et al.* 1979) could not entirely confirm these findings. Research tends to indicate positive effects of warm-up (Skubic and Hodgkins 1957; Atha and Wheatly 1976). Most coaches and athletes believe that warm-up is essential to prevent injuries, but there is very little direct research evidence to support their beliefs. Even though the scientific basis for recommending warm-up exercises is not conclusive, we advise a general warm-up prior to the main activity and prior to flexibility testing. A 5- to 10-minute moderate intensity warm-up is suggested before testing, but should be standardized.

5.4 LABORATORY SESSIONS: FLEXIBILITY MEASUREMENTS WITH GONIOMETRY

5.4.1 Definitions

(a) Goniometry

From a clinical point of view goniometry can be described as a technique for measuring human joint flexibility by expressing in degrees the range of motion, according to a given degree of freedom. Traditionally, degrees of freedom are assigned in relation to an anatomical reference frame. Hence, functional anatomical terminology is used to label different movement, such as flexion and extension, abduction and adduction, medial and lateral rotation (internal and external rotation). Clinical goniometry in most cases is restricted to the angular changes of peripheral pathways of limb segments, measured in a two-dimensional way. Although goniometry emphasizes relative angular changes between bony or body segments in joint motion, it should be mentioned that small amounts of translation occur simultaneously, and therefore are an essential part of the arthro-kinematic mechanisms.

(b) Goniometers

A goniometer measures the angle between two bony segments. When maximal amplitude of a movement is reached, this maximal amplitude is then read and recorded. Figure 5.1 shows the *international standard goniometer*.

The *Labrique goniometer* (1977) is a pendulum goniometer with a needle, constructed within the protractor and which maintains a vertical direction under the influence of gravity. This needle permits a rapid evaluation of the ROM of a joint, in relation to the vertical, or the horizontal if the scale on the reverse side of the apparatus is used. The pendulum principle is also used in the previously cited (5.2 a) Monus goniometer (Figure 5.3).

The *VUB-goniometer* was developed at the Vrije Universiteit Brussel (VUB) (Van Roy *et al.* 1985) and was applied in several projects to study the optimal duration of static stretching exercises (Borms *et al.*, 1987) and the maintenance of coxo-femoral flexibility (Van Roy *et al.* 1987). This goniometer differs from traditional protractor goniometers in that the graduation scale, the goniometer's fulcrum and the moving arm are mounted on a carriage, which slides along the stationary arm of the goniometer (Figure 5.4). This construction allows an easy orientation

Figure 5.3 The Monus goniometer.

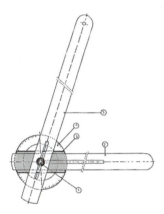

Figure 5.4 The VUB-goniometer. Patent no 899964 (Belgium)
1. Fulcrum
2. Stationary arm
3. Sliding carriage
4. Protractor scale
5. Moving arm.

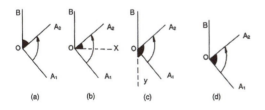

Figure 5.5 Four different ways to evaluate the angle in a joint (after Rocher and Rigaud 1964)
(a) true angle;
(b) complementary angle;
(c) supplementary angle;
(d) ROM.

of the transparent 55 cm-long arms of the goniometer along the longitudinal axes of the body segments. Joint range can then be measured without centreing the fulcrum of the goniometer of the joint axis, because considering fixed joint axes as reference points introduces systematic errors in goniometry (Van Roy 1981).

(c) Possible interpretations of a range of motion

In Figure 5.5 OA always represents the segment which moves from point 1 to point 2 over an angle of 50°. As OA rotates around a point O, it changes the angular position in relation to OB, the stationary segment. This motion over an angle of 50° can be measured in four different ways (after Rocher and Rigaud 1964):

1. The *true angle* between the skeletal segments in the end position of the motion: angle BOA_2 ($BOA_2 = BOA_1 - 50°$) (Figure 5.5a).
2. The *complementary angle* A_2OX (Figure 5.5b).
3. The *supplementary angle* A_2OY (Figure 5.5c).
4. The range of motion angle A_2OA_1 (Figure 5.5d).

From the above, it is clear that confusion can arise in the interpretation of the measurements obtained. If the measurement of the ROM is of interest, then it should also be specified from which reference point the range of motion has been measured. An important attempt to standardize goniometric techniques has been worked out by the American Academy of Orthopaedic Surgeons (1965). The standardization generalizes the 'Neutral Zero Method' of Cave and Roberts (1936). In this, the ROM is measured from a specific reference position, which for every joint is defined as the *zero starting position*. In this international convention, increasing ROM is always characterized by increasing angular values (which is not obvious in all manuals on goniometry). Moreover, rather than the anatomical position, an upright position with feet together, arms hanging alongside the body with thumbs forwards, is the basis of a reference position for measurement.

(d) Measurement without positioning of the goniometer's axis relative to the joint's axis

From the knowledge that motion does not occur around fixed axes, it is clear that attempts to let the goniometer's axis coincide with the centre of rotation or the axis of motion, generate a systematic measurement error (Van Roy, 1981). To overcome this problem, the choice of two bony reference points per segment is recommended to ensure good coincidence of the goniometer arms with the longitudinal axes of the considered bony segments. If available, the use of a modified protractor goniometer with a sliding carriage can be helpful in overcoming systematic errors caused by faulty placements of the goniometer axis.

5.4.2 General guidelines for goniometry

(a) Knowledge of anatomy of the musculoskeletal system

Measurements have to be carried out on the naked skin, whereby the examiner palpates two specific anthropometric reference points for each segment. These 'landmarks' can shift considerably under the skin as motion occurs. Therefore, all reference points should be marked in the end position of the segment. Realizing that real joint motion includes several angular components and small components of translation relative to different degrees of freedom, it is clear that two-dimensional goniometry is only a two-dimensional criterion to estimate the real flexibility, which in fact occurs three-dimensionally (Van Roy, 1981). Although the reliability and the objectivity of two-dimensional goniometry in standardized situations can be very high, the content validity very often remains restricted.

(b) Knowledge of internal factors influencing flexibility

Based on kinesiological knowledge and insights, understanding is required of the compensation movements which are to be expected in joints situated proximally and distally to the joint to be measured. It is therefore important that the starting position is described precisely and that compensatory movements are controlled. For example, lateral bending of the spine can compensate for lack of arm abduction. On the other hand, a particular degree of hip abduction should theoretically represent pure coxofemoral abduction, but in most cases hip abduction results from a combination of pure coxofemoral abduction and lateral version of the pelvis.

One should differentiate between *osteokinematic* and *arthrokinematic* readings of flexibility; the former being an expression of angular changes of a bony segment in space in relation to the anatomical reference system; the latter being an expression of angular changes between articulating bony segments. Although efforts can be made to perform arthrokinematic readings, one has to recognize that many goniometric readings reflect osteokinematic aspects of flexibility. Thus, if the inclination of the upper arm is measured relative to the trunk, the obtained goniometric result does not reflect the ROM realized between the humerus and glenoid cavity. Even when efforts are made to reduce compensatory movement, measuring arm movements relative to the trunk causes abstractions, due to the upward rotation of the scapula as a result of simultaneous motion in the shoulder girdle and the spine. If plantar flexion is measured at the ankle joint, using reference points at the fibula and at the fifth metatarsal bone, the goniometric reading reflects an angular value between shin and foot, but not between the tibiofibular mortise and the talar bone (Backer and Kofoed 1989). It is also very important to determine if the motion had been carried out actively or passively. A key factor is the type of warm-up used.

(c) Knowledge of external factors influencing flexibility

Some external factors influencing flexibility are temperature, exercise, gender, age, race, professional flexibility needs, sports flexibility needs and pathology.

(d) Scientific rigour and precision in the choice and use of the goniometer

The following recommendations are made:

1   The goniometer needs to have long arms sufficient to cover two reference points.
2   The goniometer needs to have a protractor with a precision of one degree.
3   Esch and Lepley (1974) have pointed out the danger of creating parallax errors; therefore readings should be made at eye level.
4   The presence of a thin indicator line on the goniometer's arms can be helpful for increasing the goniometer's precision.
5   No loose articulation in the goniometer should be allowed.
6   Readings should be made prior to removing the goniometer from the segments.
7   The measurements should be recorded with three figures. If a recorder assists the examiner, the values should be dictated by the examiner as, for example, 1-5-3 rather than 153. This should then be repeated and recorded on a proforma by the recorder.
8   The proforma (Figure 5.7) should contain personal details of the subject being measured (e.g. age, gender, profession, sport activities, daily habitual activity) as well as technical information regarding the measurements (starting position, room temperature).

(e) Replication of measurements and the interpretation of results

From experience, we know that data from a very large number of consecutive measurements are normally distributed around a value, which very likely approaches the true amplitude. Thus, a difference of, for example, 5° from a later measurement is not necessarily an increase in amplitude, but rather the result of a summation of small systematic errors and the absolute measurement error. Therefore, it is strongly recommended to perform triple measurements with the median or the average of the two closest results as central value to be compared with the median or the average of earlier (or later) obtained results.

The interpretation of results can be done in different ways: pre-test and post-test comparisons (athletic season, before and after treatment and so on), carry-over effect, left-right comparisons and finally comparison with norms. The latter is difficult, as few normative data exist for 'normal' populations (per age and gender) or for athletic groups. 'Normal' ROMs for athletes from different sports are not so well documented in the literature.

Tables 5.1 and 5.2 give norms based on the measurements described in this chapter for a population of over 100 physical education and physiotherapy students, male and female (as separate groups). They were all tested in the period 1984–90. A typical proforma, used by us, is displayed in Figure 5.6.

5.4.3 The measurements

Considering the limitation of space in this book, only a selection of possible measurements is presented in the following pages.

(a) Shoulder flexion

- The international protractor goniometer or the VUB-goniometer is recommended.
- The subject lies supine on a table, legs bent, thorax fixed on the table with velcro straps. The subject executes a bilateral shoulder flexion in a pure sagittal plane, hand palms turned towards each other, elbows extended (Figure 5.7).
- Landmarks are made at the middle of the lateral side of the upper arm at the level of the deltoid tuberosity and of the lateral epicondyle of the humerus.
- The stationary arm of the goniometer

PROFORMA FOR GONIOMETRIC MEASUREMENTS

01. Subject   ....
                       (Last name)   (First name)

02. Identity   Gender F=2   M=1   □
03. Date of observations   year □ □   mo □ □   day □ □   □ □ □ □
04. Date of birth   year □ □   mo □ □   day □ □   □ □ □ □
05. Room t°   □ □ □

---

06. Body Mass (kg)   □ □ □ □
07. Stature (stretched/cm)   □ □ □ □   □ □ □ □   □ □ □ □   □ □ □ □

---

08. Shoulder flexion	□ □ □	□ □ □	□ □ □	□ □ □
09. Shoulder extension	□ □ □	□ □ □	□ □ □	□ □ □
10. Shoulder lateral rotation	□ □ □	□ □ □	□ □ □	□ □ □
11. Shoulder medial rotation	□ □ □	□ □ □	□ □ □	□ □ □
12. Shoulder abduction	□ □ □	□ □ □	□ □ □	□ □ □
13. Shoulder horizontal adduction	□ □ □	□ □ □	□ □ □	□ □ □
14. Elbow flexion	□ □ □	□ □ □	□ □ □	□ □ □
15. Elbow extension	□ □ □	□ □ □	□ □ □	□ □ □
16. Forearm pronation	□ □ □	□ □ □	□ □ □	□ □ □
17. Forearm supination	□ □ □	□ □ □	□ □ □	□ □ □
18. Wrist flexion	□ □ □	□ □ □	□ □ □	□ □ □
19. Wrist extension	□ □ □	□ □ □	□ □ □	□ □ □
20. Wrist radial deviation	□ □ □	□ □ □	□ □ □	□ □ □
21. Wrist ulnar deviation	□ □ □	□ □ □	□ □ □	□ □ □
22. Hip flexion (bent leg)	□ □ □	□ □ □	□ □ □	□ □ □
23. Hip flexion (straight leg)	□ □ □	□ □ □	□ □ □	□ □ □
24. Hip extension	□ □ □	□ □ □	□ □ □	□ □ □
25. Hip abduction	□ □ □	□ □ □	□ □ □	□ □ □
26. Hip adduction	□ □ □	□ □ □	□ □ □	□ □ □
27. Hip medial rotation	□ □ □	□ □ □	□ □ □	□ □ □
28. Hip lateral rotation	□ □ □	□ □ □	□ □ □	□ □ □
29. Knee flexion	□ □ □	□ □ □	□ □ □	□ □ □
30. Knee extension	□ □ □	□ □ □	□ □ □	□ □ □
31. Knee medial rotation	□ □ □	□ □ □	□ □ □	□ □ □
32. Knee lateral rotation	□ □ □	□ □ □	□ □ □	□ □ □
33. Ankle dorsiflexion	□ □ □	□ □ □	□ □ □	□ □ □
34. Ankle plantar flexion	□ □ □	□ □ □	□ □ □	□ □ □

WARM-UP: YES □   NO □
IF YES: HOW LONG, WHAT KIND ?

....
....

SPORT:
....

DAILY PHYSICAL ACTIVITY:
....

BODY TYPE:
....

INJURIES:
....

TESTING: Passive □   Active □

Figure 5.6 Proforma for Goniometric measurements.

is positioned along the thorax parallel to the board of the table, while the moving arm is in line with the longitudinal axis of the upper arm, oriented on both landmarks.

- The result reflects an osteokinematic measurement of flexibility. An arthrokinematic reading requires the determination of angular motion between scapula and humerus.

(b) Shoulder extension

- We recommend the international protractor goniometer or the VUB-goniometer.
- The subject lies prone on a table, head in neutral position (if possible), small pillow under abdomen to avoid hyperlordosis. A bilateral shoulder extension is executed in a sagittal plane, elbows extended, hand palms in the prolongation of the forearms turned towards each other (Figure 5.8).
- The landmarks are: the middle of the lateral side of the upper arm at the level of the deltoid tuberosity and the lateral epicondyle of the humerus.
- The stationary arm of the goniometer is positioned along the thorax parallel to the board of the table and the moving arm is in line with the longitudinal axis of the upper arm, oriented on both landmarks.

(c) Shoulder lateral (external) rotation

- We recommend the Labrique goniometer and the use of its blue scale.
- The subject lies prone on a table, shoulder in 90° abduction, elbow flexed 90°, wrist in neutral position (hand in prolongation of forearm, palm towards end of table, thumb directed towards the medial axis of the body), upper arm resting on table, elbow free. The subject performs a maximal lateral rotation, fixing humerus in the same abduction angle on the table, shoulder in contact with table, head in neutral position (if possible) (Figure 5.9).
- The landmarks are the tip of the olecranon

Figure 5.7 Measurement of shoulder flexion.

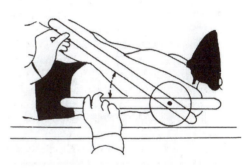

Figure 5.8 Measurement of shoulder extension.

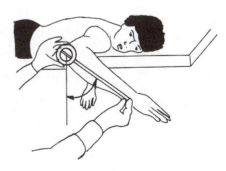

Figure 5.9 Measurement of shoulder lateral (external) rotation.

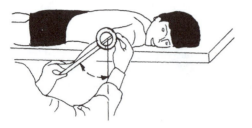

Figure 5.10 Measurement of shoulder medial (internal) rotation.

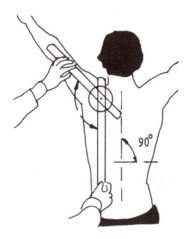

Figure 5.11 Measurement of shoulder abduction.

and the tip of the ulnar styloid process (this side is facing end of table).
- The goniometer is positioned in line with the longitudinal axis of the forearm, oriented on both landmarks.

(d) Shoulder medial (internal) rotation
- We recommend the Labrique goniometer and the use of its blue scale.
- The subject lies prone on a table, shoulder in 90° abduction, elbow flexed 90°, wrist in neutral position (hand in prolongation of forearm), palm towards end of table, thumb directed towards the medial axis of the body, upper arm resting on table, elbow free. The subject performs a maximal medial rotation, fixing humerus in the same abduction angle on the table,

shoulder in contact with table, head in neutral position (Figure 5.10).
- The landmarks are the tip of the olecranon and the tip of the ulnar styloid process (this side is facing the end of table).
- The goniometer is positioned in line with the longitudinal axis of the forearm, oriented on both landmarks.

(e) Shoulder abduction
- The protractor goniometer is recommended for this measurement.
- The subject sits on a chair, feet on the floor, hips and knees flexed 90°. The abduction is performed bilaterally in order to avoid compensatory lateral bending of the spine (Figure 5.11). The palms are kept in a pure sagittal plane, thumbs directed forwards, elbows extended, wrists in neutral position (palms in prolongation of forearms).
- Landmarks are indicated, when maximal abduction is reached, on the middle of the superior part of the upper arm and on the lateral epicondyle of the humerus. The angulus acromii and the deltoid tuberosity can be helpful in determining the middle of the upper part of the humerus.
- The stationary arm of the goniometer is positioned parallel with the spine, the moving arm is in line with the longitudinal axis of the humerus, oriented on both landmarks.

(f) Shoulder horizontal adduction
- The protractor goniometer is recommended for this measurement.
- The subject sits on a chair, feet on the floor, hips and knees flexed 90°, back against a wall; the extended arm is kept 90° horizontally forwards and the hand is in the prolongation of the forearm, palm facing the medial axis of the body. A maximal adduction of the arm is performed in a horizontal plane, while both shoulder blades remain in contact with the wall (Figure 5.12).

- When maximal horizontal adduction is reached, landmarks are indicated on the middle of the upper and the lower part of the humerus. The deltoid tuberosity and the most ventral aspect of the lateral epicondyle of the humerus can be helpful in determining these landmarks.
- The stationary arm is kept parallel with the wall; the moving arm is parallel with the longitudinal axis of the upper arm, oriented on both landmarks. It is important to read the ROM on the external (green) scale of the goniometer.

(g) Elbow flexion

- The protractor goniometer is recommended for this measurement.

  The subject lies supine on a table, knees flexed, feet on the table. The arm to be measured is held in a sagittal plane. The forearm is in a neutral position (palm directed toward the thigh). The subject performs a complete flexion of the elbow (Figure 5.13). The hand remains extended, in the prolongation of the forearm.
- The stationary arm is positioned parallel with the longitudinal axis of the humerus. The deltoid tuberosity and the ventral aspect of the lateral epicondyle of the humerus under the extensor carpi radialis longus and brevis muscles can be helpful in determining the midline of the humerus.
- The moving arm is aligned parallel with the longitudinal axis of the forearm. The middle of the radial head under the extensor carpi radialis longus and brevis muscle, and the styloid process of the radius can be helpful in determining the reference points for the forearm.

(h) Elbow extension and hyperextension

- Elbow extension is the movement from the angle of greatest flexion to the zero position. Eventually limited motion can be recorded. The protractor goniometer is recommended for this measurement.

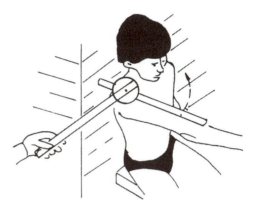

Figure 5.12 Measurement of shoulder horizontal adduction.

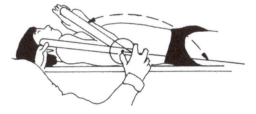

Figure 5.13 Measurement of elbow flexion.

The subject lies supine on a table, knees flexed, feet on the table. The arm to be measured is situated in a sagittal plane, the elbow is flexed, and the forearm is in a position between pronation and supination. The subject extends the elbow. The hand remains extended in the prolongation of the forearm. The thumb and fingers are kept together (Figure 5.14).
- The stationary arm is positioned parallel with the longitudinal axis of the humerus. The deltoid tuberosity and the ventral aspect of the lateral epicondyle of the humerus under the extensor carpi radialis longus and brevis muscles can be helpful in determining the midline of the humerus.
- The moving arm is aligned parallel with the longitudinal axis of the forearm. The middle of the radial head under the

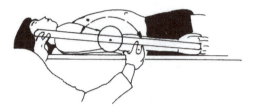

Figure 5.14 Measurement of elbow extension.

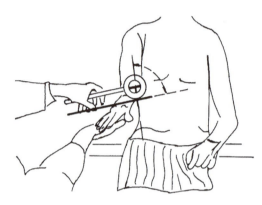

Figure 5.15 Measurement of forearm pronation.

extensor carpi radialis longus and brevis muscle, and the styloid process of the radius can be helpful in determining the reference points for the forearm.

• For the measurement of elbow hyperextension, the subject sits on a chair, preferably with the arm extended and in supination. The goniometer is aligned to the lateral side of the upper arm and forearm. The amount of hyperextension (extension beyond the zero starting position) is recorded.

(i) Forearm pronation
• The Labrique goniometer used in its holder is recommended.
• The subject sits on a chair. The upper arm of the side to be measured is held in a neutral position, the elbow is flexed 90°, and the forearm is kept in a neutral position between pronation and supination.

The hand is extended, in the prolongation of the forearm with the fingers extended and kept together. The subject performs a complete pronation (Figure 5.15), taking care that the humerus remains in a pure vertical position and that no compensatory motion occurs in the shoulder girdle and/or the spine (should this occur, bilateral pronations should be carried out).

• Eventually, landmarks can be indicated on the dorsal side of the head of the ulna and on the distal epiphysis of the radius.
• The flat side of the goniometer holder is placed against the dorsal side of the most distal part of the forearm, while the red scale is kept upwards and the pointer indicates zero degrees before pronation is performed.

(j) Forearm supination
• The Labrique goniometer used in its holder is recommended for this technique.
• The subject sits on a chair. The upper arm of the side to be measured is held in a neutral position, the elbow is flexed 90°, and the forearm is kept in a neutral position between pronation and supination. The hand is extended, in the prolongation of the forearm with the fingers extended and kept together. The subject performs a complete supination (Figure 5.16), taking care that the humerus remains in a pure vertical position and that no compensatory motion occurs in the shoulder girdle and/or the spine (should this occur bilateral supinations should be carried out).
• Eventually, landmarks can be indicated on the dorsal side of the head of the ulna and on the distal epiphysis of the radius.
• The flat side of the goniometer holder is placed against the dorsal side of the most distal part of the forearm, while the blue scale is kept upwards and the pointer

indicates zero degrees before supination is performed.

(k) Wrist flexion

- The protractor goniometer is recommended.
- The subject sits on a chair, upper arm along the trunk, elbow flexed 90°, forearm in pronation, not in support, hand and fingers are aligned with the forearm. A maximal wrist flexion is executed, metacarpals and phalanges of fingers are kept in one line, thumb kept in neutral position (Figure 5.17).
- The longitudinal axis of the third metacarpal bone, along its dorsal side between the base and the head of this metacarpal bone, serves as a first reference line. A line between the tip of the olecranon and the styloid process of the ulna reflects the longitudinal axis of the forearm. The lateral epicondyle of the humerus may serve as a guiding landmark in the determination of the more medially situated tip of the olecranon.
- The stationary arm of the goniometer is positioned parallel with the longitudinal axis of the forearm, oriented on both landmarks.
- The moving arm is in line with the longitudinal axis of the third metacarpal bone, observed at the dorsal side.

(l) Wrist extension

- The protractor goniometer is recommended.
- The subject sits on a chair, upper arm along the trunk, elbow flexed 90°, forearm in pronation, not in support, hand and fingers are aligned with the forearm. A maximal wrist extension is executed, fingers flexed to avoid passive insufficiency of the finger flexors, thumb fixed inside the closed fist (Figure 5.18).
- The longitudinal axis of the third metacarpal bone, along its dorsal side between the base and the head of this metacarpal bone, serves as a first reference line. A

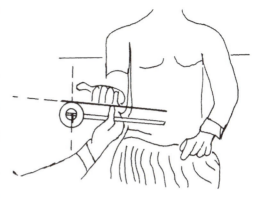

Figure 5.16 Measurement of forearm supination.

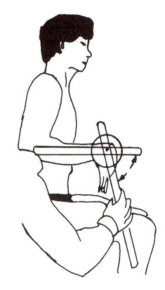

Figure 5.17 Measurement of wrist flexion.

line between the tip of the olecranon and the styloid process of the ulna reflects the longitudinal axis of the forearm. The lateral epicondyle of the humerus may serve as a guiding landmark in the determination of the more medially situated tip of the olecranon.

- The stationary arm of the goniometer is positioned parallel with the longitudinal axis of the forearm, oriented on both landmarks.

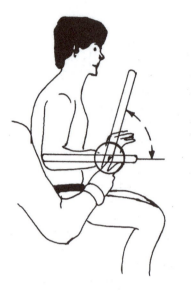

Figure 5.18 Measurement of wrist extension.

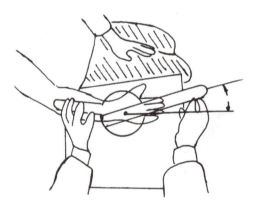

Figure 5.19 Measurement of wrist radial deviation.

- The moving arm is in line with the longitudinal axis of the third metacarpal bone, observed at the dorsal side.

(m) Wrist radial deviation
- The protractor goniometer is recommended for this measurement, which is alternatively indicated in the literature as radial abduction or radial inclination. The subject sits on a chair with upper arms

kept along the body. The elbow at the side to be measured is flexed 90°; the forearm is in pronation and in support on the table. The hand and fingers are in the prolongation of the forearm. The subject performs a radial deviation in the wrist (Figure 5.19) while the palm of the hand remains continuously in contact with the table. The fingers and thumbs are kept together. The humerus should not move.

- Landmarks are indicated at maximal radial deviation.
- The stationary arm of the goniometer is parallel with the longitudinal axis of the forearm, held in pronation. To identify this line, it can be helpful to situate the middle of the upper part of the forearm between the brachioradialis muscle and the extensor carpi radialis muscle, and to localize the middle of the connection between the radial and the ulnar styloid processes in the lower part of the forearm.
- The moving arm is held parallel with the longitudinal axis of the third metacarpal, situated between the middle of the dorsal aspect of the basis and the middle of the dorsal aspect of the head of this metacarpal bone.

(n) Wrist ulnar deviation
- The protractor goniometer is recommended for this measurement, which is alternatively indicated in the literature as ulnar abduction or ulnar inclination.
- The subject sits on a chair with upper arms kept along the body. The elbow at the side to be measured is flexed 90°; the forearm is in pronation and in support on the table. The hand and fingers are in the prolongation of the forearm.
- The subject performs ulnar deviation in the wrist (Figure 5.20) while the palm of the hand remains continuously in contact with the table. The fingers and thumbs are kept together. The humerus should not move.

- Landmarks are indicated at maximal ulnar deviation.
- The stationary arm of the goniometer is parallel with the longitudinal axis of the forearm, held in pronation. To identify this line, it can be helpful to situate the middle of the upper part of the forearm between the brachioradialis muscle and the extensor carpi radialis muscle, and to localize the middle of the connection between the radial and the ulnar styloid processes in the lower part of the forearm.
- The moving arm is held parallel with the longitudinal axis of the third metacarpal, situated between the middle of the dorsal aspect of the basis and the middle of the dorsal aspect of the head of this metacarpal bone.

(o) Hip flexion (bent leg)

- We recommend the Labrique goniometer and use of its red scale.
- The subject lies supine on a table and carries out, in a pure sagittal plane, a complete flexion in the hip, bent knee to avoid passive insufficiency of the hamstrings (Figure 5.21). When the opposite leg is beginning to lose contact with the table, a reading of the amplitude should be made, as this is a sign that the movement is continued in the spine. Therefore it is recommended to use a velcro strap at the distal end of the opposite thigh or to call for assistance.
- The landmarks are the tip of the greater trochanter and the lateral femoral epicondyle.
- The goniometer is kept with the red scale left of the examiner (the needle is then at zero degrees at the start of the motion), in line with the longitudinal axis of the thigh oriented on both landmarks.
- The result reflects an osteokinematic measurement of flexibility.

(p) Hip flexion (straight leg)

- When the effect of hamstring stretches on

Figure 5.20 Measurement of wrist ulnar deviation.

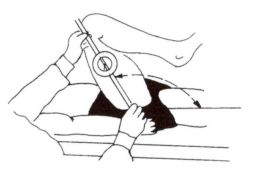

Figure 5.21 Measurement of hip flexion (bent leg).

coxo-femoral flexibility (hip flexion with a straight leg) is measured by goniometry, the examiner should take into account the angular change between the pelvis and the femur (Clayson *et al.* 1966). Straight leg-raising includes a posterior pelvic tilt and a reduction of lumbar lordosis.

- First a transverse line for the pelvis should be considered, connecting the anterior superior iliac spine with the posterior superior iliac spine (line AB in Figure 5.22). A line CD drawn perpendicular to this line in the direction of the most superior point of the greater

Figure 5.22 Reference lines for the measurement of hip extension described by Mundale *et al.* (1956).

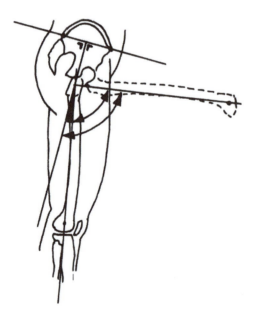

Figure 5.23 Angle beta between the reference lines considered in the position of maximal hip flexion with the straight leg.

trochanter serves as the longitudinal axis for the pelvis, and a line DE from the most superior point of the greater trochanter to the lateral epicondyle of the femur serves as the longitudinal axis of the femur. Between the lines CD and DE, an angle, α, can be measured in the resting position. An angle, β, is obtained between these reference lines in maximal flexion (Figure 5.23). Hence, in order to obtain the result of an isolated coxofemoral flexion, the value of α must be subtracted from that of β.

- We recommend the VUB-goniometer with a second carriage (Figure 5.24) which can slide along one of the arms and through which a very flexible piece of plastic can be inserted (based on previous work by Clayson *et al.* 1966).

- The subject lies sideways with the trunk aligned with the posterior edge of the table (Figure 5.25 a, b). For reasons of stability the supporting leg is slightly bent at the hip and knee joints, with the sole of the foot parallel with the posterior edge of the table. Before starting the measurements, care must be taken to ensure that the acromiale, the superior point of the greater trochanter and the lateral epicondyle of the femur are well aligned. This position offers several advantages. The reference points on the pelvis and femur can be more easily reached. It also offers stability of the subject's body while moving, and hip flexion against gravity is avoided. In a pilot study (Van Roy *et al.* 1987) a significant difference was obtained between the measurements of angle α in lying sideways and those of angle α in the normal standing position. Once angle α is determined, maximal hip flexion without bending the knee is performed. Abduction of the subject's leg can be eliminated by an assistant who supports the leg during the movement. This assistant should not push the leg into passive hip flexion and should instruct the subject not to perform hip rotation, knee flexion or movements at the ankle joint during hamstring stretching. The angle β is determined. The final score is obtained by subtracting angle α from angle β.

- The result reflects an attempt to realize an arthrokinematic measurement of flexibility.

(q) Hip extension

- The Labrique goniometer and its blue scale are used, or another inclinometer with long arm(s) is recommended.
- The subject lies prone at the end of a table, legs outside the table, feet on ground, a small pillow under the abdomen; the opposite leg is in the greatest possible flexion at the hip; hands grip the sides of the table. A maximal extension in the hip is performed while the opposite leg is kept bent (Figure 5.26).
- The landmarks are the tip of the greater trochanter and the lateral femoral condyle.
- The goniometer is kept with the blue scale left of the examiner (the needle is then at zero degrees at the start of the motion), in line with the longitudinal axis of the thigh oriented on both landmarks.

(r) Hip abduction

- A protractor goniometer (with long arms) or the VUB-goniometer is recommended.
- The subject lies supine on a table with the opposite hip in slight abduction in order to allow the lower leg of the opposite leg to hang outside the table so that the hips can be stabilized. A maximal abduction is performed with straight leg in the plane of the table, without lateral rotation of foot point at the end of the movement (Figure 5.27).
- The landmarks are the left and right superior anterior iliac spines and the lateral board of the quadriceps tendon.
- The stationary arm of the goniometer

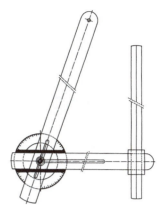

Figure 5.24 VUB-goniometer with second carriage.

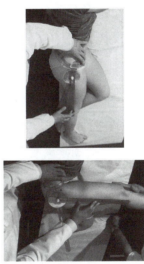

Figure 5.25 a+b Measurement of hip flexion (straight leg).

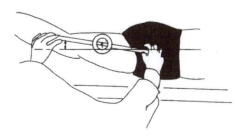

Figure 5.26 Measurement of hip extension.

Figure 5.27 Measurement of hip abduction.

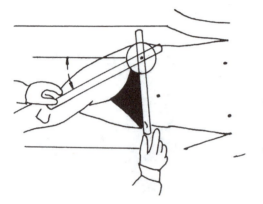

Figure 5.28 Measurement of hip adduction.

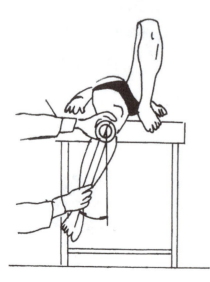

Figure 5.29 Measurement of hip medial (internal) rotation.

is positioned on the line between both spines.

- The moving arm is in line with the longitudinal axis of the thigh, oriented on the anterior iliac spine of the side to be measured and the lateral board of the quadriceps tendon.

(s) Hip adduction

- A protractor goniometer (with long arms) or the VUB-goniometer is recommended.
- The subject lies supine on a table. A maximal adduction is performed with slightly elevated thigh (about 40° hip flexion), and extended knee, without rotation in the hip (Figure 5.28).
- The landmarks are the left and right superior anterior iliac spines and lateral board of the quadriceps tendon.
- The stationary arm of the goniometer is positioned on the line between both spines.
- The moving arm is in line with the longitudinal axis of the thigh, oriented on the anterior iliac spine of the side to be measured and the lateral board of the quadriceps tendon.

(t) Hip medial (internal) rotation

- The Labrique goniometer with its blue scale is recommended for this measurement.
- The subject lies supine on a table with the contralateral leg bent at the knee and hip and with the heel supported on the table. The hip at the side to be measured is in neutral position relative to the trunk, the knee is flexed 90° and the lower leg hangs outside and at the end of the table. The pelvis is fixed on the table with a velcro strap.

  The subject performs a maximal hip medial rotation (Figure 5.29). Compensatory motion such as pelvis tilt must be avoided.
- At maximum ROM, landmarks are indicated on the ventral margin of the

tibia below the tuberosity of the tibia and on a point located about 5 cm above the tibiotarsal joint.

- The goniometer is kept so that the blue scale is positioned at the upper part of the tibia. The pointer now indicates zero degrees at the beginning of the movement. The goniometer is oriented on the landmarks.

(u) Hip lateral (external) rotation

- The Labrique goniometer with its blue scale is recommended for this measurement.
- The subject lies supine on a table with contralateral leg bent at the knee and hip and with the heel supported on the table. The hip at the side to be measured is in neutral position relative to the trunk, the knee is flexed 90° and the lower leg hangs outside and at the end of the table. The pelvis is fixed on the table with a velcro strap. The subject performs a maximal hip lateral rotation (Figure 5.30). Compensatory motion such as pelvis tilt must be avoided.
- At maximum ROM, landmarks are indicated on the ventral margin of the tibia below the tuberosity of the tibia and on a point located about 5 cm above the tibiotarsal joint.
- The goniometer is kept so that the blue scale is positioned at the upper part of the tibia. The pointer now indicates zero degrees at the beginning of the movement. The goniometer is oriented on the landmarks.

(v) Knee flexion

- The protractor goniometer (with long arms) or the VUB-goniometer is recommended.
- The subject lies supine on a table. A maximal flexion of the knee is performed, foot sole gliding over the table in the direction of the heel (Figure 5.31).
- Landmarks are the tip of the greater trochanter, the lateral femoral epicondyle,

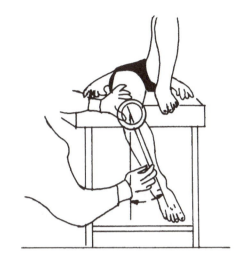

Figure 5.30 Measurement of hip lateral (external) rotation.

Figure 5.31 Measurement of knee flexion.

the tip of the fibular head and the middle of the inferior side of the lateral malleolus.

- The stationary arm of the goniometer is positioned in line with the longitudinal axis of the thigh, oriented on the tip of the greater trochanter and the lateral femoral epicondyle.
- The moving arm is in line with the

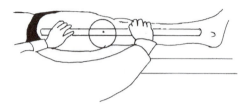

Figure 5.32 Measurement of knee extension.

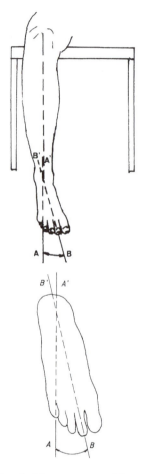

Figure 5.33 a+b Measurement of knee medial (internal) rotation.

longitudinal axis of the lower leg, oriented on both landmarks.

(w) Knee extension and hyperextension
- Knee extension is the movement from the angle of greatest flexion to the zero position. Eventually limited motion can be recorded. The protractor goniometer (with long arms) or the VUB-goniometer is recommended.
- The subject lies supine on a table, leg to be measured flexed, foot supported on the table, the opposite leg extended, arms alongside body. A maximal extension of the knee is performed, foot sole gliding over the table in the direction of the end of the table (Figure 5.32).
- Landmarks are the tip of the greater trochanter, the lateral femoral epicondyle, the tip of the fibular head and the middle of the inferior side of the lateral malleolus.
- The stationary arm of the goniometer is positioned in line with the longitudinal axis of the thigh, oriented on both landmarks.
- The moving arm is in line with the longitudinal axis of the lower leg, oriented on both landmarks.
- For the measurement of hyperextension, the amount of extension beyond the zero starting position of the knee joint) is recorded. Hereby, the heel is lifted off from the table.

(x) Knee medial (internal) rotation
- The protractor goniometer is recommended.
- The subject sits on a chair with hip and knee at the side to be measured flexed 90°. The foot is flat on a paper (size about 30 cm × 50 cm), fixed on the floor. The contralateral knee is a little more extended in order not to disturb the execution of the movement. The subject grasps with both hands the front side of the chair close to the knee to fix the lower limb. A maximal knee medial rotation is performed (Figure 5.33) without compensatory hip motion and knee flexion or extension.
- Landmarks are indicated on the projection of the middle of the calcaneal tuberosity at the bottom side of the

heel and at the longitudinal axis of the second metatarsal bone. The landmarks must be localized on the paper when the foot is in neutral position (AA'); the same landmarks must then be indicated when the medial rotation of the knee is performed (BB'). Two lines A-A' and B-B' should be drawn and continued until the junction.

- The angle between the two lines on the paper is subsequently read with the goniometer.

(y) Knee lateral (external) rotation

- The protractor goniometer is recommended.
- The subject sits on a chair with hip and knee at the side to be measured flexed 90°. The foot is flat on a paper (size about 30 cm × 50 cm), fixed on the floor. The contralateral knee is a little more extended in order not to disturb the execution of the movement. The subject grasps with both hands the front side of the chair close to the knee to fix the lower limb. A maximal knee lateral rotation is performed (Figure 5.34) without compensatory hip motion and knee flexion or extension.
- Landmarks are indicated on the projection of the middle of the calcaneus tuberosity at the bottom side of the heel and at the longitudinal axis of the second metatarsal bone. The landmarks must be localized on the paper when the foot is in neutral position (AA'); the same landmarks must then be indicated when the lateral rotation of the knee is performed (BB'). Two lines A-A' and B-B' should be drawn and continued until the junction.
- The angle between the two lines on the paper is subsequently read with the goniometer.

(z) Ankle dorsiflexion

- We recommend the international protractor goniometer with an extended stationary arm or the VUB-goniometer.

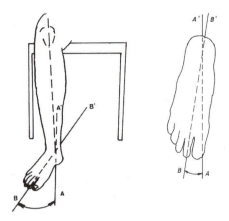

Figure 5.34 a+b Measurement of knee lateral (external) rotation.

- The subject lies supine on a table, lower legs hanging outside table, knees flexed 90° (to eliminate passive insufficiency of the gastrocnemius muscle). A maximal dorsiflexion is executed at the talocrural joint, making sure that the knee remains at 90° flexion (Figure 5.35).
- Landmarks are the tip of the fibular head at the lateral side of the lower leg; the middle of the inferior side of the lateral malleolus; a line parallel to the foot sole is drawn starting from the middle of the lateral side of the head of the fifth metatarsal.
- The stationary arm of the goniometer is in line with the longitudinal axis of the lower leg, oriented on both landmarks.
- The moving arm is in line with the longitudinal axis of the foot, oriented on the constructed reference line.

(aa) Ankle plantar flexion

- We recommend the international protractor goniometer with an extended stationary arm or the VUB-goniometer.
- The subject lies supine on a table, with lower legs hanging outside table, knees flexed 90°. A maximal plantar-flexion is executed at the talocrural joint, making sure that the knee remains at 90° flexion.

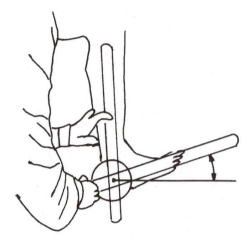

Figure 5.35 Measurement of ankle dorsiflexion.

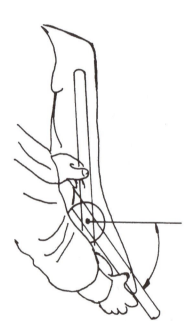

Figure 5.36 Measurement of ankle plantar flexion.

A flexion of the toes is normal with this movement (Figure 5.36).

• Landmarks are the tip of the fibular head at the lateral side of the lower leg; the middle of the inferior side of the lateral malleolus; a line parallel to the foot sole is drawn starting from the middle of the lateral side of the head of the fifth metatarsal.

• The stationary arm of the goniometer is in line with the longitudinal axis of the lower leg, oriented on both landmarks.

• The moving arm is in line with the longitudinal axis of the foot, oriented on the constructed reference line.

5.5 SUMMARY AND CONCLUSION

• From the detailed description of the measurements above, it should be clear that goniometry requires a good knowledge of anatomy and anthropometry.

• Several types of goniometers are available. The goniometer is a reliable instrument when used by experienced individuals who follow carefully the standardized protocol.

• When bony landmarks are visible or easy to determine, the goniometer usually provides an accurate and convenient clinical method for estimating joint motion. However, when the bony landmarks are not easy to locate, for whatever reasons, the goniometer may not give accurate information and satisfaction.

• Results of flexibility may reflect osteokinematics or constitute an attempt to evaluate arthrokinematics.

• Measurement precision will also improve when the examiner is assisted by a second examiner, checks and calibrates the equipment, explains the test procedures to the subject, adheres to triple measurements and notes on the proforma those factors that may affect the test results such as age, gender, body type, certain pathologies or injuries, daily physical activities, room temperature and previous warm-up.

Although most of these variables and their eventual causal relationship with flexibility have been reviewed elsewhere (Borms 1984; Hubley-Kozey 1991), it is nonetheless important to mention two factors among these, temperature and warm-up.

- In general, there has been little appreciation that flexibility is more complex than one might think. Two-dimensional goniometry is very common in the daily practice of rehabilitation medicine and physiotherapy, but these relatively simple measurement procedures have their restrictions. Although the intra-observer and inter-observer reliability of goniometric measurements generally reach high values when goniometric readings are performed in a standardized way, the content validity remains restricted. Clinical goniometry only gives a two-dimensional estimation of the range of motion, which usually results from three-dimensional joint motion.

- When additional rotation and translation components of joint motion are of interest, three-dimensional kinematic studies of the joints of the extremities and the spine represent the alternative approach in the assessment of flexibility.

Table 5.1 Flexibility norms for men (physical education and physiotherapy students 20 years of age)

	Range	P_{25}	P_{50}	P_{75}
Shoulder flexion	154–195	170	177	188
Shoulder extension	25–80	43	49	59
Shoulder lateral rotation	43–93	56	72	79
Shoulder medial rotation	16–92	47	64	75
Shoulder abduction	110–199	143	156	181
Shoulder horizontal adduction	17–60	30	35	46
Elbow flexion	130–156	139	144	151
Forearm pronation	40–98	78	85	91
Forearm supination	56–98	80	90	92
Wrist flexion	60–94	65	69	79
Wrist extension	45–88	58	67	75
Wrist radial deviation	12–38	20	27	30
Wrist ulnar deviation	19–59	33	44	50
Hip flexion (bent leg)	105–155	120	128	133
Hip flexion (straight leg)	–	–	–	–
Hip extension	9–29	18	21	26
Hip abduction	–	–	–	–
Hip adduction	9–68	16	29	31
Hip medial rotation	26–50	30	33	38
Hip lateral rotation	26–70	32	36	42
Knee flexion	130–155	136	142	146
Knee medial rotation	21–60	27	37	46
Knee lateral rotation	20–53	25	28	37
Ankle dorsiflexion	4–37	6	13	22
Ankle plantar-flexion	18–78	47	57	70

Table 5.2 Flexibility norms for women (physical education and physiotherapy students 20 years of age)

	RANGE	P_{25}	P_{50}	P75
Shoulder flexion	154–197	172	177	183
Shoulder extension	20–86	46	54	59
Shoulder lateral rotation	13–89	51	65	77
Shoulder medial rotation	24–89	52	66	74
Shoulder abduction	105–203	125	147	179
Shoulder horizontal adduction	11–55	27	36	40
Elbow flexion	128–161	136	144	151
Forearm pronation	40–99	79	88	94
Forearm supination	51–99	80	88	91
Wrist flexion	62–95	68	70	79
Wrist extension	30–89	62	69	75
Wrist radial deviation	12–49	22	29	33
Wrist ulnar deviation	19–58	39	45	50
Hip flexion (bent leg)	103–155	115	126	130
Hip flexion (straight leg)	–	–	–	–
Hip extension	8–29	10	18	24
Hip abduction	–	–	–	–
Hip adduction	20–69	21	33	40
Hip medial rotation	24–65	29	32	37
Hip lateral rotation	23–62	27	30	35
Knee flexion	131–160	139	145	152
Knee medial rotation	20–69	38	48	56
Knee lateral rotation	22–54	26	34	43
Ankle dorsiflexion	1–31	12	14	20
Ankle plantar flexion	26–90	53	70	84

FURTHER READING

Books

American Academy of Orthopaedic Surgeons (1965). *Joint Motion. Method of Measuring and Recording*. Churchill Livingstone: Edinburgh, London and New York.

Greene W. and Heckman W. *Clinical Measurement of Joint Motion*, American Academy of Orthopaedic Surgeons, Rosemont, IL USA.

Norkin C. and White J. (1985). *Measurement of Joint Motion: a guide to goniometry*. F.A. Davis Company; Philadelphia, PA.

Journals

Clinics in Rheumatic Diseases (1982); 8 (3) Measurement of joint movement, (ed. V. Wright, Eastbourne, W.B. Sounders.

REFERENCES

AAHPERD (1984). *Technical Manual: Health related Physical Fitness*. AAHPERD; Reston, VA.

Allard P., Stokes I. A. F. and Blanchi J.-P. (1995) (eds.) *Three-dimensional Analysis of Human Movement*. Human Kinetics; Champaign, IL.

American Academy of Orthopaedic Surgeons

(1965). *Joint Motion. Method of Measuring and Recording*. Churchill Livingstone; Edinburgh, London and New York.

Atha J. and Wheatly D. W. (1976). The mobilising effects of repeated measurement of hip flexion. *British Journal of Sports Medicine*; **10**: 22–5.

Backer M. and Kofoed H. (1989). Passive ankle mobility, clinical measurement compared with radiography. *Journal of Bone and Joint Surgery*; **71-B**: 696–8.

Baeyens J. P., Van Roy P., De Schepper A., Declercq G. and Clarijs J. P. (2001). Glenohumeral joint kinematics related to minor anterior instability of the shoulder at the end of the late preparatory phase of throwing, 3D intra articular dysfunctions in minor anterior glenohumeral instability. *Clinical Biomechanics*; **16**: 752–7.

Benedetti M. G., Cappozzo A. and Leardini A. (1994). Anatomical landmark definition and identification. *CAMARC II Internal Report*, 15 May.

Borms J. (1984). Importance of flexibility in overall physical fitness. *International Journal. of Physical Education*; **XXI**: 15–26.

Borms J., Van Roy P., Santens J. P. and Haentjens A. (1987). Optimal duration of static stretching exercises for improvement of coxo-femoral flexibility. *Journal of Sports Sciences*; **5**: 39–47.

Broer M. H. and Galles N. R. G. (1958). Importance of relationship between body measurements in performance of toe-touch test. *Research Quarterly*; **29**: 253–63.

Brown R. K. and Stevenson B. R. (1953) Gravity goniometer. *Journal of Bone and Joint Surgery*; **35-A**: 784–5.

Bull A. M. J. and Amis A. A. (1998). Knee joint motion: description and measurement, *Proceedings of the Institute of Mechanical Engineers*; **212**: 357–71.

Buck C. A., Dameron F. B., Dow M. J. and Skowlund H. V. (1959). Study of normal range of motion in the neck utilizing a bubble goniometer. *Archives of Physical Therapy Medicine and Rehabilitation*; **40**: 390–5.

Cappozzo A. and Della Croce U. (1994) The PGD Lexicon. *CAMARC II Internal Report*, 15 May.

Cappozzo A., Catani F., Della Croce U. and Leardini A. (1995) Position and orientation in space of bones during movement: anatomical frame definition and determination. *Clinical Biomechanics*; **10**: 171–8.

Cappozzo A., Catani F., Leardini A. *et al.* (1996). Position and orientation in space of bones during movement: experimental artefacts. *Clinical Biomechanics*; **11**: 90–100.

Cappozzo A., Della Croce U., Leardini A. and Chiari L. (2005). Human movement analysis using stereophotogrammetry. Part 1: theoretical background. *Gait and Posture*; **21**: 186–96.

Cave E. F. and Roberts S.M. (1936). A method of measuring and recording joint function. *The Journal of Bone and Joint Surgery*; **18**: 455–65.

Chiari L., Della Croce U., Leardini, A. and Cappozzo, A. (2005). Human movement analysis using stereophotogrammetry. Part 2: instrumental errors. *Gait and Posture*; **21**: 197–211.

Clark W. A. (1920). A system for joints measurements. *The Journal of Orthopaedic Surgery*; **2**: 687–700.

Claeys R. and Gomes E. K. (1968). The measurement of the pelvic movements and its applications. In: (J. Wartenweiler, E. Jokl and M. Hebbelinck, eds): *Biomechanics I: Technique of Drawing of Movement and Movement Analysis*. Basel; Karger: 238–40.

Clayson S., Mundale M. and Kottke F. (1966). Goniometer adaptation for measuring hip extension. *Archives of Physical Medicine and Rehabilitation*; **47**: 255–61.

Cleveland D. E. (1918). Diagrams for showing limitation of movement through joints. *Canadian Medical Association Journal*; **8**: 1070 (Abstract)

Council of Europe, Committee for the Development of Sport, Eurofit (1988). *Handbook for the Eurofit Tests of Physical Fitness*. Committee of the Development of Sport within the Council of Europe; Rome: 72.

Cureton T.K. (1941). Flexibility as an aspect of physical fitness. *Research Quarterly*; **12**: 381–90.

Della Croce U., Leardini A., Chiari L. and Cappozzo A. (2005). Human movement analysis using stereophotogrammetry. Part 4: assessment of anatomical landmark misplacement and its effects on joint kinematics. *Gait and Posture*; **21**: 226–37.

Ellis M. (1984) Personal communication.

Esch D. and Lepley M. (1974). *Evaluation of joint motion; methods of measurement and recording.* University of Minnesota Press; Minneapolis, MN: p. 33.

Fox R. F. (1917). Demonstration of the mensuration apparatus in use at the Red Cross Clinic for the physical treatment of officers. *Proceedings of the Royal Society of Medicine*; 10: 63–9.

Fox R. F. and van Bremen J. (1937). *Chronic rheumatism, causation and treatment.* J. & A. Churchill Ltd.: London: pp. 327–31.

Grobaker M. R. and Stull G. A. (1975). Thermal applications as a determiner of joint flexibility. *American Corrective Therapy Journal*; 25: 3–8.

Grood E. S. and Suntay W. J. (1983). A joint co-ordinate system for the clinical description of three-dimensional motions: application to the knee. *Journal of Biomechanical Engineering*; 105: 136–44.

Hand J. G. (1938). A compact pendulum goniometer. *Journal of Bone and Joint Surgery*; 20: 494–5.

Hopkins D. R. and Hoeger W. W. K. (1986). The modified sit and reach test. In: (W. W. K. Hoeger, ed) *Lifetime Physical Fitness and Wellness: A Personalised Program.* Morton Pub Co.; Englewood, CO: p. 47.

Hsiao H. and Keyserling W. M. (1990) Three-dimensional ultrasonic system for posture measurement. *Ergonomics*; 33: 1089–114.

Hubley-Kozey C. L. (1991). Testing flexibility (Chapter 7) In: (J. D. Mac Dougall, H. A. Wenger and H. J. Green, eds) *Physiological Testing of the High-Performance Athlete.* Human Kinetics Books; Champaign, IL: pp. 309–59.

Karpovich P. V. and Karpovich G. P. (1959). Electrogoniometer: a new device for study of joints in action. *Federation Proceedings*; 18 (79): 310 (Abstract)

Kottke F. J. and Mundale M. O. (1959). Range of mobility of the cervical spine. *Archives of Physical Medicine and Rehabilitation*; 47: 379–82.

Kraus H. and Hirschland R. P. (1954). Minimum muscular fitness tests in school children. *Research Quarterly*; 25: 178–88.

Labrique Ph. (1977). *Le goniomètre de Labrique.* Prodim; Brussels.

Lakie M. I, Walsh E. G. and Wright G. W. (1979)

Cooling and wrist compliance. *Journal of Physiology*; 296: 47–8.

Larson L. A. (ed.) (1974). *Fitness, Health and Work capacity: International Standards for Assessment.* MacMillan Publishing Co. Inc.; New York.

Leardini A., Chiari L., Della Croce U. and Cappozzo A. (2005). Human movement analysis using stereophotogrammetry. Part 3: soft tissue artifact assessment and compensation. *Gait and Posture*; 21: 212–25.

Leighton J. R. (1955) An instrument and technic for the measurement of range of motion, *Archives of Physical Medicine and Rehabilitation*; 36: 571–8.

Leighton J. R. (1966). The Leighton flexometer and flexibility test. *Journal of the Association for Physical and Mental Rehabilitation*; 20: 86–93.

Loebl W. Y. (1967). Measurements of spinal posture and range of spinal movements. *Annals of Physical Medicine*; 9 (33): 103–110)

Looser E. (1934). Die systematische Untersuchung des Gelenkapparates. *Schweizerische Medizinische Wochenschrift*; 64: 646–8.

Lundberg A. (1989). Kinematics of ankle and foot. *Acta Orthopaedica Scandinavica*; 60: (Suppl. 233): 8–26.

Mundale M. O., Hislop H. J., Rabideau R. J. and Kottke F. J. (1956). Evaluation of extension of the hip. *Archives of Physical Medicine*; 37: 75–80.

Moore M. L. (1949). The measurement of joint motion, Part I: introductory review of literature. *Physical Therapy Review*; 29: 195–205.

Moore M. L. (1965). Clinical assessment of joint motion. In S. Licht, ed. *Therapeutic Exercise.* Waverly Press; Baltimore: pp. 128–62.

Nicol A. C. (1987) A new flexible electrogoniometer with widespread applications. In: (B. Jonsson, ed) *Biomechanics X-B.* Human Kinetics Publishers; Champaign, IL: pp.1029–33.

Rippstein J. (1977) Vom schätzen und messen mit neuer Hilfmitteln. *Orthopäde*; 6: 81–4.

Rocher C. and Rigaud A. (1964). Fonctions et bilans articulaires. *Kinésithérapie et Rééducation.* Masson; Paris.

Russe O., Gerhardt J. J. and King P. S. (1972). *An atlas of examination, standard measurements and diagnosis in orthopedics and traumatology.* Hans Huber; Bern.

Schlaaff J. (1937). Der Messfächer, ein Zwangsmass zu Einheitlicher Gelenkmessung, *Zentralblatt für Chirurgie*; **23**: 1355–9.

Schlaaff J. (1938). Der Messfächer in neuer Form. *Münchener Medizinische Wochenschrift*; **85**: 369–70.

Scott M. G. and French E. (1950). *Evaluation in Physical Education*. C.V. Mosby; St. Louis, MO.

Skubic V. and Hodgkins J. (1957). Effect of warm-up activities on speed, strength and accuracy. *Research Quarterly*; **28**: 147–52.

Tesio L., Monzani M., Gatti R. and Franchignoni F. (1995) Flexible electrogoniometers: kinesiological advantages with respect to potentiometric goniometers. *Clinical Biomechanics*; **10**: 275–7.

Tousignant M., de Bellefeuille L., O'Donoughue S. and Grahovac S. (2000). Criterion validity of the cervical range of motion (CROM) goniometer for cervical flexion and extension. *Spine*; **25**: 324–30.

Tousignant M., Smeesters C., Breton A. M., Breton E. and Corriveau H. (2006). Criterion validity of the cervical range of motion (CROM) device for rotational range of motion on healthy adults. *Journal of Orthopedic Sports Physiotherapy*; **36**: 242–8.

Van Roy P. (1981). *Investigation on the validity of goniometry as measuring technique to assess wrist flexibility* (in Dutch). Unpublished Licentiate thesis: Vrije Universiteit Brussel.

Van Roy P., Hebbelinck M. and Borms J. (1985). Introduction d'un goniomètre standard modifié avec la graduation et la branche pivotante montées sur un chariot déplaçable. *Annales de Kinésitherapie*; **12**: 255–9.

Van Roy P., Borms J. and Haentjens A. (1987) Goniometric study of the maintenance of hip flexibility resulting from hamstring stretches. *Physiotherapy Practice*; **3**: 52–9.

Van Roy P., Barbaix E. and Clarys J. P. (2000) Anatomy of the lumbar canal, foramen, and ligaments, with references to recent insights. In: (R. Gunzburg and M. Szpalski, eds) *Lumbar Spinal Stenosis*. Lippincott Williams & Wilkins; Philadelphia, PA: pp. 7–25.

Von Richter W. (1974). Ein neues Goniometer zur messung von Gelenkbewegungen. *Beitrage zur Orthopaedie und Traumatologie*; **21**: 439–43.

Wells K. F. and Dillon E. K. (1952) The sit and reach: a test of back and leg flexibility. *Research Quarterly*; **23**: 115–18.

Wright V. (1973) Stiffness: a review of its measurement and physiological importance. *Physiotherapy*; **59**: 107–11.

Wright V. (ed.) (1982). Measurement of joint movement. *Clinics in Rheumatic Diseases*; 8 (3), Eastbourne, W.B. Saunders.

Wright V. and Johns R. J. (1960). Physical factors concerned with the stiffness of normal and diseases joints. *John Hopkins Hospital Bulletin*; **106**: 215–31.

Wu G., Siegler S., Allard P., Kirtley C., Leardini A., Rosenbaum D., Whittle M., D'Lima D., Cristofolini L., Witte H., Schmid O. and Stokes I. (2002). ISB recommendation on definitions of joint coordinate systems of various joints for the reporting of human joint motion – part I: ankle, hip, and spine. *Journal of Biomechanics*; **35**: 543–8.

Wu G., van der Helm F., Veeger H., Makhsous M., Van Roy P., Anglin C., Nagels J., Karduna A., McQuade K., Wang, X., Werner F. and Buchholz B. (2005). ISB recommendation on definitions of joint coordinate systems of various joints for the reporting of human joint motion – part II: shoulder, elbow, wrist and hand. *Journal of Biomechanics*; **38**: 981–2.

Zinovieff A. A., Harborrow R. R. (1975). Inclinometer for measuring straight-leg raising, *Rheumatology and Rehabilitation*; **14**: 114–15.

PART THREE

ASSESSMENT OF PHYSICAL ACTIVITY AND PERFORMANCE

CHAPTER 6

FIELD METHODS OF ASSESSING PHYSICAL ACTIVITY AND ENERGY BALANCE

Ann V. Rowlands

6.1 AIMS

The aims of this chapter are:

- to demonstrate the importance of measuring physical activity accurately;
- to distinguish between physical activity and energy expenditure;
- to consider the options available to measure physical activity and the appropriateness of each method of assessing physical activity for any given question (taking into consideration the population involved, the accuracy of information required, cost restrictions, sample size and the type of physical activity that needs to be quantified).

6.2 WHY ESTIMATE PHYSICAL ACTIVITY? THE NEED FOR A VALID MEASURE

The accurate and reliable assessment of physical activity is necessary for any research study where physical activity is either an outcome measure or an intervention. However, physical activity is notoriously difficult to measure, particularly when assessing activity in children. Numerous methods exist for the measurement of physical activity. Broadly, the various techniques can be grouped as self-report, observation, heart rate telemetry and motion sensors. Pragmatic considerations often lead to self-report as the tool of choice, particularly in large-scale epidemiological studies (Freedson *et al.* 2005). However, the sporadic short-burst nature of children's activity (Bailey *et al.* 1995; Baquet *et al.* 2007; Berman *et al.* 1998) makes it particularly difficult to capture data via self-report methods. The problem is compounded, as the concept of time and the ability to recall accurately are limited by the child's level of cognition and the emotion associated with the activity (Gleitman 1996). Developments in technology over the past 20 years have permitted an increase in the use of objective methods to assess habitual physical activity. Outcome measures from the available tools normally relate to the amount of activity (i.e. movement), time spent at different intensities of activity and/or indicators of energy expenditure.

6.3 ENERGY EXPENDITURE AND PHYSICAL ACTIVITY

The terms energy expenditure and physical

activity are not synonymous and cannot be used interchangeably. The same amount of energy may be expended in a short burst of strenuous exercise as in less intense endurance exercise of longer duration (Montoye *et al.* 1996). However, the physiological effect of the two activities may be quite different.

6.3.1 Effect of size on energy expenditure

Total energy expenditure is positively related to body size and is, therefore, higher in obese individuals than non-obese individuals. When total energy expenditure is normalised for fat-free mass there appears to be no difference between obese and non-obese children (Goran 1997). This indicates a lower level of actual activity in the obese children, as any given movement will demand greater energy expenditure in the heavier child. This highlights the importance of differentiating between physical activity and energy expenditure. Physical activity level (PAL) (the ratio of total energy expenditure to basal metabolic rate (BMR)) is one method of controlling for the effect of body mass on energy expenditure (Black *et al.* 1996). However, information is limited to a single number representing energy expended. No information regarding the physical activity pattern or intensity of individual activities is obtained. It is unclear which aspects of physical activity are important in controlling body mass, so it is important to measure as many of these factors as possible. Goran (1997) has suggested that intensity, activity time, metabolic efficiency, overall energy cost, and the type of physical activity are relevant factors for consideration.

6.4 METHODS OF ESTIMATING PHYSICAL ACTIVITY OR ENERGY EXPENDITURE

6.4.1 Doubly labelled water

Doubly labelled water (DLW) is considered the gold standard for the assessment of daily energy expenditure in free-living subjects (Montoye *et al.* 1996). It provides a measure of daily energy expenditure over approximately 2 weeks and has been demonstrated to have good precision in adults (Schoeller and van Santen 1982; Klein *et al.* 1984; Prentice *et al.* 1985) and in infants (Roberts *et al.* 1986).

For human participants, the measurement of energy expenditure using DLW is very simple. It does not interfere with their lifestyle and hence is relatively unlikely to affect their normal pattern of daily activity. All that is required is the consumption of a dose of isotope-enriched water followed by the collection of urine samples after 7 days and after 14 days (2-point method), or on a daily basis (multipoint method).

Water containing a known concentration of isotopes of hydrogen ($^2H_2$) and oxygen (^{18}O) is consumed. After a few hours the isotopes have re-distributed and are in equilibrium with body water (Montoye *et al.* 1996). The method is based on the measurement of carbon dioxide production from the difference between the elimination rates of the isotopes of hydrogen (deuterium $^2H_2$) and oxygen (^{18}O) with which the water is labelled. This is possible as the labelled oxygen leaves the body in the form of water ($H_2^{18}O$) and in the form of carbon dioxide ($C^{18}O_2$). However, the labelled hydrogen only leaves the body in the form of water (^2H_2O). From the difference in the elimination rates of the two isotopes it is possible to calculate the quantity of carbon dioxide produced. Together with an estimation of the respiratory quotient (RQ), the quantity of carbon dioxide produced allows the calculation of oxygen uptake for the time period. The RQ will be unknown when measuring energy expenditure in the field, hence the need for the estimation. In Western societies the RQ is usually estimated to be 0.85. A difference of 0.01 between the estimated and actual RQ would lead to an error of approximately 1% in calculated energy expenditure (Montoye *et al.* 1996)

The main disadvantage of the DLW

method is its high cost. This prevents its use in large scale studies or as a standard physiological measure of physical activity. Additionally, it can only provide a measure of total energy expenditure over a period of time. No information regarding a person's activity pattern or the intensity of activity undertaken can be obtained. Nevertheless, it is accepted as the ideal criterion method for validating alternative measures of total daily energy expenditure (Montoye *et al.* 1996). It has been used to validate measures of energy expenditure and physical activity, including triaxial accelerometers (Bouten *et al.* 1996), heart rate monitoring (e.g. Livingstone *et al.* 1990; Emons *et al.* 1992) and questionnaires (e.g. Bratteby *et al.* 1997).

6.4.2 Self-report – Questionnaires

Self-report is probably the most common method used for assessing physical activity levels. This is due to low cost, ease of use and the ability to assess large numbers of people over a relatively short period of time (Sallis and Saelens 2000). Questionnaires vary as to whether they assess activity over the previous few days (e.g. Ku *et al.* 1981, Shapiro *et al.* 1984), few weeks (e.g. Watson and O'Donovan 1977) or more general 'typical' activity (e.g. Johnson *et al.* 1956; Tell and Vellar 1988; Woods *et al.* 1992).

The types of activity assessed by questionnaire also vary. Several questionnaires for adults concentrate on leisure time physical activity alone or work time physical activity alone, others on total activity. Children's questionnaires usually concentrate on either sport participation and leisure time physical activity or total physical activity. Memory aids are frequently used in an effort to make questionnaires more accurate. Partitioning the day into portions and providing lists of activities to choose from are two of the main strategies (e.g. Gazzaniga and Burns 1993).

When assessing habitual physical activity in adults, questionnaires give a reasonably valid and reliable estimate, at least allowing

the categorisation of people into groups based on their levels of physical activity (Montoye *et al.* 1996). In children there are limitations associated with the recall of activities. Cale (1994) highlighted the limited cognitive ability of children to recall activities. This problem is exacerbated when the child is also expected to remember duration and intensity of activities. Baranowski *et al.* (1984) showed that children can only recall 55–65% of their daily activities. This finding was supported in a later study where 11- to 13-year-olds were observed for 7 days. In a subsequent recall of activities over this time period only 46% of observed activities were reported (Wallace *et al.* 1985). It is clear that care needs to be taken when using questionnaires with children. For children younger than 10–12 years, questionnaire methods appear to be inappropriate and more objective methods, such as observation or motion counters, are recommended (Montoye *et al.* 1996)

A discussion of available questionnaires is beyond the scope of this chapter. For information pertaining to specific questionnaires, or diary methods, and their reliability and validity, the reader is referred to the text by Montoye *et al.* (1996).

6.4.3 Observation

The use of observation is the logical solution to assessing physical activity. It has face validity and allows the recording of additional information related to the activity, for example, where it occurs and the social context in which it occurs. It is sometimes possible to provide information regarding motivation toward being active and which environments are conducive to increased activity levels. However, it is very time consuming and labour intensive for the observer. Consequently, it is restricted to use with small groups. Observation techniques are rarely used with adults; therefore, the rest of this section concerns methods used to assess activity in children.

Observation techniques can capture

intensity, duration and frequency of physical activity. The accuracy of the information differs according to the frequency of observations. An optimal frequency is high enough to capture activity changes and brief activities, yet long enough to allow an accurate record of the activity to be made. Children's activity is highly transitory (Welk et al. 2000) with 80%, 93% and 96% of activity bouts of moderate, vigorous and very high intensity, respectively, shorter than 10 second (Baquet et al. 2007).

Potentially, reactive behaviour could be a problem with observation techniques. Following one or two observation sessions, children appear to become habituated to the presence of the observer and reactivity is not a problem (Puhl et al. 1990; Bailey et al. 1995).

Protocols vary according to the frequency, duration of observation and the number of categories the activities can be assigned to. A comprehensive observation protocol was developed by Bailey et al. (1995) allowing the varying intervals between activities of different intensity and duration (tempo) to be recorded, as well as the frequency and duration of activities. Fourteen mutually exclusive posture codes were used, allowing the observer to describe the child's behaviour without having to make judgements about energy expenditure. Within each posture code there were three intensity levels (low, moderate and intense); the intensity level selected depended on factors such as speed, number of limbs, weight carried and incline. Observation periods were 4 hours in duration and performed in whatever setting the subject happened to be in: school days, weekend days and summer holidays were included. Observers were cued every 3 s to record activity by an audible bleep from a microcassette recorder earphone; this was considered the highest frequency possible without loss of accuracy.

More commonly, observation protocols code activities into four or five categories (Epstein et al. 1984; O'Hara et al. 1989;

Puhl et al. 1990). The Children's Activity Rating Scale (CARS) (Puhl et al. 1990) and the Children's Physical Activity Form (CPAF) (O'Hara et al. 1989) use five and four activity categories, respectively. Instead of sampling activity at set time intervals, a continuous minute-by-minute sampling method is employed in these protocols (Puhl et al. 1990). The activity level is coded at the start of each minute and any change in activity within that minute is also recorded. The time and frequency of each activity within that minute are unavailable as each activity level can only be recorded once. This is a limitation, as it is unlikely that each of the child's activities within that minute last an equal amount of time. However, Puhl et al. (1990) demonstrated that this showed only a small discrepancy when compared with a method that weighted each intensity category according to time spent.

Protocols also differ with respect to whether the outcome is a quantification of the amount of activity or whether this is converted to a prediction of energy expenditure. Energy expenditure may be predicted by taking a sub-sample of children into the laboratory and measuring the energy cost of some of the activities that could be coded (e.g. Bailey et al. 1995; Puhl et al. 1990). The limitations of predicting energy expenditure based on laboratory simulations of activities should be noted. For example, the predictions will be based on steady state activity. Children rarely reach steady state in typical play activity. Several children's and adult's activities cannot be reproduced in the laboratory and hence an energy cost for these activities has to be estimated. Alternatively, observational data can be simply categorised as low, medium or high intensity activity. This procedure avoids the assumptions associated with prediction (e.g. Bailey et al. 1995).

The CPAF was validated against heart rate with activity points as the outcome variable (O'Hara et al. 1989). The CARS can be used as a measure of activity or a prediction of energy expenditure (Puhl et al. 1990). It is important to remember that if the outcome variable is activity counts or points, this measure refers to quantity of movement and is unaffected by body mass. If the outcome variable is energy expenditure, a higher body mass will lead to higher energy expenditure for any given activity. The method of scaling energy expenditure for body mass should be considered when interpreting the results of such studies (see Chapter 11, Winter and Nevill).

When trying to capture an overall picture of a child's activity, the time spent observing the child and the variety of environments the child is observed in may be more important than the observation protocol used. Several studies have observed children during games/ physical education (PE) lessons (O'Hara et al. 1989), or while at summer camp (Epstein et al. 1984; Wallace et al. 1985). This is sufficient for validation studies or studies assessing the activity content of PE lessons or camps. To obtain a full picture of a child's activity level, the whole waking day needs to be accounted for, on several different days, at different times of the year and during school term and holidays if possible. Logistically this is very difficult, but organized games/PE lessons are far from ideal to show differences in spontaneous activity between children. Activity decreases in all children, regardless of their activity level, as activities became more organized (Corbin and Fletcher 1968).

6.4.4 Heart rate

Heart rate is not a direct measure of physical activity, but does provide an indication of the relative stress placed upon the cardiopulmonary system by physical activity (Armstrong and Welsman 2006). As it provides an objective measure, with no need for recall, heart rate monitoring has been commonly used to assess children's physical activity levels. It allows the recording of values over time, which facilitates a visual assessment of the pattern and intensity of activity. Heart rate monitoring was the first widely used objective

measure of physical activity in children. In the South West of England alone, over a 10-year period Armstrong and colleagues monitored the heart rates of over 1200 5- to 16-year-old children over three school days (Armstrong et al. 1990, 2000; Armstrong and Bray 1990, 1991; Biddle et al. 1991; McManus and Armstrong 1995; Welsman and Armstrong 1997, 1998, 2000).

The rationale for using heart rate monitoring as a measure of physical activity or energy expenditure relies on the linear relationship between heart rate and oxygen uptake. This relationship differs between individuals. Ideally, individuals' heart rate: oxygen uptake regression lines should be produced prior to measuring activity. This permits the prediction of oxygen uptake and hence energy expenditure from heart rate. This practice is time consuming, expensive and labour intensive. Hence, many authors do not carry out this calibration (Riddoch and Boreham 1995). Additionally, there are problems as the heart rate:oxygen uptake relationship of any individual is affected by the proportion of active muscle mass and whether the activity is continuous or intermittent (Klausen et al. 1985). For example, heart rate is considerably higher at similar oxygen uptake values for exercise of a static nature, and also for dynamic exercise by the arms compared with the legs (Maas et al. 1989). Thus, if a regression equation produced from a running or cycling task is used to predict the oxygen cost associated with the heart rate elicited during a task requiring upper body or static exercise, the oxygen uptake would be over-predicted.

If an oxygen uptake:heart rate regression line is not produced there are a number of ways of interpreting heart rate data. Most commonly the time spent with the heart rate above pre-determined heart rate thresholds is recorded. Elevating the heart rate above these thresholds is considered to be indicative of activity beneficial to health. This method does not take into account any individual differences in age, gender, weight, maturational level, resting heart rate or heart rate response (Riddoch and Boreham 1995; Rowlands *et al.* 1997). Some researchers have used net heart rate (Janz *et al.* 1992; Rowlands *et al.* 1999). This method controls for inter-individual differences between resting heart rate. The resting heart rate is subtracted from each heart rate recorded to give an 'activity heart rate.' The 'activity heart rate' is then averaged for the day.

Physical activity is not the only factor that causes changes in heart rate. Heart rate can also be influenced by other variables, for example, emotional stress, anxiety, level of fitness, type of muscular contraction, active muscle group, hydration and environment (Rowlands *et al.* 1997; Armstrong and Welsman 2006). These factors can have the greatest influence at low intensity activity; hence Riddoch and Boreham (1995) recommended that heart rate monitoring should be considered primarily as a tool for the assessment of moderate-to-vigorous activity and that heart rates below 120 beats.min^{-1} would not normally be considered to be valid estimates of physical activity. Children's natural activity pattern is highly transitory (Bailey *et al.* 1995; Saris 1986) and heart rates tend to be consistently low for the majority of the day (Armstrong *et al.* 1991; Gilbey and Gilbey 1995).

The method chosen for analyzing heart rate data needs careful consideration as it may affect the interpretation of the data. When activity level assessed by heart rate is expressed as net heart rate, relationships with body fat differ from when threshold heart rates are used to assess activity. For example, Janz *et al.* (1992) found inverse correlations between total activity and per cent fat in both boys and girls. However, correlations when thresholds were used were lower and not statistically significant. Rowlands *et al.* (1999) also found that results differed according to the method of analysis of the heart rate data. Low negative non-significant correlations were found between net heart rate and body fat, contrasting with relatively high significant positive correlations between

time spent above heart rate thresholds and body fat in 8- to 10-year-old girls.

A meta-analysis of 50 investigations of the relationship between activity and body fat in children and youth showed that the average effect size elicited from studies using heart rate to assess activity levels was significantly lower ($p < 0.05$) than the average effect size elicited from studies using a different method of activity assessment (questionnaire, observation, motion counter) (Rowlands *et al.* 2000). This indicated that heart rate monitoring, a physiological measure, was not measuring the same thing as the other behavioural measures. Perhaps heart rate monitoring does not capture the aspects of activity that are related to body fatness in children.

The above limitations question the suitability of heart rate telemetry for the validation of other methods that may have potential for population studies.

6.4.5 Motion counters

Motion counters provide an objective assessment of movement. They vary in cost and sophistication, from the simple, inexpensive pedometer invented approximately 500 years ago (Gibbs-Smith 1978) to sophisticated accelerometers. Generally, the pedometer gives a cumulative measure of total activity, or movements, over the time period assessed, although more sophisticated models are available. Accelerometers assess the intensity, frequency and duration of activity. Triaxial and uniaxial versions are available.

The main disadvantage of motion counters is their inability to measure static work, increased activity due to going up an incline or increased activity due to carrying a load. The contribution of static work to total daily energy expenditure has been observed to be trivial in adults (Meijer *et al.* 1989). In children, the contribution of static work to a day's energy expenditure is likely to be less than in adults, so the inability of the pedometer to measure this type of work may not be a cause for concern when assessing the activity levels of most people. The inability to measure increased activity due to going up inclines or carrying loads may be more of a problem.

a) Pedometers

Early studies using mechanical pedometers concluded that they were inaccurate at counting steps or measuring distance walked (Gayle *et al.* 1977; Kemper and Verschuur, 1977; Saris and Binkhorst, 1977; Washburn *et al.* 1980). However, during the last 10–15 years, studies have provided evidence for the reliability and validity of electronic pedometers for the quantification of distance walked, number of steps taken (Bassett *et al.* 1996), assessment of total daily activity (Sequeira *et al.* 1995) and estimation of activity intensity and duration (Tudor-Locke *et al.* 2005; Rowlands and Eston 2005). Reliability and validity do differ by brand, hence it is important to consult some of the comparative studies (e.g. Schneider *et al.* 2004; Tudor-Locke *et al.* 2006) and test the accuracy of the pedometers with the population of interest before commencing a study.

Sequeira *et al.* (1995) demonstrated that the pedometer could differentiate between varying levels of occupational activities (sitting, standing and moderate-effort occupational categories) in adults. However, the pedometer counts for the heavy work category did not differ from the counts for the moderate work category. The heavy work category was made up of a high proportion of static work, such as lifting heavy objects. As pedometers are unable to measure static work they underestimated the energy cost of the people in this occupational category.

Kilanowski *et al.* (1999) investigated the validity of pedometry as a measure of daily activity of 10- to 12-year-old children using contemporaneous measures of pedometry (Yamax Digi-walker SW-200, Yamasa, Tokyo, Japan, Figure 6.1), triaxial accelerometry (Tritrac Professional Products, Reining International, Madison,

Figure 6.1 Yamax Digi-walker SW-200 pedometer (left), ActiGraph GT1M uniaxial accelerometer (centre) and RT3 triaxial accelerometer (right).

WI, USA) and observation. Pedometer counts correlated significantly with both observation and triaxial accelerometry counts during high-intensity and low-intensity recreational activities. In the same year, a study from our laboratory showed that activity measured by pedometry or the Tritrac triaxial accelerometer, correlated positively with fitness (Tritrac r = 0.66; pedometer = 0.59, *p* < 0.01) and negatively with fatness (Tritrac r = –0.42; pedometer = –0.42 *p* < 0.05) in 34 boys and girls, aged 8–10 years (Rowlands *et al.* 1999). The simple pedometer identified the same relationships with fitness and fatness as the relatively sophisticated Tritrac. In contrast, contemporaneous measures of time spent above moderate and vigorous heart rate thresholds were not related to body fatness.

Over the last ten years, there has been a growth in the number of studies that have used pedometry to assess physical activity in children. The method is objective, cheap, unobtrusive and ideal for large population surveys or any situation where only a measure of total activity and not activity pattern is required. Recent studies have shown positive relationships between children's daily step counts and aerobic fitness (Le Masurier and Corbin 2006), bone density (Rowlands *et al.* 2002), psychological well-being (Parfitt and Eston 2005) and negative relationships with body fatness (Duncan *et al.* 2006).

There is a possibility that the act of wearing any activity monitor will cause a person to engage in reactive behaviour. This is defined as 'a change in normal activity levels because of the participants' knowledge that their activity levels are being monitored' (Welk *et al.* 2000, p. 59). The likelihood of reactive behaviour is potentially greater when activity is assessed using pedometers as people may be aware of their pedometer scores and/or able to check their score throughout the course of the day. This has led many researchers to 'blind' children to their scores by sealing the pedometers. The output can then be collated in a number of different ways. At the most controlled level, researchers may visit school each day and take pedometer scores from each child, re-sealing the pedometer after it has been read. This is problematic at weekends, so some researchers have provided one pedometer for each day of the measurement (well marked) and the child simply wears the appropriate pedometer each day and hands all the pedometers in at the end of the study. Alternatively, protocols may require parents/guardians to read the pedometer scores and re-seal the pedometer after the child has gone to bed. Other protocols make no attempt to blind the child to the pedometer output. Research has indicated little evidence for reactive behaviours whether the child is blinded to the pedometer output (Vincent and Pangrazi, 2002) or not (Ozdoba *et al.* 2004). We have assessed the difference between sealed and unsealed pedometers worn simultaneously by 9- to 11-year-old children and found no consistent discrepancy between the pedometers (unpublished data). It appears that valid measures of daily habitual activity can be obtained from sealed and unsealed pedometers. However, researchers may wish to seal pedometers during the day to minimise the risk of the pedometer accidentally being re-set and the loss of the days' data.

The pedometer also holds promise as a motivational tool to self-regulate physical activity levels. Pedometer-based intervention studies have demonstrated increased steps/day using set or individualised goals in adults (e.g. Chan *et al.* 2004; Tudor-Locke *et al.* 2004). Studies with children show that rewards based on access to television viewing combined with pedometer-based goals are effective in increasing children's activity levels (Goldfield *et al.* 2000; Roemmich *et al.* 2004), but that pedometer-based goals alone, without the rewards, are not as effective (Goldfield *et al.* 2006). We have shown that a peer-modelling, rewards (small customised toys, e.g. balls and frisbees) and pedometer-feedback intervention was successful in increasing physical activity in 9- to 11-year-old children (Horne *et al.* 2007). Therefore, evidence exists for the use of a pedometer not only as a measurement tool, but also as an intervention tool for behaviour change.

b) Time-sampling accelerometers

Early accelerometers (e.g. the Caltrac™, Hemokinetics Inc., Madison, WI, USA) enabled the assessment of intensity of activity with an output measure of total activity counts or total calories (predicted from activity counts, age, gender, height and mass). Subsequently, accelerometers with a time-sampling mechanism were developed enabling the assessment of the temporal pattern and intensity of activity as well as total accumulated activity. These units are initiated and downloaded via a computer interface and have no external controls or displays of activity levels. Since 1997, there has been a dramatic increase in the number of studies using accelerometers to assess physical activity (Troiano 2005). At the end of 2004, experts in accelerometry presented at the conference on 'Objective Monitoring of Physical Activity: Closing the Gaps in the Science of Accelerometry' held at the University of North Carolina, USA. A special issue (November 2005) of *Medicine and Science in Sports and Exercise* containing the papers from this conference was subsequently published. This collection of papers provides an excellent, thorough analysis of the accelerometer literature, areas where there is no clear consensus and where further research is required.

Accelerometers measure acceleration in one to three orthogonal planes (vertical, mediolateral and anteroposterior). Uniaxial accelerometers are normally worn so the sensitive axis is oriented in the vertical plane. Omnidirectional accelerometers are most sensitive in the vertical plane, but are also sensitive to movement in other directions with the output being a composite of the signals (Chen and Bassett 2005). In contrast, triaxial accelerometers consist of three orthogonal accelerometer units and provide an output for each plane as well as a composite measure. The commercially available accelerometers most frequently referred to in the literature are the uniaxial ActiGraph (ActiGraph, Fort Walton Beach, FL, USA, which has also been referred to as the CSA, the MTI and the WAM, Figure 6.1), the omnidirectional Actical (Mini Mitter Co., Inc., Bend OR, USA) and Actiwatch (Mini Mitter Co., Inc., Bend, OR, USA), and the triaxial RT3 (Stayhealthy, Inc., Monrovia, CA, USA, Figure 6.1), which superceded the Tritrac (Rowlands 2007).

The ActiGraph accelerometer has been validated against heart rate telemetry for use in assessing children's habitual daily activity (Janz, 1994). It was significantly correlated with heart rate telemetry (overall $r = 0.58$, $p < 0.05$), in 31 children aged 7–15 years, although the correlations between the ActiGraph movement counts and heart rate were higher during the more vigorous activities (defined as greater than 60% of heart rate reserve, $r = 0.63$, $p < 0.05$) (Janz 1994). The author suggested that the poorer relationship evident at low exercise intensities may reflect the weaknesses of heart rate telemetry in the evaluation of low exercise intensities.

When the ActiGraph accelerometer is validated in laboratory settings, higher validity correlations are found than when it is validated in field settings (Janz *et al.* 1995). Additionally, validity tends to be higher for adults compared with children (Janz 1994). Laboratory studies may elicit higher validity coefficients because the criterion variable is more valid. Oxygen consumption is normally used as the criterion in a laboratory study, whereas less valid alternatives (heart rate,

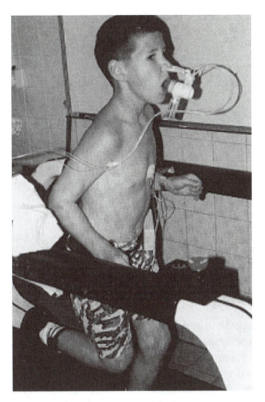

Figure 6.2 One of the children from the study by Eston *et al.* (1998). He is wearing the Tritrac on his left hip, the ActiGraph accelerometer on his right hip, a heart rate monitor (BHL 6000 Medical) and three pedometers: one on his right hip, one on his left wrist and one on his right ankle.

questionnaires) may be used in field studies. Hence, lower validity coefficients could reflect measurement error of the criterion variable as well as measurement error of the ActiGraph accelerometer. The size of validity coefficients can also be related to the variety of movement undertaken in the study. Movements are relatively ordered and controlled in laboratory studies, for example, walking and running. Similarly, adults generally undertake a lower variety of movement than children. The uniaxial system of measurement employed by the ActiGraph accelerometer may be more sensitive to common adult activities (walking/running) than children's activities (climbing/playing) (Janz 1994). This suggests that a triaxial

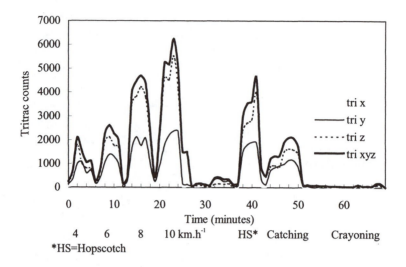

Figure 6.3 A typical plot of the Tritrac output during children's activities in the laboratory. Tri x = mediolateral plane; tri y = anteroposterior plane; tri z = vertical plane; tri xyz = vector magnitude.

accelerometer may be more appropriate for the assessment of children's activity.

The Tritrac-R3D™ (Professional Products, a division of Reining International, Madison, WI, USA) has all the benefits of the ActiGraph accelerometer, but in addition measures activity in all three dimensions. The boy in Figure 6.2 is wearing a Tritrac on the left hip and an ActiGraph accelerometer on the right hip. Figure 6.3 shows the Tritrac counts during walking, running, playing hopscotch, playing catch and crayoning (Eston *et al.* 1998). A similar validation study with adults also indicated that a triaxial accelerometer (the Tracmor unit) provided a more accurate estimate of a range of laboratory-based adult activities than uniaxial accelerometry alone (Bouten *et al.* 1994). Triaxial accelerometry has been validated as a field measure of physical activity in children using heart rate as a criterion measure (Welk and Corbin 1995), and in adults using indirect calorimetry as a criterion measure (Bouten *et al.* 1996).

Jakicic *et al.* (1999) assessed the validity of the Tritrac to predict energy expenditure in adults performing treadmill walking and running, stepping, stationary cycling and slideboard activities. The Tritrac did not differentiate between increases in energy expenditure due to increases in grade during walking or running. Nichols *et al.* (1999) also found that the Tritrac differentiated between speeds of walking and running, but not increases in gradient. Increases in workload due to increased stepping rate, increased cycling speed or increased slides per minute were detected (Jakicic *et al.* 1999). The computation of energy expenditure by the Tritrac software underestimated energy expenditure measured by indirect calorimetry during most activities, though correlated significantly for every activity except cycle ergometry. Increased energy expenditure due to carrying loads is also not detected by the Tritrac (Gotshall and DeVoe 1997).

Typical graphs showing daily activity measured by the Tritrac during a typical school day and a weekend day are shown in Figures 6.4 and 6.5. With the exception of the morning spent in a car (Figure 6.5) the rapid transition in activities, typical of children, is quite evident from these time versus movement intensity graphs.

A limitation of the Tritrac used in the above studies is its size. It measures 12.0 × 6.5 × 2.2 cm and weighs 168 g. It is supplied with a belt clip for attachment to the subject. This is an insecure method of attachment,

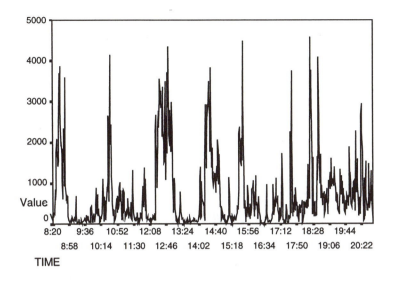

Figure 6.4 A typical Tritrac trace (vector magnitude) from a school day.

particularly when worn by children. Indeed, in trials in our laboratory, even during treadmill activities, the Tritrac rattled around, which is not ideal for an accelerometer. During initial 'hopping' activities it was liable to fly off the subject! To rectify this it was necessary to tape the Tritrac securely to a belt worn by each subject. In comparison, the smaller ActiGraph can be threaded onto a belt and therefore be held securely in position. This device does not hinder activities and is preferable for smaller children (Louie *et al.* 1999).

'Stayhealthy, Inc.' (Monrovia, CA, USA) purchased the technology and rights to the Tritrac R3D from 'Reining International.' The company developed a smaller triaxial accelerometer called the RT3 (7.1 cm × 5.6 cm × 2.8 cm, 65 g, Figure 6.1). A laboratory-based validity study showed the RT3 was as good a predictor of oxygen consumption as the Tritrac, although the resulting activity counts from the two monitors were not comparable (Rowlands *et al.* 2004).

6.5 CONSIDERATIONS WHEN USING ACCELEROMETERS TO ASSESS PHYSICAL ACTIVITY

Evidence suggests that triaxial accelerometers may provide a more valid estimate of children's physical activity than uniaxial accelerometers (Eston *et al.* 1998; Louie *et al.* 1999; Ott *et al.* 2000; Welk 2005). However, the difference appears to be small and correlations between uniaxial and triaxial output are high indicating that they are providing similar information (Trost *et al.* 2005). More recent evidence in adults and children has indicated that uniaxial accelerometry attains a plateau or even begins to decline at running speeds greater than 10 km.h^{-1} (Brage *et al.* 2003a; 2003b; Rowlands *et al.* 2007b). This is largely due to the dominance of horizontal acceleration at moderate to high running speed, rather than vertical acceleration. The incorporation of three vectors in triaxial accelerometry accounts for the variance in the relative dominance of the vectors across the different speeds. The relevance of this to the assessment of children's habitual activity, where short bursts of high-intensity activity are common (Bailey *et al.* 1995), is yet to be investigated.

The signal from an accelerometer is integrated over a given time interval, or epoch, then summed and stored. Depending on the accelerometer model, the epoch can be set as low as 1 second or as high as several minutes.

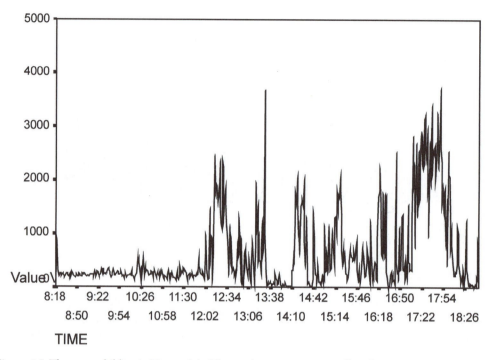

Figure 6.5 The same child as in Figure 6.4. All morning was spent travelling by car.

In the past, the vast majority of studies have set the epoch at 1 minute, although this is known to underestimate vigorous and high-intensity activity (Nilsson *et al.* 2002; Rowlands *et al.* 2006). As appreciation of the sporadic nature of children's activity has increased, studies have begun to use 10-second epochs (e.g. Hasselstrom *et al.* 2007). The arbitrary selection of a 1-minute epoch has most likely been due to the memory size of accelerometers. For example, the ActiGraph (model 7164) and triaxial RT3 are capable of collecting data at 1-second epochs for a maximum of only 9 hours. If output from each of the three vectors of the RT3 is required, as well as the composite vector magnitude, the recording time is reduced to 3 hours. However, the latest version of the ActiGraph (GT1M) has a memory size of 1 Mb and can collect data at 1-second epochs for nearly 6 days. This makes it feasible to use epochs ranging from 1 to 15 s to assess objectively the temporal pattern of children's activity over days at

a time with the uniaxial ActiGraph. At present, the RT3 can only be used in the 1-second mode for 9 hours at a time. Further research should address whether short bursts of high-intensity activity are underestimated by uniaxial accelerometry, as is the case for fast running.

Baquet *et al.* (2007), Rowlands *et al.* (2007a) and Chu *et al.* (2005) have utilized high-frequency accelerometry monitoring (1-second or 2-second epochs) to assess the pattern of children's activity. Physical activity patterns were very similar to those from the earlier observation study (Bailey *et al.* 1995). Furthermore, Chu *et al.* (2005) demonstrated that the intensity of activity bouts was positively related to fitness ($r > 0.4$, $p < 0.05$) and the interval between bouts was positively related to fatness ($r > 0.6$, $p < 0.01$) in 24 9-year-old Hong Kong Chinese children. However, the duration of the bouts was not related to fitness or fatness. This novel study highlights the potential importance of activity pattern. Further studies should investigate whether temporal aspects of the activity pattern explain variance in health and fitness in addition to that explained by composite variables (e.g. total activity, total time spent in moderate to vigorous activity). For example, total time accumulated in vigorous physical activity is related to fatness in children aged 4–6 years (Janz *et al.* 2002), 5–11 years (Abbott and Davies 2004), 8–11 years (Ekelund *et al.* 2004; Rowlands *et al.* 1999; Rowlands *et al.* 2006) and adolescents (Gutin *et al.* 2005). To what extent does the combination of frequency, intensity and duration of activity bouts matter, if the overall activity is the same?

The output from accelerometers is a dimensionless unit commonly referred to as 'accelerometer counts.' These counts are arbitrary, depending on the specifications of the accelerometer, and therefore cannot be compared between different types of accelerometer (Chen and Bassett, 2005). In order to give biological meaning to the output, these counts have been calibrated with energy expenditure (Freedson *et al.* 2005). As a result, count thresholds relating to various categories of energy expenditure (including sedentary behaviour) have been published that allow researchers to calculate the amount of time spent at differing intensities of activity for the ActiGraph (e.g. Freedson *et al.* 1997; Puyau *et al.* 2002; Trost *et al.* 2002; Treuth *et al.* 2004), the Actical (Puyau *et al.* 2004; Heil 2006), the Actiwatch (Puyau *et al.* 2004), the Tritrac (McMurray *et al.* 2004, Rowlands *et al.* 1999) and the RT3 (Rowlands *et al.* 2004). Freedson *et al.* (2005) provided a thorough discussion of the development of these thresholds. The number of available thresholds underscores the lack of agreement regarding interpretation of accelerometer output and highlights an ongoing problem with accelerometer research and comparability between studies.

Calibration studies tend to take place in the laboratory environment due to the difficulty of using a criterion measure of energy expenditure in the field. Some studies focus on walking/running activities (Freedson *et al.* 1997; Trost *et al.* 1998), while other studies incorporate 'free play' activities (Eston *et al.* 1998; Puyau *et al.* 2002; 2004; Rowlands *et al.* 2004; Pfeiffer *et al.* 2006) into the calibration. Knowledge of the activities used to develop cut-points is important, as the activities used to develop the accelerometer threshold counts have a major impact on the thresholds developed. For example, Eisenmann *et al.* (2004) demonstrated that use of a treadmill-based prediction equation (Trost *et al.* 1998) to estimate energy expenditure from the ActiGraph underestimated the energy cost of self-paced sweeping, bowling and basketball in 11-year-old boys and girls. However, activities were correctly classified as light or moderate at a group level according to thresholds based on structured activities (Puyau *et al.* 2002).

Despite the errors apparent when predicting energy expenditure from accelerometer counts, accelerometer counts are generally reported to be moderately to highly correlated with energy expenditure, assessed via a criterion method, across a range of activities. Additionally, accuracy is fair to excellent for the classification of the intensity of an activity as light, moderate or vigorous. This may be sufficient for some research questions. Currently, research is addressing methods of analyzing accelerometer data that will allow the mode of activity to be identified and the intensity to be classified once the mode is known (e.g. Crouter *et al.* 2006; Pober *et al.* 2006). This would not only improve the accuracy of the estimation of intensity, but also add some degree of qualitative information regarding activity patterns that accelerometers have always lacked.

6.6 MULTIPLE MEASURES OF PHYSICAL ACTIVITY

Physical activity is a complex behaviour and there are limitations associated with all the measurement methods described above.

The limitations associated with heart rate monitoring are mainly due to biological variance, whereas the limitations associated with accelerometry are largely biomechanical (Brage *et al.* 2004). As the errors associated with the two techniques are independent, a combination of the two methods may provide a more accurate estimate of physical activity than either method alone. The Actiheart (Cambridge Neurotechnology, Papworth, UK) is a small (10 g) heart rate recorder with an integrated omnidirectional accelerometer. It is clipped onto two ECG electrodes worn on the chest. Corder *et al.* (2005) have reported a greater accuracy in the prediction of children's energy expenditure during treadmill walking and running than either accelerometry or heart rate alone. At present, the cost of the Actiheart prohibits its use in all but small-scale studies. However, the Actiheart could provide a valid criterion measure of physical activity for use in the field.

6.7 PRACTICAL 1: RELATIONSHIP BETWEEN SELECTED MEASURES OF PHYSICAL ACTIVITY AND OXYGEN UPTAKE DURING TREADMILL WALKING AND RUNNING

6.7.1 Purpose

To assess the relationship between selected measures of physical activity and oxygen uptake during treadmill walking and running.

1   The RT3 and ActiGraph accelerometers are initialised. It is important to ensure that both units are set to the same clock, hence ensuring their internal clocks are temporally matched.
2   The participant rests for 10 minutes. Expired air is collected for 5 minutes and analyzed for resting oxygen consumption. Heart rate at rest is recorded.
3   The participant wears the RT3 accelerometer on one hip, the ActiGraph accelerometer and the pedometer (set to zero) on the other hip. One pedometer (set to zero) is also attached to a strap worn on the ankle. Heart rate is measured by radio telemetry.
4   The participant walks on the treadmill at 4 km.h^{-1} for 4 min. During the final minute, heart rate is recorded and expired air is collected and analyzed for oxygen consumption.
5   At the end of 4 minutes the pedometer readings are taken. The reading is divided by 4 to give counts.min^{-1}.
6   The above is repeated with the participant walking at 6 km.h^{-1}, running at 10 km.h^{-1} and 12 km.h^{-1}.
7   The RT3 and ActiGraph accelerometers are downloaded and the counts corresponding with the final minute of each activity recorded. For the RT3 record counts for each vector (x, y, z and vector magnitude).

6.7.2 Assignments

1   Correlate each of the activity measures (HR, ankle pedometer counts, hip pedometer counts, x RT3 counts, y RT3 counts, z RT3 counts, vector magnitude RT3 counts, ActiGraph counts) with $\dot{V}O_2$. Which activity measure has the highest correlation with $\dot{V}O_2$? (See Table 6.1 for example data.)
2   Compute the regression equation for the prediction of $\dot{V}O_2$ for each activity measure? What is the SEE associated with each regression equation?

3   Which Tritrac vector is the best predictor of oxygen uptake? (See Table 6.1 for example data.)

4   Calculate net heart rate for each activity and correlate this figure with $\dot{V}O_2$. Is the correlation between heart rate and oxygen uptake increased or decreased?

5   What would be the effect of increasing the treadmill gradient to manipulate workload, instead of changing treadmill speed, on the different correlations? Consider whether an increase or decrease in the correlation is expected.

6   What would be the effect of increasing the load carried to manipulate workload, instead of changing treadmill speed? Why do you think some of the correlations would increase or decrease?

7   Calculate the energy expenditure at rest and the energy expenditure during each activity. From these figures calculate the physical activity level associated with each activity.

Table 6.1 Example data for assignment questions 1 and 3. This should allow consideration of points raised in questions 4, 5, 6 and 7 also

	Heart rate	Pedometer (ankle)	Pedometer (hip)	RT3 x	RT3 y	RT3 z	RT3 VM	ActiGraph
$\dot{V}O_2$	0.799	0.789	0.806	0.847	0.876	0.891	0.908	0.780

8   Repeat the above methodology, but with different activities. The subject must reach steady state in each activity. Think of some appropriate activities; for example, jumping, crayoning, sitting up and down at intervals, playing catch.

FURTHER READING

Books

Montoye H. J., Kemper H. C. G., Saris W. H. M. and Washburn R. A. (1996). *Measuring Physical Activity and Energy Expenditure.* Human Kinetics; Champaign, IL.

Welk G. J. (ed.). (2002). Physical Activity Assessments for Health-Related Research. Human Kinetics; Champaign, IL.

Journals

Medicine and Science in Sports and Exercise Supplement (2005).

A Timely Meeting: Objective Measurement of Physical Activity. *Medicine and Science in Sports and Exercise*; **37**: S487–S588.

Esliger D. W., Copeland J. L., Barnes J. D. and Tremblay M. S. (2005) Standardizing and optimizing the use of accelerometer data for free-living physical activity monitoring. *Journal of Physical Activity and Health*; **3**: 366–83.

Rowlands A. V. (2007). Accelerometer assessment of physical activity in children: an update. *Pediatric Exercise Science*; **19**: 252–66.

Product websites

ActiGraph
http://www.theactigraph.com/

RT3
http://www.stayhealthy.com/products/rt3.php

Actiheart
http://www.minimitter.com/Products/Actiheart/index.html

Yamax Digi-walker SW-200
http://www.digiwalker.co.uk/SW-200.cfm

IDEEA (Intelligent device for assessment of energy expenditure and physical activity)
http://www.minisun.com/default.asp

REFERENCES

Abbott R. A. and Davies P. S. (2004) Habitual physical activity and physical activity intensity: their relation to body composition in 5.0-10.5-y-old children. *European Journal of Clinical Nutrition*; 58: 285–91.

Armstrong N. and Bray S. (1990) Primary schoolchildren's physical activity patterns during autumn and summer. *Bulletin of Physical Education*; 26: 23–6.

Armstrong N. and Bray S. (1991) Physical activity patterns defined by continuous heart rate monitoring. *Archives of Disease in Childhood*; 66: 245–7.

Armstrong N. and Welsman J. R. (2006) The physical activity patterns of European youth with reference to methods of assessment. *Sports Medicine*; 36: 1067–86.

Armstrong N., Balding J., Gentle P. and Kirby B. (1990) Patterns of physical activity among 11–16-year-old British children. *British Medical Journal*; 301: 203–5.

Armstrong N., Williams J., Balding J., Gentle P, and Kirby B. (1991) Cardiopulmonary fitness, physical activity patterns and selected coronary risk factors in 11–16 year olds. *Pediatric Exercise Science*; 3: 219–28.

Armstrong N., Welsman J. R. and Kirby B. J. (2000) Longitudinal changes in 11–13-year-olds' physical activity. *Acta Paediatrica*; 89: 775–80.

Bailey R.C., Olson J., Pepper S. L., Porszasz J., Barstow T. J. and Cooper D. M. (1995) The level and tempo of children's physical activities: an observational study. *Medicine and Science in Sports and Exercise*; 27: 1033–41.

Baquet G., Stratton G., Van Praagh E. and Berthoin S. (2007) Improving physical activity assessment in children with high-frequency accelerometry monitoring: a methodological issue. *Preventive Medicine*; 44: 143–7.

Baranowski T., Dworkin R. J., Cieslik C. J., Hooks P., Clearman D. R., Ray L., Dunn J. K. and Nader P. R. (1984) Reliability and validity of self-report of aerobic activity: Family health project. *Research Quarterly for Exercise and Sport*; 55: 309–17.

Bassett D. R., Ainsworth B. E., Leggett S. R., Mathien C. A., Main J. A., Hunter D. C. and Duncan G. E. (1996) Accuracy of five electronic pedometers for measuring distance walked. *Medicine and Science in Sports and Exercise*; 28: 1071–77.

Berman N., Bailey R., Barstow T. J. and Cooper D. M. (1998) Spectral and bout detection analysis of physical activity patterns in healthy, prepubertal boys and girls. *American Journal of Human Biology*; 10: 289–97.

Biddle S., Mitchell J. and Armstrong N. (1991) The assessment of physical activity in children: a comparison of continuous heart rate monitoring, self-report and interview techniques. *British Journal of Physical Education Research*; 10 (Suppl.): 4–8.

Black A. E., Coward W. A. and Prentice A. M. (1996) Human energy expenditure in affluent societies: an analysis of 574 doubly-labelled water measurements. *European Journal of Clinical Nutrition*; 50: 72–92.

Bouten C. V., Westerterp K. R., Verduin M. and Jansser J. D. (1994) Assessment of energy expenditure for physical activity using a triaxial accelerometer. *Medicine and Science in Sports and Exercise*; 26: 1516–23.

Bouten C. V. C., Verboeket-van de Venne W. P. H. G., Westerterp K. R., Verduin M. and Janssen, J. D. (1996) Daily physical activity assessment: comparison between movement registration and doubly labelled water. *Journal of Applied Physiology*; 81: 1019–26.

Brage S., Wedderkopp N., Anderson L. B. and Froberg K. (2003a) Influence of step frequency on movement intensity predictions with the CSA accelerometer: a field validation study in children. *Pediatric Exercise Science*; 15: 277–87.

Brage S., Wedderkopp N., Franks P. W., Anderson L. B. and Froberg K. (2003b). Reexamination of validity and reliability of the CSA monitor in walking and running. *Medicine and Science in Sports and Exercise*; 35: 1447–54.

Brage S., Brage N., Franks P. W., Ekelund U., Wong M., Anderson L. B., Froberg K. and Wareham N. J. (2004) Branched equation modelling of simultaneous accelerometry and heart rate monitoring improves estimate of directly measured physical activity energy expenditure. *Journal of Applied Physiology*; 96: 343–51.

Bratteby L-E., Sandhagen B., Fan H. and Samuelson G. (1997) A 7-day activity diary for the assessment of daily energy expenditure validated by the doubly labelled water method in adolescents. *European Journal of Clinical Nutrition*; 51: 585–91.

Cale L. (1994) Self-report measures of children's physical activity: recommendations for future development and a new alternative measure. *Health Education Journal*; 53: 439–53.

Chan C. B., Ryan D. A. J. and Tudor-Locke C. (2004) Health benefits of a pedometer-based physical activity intervention in sedentary workers. *Preventive Medicine*; 39: 1215–22.

Chen K. Y. and Bassett D. R. (2005) The technology of accelerometry-based activity monitors: current and future. *Medicine and Science in Sports and Exercise*; 37: S490–S500.

Chu E. Y. W., Hu Y., Tsang A. M. C. and McManus A. M. (2005) The influence of the distinguished pattern of locomotion to fitness and fatness in prepubertal children. XXIIIrd International Seminar on Pediatric Work Physiology, Gwatt Zentrum, Switzerland.

Corbin C. B. and Fletcher P. (1968) Diet and physical activity patterns of obese and non-obese elementary school children. *Research Quarterly*; 39: 922–28.

Corder K., Brage S., Wareham N. J. and Ekelund U. (2005) Comparison of PAEE from combined and separate heart rate and movement models in children. *Medicine and Science in Sports and Exercise*; 37: 1761–7.

Crouter S. E., Clowers K. G. and Bassett Jr. D. R. (2006) A novel method for using accelerometer data to predict energy expenditure. *Journal of Applied Physiology*; 100: 1324–31.

Duncan J. S., Schofield G. and Duncan E. K. (2006) Pedometer-determined physical activity and body composition in New Zealand children. *Medicine and Science in Sports and Exercise*; 38: 1402–9.

Eisennman J. C., Strath S. J., Shadrick D., Rigsby P., Hirsch N. and Jacobson L. (2004) Validity of uniaxial accelerometry during activities of daily living in children. *European Journal of Applied Physiology*; 91: 259–63.

Ekelund U., Sardinha L. B., Anderssen S. A., Harro M., Franks P. W., Brage S., Cooper A. R., Anderson L. B., Riddoch C. and Froberg K. (2004) Associations between objectively assessed physical activity and indicators of body fatness in 9- to 10-y-old European children: a population-based study from 4 distinct regions in Europe (the European Youth Heart Study). *American Journal of Clinical Nutrition*; 80: 584–90.

Emons H. J. G., Groenenboom D. C., Westerterp K. R. and Saris W. H. M. (1992) Comparison of heart rate monitoring combined with indirect calorimetry and the doubly labelled water ($^2H_2{}^{18}O$) method for the measurement of energy expenditure in children. *European Journal of Applied Physiology*; 65: 99–103.

Epstein L. H., McGowan C. and Woodall K. (1984) A behavioural observation system for free play activity in young overweight female children. *Research Quarterly for Exercise and Sport*; 55: 180–3.

Eston R. G., Rowlands A. V. and Ingledew D. K. (1998) Validity of heart rate, pedometry and accelerometry for predicting the energy cost of children's activities. *Journal of Applied Physiology*; 84: 362–71.

Freedson P. S., Melanson E. and Sirad J. (1997) Calibration of the Computer Science and Applications, Inc. accelerometer. *Medicine and Science in Sports and Exercise*; 29 (**Suppl.**) 5: 256 (abstract).

Freedson P. S., Pober D. and Janz K. F. (2005) Calibration of accelerometer output for children. *Medicine and Science in Sports and Exercise*; 37: S523–S530.

Gayle R., Montoye H. J. and Philpot J. (1977) Accuracy of pedometers for measuring distance walked. *Research Quarterly for Exercise and Sport*; 48: 632–6.

Gazzaniga J. M. and Burns T. L. (1993) Relationship between diet composition and body fatness, with adjustment for resting energy expenditure and physical activity, in preadolescent children. *American Journal of Clinical Nutrition*; 58: 21–8.

Gibbs-Smith C. (1978) *The Inventions of Leonardo da Vinci*. Phaidon Press Ltd.; London: pp. 31–43.

Gilbey H. and Gilbey M. (1995) The physical activity of Singapore primary school children as estimated by heart rate monitoring. *Pediatric Exercise Science*; 7: 26–35.

Gleitman H. (1996) *Basic Psychology*. 4th ed. Norton and Company; New York.

Goldfield G. S., Kalakanis L. E., Ernst M. M. and Epstein L. H. (2000) Open-loop feedback to increase physical activity in obese children. *International Journal of Obesity and Related Metabolic Disorders*; 24: 888–92.

Goldfield G. S., Mallory R., Parker T., Cunningham T., Legg C., Lumb A., Parker K., Prud'homme D., Gaboury I. and Adamo K. B. (2006) Effects of open-loop feedback on physical activity and television viewing in overweight and obese children: a randomized, controlled trial. *Pediatrics*; **118**: e157–66.

Goran M. I. (1997) Energy expenditure, body composition and disease risk in children and adolescents. *Proceedings of the Nutrition Society*; **56**: 195–209.

Gotshall R. W. and DeVoe D. E. (1997) Utility of the Tritrac-R3D accelerometer during bacpacking. *Medicine and Science in Sports and Exercise*; **29 (Suppl.)** 5: 258 (abstract).

Gutin B., Yin Z., Humphries M. C. and Barbeau P. (2005) Relations of moderate and vigorous physical activity to fitness and fatness in adolescents. *American Journal of Clinical Nutrition*; **81**: 746–50.

Hasselstrøm H., Karlsson K. M., Hansen S. E., Grønfeldt V., Froberg K. and Andersen L. B. (2007) Peripheral bone mineral density and different intensities of physical activity in children 6–8 years old: The Copenhagen School Child Intervention Study. *Calcified Tissue International*; **80**: 31–8.

Heil D. (2006) Predicting activity energy expenditure using the Actical activity monitor. *Research Quarterly for Exercise and Sport*; **77**: 64–80.

Horne P. J., Hardman C. A., Lowe C. F. and Rowlands A. V. (2007). Effects of a multi-component pedometer intervention on children's physical activity. *European Journal of Clinical Nutrition*; 1–8, doi: 10.1038/sj.ejcn.1602915.

Jakicic J. M., Winters C., Lagally K., Robertson R. J. and Wing R. R. (1999) The accuracy of the Tritrac-R3D accelerometer to estimate energy expenditure. *Medicine and Science in Sports and Exercise*; **31**: 747–54.

Janz K. F. (1994) Validation of the CSA accelerometer for assessing children's physical activity. *Medicine and Science in Sports and Exercise*; **26**: 369–75.

Janz K. F., Golden J. C., Hansen J. R. and Mahoney L. T. (1992) Heart rate monitoring of physical activity in children and adolescents: The Muscatine Study. *Pediatrics*; **89**: 256–61.

Janz K. F., Witt J. and Mahoney L. T. (1995) The stability of children's physical activity as measured by accelerometry and self-report. *Medicine and Science in Sports and Exercise*; **27**: 1326–32.

Janz K. F., Levy S. M., Burns T. L., Torner J. C., Willing M. C. and Warren J. J. (2002) Fatness, physical activity and television viewing in children during the adiposity rebound period: The Iowa bone development study. *Preventive Medicine*; **35**: 563–71.

Johnson M. L., Burke B. S. and Mayer J. (1956) Relative importance of inactivity and overeating in the energy balance of obese high school girls. *American Journal of Clinical Nutrition*; **4**: 37–44.

Kemper H. C. G. and Verschuur R. (1977) Validity and reliability of pedometers in habitual activity research. *European Journal of Applied Physiology*; **37**: 71–82.

Kilanowski C. K., Consalvi A. R. and Epstein L. H. (1999) Validation of an electronic pedometer for measurement of physical activity in children. *Pediatric Exercise Science*; **11**: 63–8.

Klausen K., Rasmussen B., Glensgaard L. K. and Jensen O. V. (1985). Work efficiency during submaximal bicycle exercise. In: (R. A. Binkhorst, H. C. G. Kemper and W. H. M. Saris, eds) *Children and Exercise XI*. Human Kinetics; Champaign IL: pp. 210–17.

Klein P. D., James W. P. T., Wong W. W., Irving C. S., Murgatroyd P. R., Cabrera M., Dallosso H. M., Klein E. R. and Nichols, B. L (1984) Calorimetric validation of the doubly labelled water method for determination of energy expenditure in man. *Human Nutrition: Clinical Nutrition*; **38C**: 95–106.

Ku L. C., Shapiro L. R., Crawford P. B. and Huenemann R. L. (1981) Body composition and physical activity in 8-year-old children. *American Journal of Clinical Nutrition*; **34**: 2770–5.

Le Masurier G. C. and Corbin C. B. (2006) Step counts among middle school students vary with aerobic fitness level. *Research Quarterly for Exercise and Sport*; **77**: 14–22.

Livingstone M. B. E., Prentice A. M., Coward W. A., Ceesay S. M., Strain J. J., McKenna P. G., Nevin, G. B., Barker, M. E. and Hickey, R. J. (1990) Simultaneous measurement of free-living energy expenditure by the doubly labeled water method and heart rate monitoring.

American Journal of Clinical Nutrition; **52**: 59–65.

Louie L., Eston R. G., Rowlands A. V., Tong K. K., Ingledew, D. K. and Fu, F. H. (1999) Validity of heart rate, pedometry and accelerometry for estimating the energy cost of activity in Hong Kong Chinese boys. *Pediatric Exercise Science*; **11**: 229–39.

Maas S., Kok M. L. J., Westra H. G. and Kemper H. C. (1989) The validity of the use of heart rate in estimating oxygen consumption in static and in combined static/dynamic exercise. *Ergonomics*; **32**: 141–8.

McManus A. and Armstrong N. (1995) Patterns of physical activity among primary school children. In: (F. J. Ring, ed) *Children in Sport*. Bath University Press; Bath, UK: pp. 17–23.

McMurray R. G., Baggett C. D., Harrell J. S., Pennell M. L. and Bangdiwala S. I. (2004) Feasibility of the Tritrac R3D accelerometer to estimate energy expenditure in youth. *Pediatric Exercise Science*; **16**:, 219–30.

Meijer G. A., Westerterp K. R., Koper H. and ten Hoor F. (1989) Assessment of energy expenditure by recording heart rate and body acceleration. *Medicine and Science in Sports and Exercise*; **221**: 343–7.

Montoye H. J., Kemper H. C. G., Saris W. H. M. and Washburn R. A. (1996) *Measuring Physical Activity and Energy Expenditure*. Human Kinetics; Champaign, IL.

Nichols J. F., Morgan C. G., Sarkin J. A., Sallis J. and Calfas K. J. (1999) Validity, reliability, and calibration of the Tritrac accelerometer as a measure of physical activity. *Medicine and Science in Sports and Exercise*; **31**: 908–12.

Nilsson A., Ekelund U., Yngve A. and Sjostrom M. (2002) Assessing physical activity among children with accelerometers using different time sampling intervals and placements. *Pediatric Exercise Science*; **14**: 87–96.

O'Hara N. M., Baranowski T., Simons-Morton B. G., Wilson B. S. and Parcel G. (1989). Validity of the observation of children's physical activity. *Research Quarterly for Exercise and Sport*; **60**: 42–7.

Ott A. E., Pate R. R., Trost S. G., Ward D. S. and Saunders R. (2000) The use of uniaxial and triaxial accelerometers to measure children's free play physical activity. *Pediatric Exercise Science*; **12**: 360–70.

Ozdoba R., Corbin C. and Le Masurier G.

(2004) Does reactivity exist in children when measuring activity levels with unsealed pedometers. *Pediatric Exercise Science*; **16**: 158–66.

Parfitt G. and Eston R. G. (2005). The relationship between children's habitual activity level and psychological well-being. *Acta Paediatrica*; **94**: 1791–7.

Pfeiffer K. A., McIver K. L., Dowda M., Almeida M. J. and Pate R. R. (2006) Validation and calibration of the Actical accelerometer in preschool children. *Medicine and Science in Sports and Exercise*; **38**: 152–7.

Prentice A. M., Coward W. A., Davies H. L., Davies H. L., Goldberg G. R., Murgatroyd P. R., Ashford J., Sawyer M. and Whitehead R. G. (1985) Unexpectedly low levels of energy expenditure in healthy women. *Lancet*; **1**: 1419–22.

Pober D.M., Staudenmayer J., Raphael C. and Freedson P. S. (2006) Development of novel techniques to classify physical activity mode using accelerometers. *Medicine and Science in Sports and Exercise*; **38**: 1626–34.

Puhl J., Greaves K., Hoyt M. and Baranowski T. (1990). Children's activity rating scale (CARS): Description and calibration. *Research Quarterly for Exercise and Sport*; **61**: 26–36.

Puyau M. R., Adolph A. L., Vohra F. A. and Butte N. F. (2002) Validation and calibration of physical activity monitors in children. *Obesity Research*; **10**: 150–7.

Puyau M. R., Adolph A. L., Vohra F. A., Zakeri I. and Butte N. F. (2004) Prediction of activity energy expenditure using accelerometers in children. *Medicine and Science in Sports and Exercise*; **36**: 1625–31.

Riddoch C. J. and Boreham C. A. G. (1995) The health-related physical activity of children. *Sports Medicine*; **19**: 86–102.

Roberts S. B., Coward W. A., Schlingenseipen K. H. *et al.* (1986) Comparison of the doubly labelled water ($^2H_2{}^{18}O$) method with indirect calorimetry and a nutrient-balance study for simultaneous determination of energy expenditure, water intake, and metabolizable energy intake in preterm infants. *American Journal of Clinical Nutrition*; **44**: 315–22.

Roemmich J. N., Gurgol C. M. and Epstein L. H. (2004).Open-loop feedback increases physical activity of youth. *Medicine Science in Sports and Exercise*; **36**: 668–73.

Rowlands A. V. (2007) Accelerometer assessment of physical activity in children: an update. *Pediatric Exercise Science*; 19: 252–66.

Rowlands A. V. and Eston R. G. (2005) Comparison of accelerometer and pedometer measures of physical activity in boys and girls, aged 8–10 yrs. *Research Quarterly for Exercise and Sport*; 76: 251–7.

Rowlands A. V., Eston R. G. and Ingledew D. K. (1997) Measurement of physical activity in children with particular reference to the use of heart rate and pedometry. *Sports Medicine*; 24: 258–72.

Rowlands A. V., Eston R. G. and Ingledew D. K. (1999). The relationship between activity levels, aerobic fitness, and body fat in 8- to 10-yr-old children. *Journal of Applied Physiology*; 86: 1428–35.

Rowlands A. V., Ingledew D. K. and Eston R. G. (2000). The relationship between body fatness and habitual physical activity in children: A meta-analysis. *Annals of Human Biology*; 27: 479–98.

Rowlands A. V., Powell S. M., Eston R. G. and Ingledew D. K. (2002) Relationship between bone mass, objectively measured physical activity and calcium intake in 8–11 year old children. *Pediatric Exercise Science*; 14: 358–68.

Rowlands A. V., Thomas P. W. M., Eston R. G. and Topping R. (2004) Validation of the RT3 triaxial accelerometer for the assessment of physical activity. *Medicine and Science in Sports and Exercise*; 36: 518–24.

Rowlands A. V., Powell S. M., Humphries R. and Eston R. G. (2006) The effect of accelerometer epoch on physical activity output measures. *Journal of Exercise Science and Fitness*; 4: 51–7.

Rowlands A. V., Pilgrim E. and Eston R. G. (2007a) Patterns of habitual activity across weekdays and weekend days in 9–11-year-old children. *Preventive Medicine*. doi.org/10.1016/j.ypmed.2007.11.004.

Rowlands A. V., Stone M. R. and Eston R. G. (2007b) Influence of speed and step frequency during walking and running on motion sensor output. *Medicine and Science in Sports and Exercise*; 39: 716–27.

Sallis J. F. and Saelens B. E. (2000). Assessment of physical activity by self-report: status, limitations and future directions. *Research Quarterly for Exercise and Sport*; 71: 1–14.

Saris W. H. M. (1986) Habitual activity in children: methodology and findings in health and disease. *Medicine and Science in Sports and Exercise*; 18: 253–63.

Saris W. H. M. and Binkhorst R. A. (1977) The use of pedometer and actometer in studying daily physical activity in man. Part I. Reliability of pedometer and actometer. *European Journal of Applied Physiology*; 37: 219–28.

Schneider P. L., Crouter S. E. and Bassett D. R. (2004) Pedometer measures of free-living physical activity: comparison of 13 models. *Medicine and Science in Sports and Exercise*; 36: 331–5.

Schoeller D. A. and van Santen E. (1982) Measurement of energy expenditure in humans by doubly labelled water method. *Journal of Applied Physiology*; 53: 955–9.

Sequeira M. M., Rickenbach M., Wietlisbach V., Tullen B. and Schutz Y. (1995) Physical activity assessment using a pedometer and its comparison with a questionnaire in a large population survey. *American Journal of Epidemiology*; 142: 989–99.

Shapiro L. R., Crawford P. B., Clark M. J., Pearson D. L., Raz J. and Huenemann R. L. (1984) Obesity prognosis: A longitudinal study of children from the age of 6 months to 9 years. *American Journal of Public Health*; 74: 968–72.

Tell G. S. and Vellar O. D. (1988) Physical fitness, physical activity and cardiovascular disease risk factors in adolescents. The Oslo Youth Study. *Preventive Medicine*; 17: 12–24.

Treuth M. S., Schmitz K., Catellier D. J., McMurray R. G., McMurray D. M., Almeida M. J., Going S., Norman J. E. and Pate R. (2004) Defining accelerometer thresholds for activity intensities in adolescent girls. *Medicine and Science in Sports and Exercise*; 36: 1259–66.

Troiano R. P. (2005). A timely meeting: objective measurement of physical activity. *Medicine and Science in Sports and Exercise*; 37: S487–S489.

Trost S. G., Ward D. S., Moorehead S. M., Watson P. D., Riner W. and Burke J. R. (1998) Validity of the computer science and applications (CSA) activity monitor in children. *Medicine and Science in Sports and Exercise*; 30: 629–33.

Trost S. G., Pate R. R., Sallis J. F., Freedson P. S., Taylor W. C., Dowda M. and Sirad J. (2002) Age and gender differences in objectively measured physical activity in youth. *Medicine and Science in Sports and Exercise*; **34**: 350–5.

Trost S. G., McIver K. L. and Pate R. R. (2005) Conducting accelerometer-based activity assessments in field-based research. *Medicine and Science in Sports and Exercise*; **37**: S531–SS543.

Tudor-Locke C., Bell R. C., Myers A. M., Harris S. B., Ecclestone S. A., Lauson N. and Rodger N. W. (2004) Controlled outcome evaluation of the First Step Program: a daily physical activity intervention for individuals with type II diabetes. *International Journal of Obesity and Related Metabolic Disorders*; **28**: 113–19.

Tudor-Locke C., Sisson S. B., Collova T., Lee S. M. and Swan P. D. (2005) Pedometer-determined step guidelines for classifying walking intensity in a young ostensibly healthy population. *Canadian Journal of Applied Physiology*; **30**: 666–76.

Tudor-Locke C., Sisson S. B., Lee S. M., Craig C. L., Plotnikoff R. C. and Bauman A. (2006) Evaluation of quality of commercial pedometers. *Canadian Journal of Public Health*; **97**: S10–S15.

Vincent S. and Pangrazi R. P. (2002) Does reactivity exist in children when measuring activity level with pedometers. *Pediatric Exercise Science*; **14**: 56–63.

Wallace J. P., McKenzie T. L. and Nader P. R. (1985) Observed vs. recalled exercise behaviour: a validation of a seven day exercise recall for boys 11–13 years old. *Research Quarterly for Exercise and Sport*; **56**: 161–5.

Washburn R., Chin M. K. and Montoye H. J. (1980) Accuracy of pedometer in walking and running. *Research Quarterly for Exercise and Sport*; **51**: 695–702.

Watson A. W. S. and O'Donovan D. J. (1977) Influence of level of habitual activity on physical working capacity and body composition of post–pubertal school boys. *Quarterly Journal of Experimental Physiology*; **62**: 325–32.

Welk G. J. (2005) Principles of design and analyses for the calibration of accelerometry-based activity monitors. *Medicine and Science in Sports and Exercise*; **37**: S501–S511.

Welk G. J. and Corbin C. B. (1995) The validity of the Tritrac-R3D activity monitor for the assessment of physical activity in children. *Research Quarterly for Exercise and Sport*; **66**: 202–9.

Welk G. J., Corbin C. B. and Dale D. (2000). Measurement issues in the assessment of physical activity in children. *Research Quarterly for Exercise and Sport*; **71**: 59–73.

Welsman J. R. and Armstrong N. (1997) Physical activity patterns of 5- to 11-year-old children. In: (N. Armstrong, B. J. Kirby and J. R. Welsman, eds) *Children and Exercise XIX: promoting health and well-being*. E & FN Spon; London: Pp. 139–44.

Welsman J. R. and Armstrong N. (1998) Physical activity patterns of 5-to-7-year-old children and their mothers. *European Journal of Physical Education*; **3**: 145–55.

Welsman J. R. and Armstrong N. (2000) Physical activity patterns in secondary schoolchildren. *European Journal of Physical Education*; **5**: 147–57.

Winter E. M. and Nevill A. M. (2009) Scaling: adjusting for differences in body size. In: (R. G. Eston and T. Reilly, Eds.) *Kinanthropometry Laboratory Manual: Anthropometry*, Routledge; Oxon.

Woods J. A., Pate R. R. and Burgess M. L. (1992) Correlates to performance on field tests of muscular strength. *Pediatric Exercise Science*; **4**: 302–11.

CHAPTER 7

ASSESSMENT OF PERFORMANCE IN TEAM GAMES

Thomas Reilly

7.1 AIMS

The aims of this chapter are:

- to outline different means of analyzing performance in field games;
- to describe field tests as used for fitness assessment in selected games;
- to exemplify two field tests for use in practical contexts.

7.2 INTRODUCTION

The ultimate goal of the athlete is to excel in performance of the sport in which he or she has specialised. In individual sports, such as running, swimming or cycling, the level of performance is gauged by the time taken to reach a set distance. In horizontal or vertical jumping, the performance is indicated by the distance or height of the jump. Similarly, in throwing events competitive performance is measured by the distance the missile is propelled, and body mass is one determinant of performance along with the acceleration of the implement prior to its release and prevailing aerodynamic factors. Anthropometric dimensions, such as body mass, are also relevant in events like rowing

where propulsion of the shell or boat is a function of the absolute power that the athlete generates.

In these individual sports not only is performance easily assessed in the competitive environment but also it is highly related to individual characteristics. These factors may include anthropometric dimensions (e.g. body mass, body size, body composition, body surface area, relative segmental lengths), physiological factors (e.g. muscle strength and power, anaerobic capacity, aerobic capacity or endurance, aerobic power as reflected in the maximal oxygen uptake) and biomechanical variables (e.g. mechanical advantage, mechanical efficiency) and so on. In sports in which complex skills and intricate team-work are required, the link between individual characteristics and performance capability is not a parsimonious relationship. The relevance of kinanthropometry is obvious in games, such as basketball and volleyball, where stature provides an advantage, but is less apparent in field hockey and association football where there can be a great degree of variability between individuals within one team (Reilly 2000a).

In the field games, success in competition is achieved by scoring more goals (or points) than the opposition. The individual team members must harmonise into an effective unit and combat the opposing team. In such contexts the assessment of how well the team is playing and how much individuals contribute to team effort presents a challenge to the sports scientist. Furthermore, there is a need in such sports for test measures that will give a reasonable prediction of performance capability in applied contexts.

In this chapter various methods for describing performance in games contexts are outlined. Such methodologies include both notation analysis and motion analysis. The emphasis in monitoring individual profiles is placed on field tests where measurements must have relevance to the sport in question and be socially convenient. For retaining scientific value such tests must be valid, reliable and objective. Examples of field tests for use with games teams are given later in this chapter.

7.3 METHOD OF ANALYZING TEAM PERFORMANCE

7.3.1 Notation analysis

Notation analysis represents a means of recording observations in an objective manner for the purpose of compiling statistical details of performance parameters. The objectives of notation systems include analysis of movements during play, technical and tactical evaluation and statistical compilation (Hughes 1988: Carling *et al.* 2005). Principles of notation date back to the use of hieroglyphs by the ancient Egyptians to read dance and primitive methods of the Romans to record gestures. In recent years they have been applied commercially in video and computer-based systems both for qualitative and quantitative analysis of performance in team sports.

Initially, behavioural events were recorded manually, utilizing short-hand codes for notation. The more sophisticated systems entailed considerable learning time. By the mid-1980s computerized notation systems had evolved. These systems were used in conjunction with video recordings, either analyzed post-event or in real-time. The game may be represented digitally with data collected directly onto the computer, which can then be queried in a structured way. The game is represented in its entirety and contains a large database for interrogation. In this way, the performance of a team as a whole, or individual team members, can be analyzed, as can particular aspects of performance, such as attack or defence.

The minutiae of performance can be detailed using notation analysis. For every event, the action concerned, the player (or players) involved, and the location of the pitch can be entered into the computer. The method has been employed in a range of field games (Hughes 1988), in squash (Hughes and Franks 1994) and other racket sports (Hughes 1998). Other uses have included identifying the characteristics of the successful patterns of play by soccer teams at the World Cup (Reilly and Korkusuz 2008), the changes in patterns of play between 1990 and 1999 in the top league in England (Williams *et al.* 1999) and the consequences for training (Carling *et al.* 2005). Another application has been the presentation of activity profiles for field-hockey players (Spencer *et al.* 2004).

The development of sports science support programmes hastened the acceptance of notation analysis by coaches. Olsen and Larsen (1997) described how notation analysis had benefited the national football team of Norway in competing with the best teams in the world. More recently Carling *et al.* (2008) provided detailed information about the range of applications across the field sports and how observations can influence preparation for matches. Currently its main use is in analyzing team performance, post-event. In conjunction with video-editing facilities it can provide interim feedback to players and coaches, for example in half-time team talks. Surveillance information may also be provided about the style of play needed to combat forthcoming opponents. Whilst largely a descriptive tool, notation analysis could be employed by sports scientists to address theory-driven questions. Such issues might include potential links between performance and individual variables characteristic of kinanthropometry.

7.3.2 Motion analysis

The physiological demands of field games can be examined by making relevant observations during match-play or by monitoring physiological responses in real or in simulated games. The type, intensity and duration (or distance) of activities can be observed by means of motion analysis. Motion analysis entails establishing work-rate profiles of players within a team according to the intensity, duration and frequency of classified activities, for example walking, moving sideways or backwards, jogging, cruising and sprinting.

The total distance covered during a game provides an overall index of work-rate, based on the assumption that energy expenditure is directly related to total work (distance covered) or power output. Several methods have been employed in attempts to determine the distance covered during match-play in soccer and other field games. Early attempts focused on the use of hand notation systems for the recording of activity patterns. Such systems tracked players' movements on a scale plan of the pitch according to conventional cartographic methods. Later systems made use of coded commentaries of activities recorded on audio tape, in conjunction with measurements based on stride characteristics taken from video recordings to evaluate the total distance covered during the 90 minutes of match-play (Reilly and Thomas, 1976). Other original methods have included cinefilm taken from overhead views of the pitch for computer-linked analysis of the movements of the whole team and synchronized cameras placed overlooking each half of the pitch to allow calculation of activities by means of trigonometry (Ohashi *et al.* 1988; Drust *et al.* 1998).

Current motion-analysis systems may be used to analyze previously recorded video footage of individual players. The total distance covered in each activity classification is estimated by determining stride frequencies on the playback of the video, provided the stride length for each activity is determined separately for the individual concerned. Where the analyst does not have direct access to players to determine individual calibration curves, a player's movement patterns around the pitch in each activity category can be plotted mechanically on a commercially available drawing tablet with estimations of the total distance covered being based on pre-determined pitch dimensions. By following the co-ordinates of the individual player's position on the scaled representation of the pitch, the velocity (and acceleration) data can be computed and distance covered over time calculated. Irrespective of the specific details of the methods employed, all methodologies used for the measurement of distance should be reliable, objective and valid (Reilly 1994).

Systems based on vision hardware utilize military optronic technology designed for the observation, detection, recognition and location of military targets, such as planes and armoury. Optronic binoculars mounted on a tripod are operated manually by the analyst in order to follow the movements of a player visually. Positional data are sampled at 5 Hz and simultaneously transferred to a laptop computer connected to the binoculars and processed in real-time. The system is portable and convenient to set up. Limitations are that only one player is monitored for each operator and the reliability of this system is yet to be established (Carling and Reilly 2008).

Contemporary systems include a range of methods from video-based technologies to global positioning systems, not all of which are suitable for application to competitive contexts (for a review, see Carling and Reilly 2008). The most sophisticated contemporary method employs six to eight cameras, three to four placed high on the stand on each side, allowing observations to be made on all players on the pitch, as well as the referee. Combined synchronized cameras and image processing lead to minimal loss of data when players enter congested areas of the pitch. This kind of facility incorporates both motion analysis and notation analysis, thereby providing information on all movements and technical actions during play. Electronic tracking of players can now be achieved automatically, so that the data for individual players are available to game commentators as play progresses. This service was first used by the Union of European Football Associations (UEFA) in its competitions during 2008; data were displayed on screen for substituted players as they left the pitch. Comparisons with traditional reference methods demonstrate good agreement, with measurement error generally below 2%.

Monitoring of multiple players at a time is also feasible with 'global positioning systems'. This method has been adopted in friendly matches and in training contexts where competitive rules can be relaxed (Edgecomb and Norton 2006). The sensors can be worn as a back-pack and six to eight players can be monitored at the same time. The low sampling frequency is a limitation of currently available systems and hence data computed for acceleration may lack validity. A positive feature is that impacts upon the player can be registered, so that the aggregate physical load associated with receiving 'hits' and tackles can be recorded.

Work-rate profiles in Association Football (soccer) and in the other field games are influenced by factors such as positional role, the style of play, environmental factors and the level of competition (Reilly 2000b). They are also influenced by physiological variables such as maximal oxygen uptake (Reilly and Thomas 1976), endurance capacity (Bangsbo 1994) and carbohydrate stores (Saltin 1973). Anthropometric variables may dictate the optimal positions of players, tall players being favoured for central roles in defence and attack. The predisposition of players for positional roles according to their anthropometric characteristics is more pronounced in Rugby Union football (Reilly 1997) than in Association Football or field hockey (Reilly and Borrie 1992). There is also an evolution of somatotypes with increased professionalisation of sports; the Rugby Union backs in contemporary international levels being more muscular than the forwards of former decades (Olds 2001).

Anthropometric characteristics are more homogenous in Rugby Sevens than in the 15-a-side version of the game, in view of the need for greater mobility around the pitch in the former. Players in a Rugby-Sevens international tournament demonstrated muscular somatotypes (2.3-5.9-1.5), with forwards on average 15 kg heavier than the backs (Rienzi et al. 1999). Anthropometric variables were reported to be significantly related to work-rate components, mesomorphy and muscle mass being negatively correlated with the amount of high intensity activity during the game. Nevertheless, neither anthropometric profiles nor work-rate measures necessarily determine whether at this level of play a game is won or lost. The same conclusion applies to Association Football at international level (Rienzi et al. 2000).

Notation and motion analysis techniques provide means of evaluating performances of athletes and are a valuable source of feedback in team games in particular. They yield data with respect to the demands that the game imposes on players. The performance capabilities of players are influenced by fitness factors and the demands that players are voluntarily prepared to impose on themselves. Whilst there has been a tradition of testing athletes in laboratory conditions for physiological functions such as maximal oxygen uptake ($\dot{V}O_2max$) and 'anaerobic threshold' or responses of blood lactate to incremental exercise, the current trend is to use field tests of fitness where possible. The use of field measures increases the social acceptability of fitness testing, saves time when group members can be accommodated together and the sports-specific elements of the test battery are obvious to the practitioners.

7.4 FIELD TESTS

7.4.1 Generic tests

Field tests refer to measures that can be implemented in the typical training environment and do not necessarily require a visit to an institutional laboratory for assessment. An implication is that the test can be performed without recourse to complex monitoring equipment. The Eurofit test battery (EUROFIT 1988) offers a range of fitness items for which norms are available to help in interpreting results. The Eurofit test battery is referred to in more detail by Beunen (2009, Chapter 3) and Barker et al. (2009, Chapter 8). Whilst the tests utilize performance measures such as runs, jumps, throws and so on, they are designed to assess physiological functions such as strength, power, muscle endurance and aerobic power albeit indirectly.

The validation of the 20-m shuttle run test for estimation of maximal oxygen uptake (Leger and Lambert 1982) marked a step forward for sports science support programmes. Athletes may be tested as a squad in a gymnasium or open ground, such as a car park or synthetic sports surface. The pace of motion between two lines 20 m apart is dictated by signals from an audio tape-recorder which has given its name 'the bleep test' to the protocol. The pace is increased progressively, analogous to the determination of $\dot{V}O_2$max on a motor-driven treadmill, until the athlete is forced to desist. The final stage reached is recorded and the $\dot{V}O_2$max can be estimated using tables provided by the National Coaching Foundation (Ramsbottom et al. 1988). For children, the prediction of $\dot{V}O_2$max has been validated by Leger et al. (1988).

Alternative tests of aerobic fitness have employed runs, either distance run for a given period of time, such as the 12-minute run of Cooper (1968) or a set distance such as

the 3-km run validated by Oja et al. (1989). The former has been used as a field test in games players whilst the latter has been used mainly for purposes of health-related fitness. The tests are essentially performance measures and have been validated against maximal oxygen uptake. The use of early running tests for predicting $\dot{V}O_2$max has been reviewed elsewhere (Eston and Brodie 1985). More recently, the progressive run test reported by Chtara et al. (2005) was intended both to estimate $\dot{V}O_2$max and establish the running velocity at which this function is reached (v-$\dot{V}O_2$max). The test takes place on a 400-m track, with cones placed 2 m apart to facilitate pacing; the initial stage is at 8.0 km.h^{-1} with increments of 0.5 km.h^{-1} each minute until the subject is no longer able to maintain the imposed speed.

7.4.2 Repeated sprint tests

The capability to reproduce high intensity sprints may be examined by means of requiring the athlete to reproduce an all-out sprint after a short recovery period. A distance of 30 m is recommended. Timing gates may be set up at the start, after 10 m and at 30 m. There is then a 10-m deceleration zone for the athlete to slow down prior to jogging back to the start line. The recovery period is variable but 25 s is recommended (Williams et al. 1997). When the interval is reduced to 15 s, test performance is significantly related to the oxygen transport system (Reilly and Doran 1999).

Seven sprints are recommended, from which peak acceleration (over 10 m) and speed (time over 30 m) can be ascertained. A fatigue index can be calculated both for acceleration and speed over 30 m, based on the drop off in performance over the seven sprints. The mean time for the seven sprints is indicative of the ability to perform several short sprints within a short period of time within a game. Generally, the best performances are in the first and second sprints; the poorest over the sixth or seventh.

7.4.3 Sports-specific tests

a) The yo-yo test

The 'yo-yo' tests were designed to test the capability to tolerate high-intensity activity for a sustained period. The test was designed by Bangsbo (1998) for relevance to field games. In the tests the player performs repeated 20-m shuttle runs interspersed with a short recovery period during which the player jogs. The time allowed for a shuttle is decreased progressively as dictated by audio bleeps from a tape recorder. The test ends when the athlete is unable to continue, the score recorded being the number of shuttles completed.

The 'yo-yo intermittent endurance' test evaluates the ability to perform intense exercise repeatedly after prolonged intermittent exercise. A 5-s rest period is allowed between each shuttle and the duration of the test in total is between 10 and 20 minutes.

The ability to recover from intense exercise is evaluated by means of the 'yo-yo intermittent recovery' test. The running speeds are higher than in the yo-yo intermittent endurance test but a 10-s period of jogging is allowed between each shuttle. The total duration of the test is between 2 and 15 minutes.

Both tests have two levels, one for elite footballers and another for recreational players. It is recommended that the tests are conducted on a football field with the players wearing football boots. The tests can be completed in a relatively short period of time and a whole squad of up to 30 players can be tested at the same time. The yo-yo intermittent recovery test is used as a compulsory test for football referees in Italy and Denmark and both tests have been employed in professional teams in a number of European countries.

An alternative means of assessing aerobic capacity and power is the two-tiered protocol reported by Svensson and Drust (2005) for application to soccer players. The '15–40' protocol refers to the varying distances in a prescribed shuttle-run, paced according to taped audio signals. The submaximal component of the test can be administered as part of the normal fitness training, with changes in fitness being indicated by heart-rate responses. The maximal component ends in voluntary exhaustion and is indicative of maximal aerobic power. Its application is restricted to critical phases of the competitive season to evaluate effects of previous training, indicate current fitness levels and provide evidence for translating the observations into training prescriptions.

b) Dribble tests for Association Football

The tests entail a run as fast as possible over a zig-zag course while dribbling a football. They incorporate an agility component, calling for an ability to change direction quickly. The tests were part of a battery designed for testing young soccer players by Reilly and Holmes (1983) and employed in talent identification programmes (Reilly et al. 2000).

The slalom dribble is a test of total body movement requiring the subject to dribble a ball round a set obstacle course as quickly as possible. Plastic conical skittles 91 cm high and with a base of diameter 23 cm are used as obstacles. Two parallel lines are drawn as reference guides 1.57 m apart. Intervals of 1.83 m are marked along each line and diagonal connections of alternate marks 4.89 m long are made. Five cones are used on the course and a sixth is placed 7.3 m from the final cone, exactly opposite it and 9.14 m from the starting line (Figure 7.1). On the command 'go' each subject dribbles the ball from behind the starting line to the right of the first cone and continues to dribble alternately round the remainder in a zig-zag fashion to the sixth where the ball is left and the subject sprints to the starting line. The time elapsed between leaving and returning past the starting line is recorded to the nearest one-tenth second and indicates the individual's score. Subjects are forced to renegotiate any displaced cones. A demonstration by the experimenter and a practice run by the subject is undertaken before four trials are performed, with a rest of 20 minutes between trials, the aggregate time representing the subject's score.

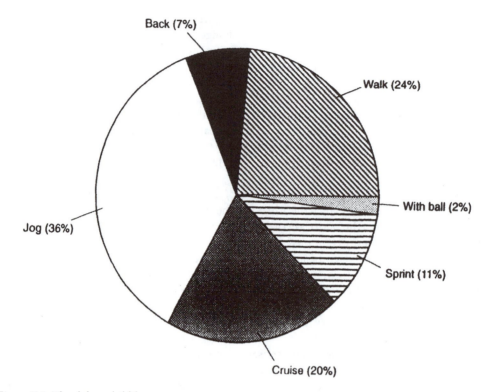

Figure 7.1 The slalom dribble.

In the straight dribble, five cones are placed in a straight line perpendicular to the start line, the first 2.74 m away, the middle two separated by 91 cm while the remainder are 1.83 m apart as shown in Figure 7.2. Subjects are required to dribble round alternate obstacles until the fifth is circled and then to return down the course in similar fashion. The ball has to be dribbled from the final obstacle to the start line which now constitutes the finish. The aggregate score from four test trials constitutes the overall test score.

c) Field test for field hockey

A battery of field tests was described by Reilly and Bretherton (1986) for use in assessing female hockey players. The tests consist of a sprint, a T-run dribbling test and a 'distance and accuracy' skill test.

The sprint over 50 (45.45 m) yards is timed to 0.01 s, the fastest of three trials being recorded. The T-run is over 60 (54.55 m) yards while dribbling a leather hockey ball around skittles. The test involves as many circuits of the T-shaped course as possible in 2 minutes. All subjects are practised in the drill, which excludes use of reversed sticks, and the best of the three trials is recorded. The distance and accuracy test involves a combination of dribbling a ball and hitting it at a target, with a set sequence being repeated as often as possible within 2 minutes. The distance travelled is calculated to the nearest 2.5 (2.27 m) yards and relative accuracy is calculated by expressing the number of accurate shots as a per cent of the number of hits. All subjects are familiarized with the drill before testing takes place.

More recently, Elferink-Gemser *et al.* (2007) have designed assessment protocols for field-hockey players, validated by the discrimination of young talented players at national elite and sub-elite levels. The assessments are

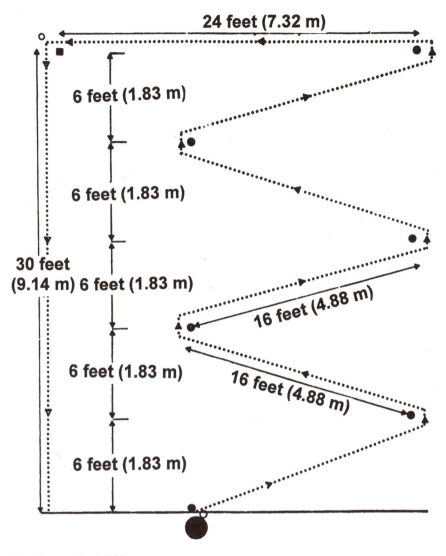

Figure 7.2 The straight dribble.

multifactorial, engage games skills and fitness components and can be used to monitor training interventions. The conditions under which the tests are administered must be controlled as far as possible for findings to have value.

d) Field test for Rugby Union football

McLean (1993) described a functional field test for application to Rugby Union. The structure and content of the test were designed so as to relate to the effort and skill patterns a player is called upon to produce in the game. The test was used by the Scotland international squad in preparing for the 1991 Rugby World Cup.

The distance run is about 99 m. The course is run twice with a 45-s recovery, which allows the drop-off in performance over the second run to be identified. Penalty points are applied for errors in the skills elements of the test.

The player starts the run with the ball in hand. Skills elements include passing the ball, running round flags, diving to win the ball

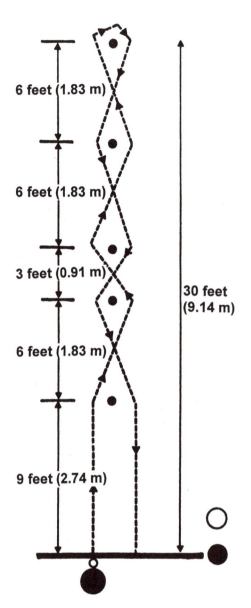

6 feet (1.83 m)

6 feet (1.83 m)

3 feet (0.91 m)

6 feet (1.83 m)

9 feet (2.74 m)

30 feet (9.14 m)

Figure 7.3 Field test for Rugby Union.

on the ground, driving a crash pad, jumping and crash-tackling, a tackle bag, picking the ball from the ground. All of these are incorporated within the test (see Figure 7.3). It was reported that players of different ability levels could be discriminated on the basis of performance in the test.

7.5 OVERVIEW

There is a rich history of performance testing for particular sports, reflected in the various test and measurement texts (e.g. Kirkendall *et al.* 1987). These tests have incorporated movements akin to patterns in the game, whether it be basketball (MacDougall *et al.* 1991) or badminton (Hughes and Fullerton 1995). The latter test is performed on a regulation badminton court; the speed of movement around a marked course being dictated by a computer-generated sound tone. The test is incremental and consists of three stages, each of 3 minutes. Heart rate and blood lactate responses are recorded and used in the interpretation of results.

The application of scientific principles to field testing has progressed to a point where existing tests are refined and new tests designed. In such instances, one difficulty is that baseline and reference data become obsolete with use of new versions of the test. Applied sports scientists ultimately have to choose between protocols that allow direct physiological interpretations of results or have proven utility for determining game-related performance.

7.6 PRACTICAL 1: THE USE OF REPEATED SPRINT TESTS

7.6.1 Aims

- to determine the athlete's running speed over 10-m and 30-m sprints;
- to examine the ability to tolerate fatigue over repeated sprints.

7.6.2 Procedure

An open 40-m stretch is marked out in a series of zones. Starting gates are set up with electronic timing devices, the timer being activated when a beam of light is broken. Additional timing gates are set up at 10 m and 30 m, the time at each of these distances being recorded as the athlete's body breaks through the light beam. The athlete continues through a 10-m deceleration zone, and then jogs back to the start line to perform the next sprint. Meanwhile the observers record the times for 10 m and 30 m and reactivate the telemetry recorder in time for the next sprint. A recovery of 25 s is permitted between sprints.

Verbal encouragement should be given to the athlete throughout the run. The athlete should also be reminded of the number of the forthcoming run and a countdown over 5 s prior to starting. It is important that the runner is stationary in the ready position when the recovery period has elapsed.

The data for two players are illustrated in Table 7.1. The first player's fastest times are 1.47 s for 10 m and 4.07 s for 30 m. Generally, the fastest times are produced in the first two runs and the slowest in one of the last two runs. Thus the player's slowest times are 1.93 s and 4.65 s, respectively. A drop-off can be calculated by expressing the slowest over the fastest time, converting to a percentage and subtracting 100 as follows:

Drop-off (fatigue index) 10 m =   (a) $(1.93/1.47) \times 100 = 131.3\%$
                                   (b) $131.3 - 100 = 31.3\%$

30 m =   (a) $(4.65/4.67) \times 100 = 114.3\%$
                                   (b) $114.3 - 100 = 14.3\%$

The fatigue index is therefore 31.3% for 10 m and 14.3% for 30 m. In a similar way the drop-off rate can be calculated for the second player. The results are 17.5% and 12.6%, for 10 m and 30 m, respectively.

7.7 PRACTICAL 2: COOPER'S 12-MINUTE RUN TEST

7.7.1 Aims

- to determine endurance capacity by means of recording distance run in 12 minutes;
- to estimate maximal oxygen uptake from performance in the 12-minute test.

7.7.2 Procedure

A measured outdoor track is required. The ideal condition would be a running track with each lap being 400 m. Alternatively, a marked course around school playing fields can be used.

As the test entails a maximal effort, it is dependent on the motivation of the subject. For this reason the pacing of effort is a potential problem. Subjects can set off at designated intervals between one another and be called to stop in turn as time is up.

The distance covered in 12 minutes should be recorded to the nearest 10 m for each individual. This distance is converted to miles, one mile being equivalent to 1603 m. For individuals of a high aerobic fitness level, the test tends to overestimate $\dot{V}O_2$max and is more useful for health-related purposes and recreational players than for serious games competitors. Maximal oxygen ($\dot{V}O_2$max) can be predicted from the formula:

$$\dot{V}O_2\text{max (ml.kg}^{-1}\text{min}^{-1}) = (\text{Distance in miles (D)} - 0.3138)/0.0278$$

For example, two athletes cover distances of 2.82 [A] and 1.98 km [B], respectively in the time allowed. Calculations are as follows:

A: $\dot{V}O_2$max (ml.kg^{-1}min^{-1}) = ((2.82/1.603) − 0.3138)/0.0278
= (1.7592 − 0.3138)/0.0278
= 1.445/0.0278
= 52 ml.kg.$^{-1}$min^{-1}

B: $\dot{V}O_2$max (ml.kg^{-1}min^{-1}) = ((1.98/1.603) − 0.3138)/0.0278
= (1.2352 − 0.3138)/0.0278
= 0.9114/0.0278
= 33 ml.kg.$^{-1}$min^{-1}

Table 7 Performance times for a games player in a repeated sprint test

		10 m (s)		30 m (s)	
		Player 1	Player 2	Player 1	Player 2
Sprints	1	1.47	1.71	4.09	4.28
	2	1.49	1.73	4.07	4.32
	3	1.60	1.82	4.20	4.41
	4	1.61	1.84	4.28	4.49
	5	1.69	1.90	4.38	4.61
	6	1.89	1.98	4.56	4.68
	7	1.93	2.01	4.65	4.82

FURTHER READING

Gore C. J. (ed) (2000) *Physiological Tests for Elite Athletes*. Human Kinetics; Champaign, IL.

Reilly T. (2005) *Science of Training – Soccer*. Routledge; Oxon.

REFERENCES

Bangsbo J. (1994) Physiology of soccer – with specific reference to intense intermittent exercise. *Acta Physiologica Scandinavica*; **151**: (Suppl.): 169.

Bangsbo J. (1998) Performance testing in soccer. *Insight: The FA Coaches Association Journal*; **2**(2): 21–3.

Barker A., Boreham C., Van Praagh E. and Rowlands A. V. (2009) Special considerations for assessing performance in young people. In: (R. G. Eston, and T. Reilly, eds) *Kinanthropometry Laboratory Manual: Anthropometry*. 3rd Edition. Routledge; Oxon: pp. 197–230.

Beunen G. (2009) Physical growth, maturation and performance. In: (R. G. Eston, and T. Reilly, eds) *Kinanthropometry Laboratory Manual: Anthropometry*, 3rd Edition. Routledge; Oxon.

Carling C. and Reilly T. (2008) The role of motion analysis in elite soccer: contemporary performance measurement techniques and work-rate data. *Sports Medicine*. In press.

Carling C., Williams A. M. and Reilly T. (2005) *Handbook of Soccer Match Analysis*. Routledge; Oxon.

Carling C., Reilly T. and Williams A. M. (2008) *Performance Assessment for Field Sports*. Routledge; Oxon.

Chtara M., Chamari K., Chaouachi M.A., Koubea D., Fexy Y., Millet G. P. and Amril M. (2005) Effects of intra-session concurrent endurance and strength training sequence on aerobic performance and capacity. *British Journal of Sports Medicine*; **39**: 555–60.

Cooper K. H. (1968) A means of assessing maximal oxygen intake correlating between field and treadmill running. *Journal of the American Medical Association*; **203**: 201–4.

Drust B., Reilly T. and Rienzi E. (1998) Analysis of work-rate in soccer. *Sports Exercise and Injury*; **4**: 151–5.

Edgcomb S. J. and Norton K. (2006) Comparison of global positioning and computer-based tracking systems for measuring player movement distance during Australian Football. *Journal of Science and Medicine in Sport*; **9**: 25–32.

Elferink-Gemser M. T., Visscher C., Lemminck K. A. P. M. and Mulder T. (2007) Multidimensional performance characteristics and standard of performance in talented youth field hockey players. *Journal of Sports Sciences*; **25**: 481–9.

EUROFIT: *European Test of Physical Fitness* (1988) Council of Europe, Committee for the Development of Sport (CDDS); Rome.

Eston R. G. and Brodie D. A. (1985) The assessment of maximal oxygen uptake from running tests. *Physical Education Review*; **8** (1): 26–34.

Hughes M. (1988) Computerised notation analysis in field games. *Ergonomics*; **31**: 1585–92.

Hughes M. (1998) The application of notation analysis to racket sports. In: (A. Lees, I. Maynard, M. Hughes and T. Reilly, eds) *Science and Racket Sports II*; E. and F. N. Spon; London: pp. 211–20.

Hughes M. and Franks I. M. (1994) Dynamic patterns of movement in squash players of different standards in winning and losing matches. *Ergonomics*; **37**: 23–9.

Hughes M. G. and Fullerton F. M. (1995) Development of an on-court test for elite badminton players. In: (T. Reilly, M. Hughes and A. Lees, eds) *Science and Racket Sports*, F. N. Spon; London: pp. 51–4.

Kirkendall D. Gruber J. J. and Johnson R. E. (1987) *Measurement and Evaluation for Physical Education*. Human Kinetics; Champaign, IL.

Leger L. and Lambert J. (1982) A maximal 20-m shuttle run test to predict $\dot{V}O_2$max. *European Journal of Applied Physiology*; **49**: 1–12.

Leger L.A., Mercier D., Gadoury C. and Lambert J. (1988) The multistage 20 metre shuttle run test for aerobic fitness. *Journal of Sports Sciences*; **6**: 93–101.

MacDougall J. D., Wenger H. A. and Green H. J. (1991) *Physiological Testing of the High-Performance Athlete*. Human Kinetics Books; Champaign, IL.

McLean D. A. (1993) Field testing in Rugby Union football. In: (D. A. D. Macleod, R. J. Maughan, C. Williams, C. R. Madeley, J. C. M. Sharp and R. W. Hutton, eds) *Intermittent High Intensity Exercise: Preparation, Stresses and Damage Limitation.* E. and F. N. Spon; London: pp. 79–83.

Ohashi J., Togari H., Isokawa M., and Suzaki S. (1988) Measuring movement speeds and distances covered during soccer match-play. In: (T. Reilly, A. Lees, K. Davids and W. Murphy, eds) *Science and Football.* E. and F. N. Spon; London: pp. 320–3.

Oja P., Laukkanen R., Pasanen M. and Vuori I. (1989) A new fitness test for cardiovascular epidemiology and exercise promotion. *Annals of Medicine*; **21**: 249–50.

Olds T. (2001) The evolution of physique in male rugby union players in the twentieth century. *Journal of Sports Sciences*; **19**: 253–62.

Olsen E. and Larsen O. (1997) Use of match analysis by coaches. In: (T. Reilly, J. Bangsbo and M. Hughes, eds) *Science and Football III.* E. and F. N. Spon; London: pp. 209–20.

Ramsbottom R., Brewer T. and Williams C. (1988) A progressive shuttle run test to estimate maximal oxygen uptake. *British Journal of Sports Medicine*; **22**: 141–4.

Reilly T. (1994) Motion characteristics. In: (B. Ekblom, ed) *Football (Soccer).* Blackwell Scientific Publications; Oxford: pp. 78–99.

Reilly T. (1997) The physiology of Rugby Union football. *Biology of Sport*; **14**: 83–101.

Reilly T. (2000a) Endurance aspects of soccer and other field games. In: (R. J. Shephard, ed). *Endurance in Sport* (2nd Edition) Blackwell Scientific Publications; London.

Reilly T. (2000b) The physiological demands of soccer. In: (J. Bangsbo, ed) *Soccer and Science: In an Interdisciplinary Perspective.* Munksgaard; Copenhagen: pp. 91–105.

Reilly T. and Borrie A. (1992) Physiology applied to field hockey. *Sports Medicine*; **14**: 10–26.

Reilly T. and Bretherton S. (1986) Multivariate analysis of fitness in female field hockey players. In: (J. A. P. Day, ed) *Perspectives in Kinanthropometry.* Human Kinetics; Champaign, IL: pp. 135–42.

Reilly T. and Doran D. (1999) Kinanthropometric and performance profiles of elite Gaelic footballers. *Journal of Sports Sciences*; **17**: 922 (Abstract)

Reilly T. and Holmes M. (1983) A preliminary analysis of selected soccer skills. *Physical Education Review*; **6**: 64–71.

Reilly T. and Korkusuz F. (2008) *Science and Football VI.* Routledge; London.

Reilly T. and Thomas V. (1976) A motion analysis of work-rate in different positional roles in professional football match-play. *Journal of Human Movement Studies*; **2**: 87–97.

Reilly T., Williams A. M., Nevill A. and Franks A. (2000) A multidisciplinary approach to talent identification in soccer. *Journal of Sports Sciences*; **18**: 695–702.

Rienzi E., Reilly T. and Malkin C. (1999) Investigation of anthropometric and work-rate profiles of Rugby Sevens players. *Journal of Sports Medicine and Physical Fitness*; **39**: 160–4.

Rienzi E., Drust B., Reilly T., Carter J. E. L. and Martin A. (2000) Investigation of anthropometric and work-rate profiles of elite South American international soccer players. *Journal of Sports Medicine and Physical Fitness*; **40**: 162–9.

Saltin B. (1973) Metabolic fundamentals in exercise. *Medicine and Science in Sports*; **5**: 137–46.

Spencer M., Lawrence S., Rechichi C., Bishop D., Dawson B. and Goodman C. (2004) Time-motion analysis of elite female hockey, with special reference to repeated sprint activity. *Journal of Sports Sciences*; **22**: 843–50.

Svensson M. and Drust B. (2005) Testing soccer players. *Journal of Sports Sciences*; **23**: 601–18.

Williams M., Lees D. and Reilly T. (1999) *A quantitative analysis of matches played in the 1991–92 and 1997–98 seasons.* The Football Association; London.

Williams M., Borrie A., Cable T., Gilbourne D., Lees A., MacLaren D. and Reilly T. (1997) *Umbro Conditioning for Football.* Ebury; London.

CHAPTER 8

SPECIAL CONSIDERATIONS FOR ASSESSING PERFORMANCE IN YOUNG PEOPLE

Alan Barker, Colin Boreham, Emmanuel van Praagh and Ann V. Rowlands

8.1 AIMS

The aims of this chapter are to:

- describe the physical performance of children in the context of growth and maturation;
- examine concepts and practices associated with the testing and interpretation of aerobic and anaerobic performance in young people;
- provide normative tables to aid in the interpretation of EUROFIT field tests of fitness in children.

8.2 INTRODUCTION

Physiological testing of children's performance may be undertaken for a number of reasons, including:

(i) *Performance Enhancement* – the regular monitoring of physiological function in young sportspersons may help in the identification of strengths and weaknesses, and as a motivation for training.

(ii) *Educational* – advocates of fitness testing in the school setting claim that it motivates children to maintain or increase fitness; promotes healthy lifestyles and physical activity; and can be used as an educational tool, particularly with regard to health-related aspects of exercise.

(iii) *Research* – there is a growing academic interest in paediatric exercise science, whether from the health, performance or growth viewpoints. For example, research can be used to investigate how children's physiologic response to exercise differs from that of adults; to inform training guidelines for young athletes; to inform therapeutic interventions for children with chronic disease and to inform recommendations regarding preventive health strategies in childhood.

(iv) *Clinical Diagnosis and Rehabilitation* – as with adults, the diagnosis and treatment of certain clinical conditions in children may be helped by exercise testing. An excellent review of this topic can be found in a recent text by Bar-Or and Rowland (2004).

The diversity of approaches outlined above is matched by the variety of methods used to measure performance in children. These vary from sophisticated laboratory-based techniques for measuring parameters of aerobic (e.g. maximal O_2 uptake [$\dot{V}O_2max$])

and anaerobic (e.g. power output profile from a Wingate anaerobic test [WAnT]) performance, to simple 'field'-based tests of fitness (e.g. sit-ups, jumping tests, timed distance runs and grip strength). However, before examining specific areas of performance testing in children, it is important to review the processes of growth and maturation, and how these may influence test results. Without doubt, a basic understanding of the biological changes that occur throughout childhood, but most particularly at adolescence, is essential if test results are to be interpreted correctly.

8.3 GROWTH, MATURATION AND PERFORMANCE

Postnatal growth may be divided into four phases: *infancy* (from birth to 2 years), *early childhood* (pre-school), *middle childhood* (to adolescence) and *adolescence* (from 8–18 years for girls and 10–22 years for boys). As children younger than 8 years are seldom engaged in competitive sport, and may not possess the motor skills or the intellectual or emotional maturity required for successful fitness testing, the remainder of this chapter will deal primarily with the immediate pre-adolescent and adolescent phases of childhood. Important gender differences will be highlighted.

Generally speaking, gender differences which may influence performance are minimal before adolescence. Both boys and girls experience relatively rapid growth in stature during infancy and steady growth (approximately 5–6 cm per year) during childhood before the initiation of the pubertal growth spurt leading to the attainment of peak height velocity (PHV). Peak height velocity is the maximum rate of growth occurring during the adolescent growth spurt (Baxter-Jones and Sherar 2007). Girls begin their adolescent growth spurt on average, 2 years before boys (8–10 years vs 10–12 years respectively), which can confer a temporary advantage of height and mass for girls around this time. However, boys have a higher PHV and experience, on average, 2 more years of pre-adolescent growth than girls. This results in adult males being, on average, 13 cm taller than adult females. During the early part of the growth spurt, rapid growth in the lower extremities is evident, while an increased trunk length occurs later, and a greater muscle mass later still. There are also noticeable regional differences in growth during adolescence. Boys, for example, have only a slightly greater increase in calf muscle mass than girls, but nearly twice the increase in muscle mass of the arm during the adolescent growth spurt (Malina *et al.* 2004).

Relatively minor somatic differences between boys and girls are magnified during adolescence. Following the growth spurt, girls generally display a broader pelvis and hips, with a proportionately greater trunk:leg ratio. Body composition also changes from approximately 20% body fat to 25% body fat over this period. Boys, in contrast, maintain a similar body fat (16% to 15%) over the adolescent growth period – a change that is accompanied by a dramatic rise in lean body mass, shoulder width (the shoulder/hip ratio is 1.40 in pre-pubertal children, but 1.45 in post-pubertal boys and 1.35 in mature girls) and leg length. Such differences between the sexes – the boys being generally leaner, more muscular, broader shouldered and narrower hipped with relatively straighter limbs and longer legs – have obvious implications for physical performance. Some examples of results from common field tests applied over the adolescent period illustrate these differences clearly (Figure 8.1). It should be borne in mind when comparing physical performances of male and female adolescents, that other factors such as motivation and changes in social interests (Malina *et al.* 2004) and the documented fall-off in physical activity, particularly in girls (Boreham *et al.* 1993) may also influence results. The disproportionate rise in strength of boys compared with girls over the adolescent growth spurt (see Figure 8.1) has been largely

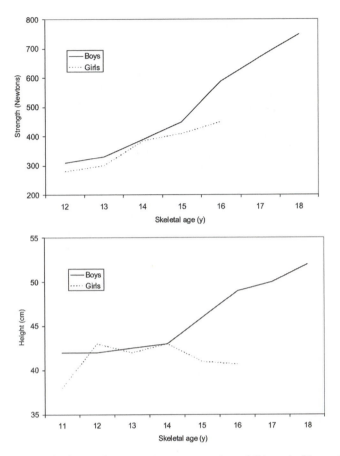

Figure 8.1 Mean and standard error for (a) static arm strength, and (b) vertical jump, in boys and girls versus skeletal age. Reproduced from Kemper (1985) with the permission of S Karger AG, Basel.

attributed to increasing levels of testosterone in the former (Round *et al.* 1999).

There is no such individual as the 'average adolescent' performer and confusion can arise as a result of the enormous individual variation inherent in the processes of biological maturation and sexual differentiation. While PHV may, on average, be between 11 and 12 years for girls and between 13 and 14 years for boys, there may be as much as 5 years difference in the timing of this phenomenon, and similar variation in the development of secondary gender characteristics, between any two individuals of the same gender. Thus, a child's chronological age is likely to bear little resemblance to his/her biological age (Figure 8.2) – the latter being of greater

significance to physical performance. This is illustrated in Figure 8.3, which demonstrates an early maturer to have a distinct advantage in most indices of physiological performance, whereas for the late maturer, performance is disadvantaged. This is particularly so for tasks requiring strength and power, possibly reflecting the tendency for early maturers to be more mesomorphic than late developers. This relationship between performance and biological maturation is also likely to be present within a single year group as a given child may be up to 11 months older than his or her peer. For example, Brewer *et al.* (1992) studied 59 members of the Swedish under-17 soccer squad and discovered that the majority of the players were born in the first

Figure 8.2 A group of 12-year-old schoolchildren illustrates typical variation in biological maturation at this age.

three months of the year, probably resulting in a slightly more advanced biological development.

Given the rapid rate of growth during the adolescent growth spurt (PHV of 9–11 cm year^{-1}), it is perhaps not surprising that there is a common perception of 'adolescent awkwardness' during this period. The temporary disruption of motor function during the growth spurt, particularly relating to balance, may be due to a segmental disproportion arising from the period early in the growth spurt, when leg length increases in proportion to trunk length. Boys in particular, but accounting only to between 10–30% of the adolescent male population, may be affected (Beunen and Malina 1988). However, the effects are temporary, lasting approximately six months, and disappear by early adulthood.

Given the above, it should be evident that the biological events associated with growth and development, particularly over the period of adolescence, highlight the complexity of interpreting performance test scores correctly in young people. Therefore, to provide a valid interpretation of physiological and performance-based measures, either in the laboratory or field environment during growth, an individual's or a group of indi-

viduals' level of maturity must be controlled for. As highlighted in Chapter 3 (Beunen, 2009), an assessment of biological maturation may be obtained from an estimation of 'skeletal' age using radiograph techniques, or 'sexual' maturation using illustrations of the development of secondary gender characteristics. However, given the invasive and intrusive nature, and the requirement for trained personnel, these techniques have limited application in young people. In contrast, Mirwald *et al.* (2002) have developed gender-specific regression algorithms that allow for the determination of the years from PHV using non-invasive, simple to administer, anthropometric measures on a cross-sectional basis. All that is required is a measure of height (cm), sitting height (cm), leg length (stature-sitting height, cm), body mass (kg) and chronological age (y), and a child's age from PHV can be estimated and used to determine the age at PHV to within ± 1 year error (95% confidence intervals). For example, for a 11.6-year-old boy with a maturity offset score of –2.2 years, his age at PHV is 13.8 (± 1) years. A distinct advantage of this technique is that the age at PHV is a common marker of maturity both within and between subject groups and across sexes, thus representing a sound method to assess biological maturation.

Boys' algorithm ($R^2 = 0.89$):

Age from PHV (years) = –9.236 + (0.0002708 · ((leg length · sitting height)) + (–0.001663 · (age · leg length)) + (0.007216 · (age · sitting height)) + (0.02292 · (body mass by height ratio expressed as percentage))

Girls' algorithm ($R^2 = 0.89$):

Age from PHV (years) = –9.376 + (0.0001882 · (leg length · sitting height) + (0.0022 · (age · leg length)) + (0.005841 · (age · sitting height)) + (–0.002658 · (age · body mass)) + (0.07693 · (body mass by height ratio expressed as a percentage))

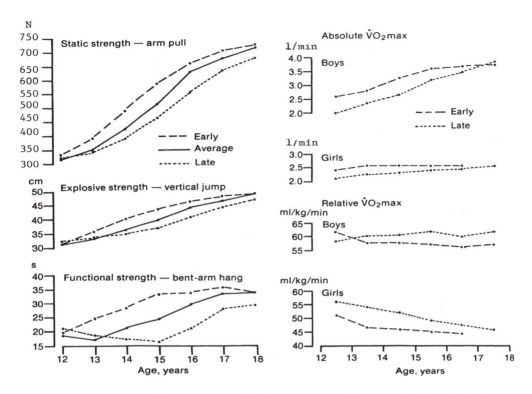

Figure 8.3 Mean motor performance scores of early-, average- and late-maturing boys in the Leuven Growth study of Belgian Boys. Modified from *Growth, Maturation and Physical Activity* (pp. 296) by RM Malina and C Bouchard (1991) Human Kinetics; Champaign, IL. Copyright 1991 by Robert M. Malina and Claude Bouchard. Reprinted by permission.

8.4 ANTHROPOMETRIC TESTS (BODY COMPOSITION)

Techniques for the anthropometric measurements commonly used with children are somewhat specialised, and are dealt with at length elsewhere (e.g. Chapters 1–5: Malina *et al*. 2004) and by Beunen in this text (Chapter 3). Nevertheless, it is worth examining measures that may be used to gauge the body composition of children in some detail.

Possibly the simplest measure of estimating body composition in adults is the Body Mass Index (BMI), or Quetelet's Index (Weight/Height²). In growing children, particularly boys, use of this index as a measure of relative obesity may be misleading, as a large proportion of weight gain during adolescence is lean rather than adipose tissue. Thus,

the BMI may increase from 17.8 kg.m^{-2} to 21.3 kg.m^{-2} in 11- and 16-year-old boys respectively, while the sum of four skinfolds (biceps, triceps, subscapular and iliac crest) falls from 33.7 mm to 31.5 mm over the same period. The increase in BMI in girls from 11 to 16 years (from 18.6 kg.m^{-2} to 21.5 kg.m^{-2} respectively) may be a better indicator of increased adipose tissue (sum of four skinfolds rises from 37.2 mm to 43.1 mm; Riddoch *et al*. 1991). Irrespective of these concerns for using the BMI as an estimate of body composition in young people, age-and gender-specific cut-off points for 'overweight' and 'obesity' are available for children between the ages of 2 and 18 years (Cole *et al*. 2000).

Many methods are available to assess body fatness in children e.g. skinfolds, bioelectrical impedance, densitometry (for a discussion of the methods used to estimate body com-

Table 8.1 Prediction equations of percentage fat from triceps and subscapular skinfolds in children and youth for males and females[a]

Triceps and subscapular skinfolds > 35 mm

%Fat = 0.783 Σ SF + *I* Males

%Fat = 0.546 SF + 9.7 Females

Triceps and subscapular skinfolds (< 35 mm)[b]

%Fat = 1.21 (Σ SF) – 0.008 (Σ SF)^2 + *I* Males

%Fat = 1.33 (Σ SF) – 0.013 (Σ SF)^2 + 2.5 Females (2.0 blacks, 3.0 whites)

I = Intercept varies with maturation level and racial group for males as follows

Age	Black	White
Prepubescent	–3.5	–1.7
Pubescent	–5.2	–3.4
Postpubescent	–6.8	–5.5
Adult	–6.8	–5.5

[a] From *Advances in Body Composition Assessment* (p. 74) by T. G. Lohman (1992), Human Kinetics; Champaign, IL: Copyright 1992 by Timothy G. Lohman. Reprinted by permission.

Calculations were derived using the equation of Slaughter *et al.* (1988).

[b] Thus for a white pubescent male with a triceps of 15 mm and a subscapular of 12 mm, the % fat would be:

%Fat = 1.21 (27) – 0.008 (27)^2 – 3.4

= 23.4%

position see Chapter 1 in this book (Eston *et al.*)). One of the most common methods of measuring body composition in children relies on the use of skinfold thicknesses (Figure 8.4). The prediction of percentage body fat from skinfold thickness relies on the relationship between skinfolds and body density. However, the changes in body composition during growth affect the conceptual basis for estimating fatness and leanness from body density (Armstrong and Welsman 1997). For example, the water content of a child's fat free mass decreases from 75.2% in a 10-year-old boy, to 73.6% at 18 years (Haschke 1983) and bone density increases during childhood. Because of the above reservations, some investigators choose simply to sum the four skinfold thicknesses for use as a comparator. Alternatively, child-specific equations can be used (Lohman 1992). These are shown in Table 8.1. These multicomponent criterion-referenced equations account for age, gender and maturational stage (see Chapter 1, Eston *et al.*, 2009).

8.5 GENERAL CONSIDERATIONS WHEN ASSESSING PERFORMANCE IN CHILDREN

While the general nature of the protocols used for assessing exercise performance in young people are similar to those used in the adult population, there are several unique aspects that the investigator should be aware of. These include the following:

• Although the risks associated with maximal testing of healthy children are low, the tester should take every reasonable precaution to ensure safety of the child. Such steps should include a carefully worded explanation of the test, adequate familiarization beforehand, extra testing staff (e.g., one standing behind a treadmill during testing)- and a simple questionnaire relating to clinical contra-indications, recent or current viral infections, asthma and so on.

• Children will be less anxious if the right

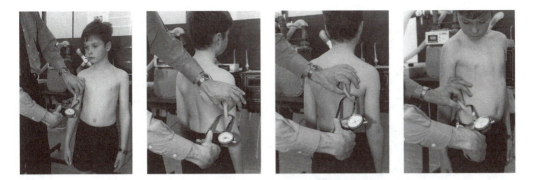

Figure 8.4 Skinfold thicknesses may be measured from (a) biceps, (b) triceps, (c) subscapular and (d) iliac sites.

environment for testing is created. If groups of children are brought to the laboratory, some bright pictures, comics, DVDs and computer games will help occupy those who are not involved. Children recover very quickly from maximal effort, and should always be generously rewarded – at least verbally.

- Be aware of the sensitivities of children, particularly in the group situation. It is wise to underplay both extremes of performance.
- Approval for testing children must be obtained from an appropriate peer-review ethics committee. Prior to participation in research, it is normal practice to obtain written informed consent from parents and written or verbal assent from children. Children should be told that they are free to withdraw at any time from the test procedures.

8.6 ASSESSMENT OF AEROBIC PERFORMANCE IN THE LABORATORY

The participation in physical activity, whether for health benefits, recreational activity, or sporting performance, requires the effective integration of the cardiovascular, respiratory and muscular systems to support the metabolic demands of exercise. As outline by Wasserman *et al.* (2005) the three fundamental parameters of aerobic function which reflect the integrated response of the body are:

- Maximal rate of O_2 uptake during exercise ($\dot{V}O_2max$), defined as the maximal rate at which ATP can be synthesised aerobically whilst exercising with a large muscle mass at sea level;
- The anaerobic threshold, which represents the $\dot{V}O_2$ (or exercise intensity) at which an inflection and sustained increase in blood lactate concentration is observed from baseline levels;
- O_2 cost of exercise or exercise economy, which represents the metabolic cost ($\dot{V}O_2$) to perform exercise at a given power output or running speed.

The collective measurement of these three parameters permits a comprehensive assessment of the aerobic function and performance of the young person. Similar to their determination in the adult population, all three parameters can be measured in children and adolescents using a single progressive, incremental exercise test to exhaustion. Although portable gas analyzers permit the measurement of $\dot{V}O_2$ during 'free-living' and therefore under more ecologically valid exercise conditions, the bulk of testing in young people takes place using standard exercise physiology laboratory equipment where gas exchange variables can be collected 'on-line'

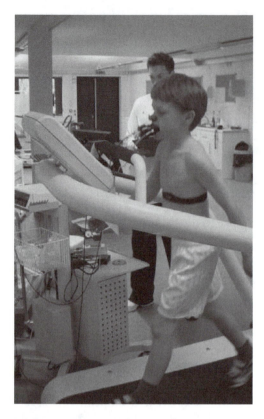

Figure 8.5 The measurement of oxygen uptake during treadmill exercise.

at high sampling resolution, providing the investigator with rich information on the child's aerobic function (Figure 8.5).

8.6.1 Equipment

Exercise tests are normally carried out using either a treadmill or cycle ergometer and are well tolerated by young people providing a familiarization session is undertaken beforehand. In general, the treadmill is the preferred instrument with children who may find pedalling difficult, particularly if asked to maintain a set cadence on a mechanically braked cycle. In addition, cycle ergometry may create local muscular fatigue in the legs of children at higher work rates when the increments in exercise intensity are too large for the child subject. Furthermore, specially built paediatric cycle ergometers with different arm crank lengths and handlebar and/or seat adjustments may be required for exercise testing of very small children. Poorly motivated children may also respond better to exercise on a treadmill, as the speed and gradient dictates the work rate as opposed to the motivation and compliance of the child (Rowland 2005). On the other hand, the use of a treadmill can hinder the measurement of supplementary variables, such as blood sampling and blood pressure during exercise. As in adults, $\dot{V}O_2$max and peak heart rates are typically higher during treadmill testing than on the cycle ergometer.

If a cycle ergometer is to be used, the seat height should be adjusted so that the extended leg is almost completely straight at the bottom of the pedal revolution (with the foot in the horizontal position). If a treadmill is to be used, in addition to the personnel operating the test, an extra person should be positioned at the side of the treadmill to support the child if he/she stumbles. This is sufficient for most children, but in some cases it may be advisable for the child to wear a safety harness and for padding to be provided at the rear of the treadmill. Front and side rails may also need adjusting for small children. Prior to testing, the child should be familiarized with the sensation of walking and running on a moving belt, and with how to mount and dismount the treadmill. This is important not only from a safety perspective, but also to control for the inflated metabolic cost of exercise typically observed in children without prior history of exercising on a treadmill. Non-verbal signals for stopping should be confirmed. During the test, the investigator should communicate in a positive, friendly manner continuously and should avoid enquiring as to whether the child feels tired – invariably the answer will be 'yes!' Instead, signs of fatigue (both subjective and objective) should be noted, and a heightened state of vigilance maintained towards the end of a test. Above intensities of approximately 85% of $\dot{V}O_2$ max, children

Table 8.2 The modified Balke treadmill protocol (2-minute stages)

Participant	Speed (km.h⁻¹)	Initial grade (%)	Grade increment(%)
Poorly fit	4.8	6	2.0
Sedentary	5.2	6	2.0
Active	8.0	0	2.5
Athlete	8.5	0	2.5

Adapted from Rowland (1999).

Table 8.3 The Bruce treadmill protocol (3-minute stages)

Stage	Speed (km.h⁻¹)	Grade (%)	Duration (min)
1	2.7	10	3
2	4.0	12	3
3	5.5	14	3
4	6.8	16	3
5	8.0	18	3
6	8.8	20	3
7	9.7	22	3

Table 8.4 The McMaster continuous cycling protocol

Body height (cm)	Initial load (Watts)	Increments (Watts)	Duration of each load (min)
<119.9	12.5	12.5	2
120–139.9	12.5	25	2
140–159.9	25	25	2
> 160	25	25 female	2
		50 male	

may suddenly stop exercising without prior warning (Rowland 1993a). Anticipation of such an event by the investigator may be helped by the use of a perceived exertion rating scale during the exercise test (Williams et al. 1994; Eston et al. 2000).

After the test, a cool down at walking speed of at least 5 minutes is recommended, to avoid peripheral venous pooling and syncope. The mouthpiece and noseclip should be removed as soon as possible, and a drink of water, or preferably juice, offered. In the unlikely event of prolonged or repeated exercise testing of prepubertal children, in whom thermoregulatory responses may not be fully developed (Sharp 1991), frequent drinking by the subject should be encouraged if possible.

8.6.2 Protocols

Protocols for maximal exercise testing in children can be classified as continuous or discontinuous (i.e. each increment in exercise intensity is followed by a brief rest period, typically of 1 minute duration). The latter may be more suitable when testing with younger children who are likely to have little prior experience of a maximal effort and may require verbal support during the rest periods (Stratton and Williams 2007). Continuous treadmill protocols for children generally involve either a modified Balke protocol (Table 8.2), in which treadmill speed is held constant, while the gradient is increased every minute by 2% (Rowland 1993a, 1999) or a modified Bruce protocol (Table 8.3). The advantages of the Balke protocol are that it only requires the child to cope with changes in one variable (grade, while speed stays constant); selection of the appropriate speed for fitness level leads to an acceptable test duration regardless of fitness level of the individual (Rowland 1999).

An appropriate continuous cycle ergometer protocol is the well-established McMaster protocol (see Table 8.4). For further details the reader is referred to Bar-0r (1983). An alternative protocol on the cycle ergometer is a ramp-incremental exercise test to exhaustion; that is, power output increases as a linear function of time rather than in step increments. This protocol is well tolerated by children of all ages and allows for the determination of all three parameters of aerobic function ($\dot{V}O_2$max, anaerobic threshold and the O_2 cost of exercise) within 6–10 minutes when using an online system for determination of gas exchanges variables (Cooper *et al.* 1984). As a ramp-incremental protocol does not require the child to tolerate the abrupt change in work rate that is engendered in protocols using step increments, the child is less likely to terminate exercise prematurely during high work intensities. The test starts with a period (usually 3 minutes) of baseline pedalling (0 watts), following which work rate is increased in a continuous fashion. For children as young as 8–10 years, a ramp increment of 10 watts per minute (1 watt every 6 s) is suitable, whereas 15 watts per minute (1 watt every 4 s) for 11- to 13-year-old children, and up to 20 watts per minute (1 watt every 3 s) for 14- to 17-year-old children are likely to be appropriate.

8.6.3 Criteria for $\dot{V}O_2$ max

The 'gold standard' criterion for determining whether a subject has attained his/her $\dot{V}O_2$max is the demonstration of a plateau in the $\dot{V}O_2$ response despite an increase in workload. Most investigators however, have found difficulty in identifying such a plateau-like behaviour in the $\dot{V}O_2$ response; not only

in the paediatric population (Armstrong and Welsman 1994), but also in adults (Day *et al.* 2003). Thus, the term 'peak $\dot{V}O_2$' rather than 'maximum $\dot{V}O_2$' has been adopted as the appropriate terminology in young people. Given that the majority of children fail to satisfy the demonstration of plateau in $\dot{V}O_2$, secondary criteria have been adopted to aid verification of a maximal effort. While no single criterion alone appears to be a valid indicator of a maximum effort, a maximal test is usually defined by a combination of the following criteria:

(i)   Heart rate around 200 beats per minute for treadmill exercise or 195 beats per minute for cycle exercise[*];

(ii) Respiratory exchange ratio (RER) $\geq$ 1.00[*];

(iii) Extreme forced ventilation, or subjective signs of exhaustion (e.g. facial flushing, intense effort).

Using these criteria, the within-subject error for determining peak $\dot{V}O_2$ in young people when expressed as a typical error score is approximately 5% variation (Welsman *et al.* 2005). The adoption of this secondary criteria was in part established from studies that have demonstrated no significant differences in the peak $\dot{V}O_2$ maximal heart rate and maximal RER between subjects demonstrating a plateau in $\dot{V}O_2$ and those not (Rowland and Cunningham 1992). Furthermore, when children who fail to demonstrate a plateau in the $\dot{V}O_2$ response are required to exercise at an intensity higher than that achieved at exhaustion during the incremental protocol (i.e. supra-maximal exercise), no further increase in $\dot{V}O_2$ is observed; thus supporting the contention that a peak score does

---

[*] It should be noted that values vary significantly between individuals with a standard deviation around the values cited of around ± 5–10 beats per minute for heart rate and ± 0.05 for RER (Rowland 2005).

represent the upper limit of $\dot{V}O_2$ (Armstrong *et al.* 1996). However, scrutiny of the data published by Rowland (1993b) indicates that on an individual basis some children may increase their peak $\dot{V}O_2$ up to 8%, whereas other children may demonstrate a decline by 5%, when completing a supra-maximal exercise bout. These data therefore support the contention that a peak $\dot{V}O_2$ score may in fact represent a maximal value in young people, but without the completion of an additional supra-maximal exercise bout to confirm the existence of a plateau, one cannot be certain. Therefore, if the verification of a 'true' maximum is sought, it may be prudent for the researcher to impose, after a brief rest period of 5–10 minutes, a supra-maximal exercise bout; for example, at 105% of the power output achieved at the end of a cycling incremental exercise test, in order to determine whether the child has truly reached a plateau in $\dot{V}O_2$ (see Armstrong *et al.* 1996 and Day *et al.* 2003 for further details).

8.6.4 Determination of the anaerobic threshold

During exercise of increasing intensity, a point is reached where the accumulation of lactate in the muscle and blood increases above baseline levels. Originally, this onset of lactate accumulation was attributed to a limited rate of oxidative phosphorylation due to a shortfall in O_2 within the contracting muscles (cell hypoxia) and was termed the anaerobic threshold (Wasserman 1984). However, as contracting muscles produce lactate under conditions of adequate cellular O_2, the increase in muscle and blood lactate does not represent the onset of O_2 limited anaerobic metabolism, but rather a complex interplay between the cellular redox and phosphorylation potential and O_2 concentration (Gladden 2004), and a balance between the lactate production and removal mechanism operating within the system (Brooks 1985). Irrespective of the physiological basis and terminology used to define the onset of lactate accumulation

within the muscle and blood, it is clear that a delayed threshold is indicative of an enhanced oxidative capacity of the muscle.

In children, the onset of the anaerobic threshold can be determined through capillary blood samples obtained at various steady-state points of a step-incremental exercise protocol. Blood lactate concentration is plotted against variables such as running speed or $\dot{V}O_2$, and the point at which an increase in blood lactate above baseline occurs is referred to as the lactate threshold (LT). Alternatively, fixed blood lactate concentrations (usually 2.0 and 4.0 mM in adults) may be a more appropriate marker of aerobic function as they may be less prone to observer error associated with the subjective determination of the LT and provide a sensitive means of quantifying the effect of training and growth and maturation on sub-maximal aerobic fitness (Figure 8.6).

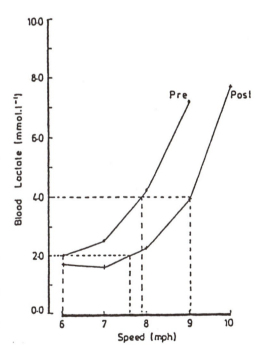

Figure 8.6 Blood lactate concentration during an incremental running test, pre and post one year's endurance training as an individual. Reproduced with permission from the BASS Position Statement on the Physiological Assessment of the Elite Competitor (1988).

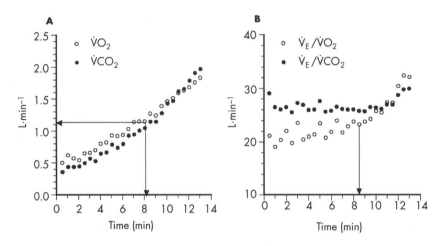

Figure 8.7 Identification of the LT using the non-invasive GET (A) and VT (B) methods in an 8-year-old child during a ramp-incremental cycle exercise test to exhaustion. Power output during the test was increased at a rate of 10 W·min⁻¹. In this example, the LT was deemed to occur at a $\dot{V}O_2$ of 1.13 L·min⁻¹, which corresponded to 61% of the child's peak $\dot{V}O_2$.

However, care should be taken in specifying sampling sites and assay media in the interpretation of blood lactate concentrations (Williams *et al.* 1992). Moreover, as the 4.0 mM fixed blood lactate concentration may occur at ~ 90% peak $\dot{V}O_2$ in 13- to 14-year-old adolescents, the 2.0 or 2.5 mM level may be a more appropriate marker of sub-maximal aerobic fitness in young people (Williams and Armstrong 1991).

Under conditions of cellular pH, approximately 99% of the lactic acid dissociates into lactate and H⁺. In order to maintain cellular pH balance, H⁺ is buffered by bicarbonate (HCO_3^-) ions giving rise to an excess of CO_2 production in addition to the liberation of CO_2 produced by the catabolism of metabolic substrate:

$$H^+ + HCO_3^- \leftrightarrow H_2CO_3 \leftrightarrow H_2O + CO_2$$

This excess liberation of CO_2 from the contracting muscle is observed at the mouth via a rise in expired CO_2 ($\dot{V}CO_2$). Consequently, during incremental exercise the LT may be estimated from the non-linear increase in $\dot{V}CO_2$ relative to $\dot{V}O_2$, which is termed the gas exchange threshold (GET). This breakpoint

in $\dot{V}CO_2$ relative to $\dot{V}O_2$ can be identified objectively using bi-linear regression modelling (Beaver *et al.* 1986) or visually. To maintain arterial pressure of CO_2, the increased CO_2 production from the muscle is detected by the carotid bodies and signals an accelerated rise in pulmonary ventilation ($\dot{V}_E$). This forms the basis of the ventilatory threshold (VT), which is also considered synonymous with the LT, and can be determined from an increase in the O_2 ventilatory equivalent ($\dot{V}_E/\dot{V}O_2$) without a contaminant increase in the ventilatory equivalent for CO_2 ($\dot{V}_E/\dot{V}CO_2$). The identification of the GET and VT is illustrated in Figure 8.7 and can be used on a collective basis to identify the LT.

The non-invasive nature of estimating the LT using either the GET or VT is particularly attractive, given the potentially uncomfortable and traumatic nature of obtaining repeat capillary blood samples in young people. Such methods are sensitive to monitoring changes in aerobic function during growth and maturity and in response to exercise training in young people (Mahon and Cheatham 2002). Importantly, both methods are highly reproducible in the paediatric population, demonstrating a coefficient of variation of

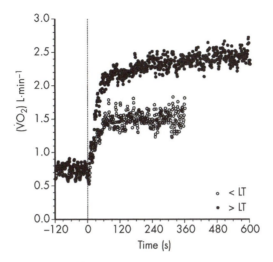

Figure 8.8 Kinetic profile of O_2 uptake ($\dot{V}O_2$) during exercise below (○) and above (●) the blood lactate threshold (LT) in a child subject exercising on a cycle ergometer. During exercise below the LT the $\dot{V}O_2$ response attains steady-state within approximately 2 minutes. However, during exercise above the LT, a steady-state profile in $\dot{V}O_2$ is not evident, even after 10 minutes of exercise. This is due to a non-linear increase in $\dot{V}O_2$ above that predicted by the $\dot{V}O_2$-power output relationship observed during sub LT work intensities.

~ 6–8% for a given subject over two repeat tests and an inter-observed reproducibility of ~ 3–6% (Fawkner *et al.* 2002). Moreover, as the GET or VT typically occurs at ~ 55–65% peak $\dot{V}O_2$ in children, its measurement may be a more judicious choice when the goal is to determine the oxidative function in children (i.e. disease states) who are contraindicated to exercise, or experience difficulties in exercising, at higher intensities (Hebestreit *et al.* 2000).

8.6.5 Determination of the O_2 cost of exercise

The O_2 cost of exercise is defined as the metabolic cost ($\dot{V}O_2$) to perform exercise at a given sub-maximal workload and can be determined using both treadmill (for measurement of running economy) and cycling exercise protocols. Due to the temporal and amplitude features of the $\dot{V}O_2$ profile in children during exercise above and below the LT (Figure 8.8), an accurate measurement of the O_2 cost of exercise requires an exercise protocol that imposes step increments in power output or

running speed that are at least 3 minutes in duration and at an exercise intensity below the LT – this ensures the attainment of steady-state exercise and the O_2 cost of exercise can then be determined from the $\dot{V}O_2$ response between the 2nd and 3rd minutes. The O_2 cost of exercise may also be determined from a ramp based incremental exercise test, where power output increases as a linear function of time. By plotting $\dot{V}O_2$ as a function of power output, the slope between the two variables measures the aerobic work efficiency and is expressed as the $\dot{V}O_2$ cost for a given change in power output (Wasserman *et al.* 2005). This technique has not only been successfully used to monitor changes in aerobic fitness during growth and maturation (Cooper *et al.* 1984) but also to monitor the dysfunction of aerobic function in children with chronic disease (Moser *et al.* 2000).

8.7 ASSESSMENT OF ANAEROBIC PERFORMANCE IN THE LABORATORY

It is well acknowledged that the habitual

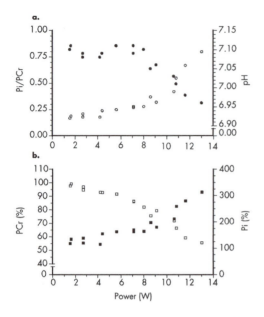

Figure 8.9 Dynamics of quadriceps muscle Pi/PCr (○) and pH (•) (figure a) and PCr (□) and Pi (■) (figure b) determined using ^{31}P-MRS in a boy subject during a single legged quadriceps step-incremental test to exhaustion. See Barker *et al.* 2006 for details and reliability of this methodology in young people.

physical activity patterns of children are dynamic and transient in nature as represented by the rapid, short-lived transitions from one metabolic state to another. In terms of cellular energetics, these patterns could be classified as ostensibly anaerobic. However, in comparison with quantifying parameters of aerobic function in young people, the direct measurement of the anaerobic energy supply during whole body exercise is restricted to invasive procedures such as the muscle biopsy technique, which is ethically questionable in the healthy child. To circumvent this issue some research groups have used ^{31}P-magnetic resonance spectroscopy (^{31}P-MRS) to determine the muscle phosphates (PCr, P_i, ATP) and cellular pH under non-invasive conditions (Figure 8.9), which allows a direct insight into anaerobic energy metabolism during exercise in young people. However, this technique is still in its infancy within the paediatric population, and has received

little investigation in children, due to the financial burden of the specialist equipment required and the restricted type of exercise that can be performed whilst lying inside the magnetic resonance scanner. Although providing valuable information regarding the muscle metabolic response during exercise in healthy (Barker *et al.* 2006; Petersen *et al.* 1999) and diseased children (Selvadurai *et al.* 2003), it has been argued this technique lacks context with exercise and performance in the 'real world' (Beneke *et al.* 2005).

Alternatively, some researchers have concentrated on measuring indirect metabolic indices of anaerobic performance in young people, such as post-exercise blood lactate or acid-base profiles (Beneke *et al.* 2005; Ratel *et al.* 2002). However, the bulk of research has focused on the power output profile generated during short-term 'all-out' cycling or treadmill exercise as a means of assessing the performance of the anaerobic energy system (Bar-Or 1996; Van Praagh 1996; Van Praagh and França 1998). That is, the mechanical power output achieved is equivalent to between two and three times the metabolic power obtained during a $\dot{V}O_2$ max test, and as such is considered to reflect the production of ATP in the muscle via anaerobic (PCr breakdown and anaerobic glycolysis) energy sources (Williams 1997).

However, interpreting the metabolic basis of the power output profile generated by the muscles during an 'all-out' short-term bout is not at all straightforward, as the elicited power output reflects not only anaerobic ATP resynthesis pathways, but also a significant contribution of ATP via oxidative metabolism. For example, it has recently been estimated that ~ 21% of the total energy turnover during a 30 s all-out cycling WAnT is provided via oxidative metabolism whereas PCr and anaerobic glycolysis represented ~ 34% and ~ 45% of the total energy turnover respectively in children (Beneke *et al.* 2007). Moreover, it is known that children can elicit >90% of their peak $\dot{V}O_2$ during short-term 'all-out' sprint cycling exercise of 90 s in duration (Williams *et al.* 2005). Collectively, these results clearly demonstrate that while the energetic provision of ATP is largely anaerobic during short-term 'all-out' exercise, it is not exclusively anaerobic and as such this should be considered when interpreting the data from such tests, especially those of longer duration (i.e. >30 s).

A significant drawback of measuring the power output profile during short-term 'all-out' exercise bouts is the lack of clear-cut objective criteria to verify a maximal response by the child participant. The researcher or trainer must therefore rely on the willing cooperation of the subject to work to his or her maximum. An adequate familiarization to the test ergometer and protocol is essential for the child to achieve this level of physical performance.

Prior to executing an 'all-out' short-term test to determine anaerobic performance, the child should undertake a standardized 5-minute warm-up period on the testing ergometer at a 'light' intensity, interspersed with a couple of short duration (5–7 s) 'all-out' practice sprints at the end of the 3rd and 4th minutes. By ensuring the warm-up is standardized within and between subject, this controls for the performance-induced benefits of a warm-up (Inbar and Bar-Or 1975), largely due to a temperature related modulation of the muscle velocity and power output curves (Williams 1997), and the potential of a learning effect on the power output measures. Following the completion of a maximal 'all-out' exercise protocol, care should be taken to ensure the safe and appropriate recovery of the child participant. This should consist of a supervised period of light intensity exercise for 10 minutes.

The measurement of mechanical power output to reflect anaerobic performance is invariably determined during an 'all-out' bout of short-term exercise, which lasts for the duration of 1–60 s. According to Bar-Or (1996), the power output indices that are subsequently used to quantify anaerobic performance are:

- Peak power, defined as the highest mechanical power output that can be elicited by the contracting muscles during a given 'all-out' short-term exercise bout. This usually occurs within 1–5 s of the onset of exercise.

- Mean power, defined as the average mechanical power that is achieved during a given 'all-out' short-term bout, which is thought to reflect the local muscle endurance or the muscles' ability to sustain power output during the exercise bout. Some authors have used the mean power output to reflect the muscles' anaerobic capacity during a 30 s WAnT (i.e. the maximal amount of ATP that can be synthesised by anaerobic pathways), although this has yet to be validated in children and as such is not recommended.

In addition, some authors have also reported the fatigue index as a measure of anaerobic performance, which represents the percentage decline in the final power output when expressed relative to peak power:

Fatigue index (%) = ((peak power – final power) / peak power) × 100

However, the fatigue index is less reliable than the peak or mean power output measures, and therefore may lack the precision to identify growth and maturity, exercise training or disease related changes in anaerobic performance (Naughton *et al.* 1992).

8.7.1 Measurement of short-term anaerobic performance

a) 30-s WAnT Cycling Test
Cumming (1973) was the first to investigate short-term power output on a cycle ergometer in 12- to 17-year-old children (the 30-s cycling test). The absolute braking force for the children to overcome in this supra-maximal test was 4 to 4.5 kg for girls and boys, respectively. This test was further developed

Table 8.5 Optimal resistance for the WAnT using the Monark cycle ergometer

Body mass (kg)	Breaking force (N)
20–24.9	17.2
25–29.9	20.9
30–34.9	24.5
35–39.9	27.7
40–44.9	31.9
45–49.9	35.6
50–54.9	39.2
55–59.9	44.1
60–64.9	49.1
65–69.9	54.0

Adapted from Bar-Or (1983) with the permission of Springer-Verlag.

by researchers of the Wingate Institute (termed the WAnT), and has subsequently developed into the most researched test of anaerobic performance in young people. The WAnT test requires the subject to pedal 'as fast as they can' against a fixed resistance on a braked ergometer (Bar-Or 1996). Typically a 'rolling start' is employed to help the child overcome the inertia of the ergometer flywheel. When a pedalling velocity of 60 rev·min^{-1} is attained, the experimenter counts down 'three, two, one and go' at which point a predetermined breaking force is applied to the ergometer and the subject sprints 'all-out' for 30 s. Peak power is attained within 3–5 s following the onset of exercise, following which a decline in power output is observed until the end of the test, reflecting the fatigue processes operating within the contracting muscles.

The braking force typically used is 0.74 Newtons (N) per kg of body mass (N·kg^{-1}) for cycling exercise, although more specific braking forces are available for a given body mass in an attempt to optimize performance during a WAnT (see Table 8.5). However, it should be acknowledged that these braking forces were developed to optimize a subject's power output profile during the entire 30 s of

the WAnT and not specifically the peak power output measure. For example, Santos *et al.* (2002) demonstrated in a group of 9- to 10-year-old children (21 males and 20 females) and 14- to 15-year-old adolescents (23 males and 22 females), that the optimal breaking force required to elicit peak power output was 0.69 ± 0.10 and 0.93 ± 0.14 N·kg^{-1} for males and 0.82 ± 0.18 and 0.82 ± 0.10 N·kg^{-1} for females, respectively, using a force-velocity test on a Monark 814 ergometer. These results indicate that the optimal breaking force for the WAnT protocol is related to age and gender in young people, and that the prescription of a fixed force (i.e. 0.74 N·kg^{-1}) is unlikely to yield the subject's optimum peak power output during a 30 s WAnT.

The WAnT has been examined more extensively than any other anaerobic performance test for several paediatric populations (abled, disabled and trained) and found to be highly valid and reliable. For example, the WAnT has been demonstrated to be a reliable measure of anaerobic performance in young people with neuromuscular disease, with test-retest reliability coefficients range from 0.89 to 0.97 (Tirosch *et al.* 1990). In healthy 10- to 11-year-old children cycling against a fixed resistance of 0.74 N·kg^{-1} on a Monark 814 ergometer, the coefficient of repeatability for the WAnT test is 45 and 42 watts for peak power and mean power, respectively (Sutton *et al.* 2000).

b) Force-velocity cycling test

Bearing in mind Wilkie's (1950) rationale that:

> Maximal power output = optimal force × optimal velocity

it is clear that a maximal power output cannot be achieved using a single braking force and, as such, sprint cycling protocols should use variable breaking forces to obtain the optimum force and velocity parameters which elicit maximal power output for a given exercise protocol. To determine 'maximal' power output, initial studies required subjects to perform multiple 'all-out' sprints of 5–7 s in duration on a Monark cycle ergometer at varying breaking forces ranging from 29.4 to 68.7 N, with 3 minutes recovery allowed between each sprint (Pirnay and Crielaard 1979). The highest value of power output was assumed to represent the 'maximum' power output, and corresponded to 7.6 and 10.1 watts·kg^{-1} in boys and men respectively. This test was the precursor of the load-optimization or force-velocity test (see Winter and MacLaren 2009 for a more in-depth discussion).

The force-velocity test has subsequently been used in the paediatric population in an attempt to determine the optimum velocity and force parameters that yield the 'maximum' power output for a given subject (Santos *et al.* 2002; van Praagh *et al.* 1989). After an adequate warm-up and familiarization procedure, the subject is required to perform a number (between 5 and 8) of 5–8 s 'all-out' sprints on a cycling ergometer each at different braking forces. For example, the study by Santos *et al.* (2002) required children and adolescents to perform 5–8 s 'all-out' cycling bouts at randomly assigned braking forces ranging from 0.30 to 1.08 N·kg^{-1} on a Monark 814 ergometer, with a 5-minute rest (1 min active recovery and 4-min rest) allowed between each bout. The relationship between pedalling velocity and breaking force can be plotted graphically, and is characterized by a negative linear function in young people (van Praagh *et al.* 1989). Using the relationship between braking force and velocity to calculate the peak power output for each sprint, the resulting values can be plotted against its corresponding breaking force. The apex of the parabolic relationship between power output and breaking force, allows the peak power output to be obtained alongside the optimal braking force that is required to elicit the 'maximal' peak power output for a subject on a given exercise ergometer (see figure 11.4 in Chapter 11, from Winter and MacLaren). The within subject reliability

(mean bias ± 95% limits of agreement) for determining the 'maximum' peak power output in children and adolescents using this technique was reported by Santos *et al.* (2002) as −16.7 ± 38.3 watts over two repeat tests conducted 1 week apart in 41 teenage subjects (14–15 years).

Although the time commitments of the force-velocity tests are a significant drawback compared to the WAnT procedure for determining peak power output (~ 40 min vs 30 s), the protocol does allow for the determination of the optimal braking force to elicit 'maximal' peak power output on an individual basis. Therefore, if time permits, the optimal braking force calculated from the force-velocity test can be used for the WAnT protocol for determination of a subject's optimal peak power output.

Due to the requirement of performing successive repeated bouts of 'all-out' exercise, a concern is the residual effects of fatigue influencing the subsequent bouts and therefore the velocity- and power output-braking force relationship. However, given the short nature of the bouts (5–7 s) and the fact that the children's muscle and blood metabolic profile recovers rapidly from intense exercise (Taylor *et al.* 1997; Hebestreit *et al.* 1993), a recovery of approximately 3–5 minutes should be sufficient to allay these concerns (Bar-Or 1996).

c) Isokinetic cycling

To obtain 'true' maximal power output, it is essential to match the external load to the capability of the active muscles to operate at their optimal velocity. As the velocity in anaerobic tests which employ a constant force is progressively reduced due to muscle fatigue, these conditions are hard to fulfil. To overcome this shortcoming, Sargeant *et al.* (1981) developed an isokinetic cycle ergometer, which enabled a constant pedalling velocity to be maintained throughout an 'all-out' short-term exercise test. As the velocity is 'fixed,' the power output will be directly related to the produced force, which is

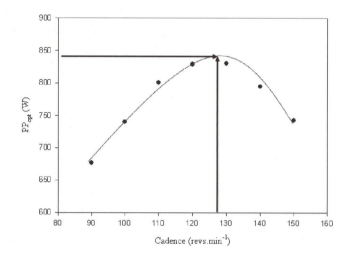

Figure 8.10 An example of a peak power output-cadence curve derived from an isokinetic cycle ergometer test. The optimum peak power (849 watts) was derived using a quadratic model and corresponded to an optimal cadence of 126 rev·min⁻¹. Figure adapted with permission from Williams *et al.* 2003.

inversely and linearly related to crank velocity over the range studied. In children, the intra-individual variation of the peak force was <6% (Sargeant *et al.* 1984).

Despite its advantages compared to a mechanically braked cycle ergometer, little research has been conducted to investigate the power output profile in children and adolescents using an isokinetic cycle ergometer. Williams and Keen (2001) developed a novel isokinetic cycle ergometer, which involved a bicycle frame being secured to a motorized treadmill, which enables the pedalling velocity to be 'set' between 0 and 170 rev·min⁻¹ with <2% error. In combination with torque measures taken from the cycle cranks, this allowed power output to be determined on a per pedal revolution basis. To determine the muscle power output-velocity relationship, subjects' performed a total of seven 'all-out' 6 s sprints. The cadence (velocity) for the initial sprint was 90 rev·min⁻¹ and increasingly incrementally by 10 rev·min⁻¹ for each subsequent bout, with 5 minutes rest allowed between each bout. The highest power output during each of the repeat 6-s sprints is then plotted against its respective cadence (velocity). The resulting relationship between peak power output and velocity is parabolic and allows determination of the optimal peak power and the optimal pedal cadence (Figure 8.10). The test-retest reliability expressed as a coefficient of variation is 5.4% for optimal peak power and 5.8% for optimal pedalling velocity in male adolescents (Williams and Keen 1997).

d) Motorized treadmill running

In a longitudinal study, Patterson *et al.* (1986) measured the responses of 19 boys, aged 10–15 years, over a 5-year period. A treadmill protocol was designed to estimate 'anaerobic capacity' using indices such as the subjects' time to exhaustion, post-exercise blood lactate concentrations and the O_2 debt (otherwise know as the excess post-exercise O_2 consumption). The boys ran on a 20% grade at speeds ranging from 7.8 km.h⁻¹ (age 10–11 years); to 11.9 km.h⁻¹ (age 14–15 years). One drawback of this method is that only 'anaerobic' endurance performance can be measured alongside physiological surrogates of 'anaerobic' metabolism. As only speed is recorded without the force component, power output cannot be calculated.

e) Non-motorized horizontal treadmill running

In adults, attempts have been made to measure maximal velocity and power output during maximal short-term running on a non-motorized treadmill (Lakomy 1987) due to the questionable generalizability of the power output profiles collected during cycling exercise to non-cycling modalities and performance. The same or adapted methodology has been used in order to examine short-term power output (5–30 s) in untrained and trained children (van Praagh et al. 1993; Sutton et al. 2000). Wearing a belt at the waist the subject develops maximal velocity while running on a non-motorized treadmill. The belt, which is attached to a horizontal bar, is connected to a potentiometer (vertical displacement) and strain gauges (horizontal traction force) allowing calculation of horizontal of force. A constant torque motor installed in the rear wheel of the treadmill is not used to drive the latter, but to compensate for belt friction or to simulate different loads. Signals from the potentiometer, the transducer and from the treadmill (belt speed) allows mechanical power (potential + kinetic power) to be calculated, thus presenting a promising model for the assessment of the child's power output profile during 'real world' locomotion where body mass is transported.

The study by Sutton et al. (2000) utilized an adapted version of the non-motorized treadmill test (called the Exeter Nonmotorized Treadmill Test [ExNMT]) to compare the obtained peak power output and mean power output values during running to the traditional cycling WAnT in a group of 10- to 11-year-old children. The average peak power output and mean power output achieved by the children during a 30-s 'all-out' sprint on the non-motorized treadmill was 211 ± 38 and 151 ± 29 watts, respectively, which was significantly lower than the performance on the cycling WAnT using a fixed braking force of 0.74 N·kg^{-1} (258 ± 80 and 228 ± 80 watts, respectively). However, the authors did notice the children elicited a higher peak blood lactate concentration 2 minutes post-exercise on the ExNMT (7.1 ± 1.3 mM) compared to the WAnT (5.6 ± 1.5 mM) suggesting a higher 'anaerobic' component during the treadmill compared to the cycling bouts. Sutton et al. (2000) also reported the test-retest reliability of the power output indices derived from the ExNMT, showing peak and mean power output to have a coefficient of repeatability of 27 and 15 watts, respectively, which compares well with the WAnT.

f) Monoarticular force-velocity tests

Movement across a single joint (e.g. elbow or knee) can be measured with devices that control the force or the velocity of the movement. One of the most commonly used ergometers is the isokinetic dynamometer – for a comprehensive review see Vandewalle et al. (1987). This technique has some drawbacks. Firstly, isokinetic dynamometer recordings are rarely generated under true constant angular velocity (Murray and Harrison 1986). Secondly, torque is measured throughout a range of motion at different limb velocities, and thus it is difficult for the subject to accelerate his/her limb voluntarily at an optimal velocity to yield a peak power output (Sargeant 1989). Thirdly, there is a need to standardize the torque-velocity relationship. Some authors report measured torque at slow (0.52 rad.s^{-1}) and/ or fast (5.23 rad.s^{-1}) angular velocities. Finally, because isokinetic dynamometers are designed for adults, modification of the equipment is required to test children. Isokinetic strength methodology and results obtained during childhood and adolescence have been addressed in great detail elsewhere (De Ste Croix 2007).

8.7.2 Considerations when assessing anaerobic performance

The assessment of power output profiles during short-term 'all-out' exercise raises several methodological problems that require consideration:

(a) Since power is the product of force and velocity, the external load (e.g. load on the cycle ergometer or body mass during jumping or running) must closely match the capability of the active muscles so that they operate at their optimal velocity (Wilkie 1960). Clearly, this is a difficult condition to fulfil or to guarantee during accelerating or decelerating (due to muscle fatigue) cycling or running sprint efforts. Several activities have been proposed for the measurement of short-term power output, including vertical jumping, running and cycle ergometry. Of these activities, only cycle ergometry allows precise measurement of power independent of body mass as the imposed load.

(b) If 'true' peak power output is to be measured, the duration of the test must be as short as possible, as power output decreases rapidly as a function of time (Wilkie, 1960; van Praagh *et al.* 1989). The measurement of 'true' peak power output requires measurements of instantaneous values of force and velocity. This condition is only satisfied in monoarticular force-velocity tests (Wilkie 1950), force platform tests (Davies and Rennie 1968; Ferretti *et al.* 1987), isokinetic cycle ergometry (Sargeant *et al.* 1981), cycling power tests including frictional force and flywheel inertia (Lakomy 1986; Arsac *et al.* 1996), and inertial-load cycling ergometry (Martin *et al.* 1997). The well known 30-s WAnT does not provide instantaneous measures and is, therefore, unable to elicit 'true' peak power output.

(c) Anaerobic glycolysis and aerobic contribution are limited during instantaneous power output tests lasting approximately 1 s in duration. As muscle lactate production starts during the first seconds of a supra-maximal exercise, glycolytic metabolism is already involved in exercise lasting less than 10 s. Therefore, only exercises lasting a few seconds can be considered as truly 'alactic' (Ferretti *et al.* 1987).

(d) Factors influencing peak power output include whether: (1) instantaneous or mean power output is measured; (2) the legs act simultaneously (vertical jumping) or successively (cycling); (3) total body mass or active muscle mass is taken into account as the relationship between these variables changes profoundly during growth and maturity and between sexes (van Praagh *et al.* 1990; Welsman *et al.* 1997); (4) peak power is measured at the beginning of exercise or after several seconds of a flying start (Vandewalle *et al.* 1987); and (5) the sampling resolution used to 'average' the power output profile (i.e. 1, 3 or 5 s).

8.8 ADJUSTING AEROBIC AND ANAEROBIC PERFORMANCE FOR BODY SIZE

The foregoing sections have provided an overview of the techniques and protocols available to the researcher for investigating aspects of aerobic and anaerobic performance in young people. However, many variables in exercise physiology, such as the peak power output achieved on a 30-s WAnT, demonstrate a strong positive relationship with body size indices. Generally speaking therefore, a child subject with a larger body mass or muscle mass will score a higher peak power output when expressed in its absolute form (watts) compared with a smaller child. Therefore, in order to understand whether differences in aerobic or anaerobic performance in subjects heterogeneous in body size are due to differences in physiology (qualitative) of body size (quantitative) characteristics, an appropriate statistical technique must be used in order to remove the influence of body size on the performance variable. This is typically achieved by the ratio standard technique (the division of Y by X), where Y is the performance variable (i.e. peak power) and X the body size variable (i.e. body mass). The adjusted physiological variable at this point is considered to be size-independent – that is, it is no longer related to body size. From this point, one can supposedly make valid comparisons – for example, of the WAnT peak power output scores between subjects of differing body size – and therefore make an inference regarding the development of anaerobic performance during growth and maturation.

However, despite its relative simplicity and intuitive appeal, the ratio standard technique is fraught with assumptions that if a given data set fails to satisfy, invalid and spurious results are yielded, which can seriously misguide the interpretation of physiological data (Welsman and Armstrong 2007). In contrast, a statistically superior technique for normalising physiological variables for body size is 'allometric modelling.' The advantage of allometry is that the model does not assume an *a priori* relationship between the Y and X variables. Rather, the allometric model describes the actual relationship between Y and X to create a power function ratio (Y/X^b), where b is the slope of a log-linear regression between Y and X, which can be subsequently used to normalise the physiological variables for body size. For an excellent discussion on the theory, application and interpretation of allometric models in physiology and performance tests the reader is referred to Chapter 11, by Winter and Nevill.

8.9 FIELD TESTS

Where the facilities or time available do not allow for laboratory testing, simple 'field' tests of fitness (e.g. sit-ups, jumping tests, timed distance runs and grip strength) can be used. Tests are available for the estimation of aerobic endurance and anaerobic power. Additionally, tests are often grouped into 'batteries' of tests, which purportedly measure a variety of fitness variables in children. Such batteries include the American Alliance for Health, Physical Education, Recreation and Dance (AAHPERD) tests (1988) and the

Council of Europe's 'EUROFIT' tests (1988). (See also Chapter 3, by Beunen, Table 3.4).

8.9.1 Field tests of aerobic endurance

Not all tests of aerobic endurance require laboratory facilities, and several field tests have been developed to cater for larger groups of children, or where time and equipment may be limited. Most of these tests, such as the 20-m multistage shuttle run (20-MST, also known as the shuttle run, bleep test or beep test), and the timed one-mile run/walk, may involve maximal effort, while the cycle ergometer test of physical work capacity (PWC_{170}) does not, requiring only approximately 85% of maximum heart rate to be achieved. The PWC_{170} is, in effect, a compromise between laboratory and field, being restricted to one child at a time, and requiring some equipment (cycle ergometer, metronome, stopwatch) and expertise on behalf of the tester. For full details of the test protocol, the EUROFIT handbook should be consulted (EUROFIT 1988).

The 20-MST and one mile run/walk tests have been employed extensively by European and North American investigators, respectively. Both have shown variable but generally moderate correlations against laboratory-measured $\dot{V}O_2$max (van Mechelen *et al.* 1986; Boreham *et al.* 1990; Safrit 1990). However, this is not surprising given that endurance running performance is governed by other factors such as the 'anaerobic threshold', running economy and motivation, as well as $\dot{V}O_2$max.

The one mile run/walk test has been incorporated into both the AAHPERD (1988) and FITNESSGRAM (1987) test batteries, and criterion-referenced standards for health developed. The standards adopted for AAHPERD are somewhat more stringent (Table 8.6).

The 20-MST, unlike the one mile run/walk test, does not require a large, marked running area, and can conveniently be carried

Table 8.6 Criterion referenced health standards for the one mile run/walk test (min)

Age	FITNESSGRAM	AAHPERD
9	12.00	10.00
10	11.00	9.30
11	11.00	9.00
12	10.00	9.00
13	9.30	8.00
14	8.30	7.45
15	8.30	7.30
16	8.30	7.30

out indoors, provided that a hall at least 20 metres long is available. Originally developed by Léger and Lambert (1982), the test consists of running to and fro between two lines, 20 metres apart, in time with a pre-recorded audio signal from a cassette tape. Starting at a pace of 8.5 km/h^{-1}, the speed progressively increases each minute until the child can no longer keep up with the required pace. A lap scoring protocol has been developed (Queen's University, Belfast, Northern Ireland) which may be particularly useful for testing children. Full details of the 20-MST are available in the EUROFIT manual (1988), and norms are also available (refer to Table 8.7 and Table 8.8).

8.9.2 Field tests of anaerobic performance

a) Vertical jump

Sargent (1921) developed the vertical jump test to measure maximal leg power in adults. Subjects are required to jump vertically as high as they can. The subject's ability to exert leg power is derived from the height of the jump. The best value from the three jumps is generally taken as the test score. The vertical jump has been accepted as a valid measure of leg power, and various vertical jump protocols have been derived from the Sargent test; for example, Jump-and-Reach test, Abalakov test (for review see Kirby 1991). The objectivity and reliability coefficients are high. Reliability

coefficients of 0.91 to 0.93 suggest high intra-individual consistency (Glencross 1966). No test-retest reliability has been reported for paediatric populations. The validity of the test, compared with the sum of four power events in track and field, is rather low ($r = 0.78$, Safrit 1990). The test does not involve high motor ability and can be easily learned by children. Norms are also available (Baumgartner and Jackson 1991). A major weakness is the lack of standardization in test administration. For instance, a counter-movement increases the vertical jump performance by about 10% (Bosco *et al.* 1983), probably due to the involvement of the stretch-shortening cycle. Moreover, a more rapid elevation of the arms also improves the height of a vertical jump.

b) Broad jump

Because of its easy execution and administration, the standing broad jump is often used instead of the vertical jump as a measure of leg muscle power. Subjects are required to jump forward as far as possible with a two-footed landing and take-off. The problem with all field-based assessments is that the tests do not reflect a single factor (leg power, in this particular case), but also learning, coordination and maturation. Thus, although the standing broad jump appears to be objective as well as reliable, its validity is questionable. Coefficients of 0.79 between standing broad jump and vertical jump assume that either can be used as a criterion measure for the other. Docherty (1996) asserted that the specific issue of validity for either test has not been examined. The test is feasible for girls and boys from 6 years on (EUROFIT 1988). Normative data are available for both age and gender groups (see Tables 8.6 and 8.7 and American Alliance for Health, Physical Education and Recreation 1975).

c) 30- to 50-metre dash

Historically, physical educators and coaches have used a 30- to 50-metre dash as a measure of running velocity. The test is easy to administer, can be done in and outdoors, and

Table 8.7 Normscales for British children: selected EUROFIT test battery items (adapted from Northern Ireland Fitness Survey, 1990)

Percentile	Age 11	12	13	14	15	16	17
Height (mm)							
Boys 80	1502	1573	1630	1686	1744	1800	1817
50	1441	1496	1560	1628	1690	1732	1756
20	1389	1436	1498	1558	1642	1668	1703
Mean	1449	1503	1566	1621	1689	1734	1760
SD	69	76	82	84	68	70	67
Girls 80	1534	1573	1617	1642	1647	1670	1679
50	1470	1510	1562	1595	1601	1617	1626
20	1408	1443	1511	1546	1555	1566	1574
Mean	1471	1511	1563	1594	1602	1620	1626
SD	75	77	67	60	60	59	63
Body mass (kg)							
Boys 80	43.7	48.7	54.5	59.3	64.4	72.0	74.2
50	36.3	41.1	44.7	50.4	57.1	63.5	66.0
20	31.8	34.1	38.4	43.2	50.9	56.4	58.5
Mean	37.7	42.1	46.5	51.7	58.0	64.2	66.5
SD	7.2	8.8	9.9	10.1	9.5	9.6	9.0
Girls 80	47.7	50.3	54.9	59.1	60.1	61.9	62.6
50	39.2	41.5	47.9	52.2	53.4	55.7	55.9
20	32.9	36.3	41.2	46.8	48.2	49.8	50.6
Mean	40.6	43.1	48.7	52.9	54.0	56.5	56.6
SD	8.9	8.8	9.3	7.9	7.4	7.7	6.9
Skinfolds (sum of four sites; biceps, triceps, subscapular, supriliac)							
Boys 80	41.9	45.9	41.4	39.0	36.7	38.8	35.7
50	29.4	30.1	26.6	27.7	26.9	28.3	27.4
20	22.8	23.3	21.2	21.9	22.7	22.8	22.8
Mean	33.7	35.6	32.3	31.9	31.6	31.5	30.0
SD	14.6	16.0	14.9	13.1	13.0	11.4	10.5
Girls 80	48.8	45.5	49.0	53.2	51.6	53.7	49.4
50	33.1	33.5	34.6	40.2	40.3	41.5	40.1
20	23.8	26.4	27.7	29.9	31.3	32.3	31.7
Mean	37.2	36.6	39.2	42.1	42.4	43.1	43.3
SD	17.0	13.0	14.4	13.8	12.7	12.5	11.7
20 Metre shuttle run (laps)							
Boys 80	80	81	90	96	102	105	110
50	61	63	72	79	86	91	97
20	44	50	55	63	68	75	81

Percentile	Age 11	12	13	14	15	16	17
Mean	61	65	72	79	86	90	96
SD	19	17	19	20	20	18	18
Girls 80	52	58	61	60	58	63	62
50	38	47	46	46	48	49	49
20	31	34	35	36	37	38	35
Mean	41	47	48	49	49	50	50
SD	13	14	15	16	14	15	16
Sit and reach (cm)							
Boys 80	21.5	21.0	22.5	22.5	26.5	28.0	30.5
50	16.0	15.0	16.0	17.0	20.0	22.0	24.0
20	11.5	9.5	10.0	11.5	13.5	15.0	17.0
Mean	16.5	15.0	16.0	17.0	19.5	22.0	23.5
SD	6.0	6.5	7.0	6.5	7.5	7.5	8.5
Girls 80	26.5	25.5	27.0	30.5	31.0	31.0	33.0
50	21.0	21.0	22.0	25.0	25.5	25.5	26.5
20	15.5	15.5	16.0	19.0	19.5	18.5	20.5
Mean	20.5	20.5	21.5	24.5	25.0	25.0	26.0
SD	6.5	6.0	6.5	6.5	6.5	7.0	7.5
Standing broad jump (cm)							
Boys 80	162	166	180	188	204	214	218
50	146	150	161	170	184	194	201
20	129	133	138	149	162	173	183
Mean	145	150	161	169	183	195	200
SD	19	20	23	25	24	24	24
Girls 80	146	153	158	165	163	168	169
50	130	136	138	143	143	147	148
20	117	121	122	126	128	128	133
Mean	131	136	140	144	459	147	151
SD	19	19	21	22	21	22	22
Sit-ups in 30 s (number completed)							
Boys 80	25	25	27	28	29	29	29
50	22	23	24	25	25	26	26
20	19	20	21	21	22	22	22
Mean	22	23	24	25	25	26	26
SD	4	4	4	4	4	4	4
Girls 80	22	23	23	23	23	23	23
50	19	20	19	20	20	20	20
20	16	17	16	17	17	17	16
Mean	19	20	19	20	20	20	19

Percentile	Age 11	12	13	14	15	16	17
SD	4	4	4	4	4	4	4
Handgrip strength (N)							
Boys 80	230	260	300	370	440	480	520
50	190	220	260	290	370	420	460
20	170	190	220	240	310	360	400
Mean	200	230	260	300	370	420	460
SD	40	50	60	70	80	70	70
Girls 80	220	240	270	300	310	320	320
50	190	200	240	260	270	280	290
20	150	160	200	230	240	240	250
Mean	190	200	230	260	270	280	290
SD	40	40	40	40	40	50	50
10 × 5 m shuttle sprint (s)							
Boys 80	23.3	23.2	21.9	21.5	20.9	20.3	20.0
50	21.7	21.4	20.6	20.1	19.8	19.1	18.7
20	20.4	20.1	19.4	18.9	18.6	17.9	17.6
Mean	21.9	21.6	20.8	20.3	19.8	19.1	18.9
SD	1.9	1.8	1.6	1.6	1.5	1.4	1.4
Girls 80	25.0	24.1	23.9	23.9	23.6	23.5	23.8
50	23.3	22.5	22.5	22.4	22.1	21.9	21.9
20	22.1	21.1	21.3	20.8	20.8	20.4	20.3
Mean	23.5	22.6	22.7	22.4	22.1	22.0	22.0
SD	1.8	2.0	1.7	1.9	2.2	1.9	2.0

Table 8.8 Normscales for Dutch children: EUROFIT test battery items (adapted from van Mechelen *et al.*, 1992)

Scale	Low score	Below average	Average	Above average	High score
Eurofit variable for boys aged 12 years					
Test					
St. broad jump (cm)	<151	152–154	155–168	169–175	from 176
Bent arm hang (s)	<10.3	10.4–15	15.1–21.6	21.7–30.7	from 30.8
10 × 5 m run (s)	<20.8	20.0–20.7	19.4–19.9	18.7–19.3	until inc. 18.6
Sit and reach (cm)	<12	13–15	16–18	19–22	from 23
Sit-ups (no. in 30 s)	<18	19–21	22–23	24–25	from 26
Body height (c)	<152	153–156	157–160	161–165	from 166
Body mass (kg)	<39	40–43	44–47	48–51	from 52
Sum 4 skinfolds (mm)	<21	22–26	27–30	31–38	from 39
20 m shuttle (steps/paliers)	<5.0	5.5–6.5	7.0–7.5	8.0–9.0	from 9.5
Handgrip (kg)	<24	25–26	27–28	29–32	from 33

Scale	Low score	Below average	Average	Above average	High score
Eurofit variables for girls aged 12 years					
Test					
St. broad jump (cm)	<139	140–149	150–157	158–165	from 166
Bent arm hang (s)	<3.8	3.9–7.5	7.6–12.6	12.7–22.0	from 22.1
10 × 5 m run (s)	<21.7	20.8–21.6	20.1–20.7	19.5–20.0	until inc. 19.4
Sit and reach (cm)	<20	21–23	24–26	27–29	from 30
Sit-ups (no. in 30 s)	<17	18–18	18–20	21–22	from 23
Body height (cm)	<153	154–158	159–162	163–166	from 167
Body mass (kg)	<40	41–45	46–50	51–55	from 56
Sum 4 skinfolds (mm)	<26	27–34	35–42	43–51	from 52
20 m shuttle (steps/paliers)	<3.5	4.0–4.5	5.0–5.5	6.0–6.5	from 7.0
Handgrips (kg)	<21	22–24	25–26	27–30	from 31
Eurofit variables for boys aged 13 years					
Test					
St. broad jump (cm)	<152	153–162	163–172	173–184	from 185
Bent arm hang (s)	<8.6	8.7–15.2	15.3–22.0	22.1–31.3	from 31.4
10 × 5 m run (s)	<20.7	19.9–20.6	19.3–19.8	18.6–19.2	until inc. 18.5
Sit and reach (cm)	<11	12–15	16–19	20–22	from 23
Sit-ups (no. in 30 s)	<18	19–21	22–23	24–25	from 26
Body height (cm)	<154	155–160	161–164	165–170	from 171
Body mass (kg)	<42	43–46	47–50	51–56	from 57
Sum 4 skinfolds (mm)	<21	22–25	26–31	32–42	from 43
20 m shuttle (steps/paliers)	<5.5	6.0–6.5	7.0–7.5	8.0–8.5	from 9.0
Handgrips (kg)	<25	26–28	29–31	32–36	from 37
Eurofit variables for girls aged 13 years					
Test					
St. broad jump (cm)	<141	142–151	152–160	161–171	from 172
Bent arm hang (s)	<3.8	3.9–7.4	7.5–13.4	13.5–20.4	from 20.5
10 × 5 m run (s)	<21.8	20.9–21.7	20.3–20.8	19.4–20.2	until inc. 19.3
Sit and reach (cm)	<20	21–24	25–28	29–32	from 33
Sit-ups (no. in 30 s)	<16	17–18	19–20	21–22	from 23
Body height (cm)	<156	157–160	161–164	165–168	from 169
Body mass (kg)	<44	45–48	49–52	53–57	from 58
Sum 4 skinfolds (mm)	<29	30–36	37–43	44–56	from 57
20 m shuttle (steps/paliers)	<4.0	4.5–4.5	5.0–5.5	60.–6.5	from 7.0
Handgrips (kg)	<23	24–26	27–29	30–31	from 32
Eurofit variables for boys aged 14 years					
Test					
St. broad jump (cm)	<157	158–170	171–181	182–194	from 195

Scale	Low score	Below average	Average	Above average	High score
Bent arm hang (s)	<10.5	10.6–17.6	17.7–25.4	25.5–38.5	from 38.6
10 × 5 m run (s)	<20.4	19.6–20.3	19.0–19.5	18.2–18.9	until inc. 18.1
Sit and reach (cm)	<11	12–17	18–21	22–26	from 27
Sit-ups (no. in 30 s)	<19	20–21	22–23	24–25	from 26
Body height (cm)	<160	161–165	166–171	172–177	from 178
Body mass (kg)	<46	47–52	53–57	58–63	from 64
Sum 4 skinfolds (mm)	<21	22–25	26–29	30–40	from 41
20 m shuttle (steps/paliers)	<6.0	6.5–7.0	7.5–8.0	8.5–9.0	from 9.5
Handgrips (kg)	<29	30–33	34–38	39–44	from 45

Eurofit variables for girls aged 14 years

Test					
St. broad jump (cm)	<143	144–152	153–162	163–171	from 172
Bent arm hang (s)	<3.1	3.2–5.9	6.0–10.5	10.6–19.6	from 19.7
10 × 5 m run (s)	<21.7	20.7–21.6	20.0–20.6	19.2–19.9	until inc. 19.1
Sit and reach (cm)	<20	21–24	25–28	29–32	from 33
Sit-ups (no. in 30 s)	<16	17–18	19–20	21–22	from 22
Body height (cm)	<161	162–164	165–168	169–171	from 172
Body mass (kg)	<49	50–52	53–56	57–62	from 63
Sum 4 skinfolds (mm)	<33	34–39	40–44	45–54	from 55
20 m shuttle (steps/paliers)	<4.0	4.5–5.0	5.5–5.5	6.0–6.5	from 7.0
Handgrips (kg)	<26	27–28	29–31	32–34	from 35

Eurofit variables for boys aged 15 years

Test					
St. broad jump (cm)	<169	170–182	183–193	194–206	from 207
Bent arm hang (s)	<15.3	15.4–25.3	25.4–35.3	35.4–46.6	from 46.7
10 × 5 m run (s)	<19.9	19.0–19.8	18.2–18.9	17.7–18.1	until inc. 17.6
Sit and reach (cm)	<12	13–18	19–23	24–27	from 38
Sit-ups (no. in 30 s)	<20	21–22	23–24	25–26	from 27
Body height (cm)	<168	169–173	174–177	178–181	from 182
Body mass (kg)	<53	54–58	59–62	63–69	from 70
Sum 4 skinfolds (mm)	<21	22–24	25–27	28–35	from 36
20 m shuttle (steps/paliers)	<6.5	7.0–7.5	8.0–9.0	9.5–9.5	from 10
Handgrips (kg)	<34	35–41	42–45	46–51	from 52

Eurofit variables for girls aged 15 years

Test					
St. broad jump (cm)	<142	143–151	152–161	162–171	from 172
Bent arm hang (s)	<3.4	3.5–6.3	6.4–10.8	10.9–17.2	from 17.3
10 × 5 m run (s)	<21.3	20.7–21.2	19.9–20.6	19.3–19.8	until inc. 19.2
Sit and reach (cm)	<21	22–27	28–30	31–34	from 35

Scale	Low score	Below average	Average	Above average	High score
Sit-ups (no. in 30 s)	<16	17–17	18–19	20–21	from 22
Body height (cm)	<161	162–165	166–169	170–173	from 174
Body mass (kg)	<51	52–55	56–59	60–64	from 65
Sum 4 skinfolds (mm)	<36	37–43	44–50	51–62	from 63
20 m shuttle (steps/paliers)	<4.0	4.5–4.5	5.0–5.5	6.0–6.5	from 7.0
Handgrips (kg)	<27	28–30	31–33	34–37	from 38

Eurofit variables for boys aged 16 years

Test	Low score	Below average	Average	Above average	High score
St. broad jump (cm)	<181	182–193	194–201	202–211	from 212
Bent arm hang (s)	<19.5	19.6–32.4	32.5–42.8	42.9–51.4	from 51.5
10 × 5 m run (s)	<19.4	18.6–19.3	18.1–18.5	17.5–18.0	until inc. 17.4
Sit and reach (cm)	<16	17–19	20–23	24–28	from 29
Sit-ups (no. in 30 s)	<20	21–22	23–24	25–26	from 27
Body height (cm)	<174	175–177	178–182	183–185	from 186
Body mass (kg)	<57	58–62	63–66	67–72	from 73
Sum 4 skinfolds (mm)	<19	20–22	23–26	27–32	from 33
20 m shuttle (steps/paliers)	<7.5	8.0–8.0	8.5–9.0	9.5–10.0	from 10.5
Handgrips (kg)	<42	43–47	48–51	52–56	from 57

Eurofit variables for girls aged 16 years

Test	Low score	Below average	Average	Above average	High score
St. broad jump (cm)	<145	146–153	154–162	163–171	from 172
Bent arm hang (s)	<3.0	3.1–6.8	6.9–12.2	12.3–20.1	from 20.2
10 × 5 m run (s)	<21.1	20.3–21.0	19.5–20.2	19.1–19.4	until inc. 19.0
Sit and reach (cm)	<24	25–29	30–31	32–34	from 35
Sit-ups (no. in 30 s)	<16	17–18	19–20	21–23	from 24
Body height (cm)	<162	163–166	167–168	169–171	from 172
Body mass (kg)	<51	52–56	57–60	61–63	from 64
Sum 4 skinfolds (mm)	<34	35–41	42–49	50–60	from 61
20 m shuttle (steps/paliers)	<4.0	4.5–5.0	5.5–5.5	6.0–6.5	from 7.0
Handgrips (kg)	<28	29–31	32–33	34–37	from 38

paediatric populations can be assessed in a short time. This simple test enables categorisation of subjects as: 'slow,' 'medium slow' or 'rapid.' However, it cannot be considered to be a 'real' power test, as the force component is not measured. Peak power (W kg^{-1}) measured by the cycle force-velocity test correlates quite well with a 30-m dash in a group of 7- and 12-year-old girls and boys. ($r = 0.80$, p<0.001), but it was significantly lower when only the girls' results were analyzed (van Praagh *et al.* 1990).

d) Field Test Batteries for Children

The use of laboratory tests to determine performance in children is not always appropriate or feasible, and several batteries of field tests have been proposed mainly to cater for large scale population studies and/or the educational testing environment.

Such test batteries include the AAHPERD 'Physical Best' programme (1988) and the more comprehensive EUROFIT test battery (Tables 8.6, 8.7 and Table 3.4 in Beunen, Chapter 3). While the purpose (Pate 1989), validity, reliability (Safrit 1990) and interpretation (Plowman 1992) of such tests have been the subject of intense debate, their expanding use, particularly in an educational setting, continues. It is likely that much of this debate is generated by an inability to (a) appreciate the limitation of the tests as scientific tools; (b) understand the underlying biological processes during growth which may contribute to a child's score on a particular test item; and (c) reach a consensus regarding criterion-referenced norms, particularly for health-related tests, such as body composition and aerobic endurance.

The limitations of such test batteries may include the high skill factor involved in performing individual test items (and hence the possibility of improvement merely reflecting the learning process rather than a 'real' change in fitness *per se*) and difficulties in validation. Nevertheless, their usefulness, particularly in an educational setting or where large numbers of individuals need to be tested with limited resources and less experienced instructors, is often underestimated (Kemper 1990).

FURTHER READING

Books

N. Armstrong (Ed) (2007) *Paediatric Exercise Physiology. Advances in Sport and Exercise Series*. (N. Spurway and D. MacLaren, eds) Elsevier; London.

Bar-Or O. and Rowland T. W. (2004) *Pediatric Exercise Medicine. From Physiologic Principles to Health Care Application*. Human Kinetics; Champaign, IL.

Tomkinson G. R. and Olds T. S. (eds) (2007) *Pediatric Fitness Secular Trends and Geographic Variability*. Medicine and Sports Science Vol 50 Series. Karger; Basel.

Journal article

Welsman J. R. and Armstrong, N. (2000). Statistical techniques for interpreting body size-related exercise performance during growth. *Pediatric Exercise Science*; **12**: 112–27.

REFERENCES

AAHPERD (1988) *Physical Best Program* American Alliance for Health, Physical Education, Recreation and Dance; Reston, VA.

American Alliance for Health, Physical Education and Recreation (1975) *Youth Fitness Test Manual*; Washington, DC.

Armstrong N. and Welsman J. R. (1994) Assessment and Interpretation of Aerobic Fitness in Children and Adolescents. In: (J. O. Holloszy, ed) *Exercise and Sport Science Reviews*. Lippincott, Williams and Wilkins; Philadelphia, PA: pp. 435–76.

Armstrong N. and Welsman J. (1997) *Young People and Physical Activity*. Oxford University Press; Oxford.

Armstrong N., Welsman J. and Winsley R. (1996) Is peak VO$_2$ a maximal index of children's aerobic fitness? *International Journal of Sports Medicine*; **17**: 356–9.

Arsac M. A., Belli A., Lacour J.-R. (1996) Muscle function during brief maximal exercise: accurate measurements on a friction-loaded cycle ergometer. *European Journal of Applied Physiology*; **74**: 100–6.

Barker A., Welsman J., Welford D., Fulford J., Williams C. and Armstrong N. (2006) Reliability of ^{31}P-magnetic resonance spectroscopy during an exhaustive incremental exercise test in children. *European Journal of Applied Physiology*; **98**: 556–65.

Bar-Or O. (1983) *Pediatric Sports Medicine for the Practitioner: from Physiologic Principles to Clinical Applications*. Springer-Verlag; New York.

Bar-Or O. (1996) Anaerobic Performance. In: *Measurement in Pediatric Exercise Science*. (D. Docherty, ed) Human Kinetics: Champaign, IL: pp. 161–82.

Bar-Or O. and Rowland T. W. (2004) *Pediatric Exercise Medicine. From Physiologic Principles to Health Care Application*. Human Kinetics; Champaign, IL.

Baumgartner T. A. and Jackson A. S. (1991) *Measurement for Evaluation in Physical Education and Exercise Science.* William C. Brown; Dubuque, IL.

Baxter-Jones A. D. G. and Sherar L. B. (2007) Growth and maturation. In: (N. Armstrong, ed) *Paediatric Exercise Physiology: Advances in Sport and Exercise Series* (N. Spurway and D. MacLaren, eds) Elsevier; London: pp. 1–26.

Beaver W. L., Wasserman K. and Whipp B. J. (1986) A new method for detecting anaerobic threshold by gas exchange. *Journal of Applied Physiology*; 60: 2020–7.

Beneke R., Hutler M., Jung M. and Leithauser R. M. (2005) Modeling the blood lactate kinetics at maximal short-term exercise conditions in children, adolescents, and adults. *Journal of Applied Physiology*; 99: 499–504.

Beneke R., Hutler M. and Leithauser R. M. (2007) Anaerobic performance and metabolism in boys and male adolescents. *European Journal of Applied Physiology*; 101: 671–7.

Beunen G. (2009) Chapter 3: Physical growth, maturation and performance. In: (R. G. Eston and T. Reilly, eds) *Kinanthropometry Laboratory Manual (3rd Edition): Anthropometry.* Routledge; Oxon.

Beunen G. and Malina R. M. (1988) Growth and physical performance relative to the timing of the adolescent spurt. *Exercise and Sports Sciences Reviews*; 16: 503–46.

Boreham C. A. G., Paliczka V. J. and Nichols A. K. (1990) A comparison of the PWC_{170} and 20-MST tests of aerobic fitness in adolescent schoolchildren. *Journal of Sports Medicine and Physical Fitness*; 30: 19–23.

Boreham C. A. G., Savage J. M., Primrose D., Cran G. and Strain J. (1993) Coronary risk factors in schoolchildren. *Archives of Disease in Childhood*; 68: 182–6.

Bosco C., Luhtanen P. and Komi P. V. (1983) A simple method for measurement of mechanical power in jumping. *European Journal of Applied Physiology*; 50: 273–82.

Brewer J., Balsom P. D., Davis J. A. and Ekblom, B. (1992) The influence of birth date and physical development on the selection of a male junior international soccer squad. *Journal of Sports Sciences*; 10: 561–2.

British Association of Sports Sciences (1988) *Position Statement on the Physiological Assessment of the Elite Competitor.* British Association of Sports Sciences; Leeds.

Brooks G. A. (1985) Anaerobic threshold: review of the concept and directions for future research. *Medicine and Science in Sports and Exercise*; 17: 22–31.

Cole T. J., Bellizzi M. C., Flegal K. M. and Dietz W. H. (2000) Establishing a standard definition for child overweight and obesity: international survey. *British Medical Journal*; 320: 1240–3.

Cooper D. M., Weiler-Ravell D. Whipp B. J. and Wasserman K. (1984) Aerobic parameters of exercise as a function of body size during growth in children. *Journal of Applied Physiology*; 56: 628–34.

Cumming G. R. (1973) Correlation of athletic performance and aerobic power in 12–17-year-old children with bone age, calf muscle, total body potassium, heart volume and two indices of anaerobic power. In: (O. Bar-Or, ed) *Pediatric Work Physiology*, Wingate Institute; Natanya, Israel: pp. 109–34.

Davies C. T. M., Rennie R. (1968). Human power output. *Nature*; 217: 770–1.

Day J. R., Rossiter H. B., Coats E. M., Skasick A. and Whipp B. J. (2003) The maximally attainable VO_2 during exercise in humans: the peak vs. maximum issue. *Journal of Applied Physiology*; 95: 1901–7.

De Ste Croix M.B.A. (2007) Muscle strength. In: (N. Armstrong, ed) *Paediatric Exercise Physiology. Advances in Sport and Exercise Series.* (N. Spurway and D. MacLaren, eds) Elsevier; London: pp. 47–70.

Docherty D. (ed.) (1996) Measurement. In: *Pediatric Exercise Science.* Human Kinetics; Champaign, IL.

Eston R. G., Parfitt C. G., Campbell L. and Lamb K. L. (2000) Reliability of effort perception for regulating exercise intensity in children using the Cart and Load Effort Rating (CALER) Scale. *Pediatric Exercise Science*; 12: 388–97.

Eston R., Williams J. G. and Faulkner J. A. (2009) Chapter 9: Control of exercise intensity using heart rate, perceived exertion and other non-invasive procedures. In: (R.G. Eston and T. Reilly, eds) *Kinanthropometry Laboratory Manual (3rd Edition): Exercise Physiology.* Routledge; Oxon: pp. 237–70.

Eston R. G., Hawes M., Martin A. D. and Reilly T. (2009): Human body composition. In: (R.

G. Eston and T Reilly, (eds) *Kinanthropometry Laboratory Manual (3rd Edition): Anthropometry (Chapter 1)*. Routledge; Oxon.

EUROFIT: *European Test of Physical Fitness* (1988) Council of Europe, Committee for the Development of Sport (CDDS); Rome.

Fawkner S. G., Armstrong N., Childs D. J. and Welsman J. R. (2002) Reliability of the visually identified ventilatory threshold and v-slope in children. *Pediatric Exercise Science*; 14: 181–92.

Ferretti G., Gussoni M., di Prampero P. E. and Cerretelli P. (1987) Effects of exercise on maximal instantaneous muscular power of humans. *Journal of Applied Physiology*; 62: 2288–94.

FITNESSGRAM *Users Manual* (1987) Institute for Aerobics Research; Dallas, TX.

Gladden L. B. (2004) Lactate metabolism: a new paradigm for the third millennium. *Journal of Physiology*; 558: 5–30.

Glencross D. J. (1966) The nature of the vertical jump test and the standing broad jump. *Research Quarterly*; 37: 353–9.

Haschke F. (1983) Body composition of adolescent males. Part 2. Body composition of male reference adolescents. *Acta Paediatrica Scandinavica*; 307: 1–12.

Hebestreit H., Mimura K. and Bar-Or O. (1993) Recovery of anaerobic muscle power following 30-s supramaximal exercise: Comparison between boys and men. *Journal of Applied Physiology*; 74: 2875–80.

Hebestreit H., Staschen B. and Hebestreit A. (2000) Ventilatory threshold: a useful method to determine aerobic fitness in children? *Medicine and Science in Sports and Exercise*; 32: 1964–9.

Inbar O. and Bar-Or O. (1975) The effects of intermittent warm-up on 7–9-year-old boys. *European Journal of Applied Physiology*; 34: 81–9.

Kemper H. C. G. (ed.), (1985) Medicine and Sports Science; vol. 20. *Growth, Health and Fitness of Teenagers*. Karger; Basel.

Kemper H. C. G. (1990) Physical fitness testing in children: is it a worthwhile activity? *Proceedings of the European EUROFIT Research Seminar*. Council of Europe; Izmir, Turkey: pp. 7–27.

Kirby R. F. (1991) *Kirby's Guide for Fitness and Motor Performance Tests*. Ben Oak; Cape Girardeau, MI.

Lakomy H. K. A. (1986) Measurement of work and power output using friction loaded cycle ergometers. *Ergonomics*; 29: 509–17.

Lakomy H. K. A. (1987) The use of a non-motorized treadmill for analyzing sprint performance. *Ergonomics*; 30: 627–38.

Léger L. and Lambert J. (1982) A maximal 20 metre shuttle run test to predict $\dot{V}O_2$max. *European Journal of Applied Physiology*; 49: 1–12.

Lohman T. (1992) Advances in body composition assessment. *Current Issues in Exercise Science Series* (Monograph Number 3). Human Kinetics; Champaign, IL.

Mahon A. D. and Cheatham C. C. (2002) Ventilatory threshold in children: a review. *Pediatric Exercise Science*; 14: 16–29.

Malina R. M. and Bouchard C. (1991) *Growth, Maturation and Physical Activity*. Human Kinetics; Champaign, IL.

Malina R. M., Bouchard C. and Bar-Or O. (2004) *Growth, Maturation and Physical Activity*. Human Kinetics; Champaign, IL.

Martin J. C., Wagner B. M. and Coyle E. F. (1997) Inertial-load method determines maximal cycling power in a single exercise bout. *Medicine and Science in Sports and Exercise*; 11: 1505–12.

Mirwald R. L., Baxter-Jones A. D., Bailey D. A. and Beunen G. P. (2002) An assessment of maturity from anthropometric measurements. *Medicine and Science in Sport and Exercise*; 34: 689–94.

Moser C., Tirakitsoontorn P., Nussbaum E., Newcomb R. and Cooper D. M. (2000) Muscle size and cardiorespiratory response to exercise in cystic fibrosis. *American Journal of Respiratory and Critical Care Medicine*; 162: 1823–7.

Murray D. A. and Harrison E. (1986) Constant velocity dynamometer: an appraisal using mechanical loading. *Medicine and Science in Sports and Exercise*; 6: 612–24.

Naughton G., Carlson J. and Fairweather I. (1992) Determining the variability of performance on Wingate anaerobic tests in children aged 6–12 years. *International Journal of Sports Medicine*; 13: 512–17.

Northern Ireland Fitness Survey (1990) *The Fitness, Physical Activity, Attitudes and Lifestyles* of *N. Ireland Post-primary Schoolchildren.* Division of Physical and Health Education. The Queen's University of Belfast; UK.

Pate R. R. (1989) The case for large-scale physical fitness testing in American youth. *Pediatric Exercise Science*; 1: 290–4.

Patterson D. H., Cunningham D. A. and Bumstead L. A. (1986) Recovery O_2 and blood lactic acid: longitudinal analysis in boys aged 11 to 15 years. *European Journal of Applied Physiology*; 55: 93–9.

Petersen S. R., Gaul C. A., Stanton M. M. and Hanstock C. C. (1999) Skeletal muscle metabolism during short-term, high-intensity exercise in prepubertal and pubertal girls. *Journal of Applied Physiology*; 87: 2151–6.

Pirnay F. and Crielaard J. M. (1979) Mesure de la puissance anaérobie alactique (Measurement of alactic anaerobic power), *Medicine and Sport*; 53: 13–16.

Plowman S. A. (1992) Criterion – referenced standards for neuromuscular physical fitness tests: an analysis. *Pediatric Exercise Science*; 4: 10–19.

Ratel S., Duche P., Hennegrave A., Van Praagh E. and Bedu M. (2002) Acid-base balance during repeated cycling sprints in boys and men. *Journal of Applied Physiology*; 92: 479–85.

Riddoch C., Savage J. M., Murphy N., Cran G. W. and Boreham C. (1991) Long-term health implications of fitness and physical activity patterns. *Archives of Disease in Childhood*; 66: 1426–33.

Round J., Jones D. A., Honour J. W. and Nevill A. M. (1999) Hormonal factors in the development of differences between boys and girls during adolescence: a longitudinal study. *Annals of Human Biology*; 26: 49–62.

Rowland T. W. (ed) (1993a) *Pediatric Laboratory Exercise Testing: Clinical Guidelines.* Human Kinetics; Champaign, IL.

Rowland T. W. (1993b) Does peak VO_2 reflect VO_2max in children? Evidence from supramaximal testing. *Medicine and Science in Sports and Exercise.* 25: 689–93.

Rowland T. W. (1999). Crusading for the Balke protocol. *Pediatric Exercise Science*; 11: 189–92.

Rowland T. W. (2005). *Children's Exercise Physiology.* Human Kinetics: Champaign, IL.

Rowland T. W. and Cunningham L. N. (1992) Oxygen uptake plateau during maximal treadmill exercise in children. *Chest*; 101: 485–9.

Safrit M. J. (1990) The validity and reliability of fitness tests for children: a review. *Pediatric Exercise Scienc*;, 2: 9–28.

Santos A. M. C., Welsman J. R., De Ste Croix M. B. A. and Armstrong N. (2002) Age- and sex- related differences in optimal peak power. *Pediatric Exercise Science*; 14: 202–12.

Sargeant A. J. (1989) Short-term muscle power in children and adolescents. In: (O. Bar-Or, ed) *Advances in Pediatric Sports Sciences, Vol. 3, Biological Issues.* Human Kinetics; Champaign, IL: pp. 41–63.

Sargeant A. J., Hoinville E. and Young A. (1981) Maximum leg force and power output during short-term dynamic exercise. *Journal of Applied Physiology.* 51: 1175–82.

Sargeant A. J., Dolan P. and Thorne A. (1984) Isokinetic measurement of maximal leg force and anaerobic power output in children. In: (J. Ilmarinen and I Välimäki, eds) *Children and Sport XII.* Springer Verlag; Berlin: pp. 93–8.

Sargent D. A. (1921) The physical test of a man. *American Physical Education Review*; 26: 188–94.

Selvadurai H. C., Allen J., Sachinwalla T., Macauley J., Blimkie C. J. and Van Asperen P. P. (2003) Muscle function and resting energy expenditure in female athletes with cystic fibrosis. *American Journal of Respiratory and Critical Care Medicine*; 168: 1476–80.

Sharp N. C. C. (1991) The exercise physiology of children. In: (V. Grisogono, ed) *Children and Sport.* W. H. Murray; London: pp. 32–71.

Slaughter M. H., Lohman T. G., Boileau R. A., Horswill C. A., Stillman R. J., Van Loan M. D. and Bemben D. A. (1988) Skinfold equations for estimation of body fatness in children and youth. *Human Biology*; 60: 709–23.

Stratton G. and Williams C. A. (2007) Children and fitness testing. In: (E. M. Winter, A. M. Jones, R. C. R. Davison, P. D. Bromley and T. H. Mercer, eds) *Sport and Exercise Physiology Testing Guidelines, Volume 2. Exercise and Clinical Testing.* Routledge; Oxon, UK: pp. 211–23.

Sutton N. C., Childs D. J., Bar-Or O. and Armstrong N. (2000) A nonmotorized treadmill test to assess children's short-term power output. *Pediatric Exercise Science*; 12: 91–100.

Taylor D. J., Kemp G. J., Thompson C. H. and Radda G. K. (1997) Ageing: effects on oxidative function of skeletal muscle *in vivo*. *Molecular and Cellular Biochemistry*; **174**: 321–4.

Tirosch E., Rosenbaum P. and Bar-Or O. (1990) A new muscle power test in neuromuscular disease: feasibility and reliability. *American Journal of Disease in Childhood*; **144**: 1083–7.

van Mechelen W., Hlobil H. and Kemper H. C. G. (1986) Validation of two running tests as estimates of maximal aerobic power in children. *European Journal of Applied Physiology*; **55**: 503–6.

van Mechelen W., van Lier W.H., Hlobil H., Cromer B. A. and Kemper H. (1992) Dutch Eurofit reference scales for boys and girls aged 12–16. In: (J. Coudert and E. van Praagh, eds) *Children and Exercise XVI: Pediatric Work Physiology. Methodological, Physiological and Pathological Aspects*. Masson; Paris: pp. 123–7.

van Praagh E. (1996) Testing of anaerobic performance. In: (O. Bar-Or, ed) *The Encyclopaedia of Sports Medicine: The Child and Adolescent Athlete*. (International Olympic Committee) Blackwell Science; London: pp. 602–16.

van Praagh, E. and França, N. M. (1998) Measuring maximal short-term power output during growth. In: (E. van Praagh, ed) *Pediatric Anaerobic Performance*. Human Kinetics; Champaign, IL: pp.155–89.

van Praagh E., Falgairette G., Bedu M., Fellmann N. and Coudert J. (1989). Laboratory and field tests in 7-year-old boys. In: (S. Oseid and K-H. Carlsen, eds) *Children and Exercise XIII*. Human Kinetics; Champaign, IL: pp.11–17.

van Praagh E., Fellmann N., Bedu, M., Falgairette G. and Coudert J. (1990) Gender difference in the relationship of anaerobic power output to body composition in children. *Pediatric Exercise Science*; **2**: 336–48.

van Praagh E., Fargeas M. A., Léger L., Fellmann N, and Coudert J..(1993) Short-term power output in children measured on a computerized treadmill ergometer. *Pediatric Exercise Science*, **5**: 482 (abstract)

Vandewalle H., Pérès G. and Monod H. (1987) Standard anaerobic exercise tests. *Sports Medicine*; **4**: 268–89.

Wasserman K. (1984) The anaerobic threshold measurement to evaluate exercise performance. *American Review of Respiration Disease*; **129**: S35–40.

Wasserman K., Hansen J. E., Sue D. Y., Stringer W. W. and Whipp B. J. (2005) *Principles of Exercise Testing and Interpretation. Including Pathophysiology and Clinical Applications* (4th edition). Lippincott Williams & Wilkins; Philadelphia, PA.

Welsman J. R. and Armstrong N. (2007) Interpreting performance in relation to body size. In: (N. Armstrong, ed) *Paediatric Exercise Physiology. Advances in Sport and Exercise Series* (N. Spurway and D. MacLaren, eds). Elsevier; London: pp. 27–46.

Welsman J. R., Armstrong N., Kirby B. J., Winsley R. J., Parsons G. and Sharpe P. (1997) Exercise performance and magnetic resonance imaging-determined thigh muscle volume in children. *European Journal of Applied Physiology*; **76**: 92–7.

Welsman J., Bywater K., Farr C., Welford D. and Armstrong N. (2005) Reliability of peak VO$_2$ and maximal cardiac output assessed using thoracic bioimpedance in children. *European Journal of Applied Physiology*; **94**: 228–34.

Wilkie D. R. (1950) The relation between force and velocity in human muscle. *Journal of Physiology*; **110**: 249–80.

Wilkie D. R. (1960) Man as a source of mechanical power. *Ergonomics*; **3**: 1–8.

Williams C. A. (1997) Children's and adolescents' anaerobic performance during cycle ergometry. *Sports Medicine*; **24**: 227–40.

Williams C. A. and Keen P. (1997) Test-retest reproducibility of a new isokinetic cycle ergometer. In: (N. Armstrong, B.J. Kirby and J. R. Welsman, eds) *Children and Exercise XIX*. E. & F. N. Spon; London: pp. 301–6.

Williams C. A. and Keen P. (2001) Isokinetic measurement of maximal muscle power during leg cycling: a comparison of adolescent boys and adult men. *Pediatric Exercise Science*; **13**: 154–66.

Williams C. A., Hammond A. and Doust J. H. (2003). Short-term power output of females during isokinetic cycling. *Isokinetics and Exercise Science*; **11**: 123–31.

Williams C. A., Ratel S. and Armstrong N. (2005) Achievement of peak VO$_2$ during a 90-s maximal intensity cycle sprint in adolescents. *Canadian Journal of Applied Physiology*; **30**: 157–71.

Williams J. R. and Armstrong N. (1991) Relationship of maximal lactate steady state to performance at fixed blood lactate reference values in children. *Pediatric Exercise Science*; 3: 333–41.

Williams J. R., Armstrong N. and Kirby B. J. (1992) The influence of the site of sampling and assay medium upon the measurement and interpretation of blood lactate responses to exercise. *Journal of Sports Sciences*; 10: 95–107.

Williams J. G., Eston R. and Furlong B. A. F. (1994) CERT: a perceived exertion scale for young children. *Perceptual and Motor Skills*; 79: 1451–8.

Winter E. M and MacLaren D. (2009) Chapter 11: Maximal intensity exercise. In: (R. G. Eston and T. Reilly, eds) *Kinanthropometry Laboratory Manual (3rd Edition): Exercise Physiology*. Routledge; Oxon.

PART FOUR

SPECIAL CONSIDERATIONS

CHAPTER 9

ANTHROPOMETRY AND BODY IMAGE

Tim S. Olds

9.1 AIMS

In this chapter the main aims are to:

- consider the anthropometric aspects of body image;
- address the question of what makes a person physically attractive or beautiful; and
- introduce anthropometric techniques.

Although the focus is on body image-related aspects of anthropometry, the theory and applications can be transferred to other areas such as sport-, health- and design-related anthropometry.

There are four laboratory experiences, each illustrating

- an aspect of recent theoretical developments in the study of body image;
- conceptual and practical aspects of anthropometry; and
- statistical and analytical techniques.

9.2 HISTORICAL PERSPECTIVE

'Body image' is perhaps best understood as a network of representations of bodies, including the image we have of our own bodies and of others' (often ideal bodies, such as those of models, movie stars and sports-people, but also of 'dystopian' bodies, such as the diseased and obese). We constantly make comparisons between our own bodies and the bodies of others, and these comparisons drive body-related behaviours such as eating, gender and exercise. The study of body image can be thought of as the intersection of anthropometry and psychology.

Traditionally, body image has been assessed and quantified using questionnaires or simple 'figure-rating' instruments. One common instrument, the 'Stunkard scale,' displays line drawings of bodies of increasing fatness, and asks respondents to choose the figures that best represent the way they look at the moment, and the way they would like to look. With the development of digital technologies, two-dimensional and three-dimensional morphing programs now exist, which allow the user to change the size and shape of body parts on photographic or three-dimensional-scan images of his/her own body, to sculpt and reconfigure their body digitally in the way they would like it to be (Stewart *et al.* 2003). Using digitally-manipulated images, Streeter and McBurney (2002) demonstrated that the preferred female waist-hip ratio (WHR) is close to 0.7 – much lower than WHRs in the population of young females.

Body-image research has dealt with a very wide variety of questions, ranging from the clinical (How can we treat body image disorders such as 'dysmorphophobia,' where people have a grossly distorted view of some part of their body?) to the historical (How have body ideals changed over time?) to the cultural (How are bodies represented in art, literature and popular culture?). In one sense, all of these questions come back to one key question: 'What makes a body beautiful or attractive?'

Some theorists (e.g. Wolf 1992) have argued that concepts of beauty change with time and place and are driven by local social and economic forces. They point to shifting ideals of female beauty, often contrasting the highly endomorphic forms of Rubens' women (estimated somatotype 7.5-3.0-0.5) and the highly ectomorphic forms of 1960s models and their 1990s analogues. Some recent research (for a summary, see Etcoff 1999) suggests that at a structural level there is a universal grammar or geometry of beauty. In other words, there are simple anthropometric characteristics that are common to all (female) bodies generally considered to be beautiful. These characteristics include symmetry, an hourglass shape and slimness.

Why is it that these characteristics may be universally desired? One attempt to answer this question uses a sociobiological or evolutionary approach, arguing that characteristics that are desired are markers or 'honest advertisements' of reproductive potential (Symons 1995). Slimness, for example, is a marker of youth and fitness, while a low WHR is a marker of health, reproductive maturity and nulliparity (i.e. not yet having borne children) (Singh and Young 1995). The preference for a low WHR is not limited to Western societies. Similar preferences are expressed by Chinese men (Dixson et al. 2007). In one study of women attending an *in vitro* fertilisation clinic, for example, those with a WHR below 0.8 had a two times greater chance of a live birth than those with a WHR above 0.8 (Zaadstra et al. 1993).

One area that has attracted a considerable amount of recent scientific attention has been symmetry. A series of animal studies have shown that both males and females are more attracted to symmetrical partners, and that symmetrical animals have greater reproductive success (Møller 1997). In humans, both males and females prefer partners with greater facial and body symmetry. Symmetrical males report becoming sexually active 3 years before non-symmetrical males and enjoying more sexual success (Thornhill and Gangestad 1994). Males also prefer women with symmetrical breasts (Møller et al. 1995). Soft-tissue symmetry in women actually increases on the day of ovulation (Manning et al. 1996). Symmetrical racehorses run faster (Manning and Ockenden 1994) and there is some evidence that athletes with greater non-functional (e.g. facial) symmetry perform better than their lopsided peers (Manning and Pickup 1998). Not all studies support this. Tomkinson and Olds (2000), for example, found no relationship between fitness and symmetry.

Why should symmetry be a desired characteristic? Evolutionary biologists argue that symmetry is an 'honest advertisement' of the ability of the organism to resist environmental insults that disrupt growth, such as parasite infections and illness. The symmetrical person is supposedly indicating to a potential mate: 'I have such good genes that I can resist these challenges unscathed. You should mate with me!' This argument has been supported by a number of studies in animals and humans (Palmer and Strobeck 1992).

9.3 THEORY AND APPLICATIONS

In this section, I will provide the background to four questions relating to standards of beauty, which form the basis of laboratory experiences. They relate to the anthropometric

Table 9.1 Mean (SD) values for the six datasets

	Reference population n = 3084	Regional models n = 11	International models n = 22–48*	Supermodels n = 12–21**	Mannequins n = 22
height (cm)	161.6	169.6	171.9	177.3	172.5
	(7.1)	(4.1)	(7.2)	(3.3)	(3.8)
ln(mass) (kg)	4.188	4.031	3.958	3.985	3.914
	[65.9]	[56.3]	[52.4]	[53.8]	[50.1]
	(0.240)	(0.104)	(0.090)	(0.094)	(0.062)
ln(BMI)	3.230	2.974	2.876	2.832	2.824
	[25.3]	[19.6]	[17.7]	[17.0]	[16.8]
	(0.227)	(.089)	(0.101)	(0.084)	(0.065)
waist/height	0.527	0.391	0.361	0.341	0.347
	(0.095)	(0.018)	(0.017)	(0.015)	(0.014)
WHR	0.841	0.714	0.705	0.687	0.680
	(0.073)	(0.037)	(0.017)	(0.028)	(0.020)

BMI = Body Mass Index; WHR = waist-hip ratio. The figures in square brackets are the antilogged values for mass and BMI. *n = 12 for ln(mass) and ln(BMI), n = 21 elsewhere. **n = 22 for waist/height and WHR, n = 48 elsewhere.

characteristics of beautiful female bodies, the relationship between somatotype and body image in men, representations of 'ideal' bodies (in this case, Ken and Barbie), and the nature of the 'ideal' face.

9.3.1 The anthropometric characteristics of beautiful female bodies

When the anthropometric characteristics, such as stature, mass and muscularity are examined in elite sports people, their mean values are found to deviate greatly from those of the general population, and the scatter of scores is much less. For example, only 1 in 1,000 women would be tall enough to play as a centre in the Women's National Basketball Association (Norton and Olds 1999). In other words, specific sportspeople form distinct and homogeneous subgroups. On moving up the ladder of ability, from novice competitors to Olympians, the deviations become greater and the scatters become less (Norton and Olds 2001).

Similar patterns are found in other groups, such as the 'ideal' bodies of fashion models, who are, in a sense, also elite 'performers.'

We would expect to find that the mean values for desirable characteristics – slimness, an hourglass shape – are more extreme in the 'ideal' bodies of regional, international and 'super' models, and in the 'hyperideal' bodies of shop mannequins, than in the general population. We should also find that there are well defined and consistent gradients as we move from average young women to hyperideal figures. In the following pages, different groups of women of varying levels of perceived beauty are considered and their anthropometric characteristics contrasted.

Consider the following five groups, chosen to represent a range of beauty:

- women aged 18–34 years from the third National Health and Nutrition Examination Survey (NHANES III) (U.S. Department of Health and Human Services 1996), an American survey conducted between 1988 and 1994. This group will form the reference population;
- regional models (n = 11; Norton et al. 1996);
- international models (n = 48), using data

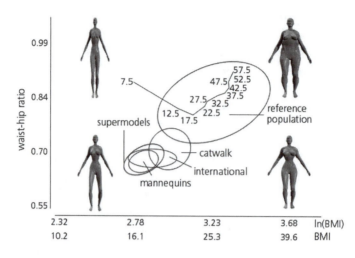

Figure 9.1 Bivariate location of each of the groups. The outline figures represent iconically the shapes of women located at the different extreme points of the anthropometric space. The ellipses are the 90% density ellipses, meaning that 90% of women in each group fall within the boundaries of the ellipse. The continuous line represents the evolution of mean ln(BMI) and WHR throughout the life cycle, in 5-year age groups with midpoints from 7.5 to 57.5 years (data from NHANES III).

provided by the 'Elite Modeling Agency' (http://www.models-online.com/);

- 'supermodels' (models earning more than $US2,000,000 in 2007), using data provided by their respective agencies (http://www.newfaces.com/super models/);
- female shop mannequins (n = 22) from an Australian mannequin warehouse (Tomkinson *et al.* 1999). Height and mass were estimated from regression equations based on segmental lengths and height-corrected girths using data from the Australian Anthropometric Database (AADBase; Norton and Olds 1996)

The data on mass, height, body mass index (BMI), height-adjusted waist girth, and WHR for each of the groups are shown in Table 9.1. The natural log of mass and BMI [ln(mass) and ln(BMI)] have been analyzed, because both of these characteristics show very skewed distributions, and log-transformation normalises them.

Fashion models are characterized by significantly (p < 0.0001) lower WHR and BMI

values than women of a comparable age in the reference population. These lumped variables are powerful discriminators between fashion models and young women in the general population. For example, only 31 of 3,084 women from the reference population have both WHRs and BMIs within 2 SDs of the average values for supermodels. This means that 99% of women would be highly unlikely to be supermodels based on these two characteristics alone.

Another interesting way of looking at these data is to situate each of the groups in a bivariate anthropometric space. By this it is meant that two variables are used conjointly – WHR and BMI. Figure 9.1 represents this space. The groups are represented as 'density ellipses' – in this case, 67% density ellipses, meaning that two-thirds of all individuals within each group will fall within the boundaries of the ellipse. The figures at each corner of the graph represent iconically what women located in those zones look like. At the bottom left-hand corner are women with a low WHR and a low BMI; i.e. women who are both thin and shapely. At the top left-hand corner are women with a low BMI

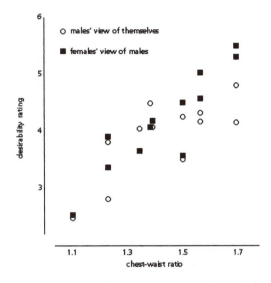

Figure 9.2 The relationship between desirability (rated on a 1–7 scale) and chest-waist ratio in men. The open circles represent men's view of themselves, and the closed squares women's view of men (plotted from data in Furnham *et al.* 1990).

but a moderate WHR – these are the very thin women with a 'straight up and down' shape. At the bottom right-hand corner are women with a moderate BMI but a low WHR – curvaceous or voluptuous women. Finally, the top right-hand corner represents women with a high BMI and a high WHR – women with a block or balloon shape.

Figure 9.1 also shows the changes in BMI and WHR in the reference population as women age. The median age in each group (from 7.5 to 57.5 years) is shown at each point on the continuous line. As women age, their BMI increases, rapidly at first and then more slowly. In fact, BMI is one of the main cues people use in assessing how old a woman is. Singh and Young (1995) found that when figures with identical faces are shown to people, they judge the heavier figures to be up to 10 years older than the slimmer ones. The waist to hip ratio decreases until adolescence and then starts to increase. The 'turning point' for these two variables, with the lowest WHR and lowest post-pubertal BMI, is during late adolescence and early adulthood; an age where reproductive potential is greatest. Younger women, models and hyperideal

bodies are located progressively closer to the bottom left-hand corner of the graph. It is interesting that porn stars, using reported body dimensions (average BMI = 18.8, average WHR = 0.69), are located close to supermodels on the graph.

9.3.2 Somatotype and body image in men

Somatotype is a way of quantifying the shape of the human body, independent of size (See Duquet and Carter 2009, Chapter 2). Somatotype is nowadays usually assessed anthropometrically, that is by taking measurements. However, the gold standard method is a combination of both visual inspection ('photoscopic' somatotyping) and measurement. Skilled anthropometrists can visually assess somatotype with surprising precision and accuracy. This has made it possible to rate figures from art and popular culture, including dolls, shop mannequins, sculptures and figures from the great painters.

In the 1940s, Sheldon developed his theory of 'constitutional psychology' (Sheldon, 1944), arguing that psychological characteristics were reflected in physical conformation. He identified three major personality types, corresponding to the extreme somatotypes:

- endotonia: governed by the viscera – indolent and hedonistic
- mesotonia: governed by the active muscles – dynamic, outgoing, aggressive
- ectotonia: withdrawn, inhibited, quiet.

Psychological health was seen as a balance between the three. Those with too little endotonia suffered from endopænia (no sense of relaxation or pleasure). Those with too little mesotonia suffered from mesopænia (lack of ambition or drive). Those with too little ectotonia suffered from ectopænia (a lack of inhibition, compulsive disorders).

Sheldon's theory built on a long tradition of pseudo-scientific and popular beliefs relating outward appearance to inner characteristics. In many cases, these attributions turned out to be self-fulfilling prophecies. For example, fat people saw themselves as lazy because everyone else saw them as lazy. Traditionally, the ideal male has been considered to be very mesomorphic, close to due north or north-north-east on the somatochart. Tucker (1984) found not only that the mesomorphic shape was preferred by both men and women, but also that men who perceived themselves as mesomorphic were more extraverted, less neurotic and had a higher self-concept. Another research group found that chest-waist ratio in men was directly related to men's satisfaction with their own body shape, and with female preferences for male body shapes (Furnham et al. 1990): the higher the chest-waist ratio, the greater the satisfaction (Figure 9.2).

Concern with body image has usually been associated mainly with women; however, there is now increasing concern among men, probably as they become more and more exposed to images of ideal male bodies. In response to a *Psychology Today* survey in 1972, 15% of men expressed overall dissatisfaction with their bodies. By 1997,

this had risen to almost 45%. The percentage of men unhappy with their waist girths had risen from 36% to 63%. Unhappiness was so great that 17% of men said they would give up 3 years of their lives to be at their ideal weight, and 11% would give up 5 years of life. Recent work by Pope et al. (1993) at Harvard has shown that some male bodybuilders may suffer from 'reverse anorexia' – a feeling that they are not big enough, in spite of very high muscularity. Increasing exposure to extremely lean and muscular ideals is probably behind the increase in the recreational use of steroids in young men. There has also been an increase in the number of males choosing to have cosmetic surgery, including chest and calf implants. About 10% of the estimated 1 million people having cosmetic surgery in the US in 1998 were males (Etcoff 1999).

9.3.3 The anthropometry of 'Ken' and 'Barbie'

Barbie is the biggest-selling doll of all time, with over one billion dollars worth of sales each year. To many people, Barbie represents a 'hyperideal' female shape. Her makers, Mattel, have been criticised for imposing unrealistic expectations of thinness on young girls. Barbie has even borne the brunt of political action. In the early 1990s a group calling itself the Barbie Liberation Organization stole talking Barbie and GI Joe dolls from toy store shelves, swapped their voice boxes, and replaced the dolls. When little girls opened their Christmas Barbies, they would come out with phrases like: 'Vengeance is mine' and 'Eat lead, cobra!' The little boys' GI Joes, on the other hand, would say things like: 'Shopping is such fun!' or 'Let's plan a dream wedding!'

Ideal bodies have often been represented as being almost impossible for most women to achieve. One famous Body Shop advertisement stated that 'There are 3 billion women who don't look like supermodels and only 8 who do.' Once we know the key anthropometric characteristics of ideal bodies, we can calculate the probability of someone randomly chosen from the reference population having characteristics as extreme as these groups. For the regional models described in Practical 1, the values range from about 2% to 11% for any single characteristic; for international models, from about 4% to 11%; for supermodels, from 0.5% to 8%; and for mannequins, from 0.5% to 6%. Unless characteristics are perfectly correlated, the chances of sharing two or more characteristics are smaller. About 1 in 25 individuals from the reference population will have both a WHR and ln(BMI) as extreme as a catwalk model, about 1 in 100 as extreme as a supermodel, and 1 in 200 as extreme as a mannequin. In the National Health and Nutrition Examination Survey (NHANES) III database, only 20 of 3,084 women aged 18–34 had a BMI less than that of the average supermodel.

A little further on, we will discuss the difficulties of 'blowing up' Barbie or Ken to life size. Let us imagine for a moment that we know Ken or Barbie's dimensions at life size. How can we make judgments about how probable or improbable their proportions are? Fortunately, many anthropometric characteristics are normally distributed. This means the likelihood of a measurement can be calculated by expressing it as a z-score relative to a reference population. Consider Barbie's upper leg length (trochanterion-tibiale laterale length). People often think that Barbie has improbably long upper legs. Is this true? At average height, Barbie would have an upper leg length of 45.5 cm (Norton et al. 1996). In the population of Australian women aged 18–34, the average upper leg length is 42.6 cm, with a standard deviation of 3.57 cm. How unlikely is an upper leg length of 45.5 cm? Barbie's value is 2.9 cm above the mean, which is $(45.5 - 42.6)/3.57 = 0.8$ SDs above the mean (i.e. a z-score of 0.8). Looking up z-tables, it is clear this is greater than about 79% of the population. So Barbie has a long, but not an improbably long, upper leg. This ratio can be compared

to Barbie's chest-waist ratio (CWR: the ratio of the chest girth taken at the level of the mesosternale, and the minimum waist girth). It is 2.0, compared to a population mean of 1.3 ± 0.06. This is $(2.0 - 1.3)/0.06 = 11.7$ SDs above the mean! This is biologically impossible however desirable it may seem.

Similar considerations apply to Ken, although Ken's dimensions are nowhere near as extreme as Barbie's (Norton et al. 1996). Ken represents a much less 'hypermesomorphic' figure than some of the 'action figures' such as GI Joe. His slim ectomorphic shape is probably designed to appeal to girls rather than to boys. A number of studies (e.g. Fallon and Rozin 1985) have shown that while men prefer mesomorphic male bodies, women favour ectomorphic body shapes in men.

The claims about Barbie's unrealistic thinness would certainly seem appropriate from a visual inspection. How can we make a scientific judgment about her proportions when she is just 27.5 cm tall? How can we 'blow Barbie up' to life size and compare her to young women in the general population? Measuring Ken and Barbie poses special problems for the anthropometrist, but also illustrates some key principles in anthropometry, including scaling and the logic of hydrostatic weighing. Practical 3 provides experience in solving these problems.

9.3.4 The anthropometry of the ideal face

People tend to be judged by their faces. We attribute personality traits – dominance, honesty, intelligence – based on facial traits alone. In one study, the success of male army cadets later in their career was strongly correlated with judgments of how dominant they looked in graduation photos (Mazur et al. 1984). A substantial body of anthropometric research has tried to establish correlations between the anthropometry of the face and the characteristics we ascribe to the person (e.g. Secord and Bevan 1956). Some recent work using digital manipulation has uncovered what appear to

Figure 9.3 Face of a shop mannequin before digital manipulation.

Figure 9.4 Face of the same mannequin as in Figure 9.3, with the following manipulations: nose-lip spacing and lip-chin spacing increased; jaw widened; eye area reduced; eyebrow arching reduced; cheekbones lowered.

be elements of a transcultural geometry of facial beauty.

One study conducted in England and Japan (Perrett *et al.* 1994) identified key points on the faces of 60 young women, and then digitised and averaged them, thereby constructing a 'mean face.' The faces of the 15 women who were rated as the most attractive were then digitised using the same key points. The differences between the two faces were calculated, and revealed six main areas of difference. In the beautiful face, the cheekbones were higher, the mouth-chin spacing was smaller, the nose-mouth spacing was smaller, the jaw line was less square, the eyebrows were more arched and the pupils were larger. These differences were consistent in both Japan and England. The beautiful face was more 'neotenous' or 'baby-like.'

Consider the faces shown in Figures 9.3 and 9.4. The original image of a shop mannequin's face (Figure 9.3) has been digitally edited to increase jaw width and nose-lip and lip-chin spacing. The eyes have been made smaller and the eyebrows less arched, and the cheekbones have been lowered (Figure 9.4). Although the altered face is still very attractive, it is not as pretty as the neotenous pouting of the original face. Women often use cosmetics to highlight exactly the characteristics identified in this study: mascara to enlarge the eyes, blusher to highlight cheek bones and lipstick to increase lip area.

Other research groups have used digital techniques to scale and superimpose photographs of different people and then average them on a pixel-by-pixel basis, thus producing a 'composite portrait.' This was a technique performed photographically by Galton (1879) over a century ago. Galton noticed that the composite or averaged faces appeared to be more attractive. Creating composite faces has the effect of evening out differences and asymmetries. Composite faces are well-balanced and have clear skin tone, because local blemishes are washed out in the averaging process.

9.4 PRACTICAL 1: THE ANTHROPOMETRIC CHARACTERISTICS OF BEAUTIFUL FEMALE BODIES

9.4.1 Rationale and purpose

In this practical, females can compare the size and shape of their bodies, quantified using the BMI and WHR, with those of supermodels and shop mannequins. This experience illustrates the sociobiological theory of physical attractiveness, and gives students practice in calculating BMI and WHR, as well as introducing statistical procedures, such as log-transformation to normalise skewed distributions and bivariate probability spaces.

9.4.2 Procedures

Step 1 All participants must be females. Weigh each participant in light indoor clothing, and measure their stretch stature without shoes. From these data, calculate the BMI

[= mass (kg)/height (m)^2]. Take the natural log of BMI. This is the X value. Example: height = 165 cm, mass = 65 kg, BMI = $65/1.65^2$ = 23.9 kg.m^{-2}, ln(BMI) = 3.1739.

Step 2 Next, measure the minimum waist girth and gluteal girth. See Chapter 1 for the exact location of these sites. From these data, calculate the WHR – this will be your Y value. Example: waist girth = 77 cm, hip girth = 97 cm, waist-hip ratio = 77/97 = 0.79.

Step 3 Plot the position on the chart provided (Figure 9.5).

Step 4 Follow Steps 1–4 for other females in your group.

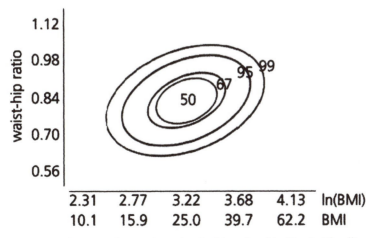

Figure 9.5 Ln(BMI) is shown on the X-axis, and waist-hip ratio of the Y-axis. The ellipses represent the 99%, 95%, 90%, 67% and 50% density ellipses for the US population.

9.4.3 Assignment

Using Figure 9.2, plot the position of the following celebrities:

- Kate Moss: height = 168.9 cm, mass = 47.5 kg, waist = 58.4 cm, hip = 88.9 cm;
- Twiggy: height = 166 cm, mass = 40.7 kg, waist = 58.4 cm, hip = 80 cm;
- Marilyn Monroe: height = 166.4 cm, mass = 53.4 kg, waist = 61 cm, hip = 91.4 cm;
- Elle MacPherson: height = 183 cm, mass = 57.9 kg, waist = 60.2 cm, hip = 88.9 cm;
- Centrefolds: height = 169 cm, mass = 51.7 kg, waist girth = 61 cm, hip = 90 cm (Tovée *et al*. 1997).

Other examples are available at the following website, where you might do some research: www.playboy.com

9.5 PRACTICAL 2: THE ANTHROPOMETRY OF THE 'IDEAL' MALE BODY

9.5.1 Rationale and purpose

Using the somatotype procedures explained by Duquet and Carter (2009) in Chapter 2, males can calculate and plot their own somatotypes, and quantify how far away they are from 'ideal' figures in somatotype space. This experience outlines recent research into male body image, and gives students practice in calculating and plotting somatotypes and in using basic somatotype statistics. The 'ideal' male figures are taken from art and popular culture.

9.5.2 Procedures

Step 1   Presented below are some somatotype ratings of figures from Renaissance and Baroque art, rated by the Czech anthropometrists Bok (1976) and Stepnicka (1983):

- Michelangelo's David: 1–7.5–2
- Bernini's David: 1–7–1
- El Greco's David: 2–6–1
- Adam (Sistine Chapel): 1.5–8–1
- Titian's Adam: 1.5–6.5–1
- Tintoretto's Adam: 1.5–6–2

Plot each of these on the somatochart provided in Chapter 2. You can also plot:

- competitive bodybuilders (Borms *et al*.1986): 1.6–8.7–1.2
- male shop mannequins (Tomkinson *et al*. 1999): 2.5–4.7–3.5

Step 2   Calculate your own somatotype and plot yourself on the graph.
Step 3   To see how well your own somatotype compares with these ideals, calculate the mean somatotype of those mentioned above. The mean somatotype is simply the average of each of the components calculated separately. Then calculate the somatotype attitudinal distance (SAD) between your own somatotype and the mean. The SAD is the three-dimensional distance between two somatotypes. You will find the equation in Chapter 2 (Duquet and Carter, Section 2.6.2b). The greater the SAD, the further you are from the 'ideal' male body.

9.5.3 Assignment

Below are the mean somatotypes of national-level athletes from a number of sports (Olds and Norton 1999). Plot each on the somatochart and calculate the SAD of each from the mean of the 'ideal' bodies. Which is closest to the 'ideal' body?

basketball:	2.4–4.4–3.7	Rugby Union – forwards:	3.4–7.0–1.0
cycling – road:	1.6–4.5–3.0	running – middle distance:	1.5–4.0–3.8
gymnastics:	1.8–6.2–2.3	soccer:	2.5–4.6–2.7
kayak – sprint:	2.0–5.4–2.3	table tennis:	3.5–3.9–2.5
orienteering:	2.0–4.7–3.5	tennis:	2.2–4.5–3.1
power lifting:	2.7–7.9–0.6	triathlon:	1.7–4.3–3.1
Rugby Union – backs:	2.5–5.8–1.9	volleyball:	2.3–4.4–3.3

9.6 PRACTICAL 3: THE ANTHROPOMETRY OF KEN AND BARBIE

Students measure the dolls Ken and Barbie using vernier callipers and dental floss, scale them to life size, and compare them to real-life people. This experience introduces novel measurement techniques, and raises theoretical issues concerning the logic of scaling and underwater weighing. Use is made of z-scores to compare Ken and Barbie to a reference population of young people.

9.6.1 Procedures

To measure Ken and Barbie you will need: a roll of dental floss, a set of vernier callipers, a basin or bucket at least 20 cm deep and 30 cm in diameter, a flat dish with a diameter greater than 30 cm, a small pair of scissors, electrical tape and a fine-tipped felt pen.
   The following dimensions will be measured: height; girths: waist (minimum); gluteal or hips (maximum posterior protuberance); chest (mesosternale); chest (nipple); ankle (minimum), breadths and lengths: biacromial; biiliocristal; foot length. Where possible, follow the measurement protocols of the International Society for the Advancement of Kinanthropometry (ISAK; Marfell-Jones et al. 2006).

Step 1   Cut off all of Barbie's hair as close to the scalp as possible. This will be important when we estimate Barbie's mass. Warning: do not do this in the presence
of small children.

Step 2   Take off Barbie's clothes.

Step 3   With a felt pen, mark as nearly as you can the following landmarks: mesosternale,
acromiale (left and right), biiliocristale (left and right).

Step 4   Cut off a length of dental floss about 10 cm long. Using it as a 'tape measure,'
measure the following sites: waist (minimum), gluteal or hips (maximum
posterior protuberance), chest (mesosternale), chest (nipple) and ankle
(minimum). Locate landmarks as nearly as you can using the descriptions in
Chapters 1 and 2 as a guide.

Step 5   Using vernier callipers, measure Barbie's biacromial and biiliocristal breadths,
and foot length. Repeat each of the measurements in Steps 4 and 5. If the
second measurement deviates by more than 5% from the first, take a third
measurement. Use the mean of two and median of three measurements as your
final value.

Step 6   Measure Barbie's height from vertex to heel. Enter all girths, heights and lengths
in the 'Barbie (raw)' column in Table 9.2.

Step 7   Tape over any gaps in Barbie's articulations to make her watertight. Fill a large
bowl or bucket to the very brim, and put it inside a larger flat dish. Submerge
Barbie completely, so that the overflow falls into the large flat dish below.
Measure the volume of water (ml) Barbie displaces either by weighing or by
using a measuring cup.

Step 8   Scale each of the linear measurements in Steps 4 and 5 by dividing them by
height, and then multiplying by 166.1 (which is the height in cm of women
in the reference population of active young Australian women). For example,
if Barbie's measured waist girth is 6.5 cm, and her height is 27.5 cm, the
scaled value will be $6.5/27.5 \times 166.1 = 39.3$ cm. This represents what Barbie's
waist girth would be if she were 166.1 cm tall. Also calculate Barbie's chest
(mesosternale)-waist ratio, and her waist-hip ratio, and also her chest (nipple)-
waist ratio. No scaling is necessary when calculating ratios. Enter these values
in the 'Barbie (adj.)' column in Table 9.2.

Step 9   We can now estimate Barbie's mass. We will assume she has 15% body fat. An
error of even 10% either way in this assumption will affect the final estimate
of mass by less than 5%. Using the Siri equation (see Eston et al. 2009 in
Chapter 1), % body fat= 495/BD − 450, where BD is body density in g.ml^{-1}.
At 15% body fat, BD = 1.0645. We now multiply Barbie's measured volume
(ml) by 1.0645 to estimate her mass (mass = volume X density).

Step 10 These values must be scaled. We now 'blow up' Barbie to the reference height
(166.1 cm). When we scale objects geometrically, mass is proportional to the
cube of height. Let Barbie's height be H cm. We multiply her estimated mass
from Step 9 by $(166.1/H)^3$ to arrive at what Barbie would weigh were she the
same height as the reference population. For example, if Barbie's estimated
mass from Step 9 were 200 g, and her measured height 28 cm, her estimated
mass at life size would be $200 \times (166.1/28)^3 = 41750$ g or 41.75 kg. We can
now calculate her BMI (assume that her height is 166.1 cm), ln(mass) and
ln(BMI) and enter those values into Table 9.2.

Step 11   Finally, we can situate Barbie relative to the reference population by calculating z-scores. The population means and SDs are given in Table 9.2. The z-scores can be converted into probability values by consulting tables in any standard statistical text.

9.6.2 Assignment

Repeat Steps 1–11 for Ken, entering data into Table 9.3. Population means and SDs are provided in Table 9.3. Ken should be standardized to a height of 179.2 cm.

Table 9.2 Datasheet for entering measurements of Barbie

Measurement	pop. mean	pop. SD	Barbie (raw)	Barbie (adj.)	z-score
chest girth (mesosternale)	87.5	5.64			
waist girth	72.2	9.59			
gluteal girth	95.5	6.67			
biacromial breadth	36.2	1.86			
biiliocristal breadth	27.4	1.67			
foot length	24.1	1.35			
ankle girth	21.4	1.30			
CWR (mesosternale)	1.27	0.057			
CWR (nipple)	NA	NA			
WHR	0.76	0.092			
ln(mass)	4.089	0.142			
ln(BMI)	3.077	0.118			

CWR = chest-waist ratio; WHR = waist-hip ratio. The population means and SDs are from a reference population of active 18- to 34-year-old Australian females (n = 475; AADBase, Norton and Olds 1996). Girths, breadths and lengths are in cm.

Table 9.3 Datasheet for entering measurements of Ken

Measurement	pop. mean	pop. SD	Ken (raw)	Ken (adj.)	z-score
chest girth (mesosternale)	97.6	7.41			
waist girth	81.1	7.20			
gluteal girth	96.7	6.72			
biacromial breadth	40.0	2.29			
biiliocristal breadth	28.3	2.09			
foot length	26.7	1.71			
ankle girth	22.9	1.93			
CWR (mesosternale)	1.23	0.057			
CWR (nipple)	NA	NA			
WHR	0.85	0.051			
ln(mass)	4.336	0.142			
ln(BMI)	3.171	0.116			

CWR = chest-waist ratio; WHR = waist-hip ratio. The population means and SDs are from a reference population of active 18- to 40-year-old Australian males (n = 677; AADBase, Norton and Olds 1996). Girths, breadths and lengths are in cm.

9.7 PRACTICAL 4: THE ANTHROPOMETRY OF THE IDEAL FACE

9.7.1 Purpose

Students measure individual female faces to see how well they embody a 'geometry of beauty'. This experience is based on recent work into digital manipulation of facial features. It introduces measurement techniques using images rather than real bodies, and touches upon issues of scaling (Figure 9.6). It is important that this practical is approved by the institution's Human Ethics Committee.

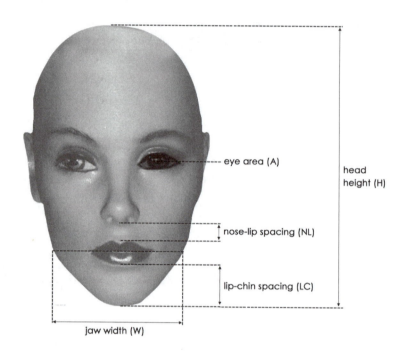

Figure 9.6 Measurement dimensions for facial characteristics.

9.7.2 Procedures

Step 1   Take a photograph of a female volunteer. Because all members of the group will be rating the attractiveness of each subject, it is probably best that the volunteers not be part of the group. The photograph can be a developed print, or taken using a digital camera. The image can then be downloaded onto a computer for digital analysis, or enlarged by photocopying for manual analysis. For the photograph, the subject should be facing the camera directly, with hair drawn back, and should assume a neutral pose.

Step 2   On the image, measure the vertical distance between the bottom of the nose and the top of the upper lip (NL on Figure 9.6).

Step 3   Measure the vertical distance between the bottom of the lower lip and the tip of the chin (LC).

Step 4   Measure the width of the jaw at the level of the middle of the lips (W).

Step 5   Measure the eye area (A). This can be done with a planimeter, if it is available, or you can calculate an area index by multiplying eye height by eye width. The eye area should include the pupil, iris and white of the eye, plus the eyelid.

Step 6   These four measures have to be standardized for facial size. Divide NL, LC and W by the height of the face (H) from the vertex to the tip of the chin. Divide the eye area (or eye area index) by the area of the whole face (determined by planimetry) or the square of the height of the face (H^2). We now have four indices of facial attractiveness: NL/H, LC/H, W/H and A/H^2.

Step 7   Repeat Steps 1–6 for a further nine female volunteers.

9.7.3 Assignments

1   Get each member of the group to rate the attractiveness of each face on a scale of 0–10 (0 = extremely unattractive; 10 = extremely beautiful). Calculate the average score for each face. This is their overall 'subjective attractiveness rating.'

2   For each of these four indices, calculate the mean and standard deviation, and convert each individual score to a z-score. Add up the z-scores for each of the 10 subjects. This is their overall 'objective attractiveness rating.'

3   We now have two attractiveness ratings – subjective and objective. To quantify the agreement between them, use Pearson's product-moment correlation coefficient. Most studies have shown strong associations between the two sets of ratings.

9.8 SUMMARY AND CONCLUSION

This chapter has focused on body image. However, anthropometric techniques can be applied in a wide range of contexts. Fortunately, we now have standardized protocols and global anthropometry accreditation schemes (Marfell-Jones et al. 2006) to assure consistency among measurers. The same analytical techniques (such as somatotyping and comparisons with reference populations) can be applied to areas as diverse as elite sport and ergonomics, body image and epidemiology. While traditional surface anthropometry using girth tapes and callipers is still very widely used, new techniques, such as three-dimensional whole-body scanning, offer exciting possibilities for future studies. Three-dimensional anthropometry has already been applied to redesigning clothing templates (Honey and Olds 2007), determining anthropometric correlates of health (Lin et al. 2004) and fitting pilots to fighter planes (Olds et al. 2007).

FURTHER READING
Books/chapters

Bruce V. and Young A. (2000) In the Eye of the Beholder. The Science of Face Perception. Oxford University Press; Oxford.

Cash T. and Pruzinsky T. (eds.) (1990) Body Images. Guilford Press; New York.

Tomkinson G. R. and Olds T. S. (1999) The size and shape of male shop mannequins. Proceedings of The Body Culture Conference. Melbourne, Australia: 27–28 July.

Journal article

Byrd-Bredbenner C., Murray J. and Schlussel Y. R. (2005) Temporal changes in anthropometric measurements of idealized females and young women in general. Journal of Women & Health; **41** (2).

Websites

http://www.bbc.co.uk/science/hottopics/love/attraction.shtml

http://www.isakonline.com/

REFERENCES

Bok V. (1976) A comparison of selected illustrations of creative works from the point of view of constitutional typology. *Acta Universitatis Carolinae (Gymnica)*; **10**: 79–91.

Borms J., Ross W. D., Duquet W. and Carter J. E. L. (1986) Somatotypes of world class bodybuilders. In: (J.A.P. Day, ed) *Perspectives in Kinanthropometry*. Human Kinetics; Champaign, IL: pp. 81–90.

Dixson B. J., Dixson A. F., Li B. and Anderson M. J. (2007) Studies of human physique and sexual attractiveness: sexual preferences of men and women in China. *American Journal of Human Biology*; **19**: 88–95.

Duquet W. and Carter J. E. L. (2009) Chapter 2: Somatotyping. In: (R. G. Eston and T. Reilly, eds.) *Kinanthropometry Laboratory Manual (3rd Edition): Anthropometry*. Routledge; Oxon: pp. 54–72.

Etcoff N. (1999) *Survival of the Prettiest: the Science of Beauty*. Doubleday; New York.

Fallon A. E. and Rozin P. (1985) Sex differences in perceptions of desirable body shape. *Journal of Abnormal Psychology*; **94**: 102–5.

Furnham A., Hester C. and Weir C. (1990) Sex differences in the preferences for specific female body shapes. *Sex Roles*; **22**: 743–54.

Eston R. G., Hawes M., Martin A. and Reilly T. (2009) Chapter 1: Human body composition. In: (R. G. Eston and T. Reilly, eds) *Kinanthropometry Laboratory Manual (3rd Edition): Anthropometry*. Routledge; Oxon: pp. 3–53.

Galton F. (1879) Composite portraits, made by combining those of many different persons in a single figure. *Nature*; **8**: 132–44.

Honey F. and Olds T. (2007) The Standards Australia sizing system: quantifying the mismatch. *Journal of Fashion Marketing and Management*; **11** (3): 320–31.

Lin J. D., Chiou W. K., Weng H. F., Fang J. T. and Liu T. H. (2004) Application of three-dimensional body scanner: observation of prevalence of metabolic syndrome. *Clinical Nutrition*; **23**: 1313–23.

Manning J. T. and Ockenden L. (1994) Fluctuating asymmetry in racehorses. *Nature*; **370**: 185–6.

Manning J. T. and Pickup L. J. (1998) Symmetry and performance in middle-distance runners. *International Journal of Sports Medicine*; **19**: 205–9.

Manning J. T., Scutt D., Whitehouse G. H., Leinster S. J. and Walton J. M. (1996) Asymmetry and the menstrual cycle in women. *Ethology and Sociobiology*; **17**: 1–15.

Marfell-Jones M., Olds T., Stewart A. and Carter J. E. L. (2006) *International standards for anthropometric assessment*. North-West University; Potchefstroom, RSA.

Møller A. P. (1997) Developmental stability and fitness: a review. *American Naturalist*; **149**: 916–32.

Møller A. P., Soler M. and Thornhill R. (1995) Breast asymmetry, sexual selection and human reproductive success. *Ethology and Sociobiology*; **16**: 207–19.

Mazur A., Mazur J. and Keating C. (1984) Military rank attainment of a West Point class: effects of cadets' physical features. *American Journal of Sociology*; **90** (1): 125–50.

Norton K. I. and Olds T. S. (eds) (1996) *Anthropometrica*. UNSW Press; Sydney.

Norton K. I. and Olds T. S. (1999) Evolution of the size and shape of athletes: causes and consequences. In: (T. S. Olds, J. Dollman and K. I. Norton, eds), *Kinanthropometry VI*. International Society for the Advancement of Kinanthropometry; Adelaide.

Norton K. I. and Olds T. S. (2001) Morphological evolution of athletes over the 20th century: causes and consequences. *Sports Medicine*; **31**: 763–83.

Norton K. I., Olds T. S., Dank S. and Olive S. C. (1996) Ken and Barbie at life size. *Sex Roles*; **34**: 287–294.

Olds T. S. and Norton K. I. (1999) *LifeSize* (software). Human Kinetics; Champaign, IL.

Olds T., Ross J., Blanchonette P. and Stratton D. (2007) Fitting the man to the machine: the ADAPT project. *Australian Defence Force Journal*; **172**: 95–102.

Palmer R. A. and Strobeck C. (1992) Fluctuating asymmetry as a measure of developmental stability: implications of non-normal distributions and power of statistical tests. *Acta Zoologica Fennica*; **191**: 57–72.

Perrett D. I., May K. A. and Yoshikawa S. (1994) Facial shape and judgements of female attractiveness. *Nature*; **368**: 239–42.

Pope H. R., Katz D. L. and Hudson J. I. (1993) Anorexia nervosa and reverse anorexia among 108 male bodybuilders. *Comprehensive Psychiatry*; **34**: 406–9.

Secord P. and Bevan W. (1956) Personality in faces: III. A cross-cultural comparison of impressions of physiognomy of personality in Faces. *Journal of Social Psychology*; **43**: 283–8.

Sheldon W. H. (1944) Constitutional factors in personality. In: (J. M. Hunt, ed) *Personality and Behavior Disorders*. Ronald Press; New York: pp. 526–49.

Singh D. and Young R. K. (1995) Body weight, waist-to-hip ratio, breasts, and hips: role in judgments of female attractiveness and desirability for relationships. *Ethology and Sociobiology*; **16**: 483–507.

Stepnicka J. (1983) The comparison of Adam's and Eve's depiction in selected style periods from the point of view of somatotype (in Czech). *Acta Universitatis Carolinæ*; **19** (1): 73–83.

Stewart A. D, Benson P. J., Michanikou E. G., Tsiota D. G. and Narli M. K. (2003) Body image perception, satisfaction and somatotype in male and female athletes and non-athletes: results using a novel morphing technique. *Journal of Sports Sciences*; **21**: 815–23.

Streeter S. A. and McBurney D. H. (2002) Waist–hip ratio and attractiveness: new evidence and a critique of 'a critical test.' *Evolution and Human Behavior*; **24** (2): 88–98.

Symons D. (1995) Beauty is in the adaptations of the beholder: the evolutionary psychology of human female sexual attractiveness. In: (P. R. Abramson and S. D. Pinkerton, eds) *Sexual Nature, Sexual Culture*. University of Chicago Press; Chicago: pp. 80–118.

Thornhill R. and Gangestad S. W. (1994) Human fluctuating asymmetry and sexual behavior. *Psychological Science*; **5**: 297–302.

Tomkinson G. R. and Olds T. S. (2000) Physiological correlates of bilateral symmetry in humans. *International Journal of Sports Medicine*; **21**: 545–50.

Tomkinson G. R., Olds T. S. and Carter J. E. L. (1999) The anthropometry of desire: the body size and shape of female shop mannequins. In: (T. S. Olds, J. Dollman and K. I. Norton, eds) *Kinanthropometry VI*. International Society for the Advancement of Kinanthropometry; Adelaide.

Tovée M. J., Mason S. M., Emery J. L., McCluskey S. E. and Cohen-Tovée E. M. (1997) Supermodels: stick-insects or hourglasses? *Lancet*; **350**: 1474–5.

Tucker L. A. (1984) Physical attractiveness, somatotype and the male personality: a dynamic interactional perspective. *Journal of Clinical Psychology*; **40**: 1226–34.

U.S. Department of Health and Human Services (1996) National Centre for Health Statistics. NHANES III Reference Manuals and Reports (CD-ROM). Centers of Disease Control and Prevention; Hyatsville, MD.

Wolf N. (1992) *The Beauty Myth: How Images of Beauty Are Used Against Women*. Anchor Press; New York.

Zaadstra B. M., Seidell J.C., van Noord P. A. H., te Velde E. R., Habbema J. D. F., Vrieswijk B. and Karbaat J. (1993) Fat and female fecundity: prospective study of effect of body fat distribution on conception rates. *British Medical Journal*; **306**: 484–7.

CHAPTER 10

STATISTICAL METHODS IN KINANTHROPOMETRY AND EXERCISE PHYSIOLOGY

Alan M. Nevill, Greg Atkinson and Mark A. Scott

10.1 AIMS

The aims of this chapter are:

- to outline the most commonly-used statistical methods that are used to describe and analyze the results of research work in exercise physiology and kinanthropometry;
- to show how such methods are applied to real examples from these disciplines;
- to show the commands for each respective test that is relevant to the popular statistical package 'SPSS 14.0'; this is also useful to illustrate the logic of the statistical procedures.

10.2 ORGANIZING AND DESCRIBING DATA IN KINANTHROPOMETRY AND EXERCISE PHYSIOLOGY

Kinanthropometry is a relatively new branch of science that is concerned with measuring the physical characteristics of human beings and the movements they perform. In our attempt to further our understanding of 'the human in motion,' there is a clear need for laboratory-based tests or experiments that will frequently involve the collection of one or more measurements or variables on a group(s) of subjects.

10.2.1 Variables in kinanthropometry and exercise physiology

A variable is any characteristic or measurement that can take on different values. When planning or designing a laboratory-based experiment, the researcher will be able to identify those measurements that can be regarded as either independent or dependent variables. A variable that is under the control of the researcher is referred to as the independent variable. The resulting measurements that are recorded on each subject as a response to the independent variable are known as the dependent variables. For example, in an experiment investigating the oxygen cost of treadmill running, the independent variable would be the running speed, set by the researcher, and the recorded oxygen cost would be the resulting dependent variable.

Classifying measurements in kinanthropometry and exercise physiology

Measurements in kinanthropometry and exercise physiology can be classified as either (i) categorical or (ii) numerical (quantitative) data.

(i) Categorical data

The simplest type of measurement is called the nominal scale where observations are allocated to one of various categories. Examples of nominal data with only two categories (binary) are: male/female, winners/losers or presence/absence of a disease. Examples of nominal data with more than two unordered categories are: country of birth, favourite sport, team supported and different equipment manufacturers. As long as the categories are exhaustive (include all cases) and non-overlapping or mutually exclusive (no case is in more than one category), we have the minimal conditions necessary for the application of statistical procedures on observations categorised on a nominal scale.

Suppose that we retain the idea of grouping from the nominal scale and add the restriction that the variable that we are measuring has an underlying continuum so that we may speak of a person having 'more than' or 'less than' another person of the variable in question. This would be an ordinal scale or rank order scale of measurement. The level of achievement at a particular sport would be an example of this type of measurement; that is, beginner, recreational participant, club standard, county representative, national or international standard.

(ii) Numerical data

Numerical data, often referred to as either interval or ratio scales of measurement, are the highest level of measurement. The distinction between interval and ratio scales (the latter has a fixed zero; the former does not) is not very useful, since most data collected in kinanthropometry and exercise physiology are measured using the ratio scale; for example, one of the few examples of an interval scale of measurement in kinanthropometry would be the results from a sit-and-reach flexibility test. An interval or ratio scale variable can be either a discrete count or a 'continuous' variable. A discrete count can only take on specific values. The number of heart beats per minute and the number of people in a team are examples of discrete variables. A 'continuous' variable may take any value within a defined range of values. Height, weight and time are examples of continuous variables. Quotation marks are used around 'continuous' because all such variables are in practice measured to a finite precision, so they are actually discrete variables with a large number of numerical values. For example, height may be measured to the nearest centimetre and the time to run 100 metres to the nearest 100'th second.

10.2.2 Frequency tables or distributions

The first step necessary to investigate and understand the results of experiments is to discover how the experimental results vary over the range of responses. Are the scores evenly spread over the entire range of responses or do they tend to be more frequent in a particular section of the range; that is, are the scores symmetric over the range or are they skewed with one or two atypical results or outliers? The scores – often referred to as the *raw data* – need to be arranged in the form of a *frequency table* to discover the distribution of measurements over the range of subjects' responses. Consider the following maximal oxygen uptake ($\dot{V}O_2$max) results given in Table 10.1 (Nevill *et al.* 1992a).

The first step in calculating a frequency table is to obtain the range of scores, i.e.

Range = highest score – lowest score = 63.0 – 48.5 = 14.5.(ml kg^{-1} min^{-1})

Table 10.1 The maximal oxygen uptake $\dot{V}O_2$max results of 30 recreationally active male subjects (Nevill *et al.* 1992a)

$\dot{V}O_2$max	$(ml\ kg^{-1}\ min^{-1})$				
60.9	59.3	59.2	58.9	58.3	58.1
55.7	53.4	53.0	51.8	50.6	54.4
63.0	60.3	59.5	57.3	57.1	57.0
56.1	55.1	55.0	54.4	54.0	53.0
52.9	52.8	52.4	51.2	48.5	53.6

Table 10.2 Frequency table for the maximal oxygen uptake results in Table 10.1

Class intervals	Mid-points (M_i)	Tally	Frequency (f_i)
47.0–48.9	47.95	I	1
49.0–50.9	49.95	I	1
51.0–52.9	51.95	IIIII	5
53.0–54.9	53.95	II IIIII	7
55.0–56.9	55.95	IIII	4
57.0–58.9	57.95	I IIIII	6
59.0–60.9	59.95	IIIII	5
61.0–62.9	61.95		0
63.0–64.9	63.95	I	1

Note: the class intervals do not overlap (there are no points in common), and do not exclude scores in the gaps between class intervals.

The next step is to divide the range into a convenient number of class intervals of equal size. Since the number of intervals should lie between 5 and 15 depending on the number of observations, we can obtain a rough estimate of the interval size. In this example, a reasonable number of intervals would be about 8 or 9 that would require an interval size of 2 ($ml\ kg^{-1}\ min^{-1}$). Hence Table 10.2 might be the result.

10.2.3 Histograms and frequency polygons

A histogram or frequency polygon is a graphical representation of a frequency table. A histogram is a set of adjacent rectangles with the class intervals forming the base of the rectangles and the areas proportional to the class frequencies. If the class intervals are all of equal size, it is usual to take the height of the rectangles as the class frequencies. If the class intervals are not of equal size, the height of the rectangles must be adjusted accordingly; for example, if one of the class intervals is twice the size of all the other intervals, then the height of this rectangle should be the frequency score divided by 2. The histogram describing the maximal oxygen uptake ($ml\ kg^{-1}\ min^{-1}$) results from Table 10.2 is given in Figure 10.1

A frequency polygon is a broken-line graph of frequencies plotted against their class intervals. It can be obtained by simply joining the mid-points of the rectangles in the histogram. In order to preserve the area representation of the frequencies, the end points of the polygon have been positioned on the base line at the mid-points of the intervals on either side of the two extreme intervals (see Figure 10.1). If the class intervals are made smaller and smaller while at the same time the number of measurements or counts further increase, the frequency polygon may

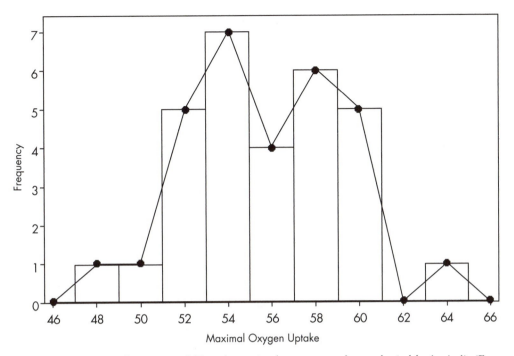

Figure 10.1 Frequency histogram of 30 male maximal oxygen uptake results (ml kg^{-1} min^{-1}). (From Nevill *et al.* 1992a.)

approach a smooth curve, called a frequency distribution. An important example of a frequency distribution that is symmetrical and bell shaped is the normal distribution. The results of tests and experiments in kinanthropometry and exercise physiology are often found to take on the form of a normal distribution. However, the normal distribution is not the only type of frequency distribution obtained when results of such tests and experiments come to be investigated. Other asymmetric or skewed frequency distributions are also obtained. An asymmetric or skewed frequency distribution has a longer tail to one side of the central maximum than the other. If the longer tail is found to the right hand side of the distribution, the data are described as positively skewed, while if the longer tail is found on the left side of the distribution, the data are described as negatively skewed. Certain transformations can be used to overcome the problems of skewed data that correct the asymmetry in

the frequency distribution; for example, a log transformation will frequently correct positively skewed data such as body mass (kg) or maximal oxygen uptake (l.min^{-1}) that have a 'log-normal' distribution.

10.2.4 The Normal plot

With a small number of observations, it is often difficult to examine the underlying distribution with a histogram. This is because the frequency in each class interval will be small, so the appearance of the histogram will change markedly in response to small fluctuations in frequencies. An alternative graphical method of exploring data which works better with small samples is the Normal plot. The exact calculations for this plot are beyond the scope of this book, but the various calculation methods are covered by Altman (1991) and Bland (2000). Suffice to say that the normal plot is based on relative cumulative frequencies plotted on non-linear axes, so

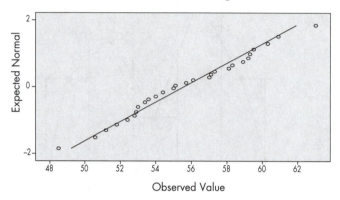

Normal Q-Q Plot of $\dot{V}O_2$max

Tests of Normality

	Kolmogorov-Smirnov [a]			Shapiro-Wilk		
	Statistic	df	Sig.	Statistic	df	Sig.
VO_2max	.099	30	.200*	.983	30	.894

*. This is a lower bound of the true significance.

[a]. Lilliefors Significance Correction

Figure 10.2 The Q-Q plot and Tests of Normality for the example data. On a Normal plot the normal probabilities are plotted against the data. The data depart from the fitted line most evidently in the extremes or distribution tails. This would indicate departure from the normal distribution. SPSS also provides the results of a statistical test, which examines the null hypothesis that the data are not normally distributed. The Shapiro-Wilk test in this example has provided a P-value of 0.894 which indicates that there is little evidence that the data do not follow a normal distribution.

that a normal distribution is judged by the points on the plot lying in a straight line. In SPSS, the type of normal plot produced by the commands given is referred to as a Q-Q plot (Quantile-Quantile plots). A departure from normality usually shows up as an s-shaped curve on the plot. An example of a Q-Q plot using the maximal oxygen uptake data is shown in Figure 10.2.

10.2.5 Measures of location or central tendency (averages)

(a) Arithmetic mean

The arithmetic mean of a set of measurements is defined as the sum of all the scores divided by the total number of measurements. When using the raw data such as the maximal

oxygen uptake measurements from Table 10.1, we need to calculate

$$\overline{X} = \frac{\Sigma X_i}{n} = \frac{(X_1 + X_2 + X_3 + ... + X_n)}{n}$$

$$= \frac{(60.9 + 59.3 + 59.2 + ... + 48.5 + 53.6)}{30}$$

$$= \frac{1666.8}{30}$$

$$= 55.560$$

where X_i refers to the individual scores and Σ is the usual 'sigma' summation notation.

If the data are available only in the form of a frequency table (secondary data), an estimate of the arithmetic mean can be obtained by assuming all the scores of each class interval are approximated by its mid-point (M_i). The estimated arithmetic mean for the maximal oxygen uptake (ml kg^{-1} min^{-1}) results given in Table 10.2 is given by,

$$\overline{X} = \frac{\Sigma(f_i M_i)}{n}$$

$$= \frac{(f_1 M_1 + f_2 + M_2 + \ldots + f_k M_k)}{n}$$

$$= \frac{\begin{array}{c}(1 \times 47.95 + 1 \times 49.95 + 5 \times 52.95 \\ + \ldots + 1 \times 63.95)\end{array}}{30}$$

$$= \frac{1670.5}{30}$$

$$= 55.68$$

where k equals the number of class intervals and M_i and f_i are the mid-point and frequency of the ith class interval respectively.

(b) Median

The median is the middle score of the ranked data. If there is an odd number of scores, the median is unique. However, if the number of scores is even, we simply take the arithmetic mean of the two middle values. To obtain the median of maximal oxygen uptake results of Table 10.1 we need to arrange the scores in order of magnitude as follows:

48.5 50.6 51.2 51.8 52.4 52.8 52.9 53.0 53.0 53.4 53.6 54.0 54.4 54.4 55.0 55.1 55.7 56.1 57.0 57.1 57.3 58.1 58.3 58.9 59.2 59.3 59.5 60.3 60.9 63.0.

Hence, the median (M) becomes

$$M = \frac{(55.0 + 55.1)}{2} = 55.05$$

(c) Mode

The mode is the most frequent observation. In small data sets, the mode is not always unique. In the case of grouped or secondary data where a frequency table has been constructed, the mode can be obtained as follows;

$$\text{Mode} = L_1 + c \, (d_1 / (d_1 + d_2))$$

where L_1 = lower class boundary of the modal class (i.e. the most frequent class interval)

c = size of the modal class interval

d_1 = excess of the modal frequency over frequency of the next lower class

d_2 = excess of the modal frequency over frequency of the next higher class

The mode for the maximal oxygen uptake results taken from Table 10.2 becomes

$$\text{Mode} = L_i + c \left(\frac{d_1}{d_1 + d_2} \right)$$

$$= 52.9 + 2 \left(\frac{2}{(2 + 3)} \right)$$

$$= 52.9 + \frac{4}{5} = 52.9 + 0.8$$

$$= 53.7$$

In summary, if the data are numerical (interval and ratio scales) and symmetric, the mean, median and mode will all tend to coincide at the centre of the frequency distribution. As such, the arithmetic mean provides the simplest and best measure of central tendency. However, if the numerical data have a skewed frequency distribution, the arithmetic mean will be distorted towards the longer tail of the distribution and the median would become a more representative average. If the observed information on a group of subjects is categorical, the calculation of the arithmetic mean is impossible. When the observed data are recorded as an ordered categorical (ordinal) scale, the median and mode are available as measures of central tendency. But if the observed information on a group of subjects is simply a nominal scale, the mode is the only measure of central tendency that remains available; for example, the most popular sports footwear manufacturer.

10.2.6 Measures of variation or dispersion

Although the arithmetic mean provides a satisfactory measure of location or central tendency, it fails to indicate the way the data are spread about this central point. Are all the observed measurements very similar, demonstrating little variation among the scores, or are the measurements spread over a wide range of observations? The degree to which the numerical data are spread out is called the variation or dispersion in the data. A number of measures of variation or dispersion is available, the most common being the range, mean deviation, the variance and the standard deviation (the standard deviation = √variance).

(a) Range
The range = highest score – lowest score, has already been introduced in Section 10.2.1, is the simplest measure of variation and has the advantage of being quick and simple to calculate. Its limitation is that it fails to represent the variation in all the data since it is obtained from just the two extreme scores.

(b) Mean deviation
The mean deviation is the sum of the deviations of a set of scores from their mean,

$$\text{Mean Deviation} = \text{MD} = \sum \frac{|X_i - \overline{X}|}{n}$$

where the notation $|X_i - \overline{X}|$ denotes the absolute value of $(X_i - \overline{X})$, without regard to its sign. The mean deviation of the

maximal oxygen uptake (ml.kg^{-1}.min^{-1}) results from Table 10.1 becomes,

$$\frac{(|60.9 - 55.56| + |59.3 - 55.56| + \ldots + |53.6 - 55.56|)}{30}$$

$$\frac{(5.34 + 3.74 + \ldots + 7.06 + 1.96)}{30}$$

$$\frac{85.71}{30}$$

$$= 2.9 \ (\text{ml kg}^{-1} \text{ min}^{-1})$$

The advantages of the mean deviation are that it includes all the scores, is easy to define and is easy to compute. Its disadvantage is its unsuitability for algebraic manipulations, since signs must be adjusted (ignored) in its definition; for example, if the mean and mean deviations of two sets of scores are known, there is no formula allowing the calculations of the mean deviations of the combined set without going back to the original data.

(c) Variance
The variance of a set of data, denoted by s^2, is defined as the average of the squared deviations from the mean.

$$s^2 = \sum \frac{(X_i - \overline{X})^2}{n} = \sum \frac{(x_i)^2}{n}$$

where $x_i = (X_i - \overline{X})$.

The variance overcomes the problem of converting positive and negative deviations into quantities that are all positive by the process of squaring. Unfortunately, whatever the units of the original data, the variance has to be described in these units 'squared'. For this reason the standard deviation= √variance, is more frequently reported. An alternative method of defining the variance is to divide the sum of squared deviations by n–1 rather than n. When we divide the sum of square deviations by n, the variance will show a systematic tendency to underestimate the variance of the entire population of scores, denoted by the Greek letter sigma (σ^2). When we divide the sum of squared deviations by n–1, however, we obtain an unbiased estimate of σ^2. Hence, the unbiased estimate of σ^2 is $s^2 = \Sigma (X_i - \bar{X})^2 / (n–1)$ where the variance estimate, s^2, has n–1 'degrees of freedom', that is, the maximum number of variates that can be freely assigned before the rest of the variates are completely determined.

(d) Standard deviation

The standard deviation, denoted by s, is the square root of the variance.

$$ s = \sqrt{\sum_i \frac{(X_i - \bar{X})^2}{n}} $$

The standard deviation of the maximal oxygen uptake (ml kg^{-1} min^{-1}) results from Table 10.1 can be found as follows,

$$ s = \sqrt{\frac{\begin{array}{c}(60.9 - 55.56)^2 + (59.3 - 55.56)^2 \\ + ... + (48.5 - 55.56)^2 + (53.6 - 55.56)^2\end{array}}{30}} $$

$$ = \sqrt{\frac{341.53}{30}} $$

$$ = \sqrt{11.38} $$

$$ = 3.373 $$

However, the calculation above requires a lot of computation. For many reasons it is more convenient to calculate the standard deviation using the alternative 'short method' formula:

$$ s = \sqrt{\sum \frac{X^2}{n} - \left(\sum \frac{X}{n}\right)^2} $$

$$ = \sqrt{\frac{92949}{30} - \left(\frac{1666.8}{30}\right)^2} $$

$$ = \sqrt{3098.3 - (55.56)^2} $$

$$ = \sqrt{3098.3 - 3086.9} $$

$$ = \sqrt{11.4} $$

$$ = 3.376 $$

The variance and standard deviation have a number of advantages over the mean deviation. In particular, they are more suitable for algebraic manipulation as demonstrated by the more convenient 'short method' formula given above.

10.2.7 Relative measure of performance or the 'z' standard score

A 'z' standard score is the difference between a particular score X_i and the mean $\bar{X}$, relative to the standard deviation s, i.e.

$$ Z_i = \frac{(X_i - \bar{X})}{s} $$

An important characteristic of a standard score is that it provides a meaningful way of comparing scores from different distributions that have different means and standard deviations. To illustrate the value of standard scores, suppose we wished to compare a decathlete's performance in two events relative to the other competitors, for example, 1,500- and 100-metre run times, at a certain competition. Suppose the athlete ran the 1,500 metres in 4 minutes 20 seconds and the 100 metres in 10.2 seconds. Clearly, a direct comparison of the two performances is impossible. However, if the mean performance (and standard deviation) of all the competing athletes at the two events were 4 minutes 30 (10) seconds and 10.5 (0.2) seconds, respectively, the decathlete's standard scores at each event, recorded in seconds, are given by,

$$ z(1500 \text{ metres}) = (260 - 270) / 10 = 10/10 = -1.0 $$

$$ z(100 \text{ metres}) = (10.2 - 10.5) / 0.2 = -0.3/0.2 = -1.5. $$

Clearly, the greater standard score, z = −1.5, indicates that the athlete performed better at the 100 metres than the 1,500 metres relative to the other competitors. Note that standard scores also play an essential role when carrying out parametric tests of significance, discussed in Section 10.4.

10.2.8 Reference intervals and description of measurement error

Another advantage of the standard deviation statistic is that it can be used to estimate the likely range that includes a certain percentage of values for the population of interest. Such 'reference intervals' are used in classical ergonomics to ensure that a piece of equipment is designed to fit a specified range of individual sizes. Reference intervals can also be used in normative studies of athletic ability to assess the population percentiles (e.g. the top 2.5%) into which individual athletes fit. About 68% of observations from a normal distribution will be within the mean ± 1 standard deviation (s). A popular reference interval covers the central 95% of observations (excludes to upper and lower 2.5% of people) and is calculated from mean ± 1.96 multiplied by s (about 2 times s above and below the mean). Interested readers are directed to Wright and Royston (1999) for a fuller discussion of how to calculate reference intervals and how to apply them to laboratory measurements.

Reference intervals can also be used to describe the error in taking measurements on a particular variable with a particular population, and can be much more informative than the conventional analysis of calculating a test-retest correlation (Atkinson and Nevill 1998). For one type of measurement error description (Bland and Altman 1999), the reference interval is calculated from the standard deviation of the test-retest differences. If this standard deviation is multiplied by 1.96 and added to and subtracted from the mean difference between test and retest, it would be expected that the majority (95%) of individuals in the population would show test-retest differences, purely due to measurement error, of no greater than this calculated reference range. It is also useful to examine the mean difference between test and retest on its own as an indicator of the degree to which measurements were affected by systematic errors (e.g. learning effects leading to an increased score).

The above '95% limits of agreement' (Bland and Altman 1999) are useful for estimating the likelihood that a change in an individual athlete's test scores is 'real' or merely due to measurement error on the test. For example, if the 95% limits of agreement for a maximal oxygen uptake test on a population of athletes are −5 to +5 $ml^{-1}kg^{-1}min$, then it is likely that a change in maximal oxygen uptake of > 5 $ml^{-1}kg^{-1}min$ for an individual athlete from the same population is a 'true' change and not due merely to measurement error on the test (Harvill 1991). In other words, only 2.5% of the population would show test-retest differences greater than 5 $ml^{-1}kg^{-1}min$ that could be attributed to random measurement error. Limits of agreement can also be employed for assessing the likelihood that different methods of measurement give similar scores for individual athletes (Bland and Altman 1999). Reference intervals should not be confused with confidence intervals, which involve the likelihood of a population mean being within a range of sample means. Most reference intervals for measurement error assume that the data are normally distributed, the errors are homoscedastic (constant throughout the range of measured values) and that the sample size is large enough to provide a precise assessment of the population interval. The first two assumptions can be explored and corrected for by logarithmic transformation (Bland and Altman 1999). The latter assumption should be controlled *a priori* by employing an adequate sample size (preferably >40). In addition, the researcher can estimate the precision of the limits of agreement by calculating the confidence intervals according to the methods of Bland and Altman (1999).

Anthropometrists may wish to calculate the 'technical error of measurement' (TEM) which is purported to represent 'the typical magnitude of measurement error that one can expect to occur' (Knapp 1992, p. 253). In reality, this statistic is similar to the standard error of measurement (Harvill 1991) in that it represents the range above and below the observed value for which there is a 68% chance of a hypothetical 'true value' existing in the 'average' subject. Whether this reference range for measurement error is considered as 'typical' is up to the researcher. It may be better to extrapolate the described measurement error to what it means for actual uses of the measurement tool. For example, researchers may be more interested in describing the measurement error so that they are more confident that the true value is within the stated reference range. This could be done by multiplying the TEM by 1.96 which gives a 95% reference range for the 'true' value (Harvill 1991). One can also estimate how the described measurement error impacts upon statistical power and estimated sample size in experiments (Atkinson *et al.* 1999; Atkinson and Nevill 2001). The TEM is calculated by summing the squared differences (d_i) between test and retest for each person (i), dividing by 2 times the sample size (n) and taking the square root (Knapp 1992):

$$TEM = \sqrt{\frac{\sum d_i^2}{2n}}$$

It is stressed that the individual differences between test and retest are involved in the calculation, rather than the individual differences from the sample mean, as is the case for the standard deviation of the differences. Practically, this would mean that TEM assumes all error is random instrument error and that no systematic learning influences are present. Kinanthropometrists should be aware that some measurements are prone to learning effects from both the subject and the tester. The TEM also assumes that the measurement error is the same, irrespective

of the general magnitude of the measured variable (homoscedasticity). This is so, even though it is known that the measurement error of some anthropometric variables is greater for subjects with higher values in general (Atkinson and Nevill 1998). This characteristic, called heteroscedasticity, can be controlled for to a certain extent by expressing the TEM as a percentage of the mean measured value for the sample:

'Relative' TEM (%) =

$$\frac{TEM}{Sample\ mean\ score} \times 100$$

We maintain that a much more informative reference range for measurement error is the 95% limits of agreement, especially for assessing individual variability, and a more thorough analysis and exploration of measurement error is through the associated methods of Bland and Altman (1999).

10.2.9 The SPSS commands to illustrate the methods of Section 10.2

SPSS is a statistical package with a very structured format for inputting the data. When you open SPSS a *Data Editor* window is opened, this contains 2 sheets *Data View* and *Variable View* (see the two tabs at the bottom of the sheet in Figure 10.3). The columns in the Data View sheet represent either different variables or repeated measures of the same variable. Each row represents a different subject's value for each of the variables. Therefore, when working with SPSS you should have the same number of rows in the sheet as there are participants in the analysis. In Figure 10.3 the $\dot{V}O_2$max data have been inputted so there is one column with 30 rows. The Variable View sheet contains information about the attributes of each column of the Data View sheet. Each row in the Variable View sheet represents each column in the Data View Sheet.

The simplest method to obtain most of the

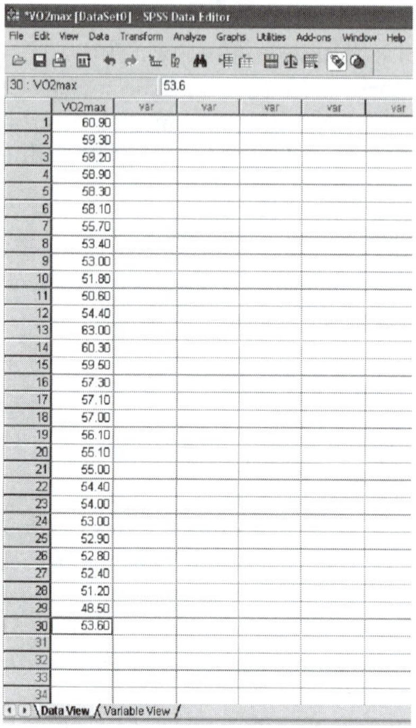

Figure 10.3 An example of data entered into the SPSS Data Editor window.

descriptive statistics given in Sections 10.2 is as follows:

1 First input the data from Table 10.1 into column 1 of the Data View sheet in a similar manner to that shown in Figure 10.3. To name the column double click 'VAR00001' at the top of the first column; this takes you on to the Variable View sheet. Now type 'VO2max' into the Name column and into the Label column of row 1.

2 Select *Analyze, Descriptives Statistics* and *Explore* via the pull down menus. Move the variable of interest – in this case VO2max [$\dot{V}O_2$max] – from the left window to the dependent list: window with the arrow button. Click *Plots ...* at the bottom of the box, and in the Descriptive box select Histogram. Also, select *Normality plots with tests*, click *continue* to return to the previous box. Now click *OK*.

A new window called 'Output1 – SPSS viewer' should have appeared. The right-hand pane of this window contains all the statistical output, in this case the descriptive statistics for the data set. As there may be a large amount of output, the left-hand pane of the window contains a tree diagram, which allows you jump between all the different output. In the first instance we are interested in the table titled 'Descriptives' (see Figure 10.4). The mean and the standard error of the mean is also provided in the first row. The standard error is defined as $s/\sqrt{n}$ and it can be used to calculate the 95% Confidence Interval for the Mean, also shown in the table. The Lower and Upper Bounds for the 95% Confidence Interval for the Mean provide an estimate of the interval within which the true population mean may actually lie. In other words, there is a 95% chance that the true population mean is encompassed by the interval 54.3 ml kg^{-1} min^{-1} to 56.8 ml kg^{-1} min^{-1}. In this instance, the upper and lower bounds are calculated in the following manner.

$$\text{Lower bound} = \overline{X} - \left(t \times \left(\frac{s}{\sqrt{n}} \right) \right)$$

$$= 55.56 - \left(2.045 \times \left(\frac{3.432}{\sqrt{30}} \right) \right)$$

$$= 55.56 - (2.045 \times 0.627)$$

$$= 55.56 - 1.282$$

$$= 54.3 \text{ ml kg}^{-1} \text{ min}^{-1}$$

$$\text{Upper bound} = \overline{X} + \left(t \times \left(\frac{s}{\sqrt{n}} \right) \right)$$

$$= 55.56 + \left(2.045 \times \left(\frac{3.432}{\sqrt{30}} \right) \right)$$

$$= 55.56 + (2.045 \times 0.627)$$

$$= 55.56 + 1.282$$

$$= 56.8 \text{ ml kg}^{-1} \text{ min}^{-1}$$

Descriptives

			Statistic	Std. Error
VO₂max	Mean		55.5600	.62655
	95% Confidence Interval for Mean	Lower Bound	54.2786	
		Upper Bound	56.8414	
	5% Trimmed Mean		55.5389	
	Median		55.0500	
	Variance		11.777	
	Std. Deviation		3.43176	
	Minimum		48.50	
	Maximum		63.00	
	Range		14.50	
	Interquartile Range		5.48	
	Skewness		.164	.427
	Kurtosis		−.515	.833

Figure 10.4 SPSS Output containing the descriptive statistics obtained via the Explore command.

The t-value in the equations is the t-distribution value for the number of degrees of freedom associated with that sample size (i.e. n–1). In the above case t was 2.045. The requirement to report confidence intervals is growing as they can be used to provide greater insight into the true value of a population parameter.

The 5% Trimmed Mean represents a mean, averaged from the middle 90% of the data, where 5% of the smallest and largest values are ignored. The standard deviation is calculated using the unbiased definition for the population variance σ^2, i.e. by dividing the sum of squared deviations by n–1. Quantification of the amount of skewness and kurtosis present in the sample data is also provided.

10.3 INVESTIGATING RELATIONSHIPS IN KINANTHROPOMETRY AND EXERCISE PHYSIOLOGY

10.3.1 Correlation

The first and most important step when investigating relationships between variables in kinanthropometry and exercise physiology

is to plot the data in the form of a scatter diagram. The eye can still identify patterns or relationships in data better than any statistical tests. If X and Y denote the independent and dependent variables respectively of our experiment, a scatter diagram describes the location of points (X,Y) on rectangular co-ordinate system. The term 'correlation' is used to describe the degree of relationship that exists between the dependent and independent variables.

(a) Positive correlation

Example 1: An example of a positive correlation is seen in Figure 10.5 between the mean power output (W) of 16 subjects, recorded on a non-motorised treadmill, and their body mass (kg) (Nevill *et al.*1992b).

The scatter diagram demonstrates a positive correlation since the subjects with a greater body mass (X) are able to record a higher mean power output (Y), i.e. as X increases, Y also increases.

(b) Negative correlation

Example 2: In contrast, an example of a negative correlation is seen in Figure 10.6 between maximal oxygen uptake (ml kg⁻¹

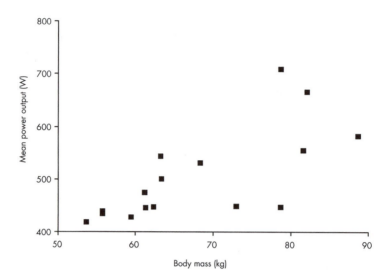

Figure 10.5 Mean power output (W) versus body mass (kg) of 16 male subjects, recorded on a non-motorized treadmill (Nevill *et al.* 1992b).

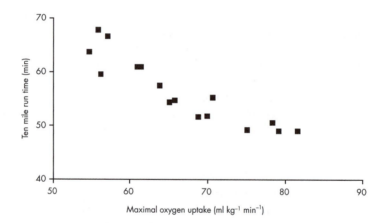

Figure 10.6 Ten-mile run times (min) versus maximal oxygen uptake (ml kg^{-1} min^{-1}) of 16 male subjects (Costill *et al.* 1973).

min^{-1}) and 10-mile (16.1 km) run times (min) of 16 male subjects, representing a wide range of distance running abilities (adapted from Costill *et al.* 1973).

The figure describes a negative correlation because the subjects with a lower 10-mile run times (X) are found to have recorded higher maximal oxygen uptake measurements (Y), i.e. as X increases Y is found to decrease. If a scatter diagram indicates no obvious pattern or relationship between the two variables, then the variables are said to have no correlation; that is, they are uncorrelated.

10.3.2 Measures of correlation

Although a scatter diagram gives a clear indication of the degree of relationship between two variables, a single numerical statistic or correlation coefficient would summarise the relationship and facilitate the comparison of several different correlations.

(a) Pearson's product-moment correlation coefficient

The most appropriate correlation coefficient for numerical variables was introduced by Karl Pearson (1857–1936) and hence, is often referred to as Pearson's product-moment correlation coefficient (Kotz *et al.*, 2004). The definition of the product-moment correlation coefficient requires a new measure of variation similar to the variance introduced in Section 10.2.6, known as the covariance, i.e.

$$s_{xy} = \frac{(X_i - \overline{X})(Y_i - \overline{Y})}{n} \qquad (10.1)$$

The covariance is a measure of the joint variation in X and Y, but its magnitude will depend on the variation in both variables. Hence, the product-moment correlation coefficient is defined as the ratio of the covariance to the product of the standard deviations of X and Y, given by

$$r = \frac{\sum (X_i - \overline{X})(Y_i - \overline{Y})}{\sqrt{[\sum (X_i - \overline{X})^2][\sum (Y_i - \overline{Y})^2]}} \qquad (10.2)$$

Note that the divisor (n) cancels in both the numerator and denominator terms in the ratio.

A more convenient formula to calculate the product-moment correlation coefficient 10.2 is given by

$$r = \frac{n\sum X_i Y_i - (\sum X)(\sum Y)}{\sqrt{[n\sum X_i^2 (\sum X)^2][n\sum Y_i^2 - (\sum Y)^2]}} \qquad (10.3)$$

The correlation coefficient for the data from Nevill *et al.* (1992b), between mean power output (W) and body mass (kg) can be obtained as follows. From the two columns 'mean power (Y)' and 'body mass (X),' three further columns are required, i.e. Y^2, X^2 and YX, given in Table 10.3.

The only additional information required to calculate the correlation coefficient, given by equation (10.3), is the number of subjects

n=16. Hence, the correlation coefficient becomes

$$r = \frac{16(558214.8) - (1088.0)(8059.2)}{\sqrt{[16(75795.12) - (1088)^2]} \sqrt{[16(4175275.3) - (8059.2)^2]}}$$

$$= \frac{8931436.8 - 8768409.6}{\sqrt{[1212721.9 - 1183744]} \sqrt{[66804405 - 64950705]}}$$

$$= \frac{163027.2}{\sqrt{[28977.9][1853699.8]}}$$

$$= \frac{163027.2}{231767.8}$$

$$= 0.703$$

The obtained value of +0.703 indicates that for this group of subjects, there was a high positive correlation between the two variables. The correlation coefficient can take any value between +1.00 and −1.00, with values of *r* close to zero indicating no linear relationship between the two variables. The above calculations are somewhat complex, due to the size or scale of the variables X and Y. However, the correlation coefficient is unaffected by adding or subtracting a constant value to or from either column. Hence, in Example 2 from Costill *et al.* (1973), by subtracting convenient constants, say 40 from the Y column, i.e. y=(Y−40) and 50 from the X column, i.e. x=(X−50) in the data in Table 10.4, an alternative 'short method' of calculating the correlation coefficient, between 10-mile run times (min) and maximal oxygen uptake or $\dot{V}O_2$max (ml kg^{-1} min^{-1}) can be used to simplify the arithmetic.

Hence, the correlation coefficient between 10-mile run times (min) and maximal oxygen uptake or $\dot{V}O_2$max (ml kg^{-1} min^{-1}) becomes

$$r = \frac{16(3593.1) - (261.4)(265.9)}{\sqrt{[16(4858.4) - (261.4)2]} \sqrt{[16(5566.3) - (265.9)2]}}$$

Table 10.3 Data required to calculate the correlation coefficient between mean power output (W) and body mass (kg) for example 1 (Nevill *et al.* 1992b)

	Mean power (Y)	Body mass (X)	(Y^2)	(X^2)	(YX)
	499.6	63.4	249600.2	4019.56	31674.6
	473.7	61.2	224391.7	3745.44	28990.4
	444.5	61.4	197580.2	3769.96	27292.3
	438.0	55.8	191844.0	3113.64	24440.4
	446.2	78.7	199094.5	6193.69	35115.9
	665.8	82.1	443289.7	6740.41	54662.2
	709.2	78.8	502964.7	6209.44	55885.0
	542.5	63.3	294306.3	4006.89	34340.2
	581.0	88.7	337561.0	7867.69	51534.7
	434.1	55.8	188442.8	3113.64	24222.8
	554.7	81.7	307692.1	6674.89	45319.0
	418.3	53.7	174974.9	2883.69	22462.7
	530.8	68.4	281748.6	4678.56	36306.7
	446.8	62.4	199630.2	3893.76	27880.3
	447.4	73.1	200166.8	5343.61	32704.9
	426.6	59.5	181987.6	3540.25	25382.7
Total	8059.2	1088.0	4175275.3	75795.12	558214.8

Table 10.4 Data required to calculate the correlation coefficient between 10-mile run time (min) and maximal oxygen uptake (ml kg^{-1} min^{-1}) for example 2 (Costill *et al.* 1973)

	Run time (Y)	$\dot{V}O_2$max (X)	$y = (Y - 40)$	$x = (X - 50)$	x^2	y^2	xy
	48.9	81.6	8.9	31.6	79.21	998.56	281.24
	49.0	79.2	9.0	29.2	81.00	852.64	262.80
	49.1	75.2	9.1	25.2	82.81	635.04	229.32
	50.5	78.4	10.5	28.4	110.25	806.56	298.20
	51.6	68.9	11.6	18.9	134.56	357.21	219.24
	51.8	70.1	11.8	20.1	139.24	404.01	237.18
	54.3	65.2	14.3	15.2	204.49	231.04	217.36
	54.6	65.9	14.6	15.9	213.16	252.81	232.14
	55.1	70.8	15.1	20.8	228.01	432.64	314.08
	57.4	63.9	17.4	13.9	302.76	193.21	241.86
	59.5	56.3	19.5	6.3	380.25	39.69	122.85
	60.8	61.0	20.8	11.0	432.64	121.00	228.80
	60.8	61.5	20.8	11.5	432.64	132.25	239.20
	63.6	54.8	23.6	4.8	556.96	23.04	113.28
	66.6	57.2	26.6	7.2	707.56	51.84	191.52
	67.8	55.9	27.8	5.9	772.84	34.81	164.02
Total	901.4	1065.9	261.4	265.9	4858.4	5566.3	3593.1

$$= \frac{57489.6 - 69506.26}{\sqrt{[77734.4 - 68329.96]}\sqrt{[89060.8 - 70702.8]}}$$

$$= \frac{-12016.7}{\sqrt{[9404.4][18358]}}$$

$$= \frac{-12016.7}{13139.48}$$

$$= -0.9145$$

In this example, the value of $r = -0.91$ indicates that for this group of subjects, there was a high negative correlation between the two variables. Pearson's product moment correlation coefficient is an appropriate statistic to describe the relationship between two variables, provided the data are approximately linear and numerical (interval or ratio scales of measurement). However, Pearson's correlation coefficient is not the only method of measuring the relationship between two variables.

(b) Spearman's rank correlation coefficient

The ranks given by two independent judges to a group of six gymnasts are given in Table 10.5. Are the two judges in agreement?

The most frequently used statistic to describe the relationship between ranks is Spearman's rank correlation coefficient r_s, given by

$$r_s = 1 - \frac{6 \times \sum D^2}{N(N^2 - 1)}$$

where D is difference between paired ranks and N is the number of pairs. For the ranks given in Table 10.5, the Spearman's rank correlation becomes,

$$r_s = 1 - \frac{6 \times 24}{6(6^2 - 1)}$$

$$= 1 - \frac{24}{35}$$

$$= 0.314$$

As with the Pearson's correlation coefficient, the value of r_s lies between +1.0 and –1.0. Suppose Judge 1 decided that gymnast 2 and gymnast 3 were equally good in their performances and should share first place. This can be incorporated into the calculation by averaging the two shared ranks in question. In this example the two gymnasts were sharing ranks 1 and 2, so the average 1.5 would be given to both performers. Note that the next best gymnast would receive the rank of 3.

10.3.3 Prediction and linear regression

Suppose we wish to predict a male endurance athlete's 10-mile (16.1 km) run time having previously recorded his maximal oxygen uptake. If we assume that our athlete is of a similar standard as the subjects used by Costill *et al.* (1973), we could use these data to predict the 10-mile run time of such an athlete. Nevill *et al.* (1990) was able to show that since maximal oxygen uptake was a rate of using oxygen per minute, that is (ml kg^{-1} min^{-1}), running performance was also better recorded as a rate, for example, average run speed in metres per second (m s^{-1}). Hence, when the 10-mile run times of the athletes studied by Costill *et al.* (1973) were recalculated as average run speeds (m s^{-1}) and correlated with their results for maximal oxygen uptake results, the relationship appeared more linear (Figure 10.7) and the correlation increased from $r = -0.91$ to $r = 0.939$.

Let us assume that we wish to predict the average running speed (Y) of an athlete from the maximal oxygen uptake (X). The predicted variable Y, is often described as the dependent variable and whilst the variable X that provides the information on which the predictions are based, is referred to as the independent variable. If we accept that the relationship in Figure 10.7 between running speed and maximal oxygen uptake is a straight line, we can write the equation of a line as follows,

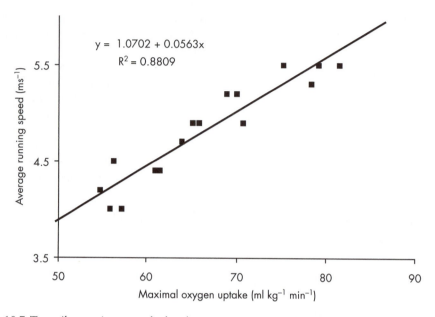

Figure 10.7 Ten-mile run times, recalculated as average run speeds (m s⁻¹), versus maximal oxygen uptake results (ml kg⁻¹ min⁻¹) (Costill *et al.* 1973).

$$Y = a + b.X$$

where a, the Y-intercept, and b, the slope of the line, are both constants.

The simplest method of estimating the constants a and b is to use 'the method of least squares.' If we denote the predicted or estimated value of the dependent variable Y as $Y_e = a + b.X$, the 'method of least squares' is the method that minimises the squared differences $d^2 = \Sigma(Y - Y_e)^2$. The equation of the line, often referred to as the *'least squares regression line of Y on X,'* fitted to n points (X,Y) by the method of least squares is given by,

$$Y_e = a + b.X$$

where $b = \dfrac{n\sum X_i Y_i - \left(\sum X\right)\left(\sum Y\right)}{n\sum X_i^2 - \left(\sum X\right)^2}$ (10.4)

$$n\,\Sigma X_i^2 - (\Sigma X)^2$$

$$a = \sum \frac{Y_i}{n} - b\sum \frac{X_i}{n}$$ (10.5)

The regression line to predict the average 10-mile run speed from an athlete's maximal oxygen uptake measurements can be obtained from the quantities in Table 10.6.

Using equation (10.4), the slope of the line becomes,

$$b = \frac{16 \times 5200.87 - (1065.9)(77.1)}{16 \times 72156.35 - (1065.9)^2}$$

$$= \frac{(83213.92 - 82180.89)}{1154501.6 - 1136142.8}$$

$$= \frac{1033.03}{18358.8}$$

$$= 0.05627$$

and the intercept a becomes,

$$a = \sum \frac{Y_i}{n} - b \times \sum \frac{X_i}{n}$$

$$a = \frac{77.1}{16} - \frac{0.05627 \times 1065.9}{16}$$

$$= 4.82 - 3.75$$

$$= 1.07$$

Table 10.5 Six gymnasts ranked on performance by two independent judges

Gymnast	Judge1 (R_1)	Judge2 (R_2)	$D = R_1 - R_2$	D^2
			Ranks given by	
1	5	6	−1	1
2	2	5	−3	9
3	1	1	0	0
4	6	3	3	9
5	3	4	−1	1
6	4	2	2	4
Totals			0	$\Sigma D^2 = 24$

Table 10.6 Data required to calculate the regression line between average 10-mile (16.1 km) run speed (m s^{-1}) and maximal oxygen uptake (ml kg^{-1} min^{-1}) for example 2 (Costill et al. 1973)

$\dot{V}O_2$max (X)	Speed (Y)	X^2	Y^2	XY
81.6	5.5	6658.56	30.25	448.80
79.2	5.5	6272.64	30.25	435.60
75.2	5.5	5655.04	30.25	413.60
78.4	5.3	6146.56	28.09	415.52
68.9	5.2	4747.21	27.04	358.28
70.1	5.2	4914.01	27.04	364.52
65.2	4.9	4251.04	24.01	319.48
65.9	4.9	4342.81	24.01	322.91
70.8	4.9	5012.64	24.01	346.92
63.9	4.7	4083.21	22.09	300.33
56.3	4.5	3169.69	20.25	253.35
61.0	4.4	3721.00	19.36	268.40
61.5	4.4	3782.25	19.36	270.60
54.8	4.2	3003.04	17.64	230.16
57.2	4.0	3271.84	16.00	228.80
55.9	4.0	3124.81	16.00	223.60
Totals 1065.9	77.1	72156.35	375.65	5200.87

Hence, the least squares regression line, required to predict the average 10-mile run speed from maximal oxygen uptake, is given by

$$Y_e = a + b.X$$

$$Y_e = 1.07 + 0.05627.X$$

An athlete who recorded a maximal oxygen uptake of 80 (ml kg^{-1} min^{-1}) would expect to run 10 miles at an average speed of 1.07 + 0.05627 × (80) = 5.57 m s^{-1} i.e. he would expect to complete the 10-mile distance in 48.14 minutes.

The quality of the regression model can also be assessed by calculating the coefficient of determination ($r^2 \times 100$), also known as R^2. In the above example, the correlation coefficient was calculated to be 0.939; therefore, the coefficient of determination was 88.1%. If there was a perfect correlation between two variables (i.e. if $r = 1$ or -1) the coefficient of determination would be 100%. A coefficient of determination of 100% would mean that the variability between the athletes in their average 10-mile run speed was due solely to their different maximal oxygen uptake values. A low coefficient of determination value means that only a small amount of variability in the dependent variable can be explained by the variability in the independent variable. This means that other unknown variables account for the unexplained variablity. In this example, maximal oxygen uptake accounted for 88.1% of the variance in the prediction of average 10-mile run speed with 11.9% being accounted for by other variables. The inclusion of more predictor variables into the regression equation can increase how much variance is accounted for by the model. These approaches will be addressed in the next section.

10.3.4 Multiple linear regression

In the previous section, we were able to predict the average running speed (Y) of an athlete from the maximal oxygen uptake (X) using linear regression, assuming the relationship between running speed and maximal oxygen uptake was linear, given by

$$Y = a + b.X.$$

Suppose we wish to predict running performance using *more* than just one independent variable. Multiple linear regression allows the researcher to predict values of a dependent variable from a collection of 'k' independent variables. The multiple linear regression equation becomes,

$$Y = a + b_1.X_1 + b_2.X_2 + \cdots + b_k.X_k$$

where X_1, X_2, $\cdots$ X_k, are the independent (or predictor) variables and b_1, b_2, $\cdots$ b_k are the unknown slope parameters. These slope parameters can be calculated using 'the method of least-squares' as described above.

In practice, statistical software, such as SPSS, can estimate these unknown parameters quickly, accurately and efficiently.

A number of methods exist for determining which independent variables should be included in a multiple regression equation. In the standard model all the predictor variables that the investigator collects are included in the equation. For example, in the previous section we calculated the regression equation for average running speed of an athlete from the maximal oxygen uptake. As well as measuring the maximal oxygen uptake as a predictor variable we also could have measured height and body mass to see if they help to predict average running speed. If we used the standard model all three predictor variables would be included in the equation. In SPSS, this method is called *enter*.

However, when predicting variables in kinanthropometry and exercise physiology, there may be certain instances when the dependent variable can be predicted, more than adequately, using a subset of the independent variables; that is, a 'reduced model'. The most common methods of producing a reduced model typically come under the general heading of *stepwise* regression. Stepwise regression methods either remove or add variables for the purpose of identifying a reduced model. The three commonly used procedures are stepwise regression (adds and removes variables), forward selection (adds variables), and backwards elimination (removes variables). The *best* of these methods, backward elimination, begins with a full or saturated model and the least important variables can then be eliminated sequentially (based on the either the size of the *F* statistic or its P-value for dropping the variable from the model). It is important to note that use of the different methods on the same data can lead to different variables being included in the final model.

The stepwise procedures have to be used with some caution as the criterion for a variable to be included in the equation is purely statistical rather than being based on the known importance of a variable from prior investigations. In situations where you want to ensure that a variable is included in the equation then hierarchical regression can be used. Here the order of entry of the variables is determined by the researcher. This option can be useful when you know from previous research that a variable makes a large contribution to the prediction of the dependent variable.

Eston *et al.* (2005) used forward elimination and hierarchical regression methods to assess which skinfolds (abdomen, iliac crest, biceps, triceps, subscapular, calf and thigh) best predicted percentage body as measured by dual energy-x-ray absorptiometry (%fatDXA) in young males (n=21) and young women (n=31). They used the forward elimination method to assess which of the seven skinfolds, along with gender, were significant predictors of %fatDXA. Thigh, calf, and iliac crest and gender were all found to be significant predictors. When the analysis was repeated on the women alone, the predictor variables remained the same. However, the thigh and iliac crest were the only significant predictor variables when the analysis was run on the data for males.

The hierarchical regression was used to assess how much variance in the prediction of %fatDXA was accounted for by the inclusion of lower-limb skinfolds when compared with a prediction model that only uses upper-body sites, specifically, Durnin and Womersley's (1974) sum of four skinfolds model (Σ4skf). The Σ4skf, thigh, calf and sum of the thigh and calf were all entered independently into the hierarchical regression in various combinations of order. The importance of the various predictor variables was assessed by comparing the change in R^2 values of the predictors for the different orders in which they were entered. The R^2 value is interpreted in exactly the same way as the coefficient of determination described at the end of the section on simple regression. The hierarchical regression allowed Eston *et al.* (2005) to examine the initial R^2 value for each variable and then to observe the amount of change after a new variable was added. For example, when Σ4skf was the first variable entered into the women's model its R^2 value 75%, when the thigh was then added it accounted for an extra 11%. When the thigh was entered first it accounted for 82% of the variance with Σ4skf only accounting for an extra 4% when added to the model. A similar pattern was observed in the male data. Based on this analysis Eston *et al.* (2005) concluded that the thigh should be included with the Σ4skf when estimating body fatness.

10.3.5 The SPSS commands to illustrate the methods of Section 10.3

One of the most important and useful statistical tools used to explore relationships is the scatter diagram. This can be obtained via the following commands;

1   First input the Mean power data from Table 10.3 into column 1 of the Data View sheet, name column 1 (i.e. VAR00001) 'Mean_power' via the Variable View sheet. Also in the Variable View sheet, type 'Mean power (W)' into the Label column of row 1.

2   Now input the Body mass data into column 2 (i.e. VAR00002). This time name the column 'Body_mass' using the Variable View sheet and type 'Body mass (kg)' into the Label column of row 2.

3   Select *Graphs* and *Scatter/Dot ...* Now select *Simple Scatter* and click on *Define*.

4   Move the variable 'Mean power (W) [Mean_power]' from the left window to the Y axis: window with the arrow button. Move the variable 'Body mass (kg) [Body_mass]' from the left window to the X axis: window with the arrow button. Now click *OK*.

5   A scatter diagram should have appeared in an output window, double click on the chart if you wish to edit it. (See Figure 10.8 for an SPSS scatterplot.) For

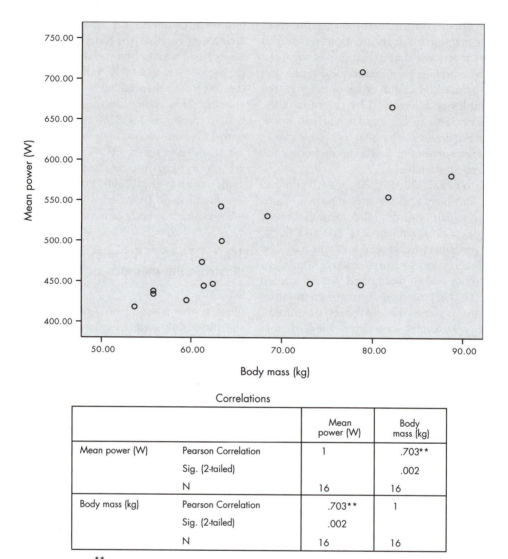

Correlations		Mean power (W)	Body mass (kg)
Mean power (W)	Pearson Correlation	1	.703**
	Sig. (2-tailed)		.002
	N	16	16
Body mass (kg)	Pearson Correlation	.703**	1
	Sig. (2-tailed)	.002	
	N	16	16

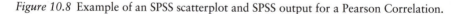

**. Correlation is significant at the 0.01 level (2-tailed).

Figure 10.8 Example of an SPSS scatterplot and SPSS output for a Pearson Correlation.

example, if you wish to add a regression line, double click on your scatter plot to open the Chart Editor, then click once on one of the data points. Then select *Elements* from the Chart Editor menu bar. Then select *Fit Line at Total*, make sure that linear regression is selected. Click *Apply*, then click *close*.

Using the same data as before the Pearson or Spearman correlation coefficient can be obtained using the following commands;

1   Select *Analyze, Correlate* and then *Bivariate*.

2   Select both the variables in the left window (i.e. 'Mean power (W) [Mean_power]' and 'Body mass (kg) [Body_mass]') and move them to the Variables: window

Model Summary

Model	R	R Square	Adjusted R Square	Std. Error of the Estimate
1	.939 [a]	.881	.872	.18735

[a] Predictors: (Constant), VO_2max

ANOVA [b]

Model		Sum of Squares	df	Mean Square	F	Sig.
1	Regression	3.633	1	3.633	103.502	.000 [a]
	Residual	.491	14	.035		
	Total	4.124	15			

[a] Predictors: (Constant), VO_2max
[b] Dependent Variable: Speed

Coefficients [a]

Model		Unstandardized Coefficients		Standardized Coefficients	t	Sig.
		B	Std. Error	Beta		
1	(Constant)	1.070	.371		2.881	.012
	VO2max	.056	.006	.939	10.174	.000

[a] Dependent Variable: Speed

Figure 10.9 SPSS output for a simple linear regression.

using the arrow button. Make sure that either the Pearson box or Spearman box is ticked and then click *OK*.

The SPSS output in Figure 10.8 shows a correlation matrix where mean power has been correlated with body mass. It also provides the probability obtaining that *r* value in the row labelled 'Sig. (2-tailed)'. In this case p = 0.002. The final row (N) in each cell is the number of pairs of scores entered into the correlation.

The least squares linear regression line to predict average 10-mile run speed from maximal oxygen uptake, can be obtained as follows,

1   Input the $\dot{V}O_2max$ data from Table 10.6 into column 1 and name the column 'VO2max'
2   Input the average speed data into column 2 and name the column 'Speed.'

3   Select *Analyze, Regression* and *Linear*.
4   Select 'Speed' and move it to the Dependent: window using the arrow button. Select 'VO2max' and move it to the Independent(s): window using the arrow button. Press *OK*.

The bottom table in Figure 10.9 provides the estimated values of the coefficients, the intercept a (Constant) and the slope b ($\dot{V}O_2max$), along with their standard errors, *t*-values for testing if the coefficients are 0, and the P-value for this test.

This first table contains the coefficient of determination, $R^2 = 0.881$ and the Adjusted $R^2 = 0.872$, adjusted for the degrees of freedom. Also in this table, the estimated standard deviation about the regression line, s = 0.1874 is given

The analysis of variance (ANOVA) table contains the component sums of squares.

The total variation of the dependent variable Speed is partitioned into that explained by the regression line (Regression) remaining unexplained variation (Residual). Note that the estimated variance about the regression line the Mean Square Residual = s^2 = $(0.1874)^2$ = 0.0351.

The multiple regression commands start the same as the regression commands described above. For example, similar to Eston *et al.* (2005), suppose we wished to predict %fatDXA from three variables (Σ4skf, thigh and Calf). To use the enter method you would move all three of these variables into the Independent(s): window when setting up the model (see step 4 of the previous SPSS regression instructions) and then run the analysis. To perform any of the stepwise procedures you would move the data across in a similar manor to the enter method, but you would change the model from Enter (see the box below Independent(s): window) to either Stepwise, Forward or Backwards. For the hierarchical regression you would enter the variable(s) that you would want to go into the model first by moving it or them into Independent(s): window. You then click on the Next button above the Independent(s): window. The next variable to be entered into the equation can be moved into Independent(s): window.

There are some key assumptions that need to be considered when running multiple regression procedures which are beyond the scope of this text. For a more detailed general introduction to regression procedures see Field (2005), and for a discussion of the use regression procedures specifically in relation to exercise physiology and kinanthropometry, see Winter *et al.* (2001).

10.4 COMPARING EXPERIMENTAL DATA IN KINANTHROPOMETRY

Laboratory-based experiments are not conducted simply to describe the results of the experiment as outlined in Sections 10.2 and 10.3. The researcher will often wish to 'test' whether the experimental results (dependent variable) have been affected by different experimental conditions (the independent variable). This important step is the function of *inferential statistics*. For further reading in the methods of inferential statistics, see Snedecor and Cochran (1989).

10.4.1 Drawing inferences from experimental data; independent subjects

The simplest experiment to design involves a group of subjects that require to be divided into two or more groups on a random basis. We shall describe the three most frequently used tests that adopt this design:

- The *t*-test for independent samples.
- One-way ANOVA for independent samples
- The Mann-Whitney test for independent samples.

These tests will be introduced together with some general points about inferential statistics with examples from kinanthropometry and exercise physiology.

(a) The t-test for independent samples
Example 3: A group of 13 male subjects was divided into two groups at random. One group of six subjects were given an exercise training programme for 6 months whilst the remaining seven subjects acted as a control group. The blood lactate concentrations (mM) of seven untrained and six trained male subjects were measured whilst running at 70% of $\dot{V}O_2$max and are given in Table 10.7.

The requirements of the independent *t*-test are as follows:
i)   That the samples are drawn from a normal population with equal variance.
ii) The variable is measured using either an interval or ratio scale.

Table 10.7 Blood lactate concentrations recorded at 70% of $\dot{V}O_2$max

Lactate concentration $(mmol \, l^{-1})$	
Untrained subjects	Trained subjects
2.5	1.8
2.9	2.6
1.9	2.4
3.6	1.5
2.9	2.4
3.7	2.0
2.6	

Clearly the blood lactate measurements can take any value within a certain range of observations and hence, we can assume the measurements are recorded on an interval scale. Also by simply producing a frequency table, the two sets of data can be checked to demonstrate an approximate normal distribution: symmetric and bell shaped. All these characteristics are described in Section 10.2.

The steps required to implement the *t*-test for independent samples are as follows.

Step 1: Calculate the mean, standard deviation and variance for both samples.

	Untrained Subjects (n_1=7)	Trained subjects (n_2=6)
Mean	X_1=2.87	X_2=2.12
Standard deviation	s_1=0.63	s_2=0.42
Variance	$(s_1)^2$=0.3969	$(s_2)^2$=0.1764

Step 2: The assumption of equal variances can be confirmed using the *F* ratio test. For this test we need to calculate the ratio of variances, taking care to put the largest variance on top, i.e.

$$F = \frac{(s_1)^2}{(s_2)^2} = \frac{0.3969}{0.1764} = 2.25$$

The value of the *F* ratio has two 'degrees of

freedom' parameters. The degrees of freedom associated with the numerator variance is n_1-1 = 6, whilst the degrees of freedom associated with the denominator variance is n_2-1 = 5.

If the two variances are similar, the value of *F* would be expected to be near unity. If a very large value of *F* (a small *F* ratio, less than unity, has been precluded by always requiring the largest variance to be the numerator term) is obtained, the assumption of equal variances should be rejected. From the *F* tables (Table 10.A.2) in the Appendix, we find that the critical value of *F* is given by $F_{0.025}$ (6,5) = 6.98. Hence, we conclude that the two variances are not significantly different (5% level of significance).

Step 3: Since the population variances are assumed to be the same, the variances of the two samples can now be combined to produce a single (pooled) estimate for the population variance σ^2. As in our example the sample sizes are not equal. Hence, a weighted average must be used to obtain the pooled estimate of the variance s^2, i.e.

$$s^2 = \frac{(n_1 - 1) \times (s_1)^2 + (n_2 - 1) \times (s_2)^2}{(n_1 + n_2 - 2)}$$

$$s^2 = \frac{(6) \times (0.3969) + (5) \times (0.1764)}{(7 + 6 - 2)}$$

$$s^2 = \frac{2.38 + 0.882}{(11)}$$

$$s^2 = \frac{3.262}{11} = 0.297$$

Step 4: We can now proceed to test for differences between the sample means. Provided the population means are normally distributed with a common variance, the distribution of differences between means is known as the *t*-distribution. Under the assumption that no difference exists between the two population mean (commonly referred to as the Null hypothesis), the standard score *t*-value (and therefore a probability value) can be found for any difference, as follows:

$$t = \frac{\overline{X}_1 - \overline{X}_2}{\sqrt{\dfrac{s^2}{n_1} + \dfrac{s^2}{n_2}}}$$

$$t = \frac{2.87 - 2.12}{\sqrt{\dfrac{0.297}{7} + \dfrac{0.297}{6}}}$$

$$t = \frac{0.75}{\sqrt{0.0424 + 0.0494}}$$

$$t = \frac{0.75}{\sqrt{0.0918}}$$

$$t = \frac{0.75}{0.303} = 2.48$$

The degrees of freedom associated with this value of t is determined from the estimate of the population variance in Step 3 above, i.e. df = $n_1 + n_2 - 2 = 11$. If the two sample means are similar, the value of t would be expected to be near zero. If a large value of t is obtained, the assumption of equal means should be rejected. From the t tables (Table 10.A.1) in the Appendix, we find that the critical value of t is given by $t_{0.025}$ (11) = 2.201. Hence, we conclude that the two means are significantly different (5% level of significance); that is, there is evidence to suggest that there is a significant difference in blood lactate concentrations between trained and untrained subjects whilst running at 70% of $\dot{V}O_2$max.

The above t-test is called a *two-tailed* test of significance. The assumption of equal means would have been rejected if the t-value was either greater than the critical $t_{.025}$ (df) value or less than $-t_{.025}$ (df). On the other hand, if we suspect that a difference between the mean blood concentrations *does* exist, the trained subjects would have lower scores than the untrained subjects, a *one-tailed* test can be used. For this one-tailed test, the critical value of t is given by $t_{.05}$ (11) = 1.796, allowing the 5% level of significance to remain in one tail of the t-distribution. In our example, the

observed t-value of 2.48 still exceeds this critical value of 1.796 and the conclusion remains the same.

The confidence interval to estimate the true mean difference between the population can be calculated in the following manner, where $\overline{X}_D$ is the difference between the two sample means (i.e. 0.75 mM), and where t is 2.201 as there are 11 degrees of freedom (Table 10.A.1).

$$\text{Lower bound} = \overline{X}_D - \left(t \times \sqrt{\left(\frac{s^2}{n_1} + \frac{s^2}{n_2}\right)} \right)$$

$$= 0.75 - (2.021 \times 0.303)$$
$$= 0.08 \text{ mM}$$

$$\text{Upper bound} = \overline{X}_D + \left(t \times \sqrt{\left(\frac{s^2}{n_1} + \frac{s^2}{n_2}\right)} \right)$$

$$= 0.75 + (2.021 \times 0.303)$$
$$= 1.42 \text{ mM}$$

There is a 95% chance that the actual mean difference between these two populations is encompassed by the confidence interval of 0.08 mM to 1.42 mM.

b) One-way ANOVA for k independent samples

One-way ANOVA, a natural extension to the t-test for two independent samples, is used to test the significance of the differences between the means from two or more (k) populations.

Example 4: The maximal oxygen uptake results (ml kg^{-1} min^{-1}) of five groups of elite Olympic sportsmen (n=6) are given in Table 10.8 (Johnson *et al.* 1998).

The analysis of variance is based on the supposition (or null hypothesis) that all N = 30 observations are distributed about the same mean population μ, with the same variance σ^2. Based on this assumption, we can make three different estimates of the population variance, σ^2, using the data in Table 10.8. The first is based on the total sum

Table 10.8 The maximal oxygen uptake results (ml kg⁻¹ min⁻¹) of five groups of elite Olympic sportsmen (n=6), results from Johnson et al. (1998)

Groups (j)	Middle Distance Runners	Long Distance Runners	Heavy-weight Rowers	Light-weight Rowers	Triathletes	Total
	73.8	79.5	65.1	71.1	76.6	
	79.9	76.7	67.7	67.9	69.9	
	75.5	80.4	69.1	67.1	69.3	
	72.5	82.3	61.5	73.8	73.6	
	82.2	81.8	63.1	75.7	68.8	
	78.3	75.9	64.1	74.4	63.2	
$T_j = \sum X$	462.2	476.6	390.6	430.0	421.4	T=2180.8
Mean X_j	77.03	79.43	65.10	71.67	70.23	72.69
$\sum X_j^2$	35674.7	37892.6	25468.8	30880.3	29700.7	159617
$(T_j)^2/n$	35604.8	37857.9	25428.1	30816.7	29596.3	158530

of squared deviations (TSS) from a common mean, given by

$$TSS = \sum (X - \overline{X})^2$$

$$= \sum X^2 - \frac{(\sum X)^2}{N}$$

$$= \sum X^2 - \frac{(T)^2}{N}$$

$$73.8^2 + 79.9^2 + 75.5^2 + \ldots + 68.8^2 + 63.2^2$$
$$- 2180.8^2/30$$
$$= 159617.1 - 158530 = 1087.1$$

This sum of squares has 29 degrees of freedom (df). The mean square (MS), 1087/29 = 37.48, is the first estimate of the population variance σ^2.

The second estimate is based on the pooled within-group variance, similar to the pooled estimate of the population variance used in the independent t-test above. For each group (j), we can estimate the within-group sum of squares as follows,

$$\sum (X - X_j)^2 = \sum X^2 - \frac{(\sum X^2)}{n}$$

$$= \sum X^2 - \frac{(T_j)^2}{n}$$

For example (see Table 10.8), the middle

distance runners within group sum-of-squares is 35674.7 − 35604.8 = 69.9. Since we can assume that all the variances within each group are the same, the sum of squared deviations within each group can be added, to give a quantity known as the within sum of squares (WSS),

$$WSS = 69.9 + 34.7 + 40.7 + 63.6 + 104.4$$
$$= 313.3,$$

and subsequently divided by its degrees of freedom, $k \times (n-1) = 5 \times 5 = 25$, to give the mean square within-groups (MS), 313.3/25=12.53, to estimate of the population variance.

The third estimate for σ^2 is based on the variance between the k group means X_j (77.03, 79.43, …, 70.23). The between groups' sum-of-squares (BSS) is estimated as

$$BSS = \sum (X_j - X)^2$$

$$= \sum \left(\frac{(T_j)^2}{n} - \frac{T^2}{N} \right)$$

$$= (462.2^2 + 476.6^2 + 390.6^2 + 430.0^2$$
$$+ 421.4^2)/6 - 2180.8^2/30 = 159303.8$$
$$- 158530 = 773.8$$

where

$$N = k \times n = 5 \times 6 = 30 \text{ (for } n = 6)$$

The 'between sum of squares' has k−1 = 4 df and hence the third estimate of the population variance σ^2 or mean square (MS) is 773.8/4= 193.45.

Clearly, these three estimates of the population variance σ^2, based on the TSS (σ^2=37.48), WSS (σ^2=12.53) and BSS (σ^2=193.45), would lead us to question the original supposition that the population variances were the same. We can formally test this assumption in precisely the same way that we were able to test the assumption of equal variances, prior to performing an independent *t*-test described in part (i), using the *F* ratio test. In this example, we would compare the variance estimate between-groups with the variance estimate within-groups, i.e. calculate the *F* ratio $F = 193.45/12.53 = 15.44$. Traditionally, this is set out in a standard table, known as the ANOVA table (Table 10.9), given below.

As with the independent *t*-test, the value of the *F* ratio, $F = 15.44$, has two degrees of freedom (df) parameters. The degrees of freedom associated with the between groups (BSS) variance is the number of groups (k) − 1 = 4, whilst the degrees of freedom associated with the the within groups (WSS) variance is k × (n−1) = 25. From the *F* tables (Table 10.A.2) we find that the critical values of *F* are given by $F_{.05}(4,25) = 2.76$ and $F_{.025}(4,25) = 3.35$. Hence, we conclude that the two variances are significantly different (using both 5% and 2.5% levels of significance) and we must reject the supposition that the variances are the same and conclude that the mean maximal oxygen uptake results (ml kg^{-1} min^{-1}) differ significantly between the five groups of elite Olympic sportsmen.

(c) The Mann-Whitney test for independent samples

If any of the normality or homogeneity of variance assumptions of the independent *t*-test are not satisfied, the Mann-Whitney test will provide a similar test but make no assumptions about the shape and size of the population distributions. It can also be used on ordinal data.

Example 5: The calf muscle's time-to-peak tension (TPT) values of eight male sprint-trained athletes and eight male endurance-trained athletes are given in Table 10.10. (A muscle's time-to-peak tension is thought to be an indicator of its fibre type).

The steps required to implement the Mann-Whitney test for independent samples are:

Step 1: Let n_1 be the size of the smaller group of scores, and n_2 be the size of the larger group. In our example, the sample sizes are equal. Hence, either group can be arbitrarily assigned as the group with n_1 scores.

Step 2: Rank the combined set of $n_1 + n_2$ results. Use rank 1 for the lowest, 2 for the next lowest, and so on (if two or more scores have the value, give each score the arithmetic mean of the shared ranks).

Step 3: Sum of the ranks of the group with n_1 scores. Let this sum be called R_1. For our example, the sprint trained athletes ranks sum to R_1=45.

Step 4; Calculate the Mann-Whitney U statistic as follows:

$$U = n_1 \times n_2 + \frac{n_1(n_1+1)}{2} - R_1$$

$$= 8 \times 8 + \frac{8(8+1)}{2} - 45$$

$$= 64 + 36 - 45 = 55$$

Step 5: Calculate U' statistic, given by

$$U' = n_1.n_2 - U$$
$$= 64 - 55 = 9$$

Step 6: Using the tables for the Mann-Whitney U statistic (Table 10.A.4 in the Appendix), assuming a two-tailed test (5% level of significance), we find the critical value is 13. If the observed value of U or U' (whichever is the smaller) is *less than or equal* to the critical value of U, the assumption that the two samples have identical distributions can be rejected.

In our example, $U' = 9$ (the smaller of 55

Table 10.9 ANOVA to compare the maximal oxygen uptake results (ml.kg^{-1}.min^{-1}) of five groups of elite Olympic sportsmen

Source of variation	df	SS	MS	F	P
BSS	4	773.8	193.45	15.44	<0.05
WSS	25	313.3	12.53		
TSS	29	1087.1			

where P is the probability, taken from the F Tables (Table 10.A.2).

Table 10.10 The calf muscle's time-to-peak tension recorded in milliseconds (ms) of elite sportsmen

	Sprint trained athletes (n^1= 8)		Endurance trained athletes (n$_2$= 8)	
	TPT	Rank	TPT	Rank
	110	4	118	12.5
	117	10	109	3
	111	5	122	15
	112	6	114	8
	117	10	117	10
	113	7	120	14
	106	1	124	16
	108	2	118	12.5
Total		45		91

and 9) is less than the critical value 13. Hence, there is a significant difference between the sprint-trained and endurance-trained athletes' time-to-peak tension of the calf muscle.

10.4.2 Drawing inferences from experimental data; correlated samples

In the previous section, we considered experiments that use independent groups of subjects. The problem with this type of design is that subjects can vary dramatically in their response to the task; that is, the differences between subjects tend to obscure the experimental effect. Fortunately 'correlated sample' experimental designs will overcome these problems of large variations between subjects. For example, between-subject variation can be 'partioned out' by adopting a repeated measures design, where the same subject performs both experimental conditions. Alternatively, subjects can be paired-off on the basis of relevant characteristics and the

subjects from each pair are then allocated at random to one or the other experimental condition. This type of experimental design is known as the *paired subjects design*.

Three of the most frequently used tests to investigate correlated sample experimental designs are:

- The *t*-test for correlated samples
- One-way ANOVA with repeated measures
- The Wilcoxon test for correlated samples

As in Section 10.4.1, these tests will be introduced using examples from kinanthropometry and exercise physiology.

a) The t-test for correlated samples
Example 6: Ten subjects were randomly selected to take part in an experiment to determine if isometric training can increase leg strength. The results are given in Table 10.11.

The requirements of the correlated *t*-test are as follows:

i)   That the differences between each pair of scores are drawn from a normal population.

ii) These differences are measured in the interval scale.

Clearly, the differences in the strength measurements can take any value within a continuous range, confirming an interval scale. A simple frequency table can be used to check the differences have an approximate normal distribution; that is, symmetric and bell shaped (in particular, no obvious outliers). Again, all these characteristics are described in Section 10.2.

Table 10.11 Leg strength in newtons (N) before and after isometric training

Before training (Xi)	After training (Yi)	Differences (Di = Yi – Xi)
480	484	4
669	676	7
351	355	4
450	447	–3
373	372	–1
320	322	2
612	625	13
510	517	7
480	485	5
492	502	10

The steps required to implement the *t*-test for correlated samples are as follows:

Step 1: Calculate the differences between each pair of scores, i.e. $D_i = X_i - Y_i$. Care should be taken to subtract consistently, recording any negative differences.

Step 2: Calculate the mean and standard deviation of the differences D_i using the unbiased estimate for the population standard deviation, i.e. $s = \Sigma (D_i - D)^2 /(n-1)$. In our example the mean and standard deviation was D=4.8 and s=4.8.

Step 3: Calculate the *t* standard score given by

$$t = \frac{D}{\left(\dfrac{s}{\sqrt{n}}\right)}$$

$$= \frac{4.8}{\left(\dfrac{4.8}{\sqrt{10}}\right)}$$

$$= \frac{4.8}{\left(\dfrac{4.8}{3.16}\right)} = \frac{4.8}{1.52}$$

$$= 3.16$$

Step 4: The degrees of freedom associated with this value of *t* is determined from the estimate

of the population variance in Step 3 above, i.e. df = n–1 = 9. If the two experimental conditions produce a similar response to the given task, the differences D_i will be relatively small and the value of *t* would be expected to be near zero. If a large value of *t* is obtained, the assumption of equal differences should be rejected. From the *t* tables (Table 10.A.1) we find that the critical value of *t* is given by $t_{.025}(9) = 2.262$. Hence, we conclude that the two experimental conditions are significantly different (5% level of significance); i.e. it would appear that leg strength measurements before and after isometric training are significantly different. Clearly, by observing the differences in Table 10.11, the leg strength had improved, on average, by 4.8 N.

As with the tests for independent samples, if we assume that isometric training will improve leg strength, a *one-tailed* test can be used. For this one-tailed test, the critical value of *t* is given by $t_{.05}(9) = 1.833$, allowing the 5% level of significance to remain in one tail of the *t*-distribution. In this case, the observed *t*-value of 3.16 still exceeds this critical value of 1.833 and our conclusion remains the same.

Similar to the independent *t*-test, a confidence interval can be calculated to give an estimation of the actual population mean difference. The t-value used in the calculation is 2.262 (see Table 10.A.1).

$$\text{Lower bound} = D - \left(t \times \left(\frac{s}{\sqrt{n}} \right) \right)$$

$$= 4.8 - (2.262 \times 1.52)$$
$$= 1.36 \text{ N}$$

$$\text{Upper bound} = D + \left(t \times \left(\frac{s}{\sqrt{n}} \right) \right)$$

$$= 4.8 + (2.262 \times 1.52)$$
$$= 8.24 \text{ N}$$

(b) One-way ANOVA with repeated measures.

Many experiments in kinanthropometry and exercise physiology require more than two repeated measurements to be taken from the same subjects.

Example 7: Eight volunteers take part in a study to assess the effect of a six-month recreational cycling programme on weight control. Estimates of percentage body fat were determined at the beginning of the study (baseline), after 3 months and at the end of the study, after 6 months. The results are given in Table 10.12.

The rows are the eight subjects ($n=8$), denoted by the subscript i, and columns are treatments or time points ($k = 3$), denoted by the subscript j. Note that the total number of observations (N) is 24. In effect, the one-way analysis of variance with repeated measures is a two-way ANOVA with three sources of variation/variance and associated sums of squares. These are the sums of squares due to the subjects (rows), treatments (columns) and an interaction (or error). These can be calculated as follows:

Rows effects (subjects)

$$\frac{\left(\sum T_i^2 \right)}{k} - \frac{(T)^2}{N}$$

$$= \frac{(90.22 + 77.82 + \ldots + 105.82)}{3} - \frac{(774.4)^2}{24}$$

$$= \frac{(77143.74)}{3} - \frac{(599695.36)}{24}$$

$$= 25714.58 - 24987.3$$
$$= 727.28$$

Columns effects (treatments or time)

$$\frac{\left(\sum T_j^2 \right)}{n} - \frac{(T)^2}{N}$$

$$= \frac{\left(264.7^2 + 257.8^2 + 251.9^2 \right)}{8} - \frac{(774.4)^2}{24}$$

$$= \frac{199980.54}{8} - \frac{599695.36}{24}$$

$$= 24997.57 - 24987.3$$
$$= 10.27$$

Interaction (error)

$$\left(\sum X^2 \right) - \frac{\left(\sum T_i^2 \right)}{k} - \frac{\left(\sum T_j^2 \right)}{n} + \frac{(T)^2}{N}$$

$$= (31.6^2 + 26.5^2 + \ldots + 35.27^2) - 25714.58$$
$$- 24997.57 + 24987.3$$
$$= 25735.0 - 25714.58 - 24997.57 +$$
$$24987.3$$
$$= 10.15$$

As with the one-way ANOVA for k independent samples, these results can be summarised in an ANOVA table (Table 10.13).

The data from this study are presumed to represent a random sample of subjects observed under three different treatment conditions or time points. The term used to describe such a study with repeated measurements is known as a mixed model; that is, the treatments are thought to be a fixed effect whilst the subjects are thought to be a random effect. The F ratio for the treatment or time effects is $F = 7.08$. From the F tables (Tables 10.A.2 and 10.A.3) we find that the critical values of F are given by $F_{.05} (2,14) = 3.74$ and $F_{.025} (2,14) = 4.86$. Clearly, the time effect F ratio (7.08) exceeds both these

Table 10.12 Estimates of percentage (%) body fat at baseline, 3 months and 6 months into the cycling programme

	Baseline	*3 months*	*6 months*	*Mean (X_i.)*	*Total (T_i.)*
Subject 1	31.6	30.5	28.1	30.07	90.2
Subject 2	26.5	25.8	25.5	25.93	77.8
Subject 3	35.9	34.0	32.1	34.00	102.0
Subject 4	35.1	34.6	34.9	34.87	104.6
Subject 5	43.2	40.9	41.0	41.70	125.1
Subject 6	33.8	33.1	33.4	33.43	100.3
Subject 7	22.5	23.8	22.3	22.87	68.6
Subject 8	36.1	35.1	34.6	35.27	105.8
Mean ($X_{.j}$)	33.09	32.23	31.49	32.27	
Total ($T_{.j}$)	264.7	257.8	251.9		T=774.4

Table 10.13 ANOVA table to compare the estimates of percentage body fat (%) recorded during the cycling programme

Source of variation	*df*	*SS*	*MS*	*F*	*P*
Treatments or time	2	10.27	5.135	7.08	<0.05
Subjects	7	727.28	103.897		
Interaction/error	14	10.15	0.725		
Total	23	747.70			

where P is the probability, taken from the F Tables (Table 10.A.2).

critical values. Hence, we can conclude that the mean estimated percentage body fat of the subjects has declined significantly during the 6-month recreational cycling programme (from 33.09% at baseline, to 32.23% at 3 months, and 31.49% at the end of the study). Note that, since the subjects constitute a random factor, there is no meaningful test of row (subject) effects.

An additional assumption associated with repeated measures ANOVA is that of compound symmetry or 'sphericity' of the covariance matrix. Discussion of this topic is beyond the scope of this book, but interested readers are directed towards the guidelines provided by Atkinson (2001) for exploring and correcting for violations of this assumption. For cases in which this assumption is extremely violated, readers may be interested in adopting the 'analysis of summary statistics' approach (Matthews *et al.* 1990), which involves the recording of statistics which describe the nature of the repeated measures

factor and analyzing these separately. For example, rather than treating 10 measurements over time as a repeated measures factor in an ANOVA model, the researcher could record the peak value, mean and time of peak value to describe the time factor. These statistics could then be compared between groups with a two-sample *t*-test for example.

(c) The Wilcoxon test for correlated samples

If the normality requirement of the correlated *t*-test is not satisfied, the Wilcoxon matched-pairs sign-ranks test will provide the same function as the correlated *t*-test but would make no assumptions about the shape of the population distributions.

Example 8: A study was designed to investigate the effects of an aerobics class on reducing percentage body fat. The percentage body fat measurements of 10 subjects, before and after the aerobics course, are given in Table 10.14.

Table 10.14 The percentage body fat, before and after an aerobics course, and the corresponding differences and ranked differences (ignoring signs)

Subject	Before (X_i)	After (Y_i)	Differences (D_i = Y_i − X_i)	Ranks
1	34.4	33.5	−0.9	4
2	37.9	34.7	−3.2	10
3	35.2	35.3	0.1	1
4	37.2	34.2	−3.0	9
5	45.1	43.9	−1.2	5
6	34.1	35.7	1.6	6
7	36.0	34.2	−1.8	7
8	38.9	36.2	−2.7	8
9	36.1	35.9	−0.2	2
10	28.3	27.8	−0.5	3

The steps required to implement the Wilcoxon test for correlated samples are as follows:

Step 1: Calculate the differences between each pair of scores, i.e. $D_i = X_i - Y_i$. As with the correlated *t*-test, care should be taken to subtract consistently, recording any negative differences.

Step 2: Ignoring the sign, rank the differences using rank 1 for the lowest, 2 for the next lowest, and so on (if two or more differences have the value, give each score the arithmetic mean of the shared ranks. Any pairs with differences equal to zero are eliminated from the test).

Step 3: Sum of the ranks of the less frequent sign and calling this sum T. For our example, the positive ranks are less frequent and give $T = 1 + 6 = 7$.

Step 4: Using the critical tables for the Wilcoxon T statistic (Table 10.A.5 in the Appendix), assuming a two-tailed test (5% level of significance), we find the critical value (n = 10) is 8. If the observed value of T is *less than or equal* to the critical value of T, the assumption that the experimental conditions are the same can be rejected.

In our example, the observed T = 7 value is less than the critical value 8. Hence, there is a significant reduction in percentage body fat during the aerobics course.

10.4.3 Multifactorial analysis of experimental data

Sometimes experimenters may want to examine the influence of a number of independent variables on a dependent variable. To illustrate this we will use data taken from an investigation by Marginson *et al.* (2005), which was designed to compare the symptoms experienced by adult males (n = 10) and boys (n = 10) to exercise-induced muscle damage. As part of their investigation, they measured the isometric strength of the quadriceps for both age groups at six different knee angles (20, 40, 60, 80, 90 and 100° away from full extension).

Such a design is defined as a two-factor experiment, since there is one factor of *age* and another factor of *knee angle*. The comparison of the two age groups is classed as a 'between subjects' factor. The time factor is a 'within-subjects' or 'repeated measures' factor, since all subjects are tested more than once. The numbers of groups or repeated measures within the experimental factors are known as the 'levels.' In the 'between subject' factor there are two levels (men and boys), whereas in the within-subjects factor there are six levels. The appropriate statistical test in this context is a factorial ANOVA, more specifically, a two-way mixed model ANOVA.

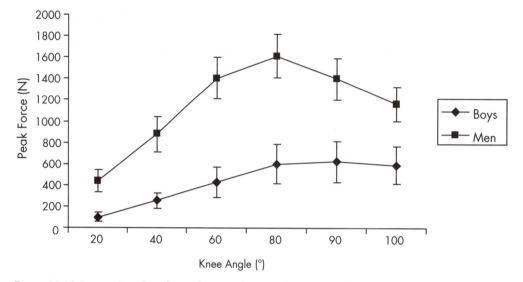

Figure 10.10 Interaction plot of age x knee angle on peak isometric force production in the quadriceps (Marginson *et al*. 2005).

Generally, in multifactorial experiments, the experimenters are interested in the 'main effect' of each factor together with 'interactions' between factors. These are given as part of the results of a factorial analysis of variance. A significant main effect infers that the factor in question has a significant influence on the dependent variable, irrespective of the influence of any other factors in the experiment. For example, a 'knee angle main effect' in the above study implies that isometric force has changed significantly across the difference angles. An interaction between factors describes the combined influence of the independent variables. Main effects and interactions should be examined together to arrive at conclusions. A graphical method of interpreting the results of multifactorial analyses is the 'interaction plot' (Figure 10.10). In the above example, there was a significant interaction of age and knee angle on isometric force ($F_{(2.01, 37.02)} = 33.17$, $P < 0.05$). Examination of the interaction plot (see Figure 10.10) reveals that the men and the boys responded differently across the range of knee angles. The men showed a much steeper increase in force production when the knee angle increased from 20°

to 80°, whereas the increase for the boys was much less. After 80° the men's force production declines but the boys' remains at a similar level. There were also main effects for age ($F_{(1,18)} = 148.85$, $P < 0.05$) and angle ($F_{(2.01,37.02)} = 198.05$, $P < 0.05$). In a main effect the mean value for each level of the factor are compared. In the main effect for age two means being compared, an overall mean for the boys (432 N) and one for men (1150 N). The influence of knee angle is not considered. The same applies for the main effect of knee angle. Six separate means are calculated and compared, one for each angle, ignoring the influence of age. If there is a significant main effect where there are more than two levels, it can be examined further by the use of post-hoc testing in a similar manner to its one-way ANOVA equivalent. In the case of knee angle, pairwise comparisons with a bonferroni correction could be used. The main effect for age does not need further post-hoc analysis, as only two means are being compared; but if there was a third level, Tukey tests could be used to determined where the significant differences occurred. SPSS does not allow you to run post–hoc tests on significant interactions. Some interaction effects may be more complicated than this example, and therefore may need multiple comparisons to unravel the results (Kinnear and Gray 1997). It is stressed that, ideally, such comparisons should be decided a priori with a specific research question in mind.

10.4.4 The SPSS commands to illustrate the methods of Section 10.4

To distinguish between the groups in between groups designs SPSS uses a coding column (see Figure 10.10). The independent *t*-test, Mann-Whitney *U* test, one-way ANOVA for k independent samples and Mixed Design ANOVA will all require a coding column. The *t*-test for independent samples is obtained in SPSS as follows.

1 Input all the Lactate data from Example 3 into the second column of the *Data View* sheet (see Figure 10.11).

2 Double click 'VAR00002' at the top of the second column; this takes you on to the *Variable View* sheet.

3 Type 'Lactate' into the Name column, this will name the column in the Data View sheet.

4 Click on the 'Data View' tab at the bottom of the sheet

5 Input the number '1' seven times in the first seven rows of VAR00001 and the number '2' in the next six rows.

6 Double click 'VAR00001', this takes you on to the *Variable View* sheet, type 'Groups' into the Name column.

7 Click on the 'None' in the Values column. Click on the grey square on the right hand side of the box.

8 In Value type '1', in Value Label type 'Untrained' and then click add. Now type '2' in the Value, and in the Value Label type 'Trained' and then click add. Click *OK*.

9 Select *Analyze, Compare Means* and *Independent-Samples t-test*. Move the variable 'Groups' from the left window to the Grouping Variables: window with

the arrow button. Now click on *Define Groups* ... Put the number '1' in group one and the number '2' in group 2, click *continue* to return to the previous box.

10 Move the variable 'Lactate' from the left window to the Test Variable[s]: window with the arrow button. Now click *OK*.

In columns 2 and 3 of the output table (see Figure 10.12) the *F* value and the probability value (sig) for the Levene's Test of Equality Variances are provided. Similar to the Variance Ratio test presented earlier, the Levene's test is another method of checking the assumption that both samples have come from populations with equal variances. If the sig value was below 0.05, it is more appropriate to use the Equal Variances not assumed row. However, in this case the sig value was above 0.05 at 0.529. There was no significant difference between variances; therefore, the output in the Equal Variances assumed row can be used.

Independent t test [DataSet2] - SPSS Data

File Edit View Data Transform Analyze Graphs

13 : Lactate   2

	Groups	Lactate	var
1	1.00	2.50	
2	1.00	2.90	
3	1.00	1.90	
4	1.00	3.60	
5	1.00	2.90	
6	1.00	3.70	
7	1.00	2.60	
8	2.00	1.80	
9	2.00	2.60	
10	2.00	2.40	
11	2.00	1.50	
12	2.00	2.40	
13	2.00	2.00	
14			

Figure 10.11 An example of how to code between groups in SPSS.

Independent Samples Test

		Levene's Test for Equality of Variances		t-test for Equality of Means						
		F	Sig.	t	df	Sig. (2-tailed)	Mean Difference	Std. Error Difference	95% Confidence Interval of the Difference	
									Lower	Upper
Lactate	Equal variances assumed	.423	.529	2.491	11	.030	.75476	.30299	.08788	1.42165
	Equal variances not assumed			2.572	10.481	.027	.75476	.29350	.10485	1.40467

Figure 10.12 SPSS output for an independent *t*-test.

The remaining columns show the same statistics as were calculated in Section 10.4.1 (a) and therefore have the same interpretation. The probability value returned in the column 'Sig (2 tailed)' refers to the exact probability of gaining a *t*-value of 2.491 when there are 11 degrees of freedom. As this is below 0.05 (5%), there was a significant difference between the trained and untrained.

For the one-way ANOVA for k independent samples, input the data into SPSS in a similar manner to the independent *t*-test. For example 4 used in Section 10.4.1 (b) there should be 2 columns and 30 rows of data in the SPSS Data View Sheet. The first column should identify the groups, so there should be six of the each of the numbers 1, 2, 3, 4 and 5 the column (where 1 = middle distance runners, 2 = long distance runners, etc) name this column Groups. The second column should contain all of the $\dot{V}O_2$max data, and use VO2max as the column name.

1   Select *Analyze, Compare Means* and *One Way ANOVA*. Move the variable Groups from the left window to the Factor: window with the arrow button.
2   Move the variable VO2max from the left window to the Dependent List: window with the arrow button.
3   Now click on *Options ...* Select Homogeneity of Variance, Descriptives and Means plot, click *continue* to return to the previous box.
4   Now click on *Post Hoc ...* Select Tukey, click *continue* to return to the previous box. Now click *OK*.

The Levene's test (see the first table in Figure 10.13) shows that there was no violation of the assumption of Homogeneity of Variance. There was a significant difference between the 5 means of the different groups as the sig value in the ANOVA table was below 0.05. A post hoc test was run to determine where the exact differences occur between the five groups. In this instance the Tukey test was used. (For descriptions of the different types of post-hoc tests, see Howell 2007.) SPSS produces a table where each row takes one of the groups in the experiment and determines the mean difference between that group and each of the other groups individually (see column 2 of the Multiple Comparisons table). It then determines whether each of these comparisons was statistically significant (see column 4 of Multiple Comparisons table). For instance, row two of the table compares the middle distance runners to the other four groups. Sig values below 0.05 identify where the significant differences occurred. For example, the mean $\dot{V}O_2$max of the middle distance runners was significantly higher than the Heavy-weight rowers and the Triathletes.

Overall, the long distance runners $\dot{V}O_2$max was significantly higher than the all of the other groups apart from the middle distance runners. The $\dot{V}O_2$max of the heavy-weight rowers was significantly lower than all the other groups except for the Triathletes. The middle distance runners $\dot{V}O_2$max was significantly higher than the heavy-weight rowers and the Triathletes.

The method of inputting the data for the Mann-Whitney test for independent samples is the same as for the previous two tests as

Test of Homogeneity of Variances

VO$_2$max

Levene Statistic	df1	df2	Sig.
.510	4	25	.729

ANOVA

VO$_2$max

	Sum of Squares	df	Mean Square	F	Sig.
Between Groups	774.165	4	193.541	15.442	.000
Within Groups	313.333	25	12.533		
Total	1087.499	29			

Multiple Comparisons

Dependent Variable: VO$_2$max

Tukey HSD

(I) Groups	(J) Groups	Mean Difference (I-J)	Std. Error	Sig.	95% Confidence Interval	
					Lower Bound	Upper Bound
Middle Distance Runners	Long Distance Runners	-2.40000	2.04396	.766	-8.4029	3.6029
	Heavy-weight Rowers	11.93333 *	2.04396	.000	5.9305	17.9362
	Light-weight Rowers	5.36667	2.04396	.096	-.6362	11.3695
	Triathletes	6.80000 *	2.04396	.021	.7971	12.8029
Long Distance Runners	Middle Distance Runners	2.40000	2.04396	.766	-3.6029	8.4029
	Heavy-weight Rowers	14.33333 *	2.04396	.000	8.3305	20.3362
	Light-weight Rowers	7.76667 *	2.04396	.007	1.7638	13.7695
	Triathletes	9.20000 *	2.04396	.001	3.1971	15.2029
Heavy-weight Rowers	Middle Distance Runners	-11.93333 *	2.04396	.000	-17.9362	-5.9305
	Long Distance Runners	-14.33333 *	2.04396	.000	-20.3362	-8.3305
	Light-weight Rowers	-6.56667 *	2.04396	.027	-12.5695	-.5638
	Triathletes	-5.13333	2.04396	.120	-11.1362	.8695
Light-weight Rowers	Middle Distance Runners	-5.36667	2.04396	.096	-11.3695	.6362
	Long Distance Runners	-7.76667 *	2.04396	.007	-13.7695	-1.7638
	Heavy-weight Rowers	6.56667	2.04396	.027	.5638	12.5695
	Triathletes	1.43333	2.04396	.954	-4.5695	7.4362
Triathletes	Middle Distance Runners	-6.80000 *	2.04396	.021	-12.8029	-.7971
	Long Distance Runners	-9.20000 *	2.04396	.001	-15.2029	-3.1971
	Heavy-weight Rowers	5.13333	2.04396	.120	-.8695	11.1362
	Light-weight Rowers	-1.43333	2.04396	.954	-7.4362	4.5695

*. The mean difference is significant at the .05 level.

Figure 10.13 SPSS output for the one-way ANOVA for k independent samples.

they are all between subjects designs, so input the TPT data for the example 5 given in section 10.4.1 (c) into the Data View sheet. In this example there should be two columns and 16 rows in use with the first column identifying the groups (1 = sprint-trained and 2 = endurance trained) and the second column containing the TPT data. Name the first column 'groups' and name the second column 'TPT'.

1 Select *Analyze, Nonparametric Tests* and *2 Independent Samples.* Move the variable Groups from the left window to the Grouping Variables: window with the arrow button. Now click on *Define Groups* … Put the number '1' in group one and the number '2' in group 2, click *continue* to return to the previous box.

2 Move the variable TPT from the left window to the Test Variable List: window

Test Statistics [b]

	TPT
Mann-Whitney U	9.000
Wilcoxon W	45.000
Z	−2.424
Asymp. Sig. (2-tailed)	.015
Exact Sig. [2*(1-tailed Sig.)]	.015 [a]

a. Not corrected for ties.

b. Grouping Variable: Groups

Figure 10.14 SPSS output for the Mann-Whitney test for independent samples.

with the arrow button. Make sure that the box next to Mann-Whitney *U* is selected. Then click *OK*.

As shown in Figure 10.14, SPSS produces the Mann-Whitney *U* test statistic ($U = 9$) in the top row of the table. For a total sample size of 40 or under, SPSS provides the exact probability of gaining a *U* value of that magnitude in the row labelled 'Exact Sig. [2*(1-tailed Sig.)]'. As the probability value was below 0.05, we conclude there was a significant difference between the sprint trained and endurance trained athletes' time-to-peak tension of the calf muscle. For larger sample sizes (N>20 for one or both samples), instead of using the exact probability of gaining *U* to determine whether a significant difference exists, the normal distribution curve can be used. This is because the *U* distribution approximates a normal distribution with the use of larger samples. To determine whether there was a significant difference the *U* value is converted into a Z value (see Cohen and Holliday, 1982). SPSS returns the Z value and the probability of gaining that value is reported in the row labelled 'Asymp. Sig. (2 tailed).'

The method for inputting data for repeated measures (within subject) designs is different than for independent groups (between subject) designs. The columns in the Data View also represent repeated measures of a dependent variable. The rows in the data file represent an individual subject's scores on each of the variables. Therefore, we do not need to code these groups; instead, we put the repeated measures into different columns.

The first example of a repeated measures design in Section 10.4.2 (a) demonstrated the calculation of the *t*-test for correlated samples. Ten subjects were randomly selected to take part in an experiment to determine if isometric training can increase leg strength. They had their leg strength measured before and after the training programme.

1 Input the 'Before' data from Table 10.11 into the first ten rows of column one, in the Variable View Sheet input 'Before' into the name column. Input the 'After' data into the first ten rows of column 2 in the Data View sheet and name the column 'After'.

2 Select *Analyze, Compare Means* and *Paired-Samples t-test*.

3 Select both the variables in the left window (i.e. click on both Before and After) and move them to the Paired Variables: window using the arrow button. Now click *OK*.

The output table (see Figure 10.15) gives the same values as were calculated in Section 10.4.2 (a), but will only return the significance value for a two-tailed test. To determine the one-tailed probability, divide the two-tailed probability by 2 (Field 2005). In this instance, the one-tailed probability is 0.006; still less than 0.05. The negative sign before the *t*-value is due to the order of the columns in SPSS. If the order of the columns had been reversed the *t*-value would have been positive, similar to the worked example.

The one-way ANOVA with repeated measures is used when there are more than two repeated measures. Therefore, if we input the data for Example 7 into the Data View sheet we will have three columns (i.e. baseline, 3 months and 6 months) and eight rows as there were eight subjects.

1 Input the Baseline data from Table 10.12 into column 1; name the column

Paired Samples Test

		Paired Differences							
					95% Confidence Interval of the Difference				
		Mean	Std. Deviation	Std. Error Mean	Lower	Upper	t	df	Sig. (2-tailed)
Pair 1	Before – After	–4.80000	4.80278	1.51877	–8.23570	–1.36430	–3.160	9	.012

Figure 10.15 SPSS output for the *t*-test correlated samples.

'Baseline'. Input the data at 3 months and name the column 'Three.' Input the data at 6 months into column 3, name the column 'Six.'

2 Select *Analyze, General Linear Model* and *Repeated Measures*. Name your Within-Subject factor as 'Time,' identify the number of levels at 3. Click *Add* and then click *Define*.

3 Select the 3 variables in the left window (i.e. Baseline, Three and Six) and move them to the Within-Subject: window using the arrow button.

4 Now click on *Options* ... Move 'Time' into the Display Means for: box, select the Compare Main Effects Box, select Bonferroni as the confidence interval adjustment. Click *continue* to return to the previous box. Now click *OK*.

The initial table of interest from the SPSS output is the one entitled Mauchly's Test of Sphericity. The Greenhouse-Geisser Epsilon is the main value of interest. Atkinson (2001) recommended that if Greenhouse-Geisser Epsilon is greater than 0.75 then the Huynh-Feldt corrected output should be used from the Tests of Within-Subjects Effects Table (see Figure 10.16). If the Greenhouse-Geisser Epsilon value is below 0.75 then it is the Greenhouse-Geisser corrected output that should be used. In this instance, the value is 0.841.

SPSS will not perform post hoc tests on repeated measures ANOVA. To determine where the significant differences are it can perform pairwise comparsions. The Pairwise Comparisons table is interpreted in the same way as the Multiple Comparisons table

produced for the one-way ANOVA for k independent samples described earlier in this section.

The nonparametric equivalent of the *t*-test for correlated samples is the Wilcoxon test. The data are inputted in exactly the same manner as their *t*-test equivalent. Input the Before and After data from example 8 (see Table 10.14) into SPSS.

1 Select *Analyze, Nonparametric Tests* and *2 Related Samples*.

2 Select both the variables in the left window (i.e. Before and After) and move them to the Test Pair(s) List: window using the arrow button.

3 Make sure that the tick box next to Wilcoxon is selected. Now click *Exact* and change the setting to 'Exact'. Click *Continue* to return to the previous box. Now click *OK*.

The Wilcoxon *t*-value is the lowest sum of the ranks in the Ranks table (see Figure 10.17). Similar to the Mann-Whitney *U* test, with smaller samples the exact significance value should be used to determine if there was a significant difference, see the 'Exact Sig. (2-tailed)' row of the Test Statistics table. For larger samples (N>25, see Cohen and Holliday 1982), a Z approximation can be used which means the probability value in the row labelled 'Asymp. Sig. (2-tailed)' should be used to assess statistical significance.

To perform a two-way mixed model ANOVA input the data from Figure 10.18 and label the columns as shown in the figure.

1 Select *Analyze, General Linear Model* and *Repeated Measures*. Name your

Mauchly's Test of Sphericity[b]

Measure: MEASURE_1

Within Subjects Effect	Mauchly's W	Approx. Chi-Square	df	Sig.	Epsilon[a]		
					Greenhouse-Geisser	Huynh-Feldt	Lower-bound
Time	.811	1.254	2	.534	.841	1.000	.500

Tests the null hypothesis that the error covariance matrix of the orthonormalized transformed dependent variables is proportional to an identity matrix.

[a.] May be used to adjust the degrees of freedom for the averaged tests of significance. Corrected tests are displayed in the Tests of Within-Subjects Effects table.

[b.] Design: Intercept
Within Subjects Design: Time

Tests of Within-Subjects Effects

Measure: MEASURE_1

Source		Type III Sum of Squares	df	Mean Square	F	Sig.
Time	Sphericity Assumed	10.261	2	5.130	7.084	.007
	Greenhouse-Geisser	10.261	1.683	6.098	7.084	.012
	Huynh-Feldt	10.261	2.000	5.130	7.084	.007
	Lower-bound	10.261	1.000	10.261	7.084	.032
Error(Time)	Sphericity Assumed	10.139	14	.724		
	Greenhouse-Geisser	10.139	11.778	.861		
	Huynh-Feldt	10.139	14.000	.724		
	Lower-bound	10.139	7.000	1.448		

Pairwise Comparisons

Measure: MEASURE_1

(I) Time	(J) Time	Mean Difference (I-J)	Std. Error	Sig. [a]	95% Confidence Interval for Difference[a]	
					Lower Bound	Upper Bound
1	2	.863	.380	.172	-.325	2.050
	3	1.600 *	.510	.049	.006	3.194
2	1	-.863	.380	.172	-2.050	.325
	3	.738	.373	.266	-.430	1.905
3	1	-1.600 *	.510	.049	-3.194	-.006
	2	-.738	.373	.266	-1.905	.430

Based on estimated marginal means

*. The mean difference is significant at the .05 level.

[a.] Adjustment for multiple comparisons: Bonferroni.

Figure 10.16 SPSS output for the one-way ANOVA with repeated measures.

Within-Subject factor as 'angle', and identify the number of levels as 6. Click *Add* and then click *Define*.

2 Move 'group' into the Between-Subjects Factor(s): Box. Move the six remaining variables into the Within-Subjects Variable box.

3 Now click on *Options* ... Move group,

angle and group*angle into the Display Means for: box, select the Compare Main Effects Box, select Bonferroni as the confidence interval adjustment. Click *continue* to return to the previous box.

4 Select *Plots*. Place angle in the Horizontal Axis: box, and place group into the separate lines: box, press add. Click *continue*

Ranks

		N	Mean Rank	Sum of Ranks
After – Before	Negative Ranks	8 [a]	6.00	48.00
	Positive Ranks	2 [b]	3.50	7.00
	Ties	0 [c]		
	Total	10		

a. After < Before
b. After > Before
c. After = Before

Test Statistics [b]

	After – Before
Z	–2.090 [a]
Asymp. Sig. (2-tailed)	.037
Exact Sig. (2-tailed)	.037
Exact Sig. (1-tailed)	.019
Point Probability	.005

a. Based on positive ranks.
b. Wilcoxon Signed Ranks Test

Figure 10.17 SPSS output for the Wilcoxon test for correlated samples.

*strength boys v men by knee flexion angle [DataSet1] - SPSS Data Editor

File   Edit   View   Data   Transform   Analyze   Graphs   Utilities   Add-ons   Window   Help

1 : group   1

	group	b1str20	b1str40	b1str60	b1str80	b1str90	b1str100	var
1	1.00	73.0	215.5	491.5	680.0	730.0	638.0	
2	1.00	93.0	235.5	394.0	554.0	633.5	627.0	
3	1.00	188.0	408.0	509.0	798.5	798.5	747.0	
4	1.00	70.5	210.0	389.0	589.0	624.5	663.5	
5	1.00	119.0	240.0	408.0	569.0	569.0	538.0	
6	1.00	86.5	218.0	218.0	378.5	458.0	412.0	
7	1.00	72.0	197.5	371.5	505.5	479.5	542.5	
8	1.00	99.5	256.0	537.5	740.0	726.0	615.0	
9	1.00	129.0	352.0	700.5	903.0	950.0	878.0	
10	1.00	43.0	185.5	251.5	293.5	266.0	255.5	
11	2.00	506.5	745.5	1195.5	1573.5	1438.0	1137.0	
12	2.00	395.0	870.0	1339.0	1507.0	1186.5	943.5	
13	2.00	448.0	1005.0	1644.5	1875.0	1501.5	1127.0	
14	2.00	314.0	600.0	1085.0	1146.0	1063.5	976.0	
15	2.00	442.0	852.5	1334.0	1630.0	1455.0	1258.0	
16	2.00	579.0	1125.0	1526.0	1680.0	1527.5	1253.3	
17	2.00	604.0	1033.0	1538.5	1502.5	1187.0	1040.5	
18	2.00	427.5	985.0	1486.5	1730.0	1518.0	1341.5	
19	2.00	284.0	690.5	1275.0	1686.5	1439.5	1122.5	
20	2.00	339.5	885.0	1647.5	1827.0	1696.5	1446.0	
21								

Figure 10.18 Data entered into the SPSS Data View sheet for the two-way mixed design ANOVA. Where 1.00 = Boys, 2 = Men in the column labelled group (Marginson *et al.* 2005).

Mauchly's Test of Sphericity [b]

Measure: MEASURE_1

Within Subjects Effect	Mauchly's W	Approx. Chi-Square	df	Sig.	Epsilon [a]		
					Greenhouse-Geisser	Huynh-Feldt	Lower-bound
angle	.015	67.210	14	.000	.411	.491	.200

Tests the null hypothesis that the error covariance matrix of the orthonormalized transformed dependent variables is proportional to an identity matrix.

a. May be used to adjust the degrees of freedom for the averaged tests of significance. Corrected tests are displayed in the Tests of Within-Subjects Effects table.

b. Design: Intercept+group
   Within Subjects Design: angle

Tests of Within-Subjects Effects

Measure: MEASURE_1

Source		Type III Sum of Squares	df	Mean Square	F	Sig.
angle	Sphericity Assumed	10002328.0	5	2000465.601	198.046	.000
	Greenhouse-Geisser	10002328.0	2.057	4863630.064	198.046	.000
	Huynh-Feldt	10002328.0	2.454	4075312.657	198.046	.000
	Lower-bound	10002328.0	1.000	10002328.01	198.046	.000
angle * group	Sphericity Assumed	1675082.760	5	335016.552	33.167	.000
	Greenhouse-Geisser	1675082.760	2.057	814508.669	33.167	.000
	Huynh-Feldt	1675082.760	2.454	682489.713	33.167	.000
	Lower-bound	1675082.760	1.000	1675082.760	33.167	.000
Error(angle)	Sphericity Assumed	909090.935	90	10101.010		
	Greenhouse-Geisser	909090.935	37.018	24558.072		
	Huynh-Feldt	909090.935	44.179	20577.597		
	Lower-bound	909090.935	18.000	50505.052		

Measure: MEASURE_1

Tests of Between-Subjects Effects

Transformed Variable: Average

Source	Type III Sum of Squares	df	Mean Square	F	Sig.
Intercept	75117793.9	1	75117793.93	722.508	.000
group	15475630.0	1	15475629.99	148.850	.000
Error	1871426.021	18	103968.112		

Figure 10.19 SPSS output for the two-way mixed model ANOVA from the study of Marginson *et al.* (2005).

to return to the previous box. Now click *OK*.

The SPSS output in Figure 10.19 contains the tables required to identify the main effect for age (Tests of Between-Subject Effects), the main effect for knee angle and the age × knee angle interaction (Tests of Within-Subject

Effects). The Mauchly's Test of Sphericity table provides the relevant Greenhouse-Geisser epsilon value (0.41) to determine if violations to sphericity need to be corrected for. In this case, Greenhouse-Geisser line of the output was the most appropriate.

Stages 3 and 4 in the above instructions will produce additional output that is not shown in Figure 10.19. Stage 3 will provide means for the different levels of each main effect and will run pairwise comparisons between them. Stage 4 will produce an interaction plot to allow for interpretation of the interaction.

10.5 SUMMARY

This chapter has illustrated some of the basic procedures which are frequently adopted to describe and interpret data from exercise physiology and kinanthropometry studies. For additional information on some of the issues associated with studies involving multiple regression and experimental designs in exercise physiology and kinanthropometry research, you are referred to Eston and Rowlands (2000), Winter *et al.* (2001) and Atkinson and Nevill (2001).

APPENDIX: CRITICAL VALUES

Table 10.A.1 The critical values of the *t*-distribution

df	0.10	0.05	Level of significance for one-tailed test 0.025	0.01	0.005	0.0005
	0.20	0.10	Level of significance for two-tailed test 0.05	0.02	0.01	0.001
1	3.078	6.314	12.706	31.821	63.657	636.619
2	1.886	2.920	4.303	6.965	9.925	31.598
3	1.638	2.353	3.182	4.541	5.841	12.941
4	1.533	2.132	2.776	3.747	4.604	8.610
5	1.476	2.015	2.571	3.365	4.032	6.859
6	1.440	1.943	2.447	3.143	3.707	5.959
7	1.415	1.895	2.365	2.998	3.499	5.405
8	1.397	1.860	2.306	2.896	3.355	5.041
9	1.383	1.833	2.262	2.821	3.250	4.781
10	1.372	1.812	2.228	2.764	3.169	4.587
11	1.363	1.796	2.201	2.718	3.106	4.437
12	1.356	1.782	2.179	2.681	3.055	4.318
13	1.350	1.771	2.160	2.650	3.012	4.221
14	1.345	1.761	2.145	2.624	2.977	4.140
15	1.341	1.753	2.131	2.602	2.947	4.073
16	1.337	1.746	2.120	2.583	2.921	4.015
17	1.333	1.740	2.110	2.567	2.898	3.965
18	1.330	1.734	2.101	2.552	2.878	3.922
19	1.328	1.729	2.093	2.539	2.861	3.883
20	1.325	1.725	2.086	2.528	2.845	3.850
21	1.323	1.721	2.080	2.518	2.831	3.819
22	1.321	1.717	2.074	2.508	2.819	3.792
23	1.319	1.714	2.069	2.500	2.807	3.767
24	1.318	1.711	2.064	2.492	2.797	3.745
25	1.316	1.708	2.060	2.485	2.787	3.725
26	1.315	1.706	2.056	2.479	2.779	3.707
27	1.314	1.703	2.052	2.473	2.771	3.690
28	1.313	1.701	2.048	2.467	2.763	3.674
29	1.311	1.699	2.045	2.462	2.756	3.659
30	1.310	1.697	2.042	2.457	2.750	3.646
40	1.303	1.684	2.021	2.423	2.704	3.551
60	1.296	1.671	2.000	2.390	2.660	3.460
120	1.289	1.658	1.980	2.358	2.617	3.373
μ	1.282	1.645	1.960	2.326	2.576	3.291

Adapted from the following original source: Table III of R.A. Fisher and F. Yates, *Statistical Tables for Biological, Agricultural and Medical Research* (1948 ed.), Oliver and Boyd, Edinburgh and London.

Table 10.A.2 The critical values of the F-distribution at the 5% level of significance (one-tailed)

df a	Degrees of freedom for numerator																		
	1	2	3	4	5	6	7	8	9	10	12	15	20	24	30	40	60	120	μ
1	161	200	216	225	230	234	237	239	241	242	244	246	248	249	250	251	252	253	254
2	18.5	19.0	19.2	19.3	19.3	19.4	19.4	19.4	19.4	19.4	19.4	19.4	19.4	19.5	19.5	19.5	19.5	19.5	19.5
3	10.1	9.55	9.28	9.12	9.01	8.94	8.89	8.85	8.81	8.79	8.74	8.70	8.66	8.64	8.62	8.59	8.57	8.55	8.53
4	7.71	6.94	6.59	6.39	6.26	6.16	6.09	6.04	6.00	5.96	5.91	5.86	5.80	5.77	5.75	5.72	5.69	5.66	5.63
5	6.61	5.79	5.41	5.19	5.05	4.95	4.88	4.82	4.77	4.74	4.68	4.62	4.56	4.53	4.50	4.46	4.43	4.40	4.37
6	5.99	5.14	4.76	4.53	4.39	4.28	4.21	4.15	4.10	4.06	4.00	3.94	3.87	3.84	3.81	3.77	3.74	3.70	3.67
7	5.59	4.74	4.35	4.12	3.97	3.87	3.79	3.73	3.68	3.64	3.57	3.51	3.44	3.41	3.38	3.34	3.30	3.27	3.23
8	5.32	4.46	4.07	3.84	3.69	3.58	3.50	3.44	3.39	3.35	3.28	3.22	3.15	3.12	3.08	3.04	3.01	2.97	2.93
9	5.12	4.26	3.86	3.63	3.48	3.37	3.29	3.23	3.18	3.14	3.07	3.01	2.94	2.90	2.86	2.83	2.79	2.75	2.71
10	4.96	4.10	3.71	3.48	3.33	3.22	3.14	3.07	3.02	2.98	2.91	2.85	2.77	2.74	2.70	2.66	2.62	2.58	2.54
11	4.84	3.98	3.59	3.36	3.20	3.09	3.01	2.95	2.90	2.85	2.79	2.72	2.65	2.61	2.57	2.53	2.49	2.45	2.40
12	4.75	3.89	3.49	3.26	3.11	3.00	2.91	2.85	2.80	2.75	2.69	2.62	2.54	2.51	2.47	2.43	2.38	2.34	2.30
13	4.67	3.81	3.41	3.18	3.03	2.92	2.83	2.77	2.71	2.67	2.60	2.53	2.46	2.42	2.38	2.34	2.30	2.25	2.21
14	4.60	3.74	3.34	3.11	2.96	2.85	2.76	2.70	2.65	2.60	2.53	2.46	2.39	2.35	2.31	2.27	2.22	2.18	2.13
15	4.54	3.68	3.29	3.06	2.90	2.79	2.71	2.64	2.59	2.54	2.48	2.40	2.33	2.29	2.25	2.20	2.16	2.11	2.07
16	4.49	3.63	3.24	3.01	2.85	2.74	2.66	2.59	2.54	2.49	2.42	2.35	2.28	2.24	2.19	2.15	2.11	2.06	2.01
17	4.45	3.59	3.20	2.96	2.81	2.70	2.61	2.55	2.49	2.45	2.38	2.31	2.23	2.19	2.15	2.10	2.06	2.01	1.96
18	4.41	3.55	3.16	2.93	2.77	2.66	2.58	2.51	2.46	2.41	2.34	2.27	2.19	2.15	2.11	2.06	2.02	1.97	1.92
19	4.38	3.52	3.13	2.90	2.74	2.63	2.54	2.48	2.42	2.38	2.31	2.23	2.16	2.11	2.07	2.03	1.98	1.93	1.88
20	4.35	3.49	3.10	2.87	2.71	2.60	2.51	2.45	2.39	2.35	2.28	2.20	2.12	2.08	2.04	1.99	1.95	1.90	1.84

cont.

df a	Degrees of freedom for numerator																		
	1	2	3	4	5	6	7	8	9	10	12	15	20	24	30	40	60	120	μ
21	4.32	3.47	3.07	2.84	2.68	2.57	2.49	2.42	2.37	2.32	2.25	2.18	2.10	2.05	2.01	1.96	1.92	1.87	1.81
22	4.30	3.44	3.05	2.82	2.66	2.55	2.46	2.40	2.34	2.30	2.23	2.15	2.07	2.03	1.98	1.94	1.89	1.84	1.78
23	4.28	3.42	3.03	2.80	2.64	2.53	2.44	2.37	2.32	2.27	2.20	2.13	2.05	2.01	1.96	1.91	1.86	1.81	1.76
24	4.26	3.40	3.01	2.78	2.62	2.51	2.42	2.36	2.30	2.25	2.18	2.11	2.03	1.98	1.94	1.89	1.84	1.79	1.73
25	4.24	3.39	2.99	2.76	2.60	2.49	2.40	2.34	2.28	2.24	2.16	2.09	2.01	1.96	1.92	1.87	1.82	1.77	1.71
30	4.17	3.32	2.92	2.69	2.53	2.42	2.33	2.27	2.21	2.16	2.09	2.01	1.93	1.89	1.84	1.79	1.74	1.68	1.62
40	4.08	3.23	2.84	2.61	2.45	2.34	2.25	2.18	2.12	2.08	2.00	1.92	1.84	1.79	1.74	1.69	1.64	1.58	1.51
60	4.00	3.15	2.76	2.53	2.37	2.25	2.17	2.10	2.04	1.99	1.92	1.84	1.75	1.70	1.65	1.59	1.53	1.47	1.39
120	3.92	3.07	2.68	2.45	2.29	2.18	2.09	2.02	1.96	1.91	1.83	1.75	1.66	1.61	1.55	1.50	1.43	1.35	1.25
μ	3.84	3.00	2.60	2.37	2.21	2.10	2.01	1.94	1.88	1.83	1.75	1.67	1.57	1.52	1.46	1.39	1.32	1.22	1.00

Adapted from the following original source: Table V of R. A. Fisher and F. Yates, *Statistical Tables for Biological, Agricultural and Medical Research* (1948 ed.), Oliver and Boyd, Edinburgh and London.

[a] Degrees of freedom for denominator

Table 10.A.3 The critical values of the *F*-distribution at the 2.5% level of significance (one-tailed) or 5% level of significance for a two-tailed test

df	Degrees of freedom for numerator																		
	1	2	3	4	5	6	7	8	9	10	12	15	20	24	30	40	60	120	μ
1	648	800	864	900	922	937	948	957	963	969	977	985	993	997	1,001	1,006	1,010	1,014	1,018
2	38.5	39.0	39.2	39.2	39.3	39.3	39.4	39.4	39.4	39.4	39.4	39.4	39.4	39.5	39.5	39.5	39.5	39.5	39.5
3	17.4	16.0	15.4	15.1	14.9	14.7	14.6	14.5	14.5	14.4	14.3	14.3	14.2	14.1	14.1	14.0	14.0	13.9	13.9
4	12.2	10.6	9.98	9.60	9.36	9.20	9.07	8.98	8.90	8.84	8.75	8.66	8.56	8.51	8.46	8.41	8.36	8.31	8.26
5	10.0	8.43	7.76	7.39	7.15	6.98	6.85	6.76	6.68	6.62	6.52	6.43	6.33	6.28	6.23	6.18	6.12	6.07	6.02
6	8.81	7.26	6.60	6.23	5.99	5.82	5.70	5.60	5.52	5.46	5.37	5.27	5.17	5.12	5.07	5.01	4.96	4.90	4.85
7	8.07	6.54	5.89	5.52	5.29	5.12	4.99	4.90	4.82	4.76	4.67	4.57	4.47	4.42	4.36	4.31	4.25	4.20	4.14
8	7.57	6.06	5.42	5.05	4.82	4.65	4.53	4.43	4.36	4.30	4.20	4.10	4.00	3.95	3.89	3.84	3.78	3.73	3.67
9	7.21	5.71	5.08	4.72	4.48	4.32	4.20	4.10	4.03	3.96	3.87	3.77	3.67	3.61	3.56	3.51	3.45	3.39	3.33
10	6.94	5.46	4.83	4.47	4.24	4.07	3.95	3.85	3.78	3.72	3.62	3.52	3.42	3.37	3.31	3.26	3.20	3.14	3.08
11	6.72	5.26	4.63	4.28	4.04	3.88	3.76	3.66	3.59	3.53	3.43	3.33	3.23	3.17	3.12	3.06	3.00	2.94	2.88
12	6.55	5.10	4.47	4.12	3.89	3.73	3.61	3.51	3.44	3.37	3.28	3.18	3.07	3.02	2.96	2.91	2.85	2.79	2.72
13	6.41	4.97	4.35	4.00	3.77	3.60	3.48	3.39	3.31	3.25	3.15	3.05	2.95	2.89	2.84	2.78	2.72	2.66	2.60
14	6.30	4.86	4.24	3.89	3.66	3.50	3.38	3.28	3.21	3.15	3.05	2.95	2.84	2.79	2.73	2.67	2.61	2.55	2.49
15	6.20	4.77	4.15	3.80	3.58	3.41	3.29	3.20	3.12	3.06	2.96	2.86	2.76	2.70	2.64	2.59	2.52	2.46	2.40
16	6.12	4.69	4.08	3.73	3.50	3.34	3.22	3.12	3.05	2.99	2.89	2.79	2.68	2.63	2.57	2.51	2.45	2.38	2.32
17	6.04	4.62	4.01	3.66	3.44	3.28	3.16	3.06	2.98	2.92	2.82	2.72	2.62	2.56	2.50	2.44	2.38	2.32	2.25
18	5.98	4.56	3.95	3.61	3.38	3.22	3.10	3.01	2.93	2.87	2.77	2.67	2.56	2.50	2.44	2.38	2.32	2.26	2.19
19	5.92	4.51	3.90	3.56	3.33	3.17	3.05	2.96	2.88	2.82	2.72	2.62	2.51	2.45	2.39	2.33	2.27	2.20	2.13
20	5.87	4.46	3.86	3.51	3.29	3.13	3.01	2.91	2.84	2.77	2.68	2.57	2.46	2.41	2.35	2.29	2.22	2.16	2.09

cont.

df^a	\multicolumn{19}{c}{Degrees of freedom for numerator}
	1	2	3	4	5	6	7	8	9	10	12	15	20	24	30	40	60	120	μ
21	5.83	4.42	3.82	3.48	3.25	3.09	2.97	2.87	2.80	2.73	2.64	2.53	2.42	2.37	2.31	2.25	2.18	2.11	2.04
22	5.79	4.38	3.78	3.44	3.22	3.05	2.93	2.84	2.76	2.70	2.60	2.50	2.39	2.33	2.27	2.21	2.14	2.08	2.00
23	5.75	4.35	3.75	3.41	3.18	3.02	2.90	2.81	2.73	2.67	2.57	2.47	2.36	2.30	2.24	2.18	2.11	2.04	1.97
24	5.72	4.32	3.72	3.38	3.15	2.99	2.87	2.78	2.70	2.64	2.54	2.44	2.33	2.27	2.21	2.15	2.08	2.01	1.94
25	5.69	4.29	3.69	3.35	3.13	2.97	2.85	2.75	2.68	2.61	2.51	2.41	2.30	2.24	2.18	2.12	2.05	1.98	1.91
30	5.57	4.18	3.59	3.25	3.03	2.87	2.75	2.65	2.57	2.51	2.41	2.31	2.20	2.14	2.07	2.01	1.94	1.87	1.79
40	5.42	4.05	3.46	3.13	2.90	2.74	2.62	2.53	2.45	2.39	2.29	2.18	2.07	2.01	1.94	1.88	1.80	1.72	1.64
60	5.29	3.93	3.34	3.01	2.79	2.63	2.51	2.41	2.33	2.27	2.17	2.06	1.94	1.88	1.82	1.74	1.67	1.58	1.48
120	5.15	3.80	3.23	2.89	2.67	2.52	2.39	2.30	2.22	2.16	2.05	1.95	1.82	1.76	1.69	1.61	1.53	1.43	1.31
μ	5.02	3.69	3.12	2.79	2.57	2.41	2.29	2.19	2.11	2.05	1.94	1.83	1.71	1.64	1.57	1.48	1.39	1.27	1.00

Adapted from the following original source: Table V of R. A. Fisher and F. Yates, *Statistical Tables for Biological, Agricultural and Medical Research* (1948 Edition), Oliver and Boyd; Edinburgh and London.

^{a} Degrees of freedom for denominator

Table 10.A.4 The critical values of the Mann–Whitney U statistic at the 5% level of significance (two-tailed)

N_s \ N_2	5	6	7	8	9	10	11	12	13	14	15	16	17	18	19	20
5	2	3	5	6	7	8	9	11	12	13	14	15	17	18	19	20
6		5	6	8	10	11	13	14	16	17	19	21	22	24	25	27
7			8	10	12	14	16	18	20	22	24	26	28	30	32	34
8				13	15	17	19	22	24	26	29	31	34	36	38	41
9					17	20	23	26	28	31	34	37	39	42	45	48
10						23	26	29	33	36	39	42	45	48	52	55
11							30	33	37	40	44	47	51	55	58	62
12								37	41	45	49	53	57	61	65	69
13									45	50	54	59	63	67	72	76
14										55	59	64	67	74	78	83
15											64	70	75	80	85	90
16												75	81	86	92	98
17													87	93	99	105
18														99	106	112
19															113	119
20																127

Adapted from the following original source: Table 5.3 of H. R. Neave (1978) *Statistical Tables*. George, Allen and Unwin: London.

Table 10.A.5 The critical values of the Wilcoxon T statistic for correlated samples (two-tailed)

N	Level of significance		
	0.05	0.02	0.01
6	0	–	–
7	2	0	–
8	4	2	0
9	6	3	2
10	8	5	3
11	11	7	5
12	14	10	7
13	17	13	10
14	21	16	13
15	25	20	16
16	30	24	20
17	35	28	23
18	40	33	28
19	46	38	32
20	52	43	38
21	59	49	43
22	66	56	49
23	73	62	55
24	81	69	61
25	89	77	68

Adapted from the following original source: Table 1 of F Wilcoxon (1949) *Some Rapid Approximate Statistical Procedures*. The American Cyanamind Company; New York.

FURTHER READING

Book

Field A. (2005). *Discovering Statistics using SPSS for Windows*. Sage; London. This is a very useful text as it provides the theory of the tests and the commands for running them in SPSS.

Website

In a recent review of statistics websites published in *The Sport and Exercise Scientist*, the *Statsoft Electronic Textbook* (http://www.statsoft.com/textbook/stathome.html) was rated the highest. It provides detailed descriptions of a wide number of topics and is easy to navigate. However, the reader should be aware that the statistical output examples are taken from the Statistica software package, not SPSS. Readers are also directed towards Andy Field's website (http://www.statisticshell.com/statisticshell.html), as it contains a large number of lecture slides and examples that incorporate the use of SPSS.

REFERENCES

Altman D. G. (1991). *Practical Statistics for Medical Research*. Chapman and Hall; London.

Atkinson G. (2001). Analysis of repeated measurements in physical therapy research. *Physical Therapy in Sport*; 2: 194–208.

Atkinson G. and Nevill A. M. (1998) Statistical methods for assessing measurement error (reliability) in variables relevant to sports medicine. *Sports Medicine*; 26: 217–38.

Atkinson G. and Nevill A. M. (2001). Selected issues in the design and analysis of sport performance research. *Journal of Sports Sciences*; 19: 811–27.

Atkinson G., Nevill A. and Edwards B. (1999). What is an acceptable amount of measurement error? The application of meaningful 'analytical goals' to the reliability analysis of sports science measurements made on a ratio scale. *Journal of Sports Sciences*; 17: 18.

Bland M. (2000). *An Introduction to Medical Statistics*. Oxford University Press; Oxford.

Bland J. M. and Altman D. G. (1999). Measuring agreement in method comparison studies. *Statistical Methods in Medical Research*; 8: 135–60.

Cohen L. and Holliday M. (1982). *Statistics for Social Scientists*. Harper & Row; London.

Costill D. L., Thomason H. and Roberts E. (1973) Fractional utilization of the aerobic capacity during distance running. *Medicine and Science in Sports*; 5: 248–52.

Durnin J. V. G. A. and Womersley J. (1974). Body fat assessment from total body density and its estimation from skinfold thickness: measurements on 481 men and women aged from 16 to 72 years. *British Journal of Nutrition*; 32: 77–97.

Eston R. G. and Rowlands A. V. (2000). Stages in the development of a research project: putting the idea together. *British Journal of Sports Medicine*; 34: 59–64.

Eston R. G., Rowlands A. V., Charlesworth S., Davies A. and Hoppitt T. (2005). Prediction of DXA-determined whole body fat from skinfolds: importance of including skinfolds from the thigh and calf in young, healthy men and women. *European Journal of Clinical Nutrition*; 59: 695–702.

Field A. (2005). *Discovering Statistics using SPSS for Windows*. Sage; London.

Harvill L. M. (1991). An NCME instructional module on standard error of measurement. *Educational Measurement: Issues and Practice*; 10: 33–41.

Howell D. C. (2007) *Statistical Methods for Psychology*. Thomson Wadsworth; Belmont, CA.

Johnson P. J., Godfrey R., Moore J., Nevill A. M., Romer L. and Winter E. M. (1998). Scaling maximal oxygen uptake of elite endurance sportsmen. *Journal of Sports Sciences*; 16: 27–8.

Kinnear, P.R and Gray, C.D (1997). *SPSS for Windows Made Simple*. London, Psychology Press.

Knapp T. R. (1992) Technical error of measurement: a methodological critique. *American Journal of Physical Anthropometry*; 87: 235–6.

Kotz S., Read C. B, Balakrishnan N. and Vidakovic B. (2004) *Encyclopedia of Statistical Sciences*. Hoboken, New Jersey.

Marginson V., Rowlands A. V., Gleeson N. P. and Eston R. G. (2005). Comparison of the symptoms of exercise-induced muscle damage after an initial and repeated bout of plyometric exercise in men and boys. *Journal of Applied Physiology*; **99**: 1174–81.

Matthews J. N. S., Altman D. G., Campbell M. J. and Royston P. (1990). Analysis of serial measurements in medical research. *British Medical Journal*; **300**: 230–5.

Nevill A. M., Ramsbottom R. and Williams C. (1990). The relationship between athletic performance and maximal oxygen uptake. *Journal of Sports Sciences*; **8**: 290–2.

Nevill A. M., Cooke C. B., Holder R. L., Ramsbottom, R. and Williams, C. (1992a). Modelling bivariate relationships when repeated measurements are recorded on more than one subject. *European Journal of Applied Physiology*; **64**: 419–25.

Nevill A. M., Ramsbottom R. and Williams C. (1992b). Scaling physiological measurements for individuals of different body size. *European Journal of Applied Physiology*; **65**: 110–17.

Snedecor G. W. and Cochran W. G. (1989). *Statistical Methods* (8th Edition). Iowa State University Press; Ames, IA.

Winter E., Eston R. G. and Lamb K. L. (2001). Statistical analyses in the physiology of exercise and kinanthropometry. *Journal of Sports Sciences*; **19**: 761–75.

Wright E. M. and Royston P. (1999). Calculating reference intervals for laboratory measurements. *Statistical Methods in Medical Research*; **8**: 93–112.

CHAPTER 11

SCALING: ADJUSTING FOR DIFFERENCES IN BODY SIZE

Edward M. Winter and Alan M. Nevill

11.1 AIMS

The principal aim of this chapter is to develop knowledge and understanding of how performance and physiological measures can be adjusted for differences either in the size of the body as a whole or of its exercising segments. Specifically, in this chapter we will:

- describe the historical background to scaling;
- outline imperfections of ratio standards;
- explain principles that underly allometric modelling;
- select and apply statistical analyses that compare physiological and performance measures in groups adjusted for differences in size;
- evaluate techniques for use in cross-sectional and longitudinal studies;
- outline implications of non-isometric growth.

11.2 INTRODUCTION

At a time when molecular and sub-cellular biology are pre-eminent, the importance of macro biology can be overlooked. It is important that this does not become the case (Winter and Brooks 2007).

Physiological and performance variables are frequently influenced by body size. For instance, the performance capabilities of children are less than those of adults. Similarly, there are track and field events such as hammer, discus and shot in which high values of body mass are especially influential. Furthermore, oxygen uptake ($\dot{V}O_2$) during a particular task in a large person will probably be greater than in a small person. These observations give rise to a simple question: to what extent are performance differences attributable to differences in size or to differences in qualitative characteristics of the body's tissues and structures?

To help answer this question, differences in body size have to be partitioned out. This partitioning is called *scaling* (Schmidt-Nielsen 1984) and is a key issue in kinanthropometry. There are four main uses (Winter 1992):

1. to compare an individual against standards for the purpose of assessment;
2. to compare groups;
3. to use in longitudinal studies of the effects of growth or training;
4. to explore possible relationships between

physiological characteristics and performance.

11.3 HISTORICAL BACKGROUND

Scaling has a long history that can be traced back to at least Euclid of Alexandria (circa. 325–265BC). Euclid is probably better known for his contributions to our understanding of the geometry of planes and solids, but the relationships between length, surface area and volume in objects have profound implications for living things. These implications apply in particular to metabolism and thermoregulation in metazoan, that is, multi-cellular organisms. Moreover, scaling is also an issue in sculpture and was well known to Greek artists at that time and those of the early Renaissance, especially Leonardo da Vinci (1452–1519) and later, Galileo Galilei (1564–1642).

Representation of the human form in large-scale sculptures is not as simple as it sounds because to support the torso and the rest of the upper body, legs can become disproportionately large, especially if movement is depicted and upper torso mass is outside the base of support. Both da Vinci and Galileo were aware of this, and also how upscaling models of machines to full-size working versions was not a simple one-for-one procedure.

Interest in scaling in the context of kinanthropometry and the physiology of exercise underwent a revival (Nevill *et al.* 1992a; Jakeman *et al.* 1994; Nevill 1994; Nevill and Holder 1994; Winter 1996) that has continued (Nevill *et al.* 2004; Winter and Brookes 2007), although it is by no means a new area of interest and is well established in biological science. One of the earliest scientific papers on the subject was by Sarrus and Rameaux (1838), but even that was predated by Jonathan Swift's *Gulliver's Travels* published in 1726. Lilliputian mathematicians were faced with a challenge: they had to calculate how much food their captive would require each day. Because Gulliver was 12 times taller

than the Lilliputians, they surmised – not unreasonably – that he would need 1728 times (i.e. 12^3) the amount consumed by his diminutive tormentors.

In 1917 D'Arcy-Thompson's *Growth and Form* was published and 15 years later so too was Huxley's (1932) *Problems of Relative Growth*. These texts made a marked contribution to the development of our understanding of the ways in which the size and function of living organisms are intimately related. Also noteworthy are the works of Sholl (1948), Tanner (1949) and Tanner (1964). The area was revisited in the early 1970s (Katch, 1973), but it was some 20 years later before concerted interest in applications of scaling to exercise science was revived.

This revival was partly attributable to advances in microcomputing that made otherwise complex and unwieldy analyses much quicker and easier to perform. Established debate about model specifications continued enthusiastically (Kermack and Haldane 1950; Ricker 1973; Rayner 1985; Sokal and Rohlf 1995; Nevill 1994; Batterham *et al.* 1997). It is now generally recognised that scaling has an important role in the development of our understanding of how the body responds and adapts to exercise.

11.4 THE RATIO STANDARD: THE TRADITIONAL METHOD

The most commonly used scaling technique is termed a *ratio standard* (Tanner 1949) in which a performance or physiological variable is simply divided by an anthropometric characteristic, such as body mass. A well-known ratio standard is $\dot{V}O_2$ expressed in ml·kg^{-1}·min^{-1}. This is used to compare groups using *t*-tests or analysis of variance (ANOVA) as appropriate, to explore relationships between aerobic capabilities and performance and to evaluate the physiological status of participants.

More than 40 years ago, Tanner (1949) warned against the use of these standards

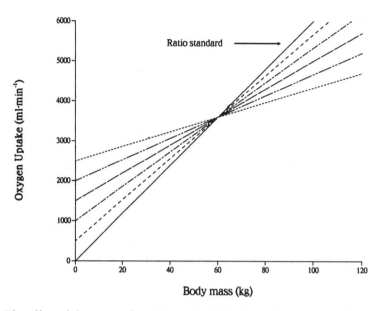

Figure 11.1 The effect of departures from Tanner's (1949) 'special circumstance' on the difference between regression standards and the ratio standard.

for evaluative purposes and demonstrated that they were, '... theoretically fallacious and, unless in exceptional circumstances, misleading' (p. 1). Furthermore, he later stated (Tanner 1964) that comparisons of groups based on mean values of ratio standards were also misleading because they, '... involve some statistical difficulties and are neither as simple nor as informative as they seem' (p. 65). What is the problem?

A ratio standard is valid only when:

$$\frac{\upsilon_x}{\upsilon_y} = r$$

where: υ_x = coefficient of variation of x i.e. $(SDx/\bar{x}) \times 100$

υ_y = coefficient of variation of y i.e. $(SDy/\bar{y}) \times 100$

r = Pearson's product-moment correlation coefficient

This expression illustrates Tanner's (1949) 'exceptional circumstance' and is equivalent to the regression standard with an intercept of 0 and a slope the same as the ratio standard.

If it is not satisfied, a distortion is introduced. Figure 11.1 illustrates the principle. The solid line represents the ratio standard whereas the other lines represent regression lines of $\dot{V}O_2$ on body mass for various values of r. The only point through which all the lines pass – the intersection point – is where the mean values for x and y occur. As r increases, the ratio standard and regression line get closer, but they will be coincident only when the special circumstance is satisfied. Rarely, if ever, is this test made, and arguably rarer still is it actually fulfilled. In fact, there are several instances where it simply cannot be satisfied. As the value of r reduces, the regression line rotates clockwise. The further data points are from the intersection, the more the ratio standard distorts the 'true' relationship.

If the ratio standard is used for evaluative purposes, those with body mass values below the mean will be ascribed high aerobic capability, whereas those whose body mass is greater than the mean will tend to be ascribed low aerobic capability, especially if the $\dot{V}O_2$ is $\dot{V}O_2$max. In other words, little people receive an artefactual arithmetic advantage, whereas large people are similarly disadvantaged.

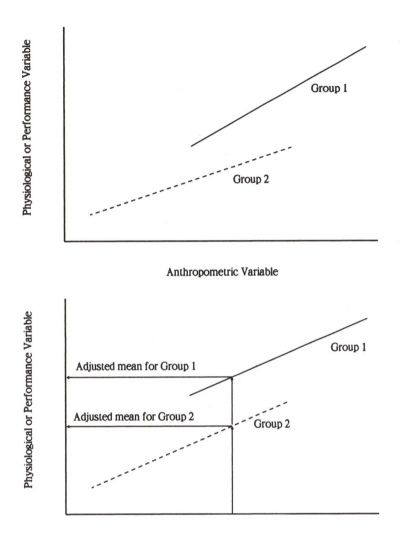

Figure 11.2a and Figure 11.2b The identification of 'adjusted means'. Actual slopes are constrained to be parallel.

The opposite occurs if economy is being investigated: large people now appear to be markedly economical, whereas small people appear to have extravagant expenditures of energy. The greater the distance of the point from the mean, the greater the distortion will be. Later, Packard and Boardman (1987) provided support for this tenet and elaborated on the theme.

For this reason, Tanner (1964) suggested that *regression standards* should be used

for evaluation and that groups should be compared via the comparison of regression lines through the statistical technique *analysis of covariance* (ANCOVA) (Snedecor and Cochran 1989).

11.5 REGRESSION STANDARDS AND ANCOVA

For the purposes of evaluation, a regression standard is straightforward. If an individual is above the regression line, he or she is above average; if below the line, he or she is below average. Norms can be established on the basis of how far above or below the line particular values lie. Comparisons of regression lines via ANCOVA so as to compare groups are more involved, although the principles are actually simple. Computer packages such as SPSS (Norusis 1992) can be used and texts such as Snedecor and Cochran (1989) and Tabachnick and Fidell (2007) provide a useful theoretical background.

Figure 11.2a illustrates the basis for comparing two groups, 1 and 2. Regression lines for each group identify the linear relationship between variables. The x variable – the predictor – is called a *covariate* because as it increases; so too does y – the response variable sometimes called the outcome measure or dependent variable. The effect of x is partitioned out and what are called *adjusted means* are calculated. In the comparison of regression lines, three tests are made:

1   variance about regression
2   equality of slopes
3   comparison of elevations of the lines.

Ideally there should be *homogeneity* of variance about regression; that is, the variance about regression should be the same in both (or all) groups. (*Heterogeneity* means that the variances are not the same.) If this test is satisfied, the slopes are compared. If there are no statistical differences between the slopes, the lines are recast and constrained to be parallel. If the slopes of the lines are different, the analysis stops; the groups are qualitatively different. The parallel slopes are used to calculate the adjusted means (Figure 11.2b). For the overall mean value of x, equivalent values of y are calculated for each group. The error term for each group is the standard error of the estimate (SEE).

11.5.1 ANCOVA – a worked example

Table 11.1 contains data for lean leg volume and peak power output in men and women (Winter *et al.* 1991).

Figure 11.3 illustrates the regression lines and raw data plots for the two groups. Comparison of the ratio standards peak power output/lean leg volume showed that there was no difference between the groups (136, 3 W·l^{-1} vs 131, 3 W·l^{-1} in men and women respectively (mean, SEM) $P = 0.206$). This suggests that there is no difference in the qualitative characteristics of the groups. In marked contrast, ANCOVA produced adjusted means of 902, 108 W in men and 748, 94 W in women (mean, SEE) $P < 0.001$). This suggests that there are qualitative differences between men and women. (See Appendix A to carry out the appropriate analysis using SPSS.)

The technique has also been applied in several other studies. For example, Winter and Maughan (1991) investigated strength and cross-sectional area of muscle with the same outcome. It has been used to adjust oxygen uptake values of children and adults to compensate for the large differences in body mass. Using this procedure, the difference in mass-relative oxygen uptake calculated by the simple ratio standard (ml·kg^{-1}·min^{-1}) at any given running speed is removed (Eston *et al.* 1993; Armstrong *et al.* 1997). With an elaborate use of the technique, Nevill *et al.* (2003) compared maximum oxygen uptake (V̇O$_2$max) in elite-standard endurance athletes. They found that large athletes such as heavyweight rowers had in fact the highest V̇O$_2$max. Considering the aerobic nature of 2000-m rowing and that just about all muscles in the body are recruited, this is physiologically plausible. Similarly, Johnson *et al.* (2000) successfully used the same procedure to examine V̇O$_2$ in 55- to 85-year-old participants in whom body mass reduces with increasing age.

Table 11.1 Absolute and natural logarithm values (ln) for lean leg volume (LLV) and optimized peak power output (OPP) in men and women

Men				Women			
LLV	lnLLV	OPP	lnOPP	LLV	lnLLV	OPP	lnOPP
(l)	(lnl)	(W)	(lnW)	(l)	(lnl)	(W)	(lnW)
7.03	1.950	928	6.833	4.79	1.567	658	6.489
7.47	2.011	825	6.715	4.55	1.515	490	6.194
8.80	2.175	1113	7.015	4.94	1.597	596	6.390
7.44	2.007	950	6.856	5.26	1.660	491	6.196
7.16	1.969	1231	7.116	5.54	1.712	717	6.575
7.69	2.040	942	6.848	4.95	1.599	467	6.146
7.50	2.015	889	6.790	4.50	1.504	534	6.280
6.43	1.861	904	6.807	7.32	1.991	769	6.645
8.41	2.129	1235	7.119	5.09	1.627	644	6.468
7.73	2.045	889	6.790	3.57	1.273	427	6.057
6.70	1.902	917	6.821	4.63	1.533	664	6.498
6.72	1.905	850	6.745	4.93	1.595	624	6.436
6.41	1.858	997	6.905	4.33	1.466	573	6.351
8.26	2.111	1003	6.911	7.89	2.066	821	6.711
7.97	2.076	1205	7.094	6.82	1.920	733	6.597
8.46	2.135	1211	7.099	5.46	1.697	800	6.685
8.47	2.137	978	6.886	4.54	1.513	672	6.510
6.91	1.933	1087	6.991	5.85	1.766	590	6.380
8.50	2.140	1082	6.987	5.38	1.683	679	6.521
7.82	2.057	1026	6.933	5.68	1.737	607	6.409
7.45	2.008	970	6.877	5.09	1.627	714	6.571
7.74	2.046	1131	7.031	4.66	1.539	755	6.627
6.83	1.921	902	6.805	5.97	1.787	755	6.627
7.72	2.044	1129	7.029	4.95	1.599	561	6.330
6.04	1.798	832	6.724	5.10	1.629	518	6.250
8.29	2.115	1242	7.124	5.91	1.777	680	6.522
6.08	1.805	938	6.844	4.19	1.433	634	6.452
6.36	1.850	856	6.752	5.00	1.609	734	6.599
7.43	2.006	939	6.845	4.35	1.470	784	6.664
5.83	1.763	801	6.686	4.62	1.530	632	6.449
6.64	1.893	919	6.823	5.76	1.751	709	6.564
8.87	2.183	1091	6.995	5.35	1.677	712	6.568
7.46	2.010	977	6.884	4.75	1.558	639	6.460
7.48	2.012	1248	7.129	5.58	1.719	726	6.588
				5.60	1.723	815	6.703

cont.

Men				Women			
LLV	lnLLV	OPP	lnOPP	LLV	lnLLV	OPP	lnOPP
(l)	(lnl)	(W)	(lnW)	(l)	(lnl)	(W)	(lnW)
				5.70	1.740	847	6.742
				5.45	1.696	701	6.553
				3.92	1.366	653	6.482
				4.09	1.409	550	6.310
				5.22	1.653	835	6.727
				4.89	1.587	893	6.795
				5.13	1.635	760	6.633
				4.40	1.482	564	6.335
				5.70	1.740	758	6.631
				4.60	1.526	630	6.446
				4.90	1.589	657	6.488
				7.06	1.954	841	6.735

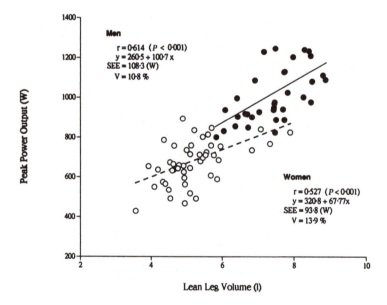

Figure 11.3 The relationship between optimized peak power output and lean leg volume in men (●————) and women (o – – – – – –) (Winter *et al.* 1991).

11.6 ALLOMETRY AND POWER FUNCTION STANDARDS

It appears that ANCOVA on regression lines solves the problems associated with scaling. This is not necessarily the case. Nevill *et al.*

(1992a) identified two major weaknesses in the use of linear modelling techniques on raw data:

1 data are not necessarily related linearly;
2 error about regression is not necessarily additive; it might be multiplicative.

Non-linear relationships between variables are well known to biologists (Schmidt-Nielsen 1984) and curiously, although they receive attention in notable texts (MacDougal *et al.* 1991; Åstrand *et al.* 2003), have not been used widely by sport and exercise scientists.

Growth and development in humans and other living things are accompanied by differential changes in the size and configuration of the body's segments (Tanner, 1989). These changes are said to be *allometric* (Schmidt-Nielsen 1984), a word derived from the Greek *allios* which means to change and *metry* to measure. Physiological variables *y* are scaled in relation to an index of body size *x* according to allometric equations. These are of the general form:

$$y = ax^b$$

where: a = constant multiplier
b = exponent

An example is described in Practical 1.

11.7 PRACTICAL 1: THE IDENTIFICATION OF ALLOMETRIC RELATIONSHIPS

The principles can be illustrated by using spheres as examples and Table 11.2 contains relevant data.

Table 11.2 Absolute and natural logarithm values (ln) of radii, surface areas and volumes in spheres

Radius (cm)	ln Radius (ln cm)	Area (cm²)	ln Area (ln cm³)	Volume (cm³)	ln Volume (ln cm³)
0.125	–2.079	0.2	–1.628	0	–4.806
0.25	–1.386	0.8	–0.242	0.1	–2.726
0.5	–0.693	3.1	1.145	0.5	–0.647
1	0	12.6	2.531	4.2	1.433
2	0.693	50.3	3.917	33.5	3.512
3	1.099	113.1	4.728	113.1	4.728
4	1.386	201.0	5.303	268.1	5.591
5	1.609	314.1	5.750	523.7	6.261
6	1.792	452.3	6.114	904.9	6.808
7	1.946	615.6	6.423	1436.9	7.270
8	2.079	804.1	6.690	2144.9	7.671

In spheres:

$$\text{Area} = 4\,\pi r^2 \text{ and Volume} = \frac{4\pi r^3}{3}$$

where: r = radius

For area, the numerical value of a, the constant multiplier, is 12.566 i.e 4π, and the exponent is 2. Similarly, for volume, the constant multiplier is 4.189 ($4\pi/3$) and the exponent is 3.

1   With radius on the abscissa, draw two graphs: one for surface area and one for volume. You should have something like Figures 11.4 and 11.5. How can these

relationships be identified? The answer is simple. The raw variables are converted into natural logarithms and ln y is regressed on ln x. This linearizes the otherwise non-linear relationship and produces an expression that is of the form:

$$\ln y = \ln a + b \ln x$$

The antilog of ln a identifies the constant multiplier in the allometric equation and the slope of the line is the numerical value of the exponent.

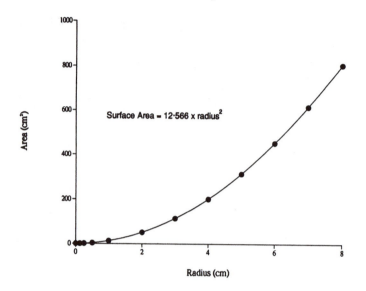

Figure 11.4 The relationship between surface area and radius in spheres.

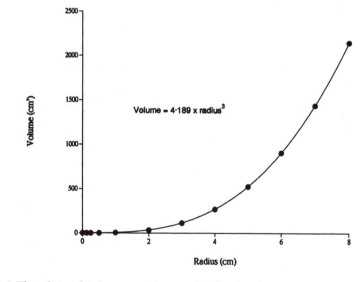

Figure 11.5 The relationship between volume and radius in spheres.

2   Using the values in Table 11.2, with ln radius on the abscissa, plot two graphs: one for surface area and one for volume.

3   Calculate the regression equations for each graph. You should have something like Figures 11.6 and 11.7. For the graph of ln surface area regressed on ln radius, a (the constant multiplier in the allometric equation that relates the raw variables) is the antilog of 2.531. This value is 12.566. Similarly, the exponent is given by the slope of the log-log regression equation, i.e. 2. In the same way, the constant multiplier in the volume–radius relationship is the antilog of 1.432. This value is 4.189. The exponent given by the log-log regression equation is 3.

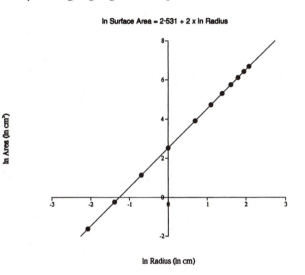

Figure 11.6 The relationship between ln surface area and ln radius in spheres.

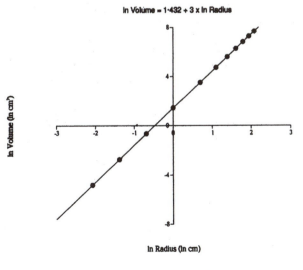

Figure 11.7 The relationship between ln volume and ln radius in spheres.

From these known relationships, we can explore an unknown one: the relationship between surface area and volume.

4   Again using the data in Table 11.2, identify the allometric relationship between surface area and volume. Make surface area the response variable. You should have something like Figures 11.8 and 11.9.

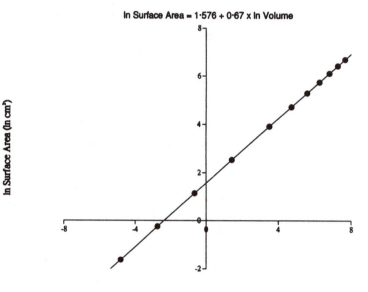

Figure 11.8 The relationship between ln surface area and ln volume in spheres.

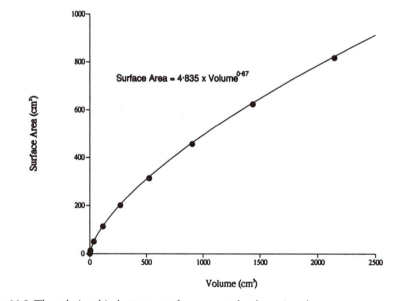

Figure 11.9 The relationship between surface area and volume in spheres.

11.8 PRACTICAL 2: POWER FUNCTION RATIO STANDARDS

The relationship in Figure 11.9 illustrates an important principle: the *surface law* (Schmidt-Nielsen, 1984). The surface area of a body is related to its volume raised to the power 0·67. In other words, as the volume of a body increases, its surface area actually reduces in proportion. Nevill *et al.* (1992a) and Nevill and Holder (1994) provided compelling evidence that measures such as O_2 are related to body mass raised to this 0·67 power. To scale correctly, a predictor variable should be raised to a power that is identified from log-log transformations. This value is called a *power function*.

The power function can then be divided into the response variable to produce a *power function ratio standard*.

Another important point about allometric relationships concerns the error term. In linear models, error about the regression line is assumed to be constant. Such error is said to be additive or *homoscedastic*. Allometric models do not make this assumption; error is assumed to be multiplicative or *heteroscedastic*. In this case, error increases as the magnitude of the predictor variable increases. This is what tends to happen with living things (Nevill and Holder 1994).

Groups can be compared by using power function ratios and *t*-tests or analysis of variance as appropriate. They can also be compared using ANCOVA on the log-log transformations. These transformations constrain error to be additive and so allow the use of ANCOVA.

11.8.1 A worked example

The data in Table 11.1 can be revisited. The natural logarithms of lean leg volume and peak power output can now be used to compare performance in men and women. This is the analysis reported by Nevill *et al.* (1992b).

1   With ln Lean Leg Volume on the abscissa, plot a graph with ln Peak Power Output for men and women. Calculate the regression equations. You should have something like Figure 11.10.

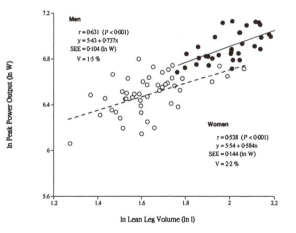

Figure 11.10 The relationship between ln peak power output and ln lean leg volume in men (•————) and women (o –––––––) (Nevill *et al.* 1992b).

2   ANCOVA on these data (Nevill 1994) confirms that for a given lean leg volume, peak power output in men is greater than in women ($P < 0.001$). (See Appendix B to implement ANCOVA using SPSS.)

3   Plot the allometric relationships for men and women. You should have something like Figure 11.11.

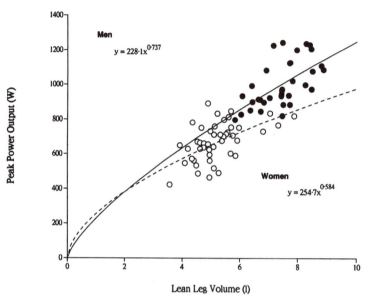

Figure 11.11 The allometric relationship between peak power output and lean leg volume in men (• ———) and women (o — — — — — —) (Nevill *et al.* 1992b).

4   ANCOVA also demonstrates that the slopes of the log/log transformations (0.737 in men vs 0.584 in women) do not differ ($P = 0.515$). A common slope of 0.626 can be used for both groups. Note that this approximates to a theoretical value of 0.67 suggested by the surface law.

5   Produce power function ratio standards ($W \cdot l^{-0.626}$) for men and women and compare the groups. This should give means, SEM of 286, 5 $W \cdot l^{-0.626}$ and 239, 5 $W \cdot l^{-0.626}$ respectively ($P < 0.001$). Similar results were reported by Eston *et al.* (1997). They also reported a common exponent of 0.60 to describe the relationship between lean upper leg volume and peak power output. Mean values, SEM were 376, 14 $W \cdot l^{-0.60}$ and 296, 13 $W \cdot l^{-0.60}$ for men and women, respectively ($P < 0.01$).

11.9 ELASTICITY

All of this seems straightforward and implies that the surface law alone affects performance, metabolism and related energetics; however, this not the case. Kleiber (1961) and others have shown that in comparisons of species that differ markedly in body mass; for example, from mice to elephants, the body-mass exponent approximates to 0.75, not 0.67.

One suggested explanation for this (McMahon 1973) is that in living things, the elasticity of their structures can absorb and then release energy in ways that rigid bodies cannot.

11.10 ALLOMETRIC CASCADE

Another attempt to explain the departure from the surface law's 0.67 exponent was proposed by Darveau et al. (2002) in the context of $\dot{V}O_2$max. The $\dot{V}O_2$max is tripartite in nature and represents the body's ability to: i) extract oxygen from the atmosphere (by the lungs); and ii) deliver it to exercising muscle (by the cardiovascular system) and use it in that muscle. Darveau et al. (2002) attempted to model this system and ascribed a weighting to each of three components. By doing so, they calculated that the exponent for body mass by which to create a power function ratio should be between 0.82 and 0.92. They also did the same for $\dot{V}O_2$ and found that the exponent was between 0.76 and 0.79. Attempts to validate this model have been encouraging (Batterham and Jackson 2003), although not without some reservations (Nevill and Bate 2005).

11.11 GEOMETRIC SIMILARITY AND NON-ISOMETRIC GROWTH

There is one more possible explanation for the surface law's exponent of 0.67 not holding true. If participants are geometrically similar, individual body components (e.g. homologous muscles, hearts, lungs) should have masses that are proportional to body mass (M), cross-sectional or surface areas proportional to $M^{0.67}$ and linear dimensions, such as stature or limb girths, proportional to $M^{0.33}$. However, this assumption has only recently been fully tested in athletic and non-exercising human populations (Nevill et al. 2004). The authors explored the assumption of geometric similarity by comparing the mass exponents associated with girth measurements taken at 13 sites throughout the body in 478 participants (279 athletic and 199 non-exercising controls). The study's findings confirmed that human adult physiques are not geometrically similar to each other.

Both in athletic and non-exercising controls, body circumferences/limb girths

develop at a greater rate than that anticipated by geometric similarity in fleshy sites containing both muscle and fat (upper arms and legs) and less than anticipated in bony sites (head, wrists and ankles). The results also suggest that thigh muscle girths of athletes and controls increase at a greater rate than that predicted by geometric similarity, proportional to body mass, $M^{0.439}$ and $M^{0.377}$ respectively. Let us assume that the thigh muscle mass (M_T) of controls increases in proportion to body mass, $M_T = (M^{0.377})^3 = M^{1.13}$ and the thigh muscles make a major and/or representative contribution to $\dot{V}O_2$max. Then, if the contribution of thigh muscle mass to $\dot{V}O_2$max obeys the surface area law ($M_T)^{0.67}$, the controls will expend a similar disproportionate increase in energy expenditure (proxied by $\dot{V}O_2$max), given by,

$$\dot{V}O_2\text{max} \sim (M_T)^{0.67} \sim (M^{1.13})^{0.67} \sim M^{0.753},$$

not dissimilar to the mass exponent b = 0.75, proposed by Kleiber (1961).

11.12 SCALING LONGITUDINAL DATA

In the previous sections we investigated the difference in peak power output between men and women having scaled for differences in lean leg volume; that is, by using lean leg volume as a covariate. The study was a cross-sectional design since the participants – physical education and sports studies students in their early twenties – were measured on one occasion. To identify and separate the relative contribution of factors such as gender or physical activity from changes attributable to growth, maturation and ageing, 'growth' data should be collected longitudinally. An appropriate method for subsequent analysis is some form of multilevel modelling (Goldstein 1995; Rasbash and Woodhouse 1995).

Multilevel modelling is an extension of ordinary multiple regression where the data have a hierarchical or cluster structure. The hierarchy consists of units or measurements that are grouped at different levels. An example is repeated-measures data in which individuals are assessed on more than one occasion. Here, the individuals are assumed to be a random sample and represent level-two units; the participants' repeated measurements recorded at each visit are level-one units. In contrast to traditional repeated-measures analyses, visit occasions are modelled as a random variable over time for each participant. The two levels of random variation take account of the fact that growth or ageing characteristics of individual participants, such as their mean growth (or decay) rate, vary around a population mean, and also that each participant's observed measurements vary around his or her own growth (or decay) trajectory.

Adapting these methods, Nevill et al. (1998) fitted allometric models to the results of two studies: the first by Baxter-Jones et al. (1993) who investigated developmental changes in aerobic power of young athletes and the second by Round et al. (1999) who investigated developmental changes in the strength of school children from North London. Not only did the allometric models provide a superior fit than traditional ANCOVA methods, but also they provided a simpler and more plausible interpretation of the data. For example, in the first study, the body mass exponents for boys and girls were close to the anticipated theoretical values, $m^{2/3}$. Armstrong et al. (1999) confirmed the suitability of allometric multilevel modelling when describing longitudinal changes in peak oxygen uptake in 11- to 13-year-olds.

11.13 SUMMARY

Five simple points can be stated about techniques that partition out differences in body size:

1   The a priori use of ratio standards is incorrect. These standards should only be used when Tanner's (1949) special circumstance is satisfied.
2   Allometric modelling should be used to partial out differences in body size.
3   Allometric cascade might be a suitable technique to investigate energy expenditure and metabolism.
4   Non-isometric growth and development influences allometric relationships.
5   Multilevel modelling is useful in the analysis of longitudinal data.

APPENDIX A: ANALYSIS OF DATA IN TABLE 11.1 USING SPSS VERSION 15.0

1. Entering the data given in Table 11.1

1.1 Create three columns: gender, llv and OPP.
1.2 Code the men as 1 and the women as 2 in the gender column (column 1).
1.3 Put the llv data into column 2.
1.4 Put the OPP data into column 3.

This codes the data according to gender.

2. Splitting the data by gender

2.1 Single click Data on the menu bar.
2.2 Single click on Split File.
2.3 Single click on Compare groups.
2.4 Double click on gender so it is contained within the Groups Based on box.
2.5 Single click on OK.

This splits the data on the basis of gender.

3. Descriptives

3.1 Single click on Analyze on the tool bar.
3.2 Single click on Descriptive Statistics.
3.3 Single click on Descriptives.
3.4 Double click on variables OPP and LLV in the variable(s) box.
3.5 Single click on options.
3.6 Single click on S.E. Mean.
3.7 Single click on Continue.
3.8 Single click on OK.

This gives descriptive data for llv and OPP in the men and women. You should have values of (mean, SEM) 7.41, 0.14 l and 1007, 23 W for the men and 5.19, 0.12 l and 673, 16 W for the women.

Remember to remove the split after you have obtained the descriptives. Do this by:

3.9 Single click Data on the menubar
3.10 Single click on Split File.
3.11 Single click on 'Analyze all cases, do not compare groups.'

3.12 Single click on OK.

4. Calculate ratio standards

4.1 Single click Transform on the menu bar.
4.2 Single click on Compute Variable.
4.3 In the Target Variable box, type a name; e.g. Oppratio.
4.4 In the Numeric Expression box type OPP/llv.
4.5 Single click on OK.

This calculates simple ratio standards OPP/llv in the men and women.

5. Recoding the gender variable

5.1 Single click on Transform on the menu bar.
5.2 Single click on Compute Variable.
5.3 In the Target Variable box, type gender.
5.4 In the Numeric Expression Box type 1.
5.5 Single click on If ...
5.6 Single click on 'Include if case satisfies condition'.
5.7 Type gender=1 in the dialogue box.
5.8 Single click on continue.
5.9 Single click on OK.
5.10 Repeat steps above (5.1–5.9), but this time at step 5.4 type 0 in Numeric Expression, and at step 5.7 type gender =2 in the dialogue box.

This recoding is necessary for the regression and ANCOVA analyses

6. Using ANOVA to compare the ratio standards

6.1 Single click on Analyze in the menu bar.
6.2 Single click on Compare Means.
6.3 Single click on One-way ANOVA.
6.4 Put Oppratio into the Dependent Box and gender into the Factor Box.
6.5 Single click on Options.
6.6 Single click in the Descriptive and Homogeneity of variance check box.

6.7 Single click on Continue
6.8 Single click on OK.

This should give (mean, SEM) 136, 3 W.l⁻¹ for the men and 131, 3 W.l⁻¹ for the women (P = 0.206).

7. Creating gender interaction

7.1 Single click Transform on the menu bar.
7.2 Single click on Compute Variable.
7.3 Remove the If ... command that created the gender variable by single clicking on 'If ...' and then single clicking on 'Include all cases'. Single click on Continue.
7.4 In the Target Variable box, type gender_llv.
7.5 In the Numeric expression box, type gender*llv
7.6 Single click on OK.

This might seem to be curious but we will use this interaction to compare the gradients of the regression lines.

8. Testing interaction

8.1 Single click on Analyze in the menu bar.
8.2 Single click on Regression.
8.3 Single click on Linear
8.4 Put llv, gender and gender_llv into the Independent box.
8.5 Put opp in the Dependent box.
8.6 Single click OK.

You should see that the interaction term – gender × llv – does not make a significant contribution to the regression equation (P = 0.233) and, hence, the need for separate slopes for the male and female covariates (llv) can be rejected.

9. Regression

9.1 Single click on Analyze in the menu bar.
9.2 Single click on Regression.
9.3 Single click on Linear.
9.4 Put llv and gender into the Independent box (put gender*llv back into the variable list).
9.5 Put opp in the dependent box.
9.6 Single click on OK.

This regression analysis is, in effect, an analysis of covariance that identifies both the covariate – llv – and the gender main effect as highly significant (P < 0.001) in both cases. This result can be confirmed using the SPSS ANCOVA commands as follows:

10. ANCOVA (Linear)

10.1 Single click on Analyze in the menu bar.
10.2 Single click on General Linear Model.
10.3 Single click on Univariate...
10.4 Put opp in the Dependent Variable box.
10.5 Put gender into the Fixed Factor(s) box.
10.6 Put llv into the Covariate(s) box.
10.7 Single click on options.
10.8 Include gender in the Display Means For box.
10.9 Single click on Continue.
10.10 Single click on OK.

This completes the analysis and calculates adjusted means; i.e. values for opp adjusted for differences in llv. The values should be (mean, SEM) 748, 19 W for the women and 902, 24 W for the men (P < 0.001).

APPENDIX B

1. Log transformation

1.1 Single click on Transform in the menu bar.
1.2 Single click on Compute Variable.
1.3 In the Target Variable box, type lnllv.
1.4 In the Numeric Expression box type LN(llv).
1.5 Single click on OK.

This takes the natural logarithm of llv and creates an lnllv column.

2. Repeat for OPP

Similarly, this takes the natural logarithm of opp and creates an lnopp column.

3. Creating gender interaction

3.1 Single click Transform on the menu bar.
3.2 Single click on Compute Variable.
3.3 In the Target Variable box, type gender_lnllv.
3.4 In the Numeric Expression box, type gender*lnllv.
3.5 Single click on OK.

*As before, this creates a variable – gender*lnllv – that can be used to test for interaction.*

4. Testing interaction

4.1 Single click on Analyze in the menu bar.
4.2 Single click on Regression.
4.3 Single click on Linear.
4.4 Put lnllv, gender and gender_lnllv into the independent box.
4.5 Put lnopp in the Dependent box.
4.6 Single click on OK.

As with the raw variables, you should see that the interaction term – gender × lnllv – does not make a significant contribution to the regression equation ($P = 0.515$) and, hence, the need for separate slopes for the male and female covariates (lnllv) can be rejected. A common slope can be used.

5. Regression

5.1 Repeat 4 above but remove gender_lnllv from the Independent box.

Again as before, this analysis is equivalent to an analysis of covariance and there is a main effect both for the covariate lnllv and gender ($P < 0.001$). The analysis also identifies the allometric models that describe the relationship between OPP and lnLLV for the men and women. By taking antilogs of the constant (5.475) and the constant plus the gender indicator variable (5.475 + 0.182

= 5.657), the constant multipliers – a – for the men (286.3) and the women (238.7) are obtained. Note that b, the common gradient and hence exponent in the allometric model is also obtained (0.626). So, in the men, OPP = $286.3 \times llv^{0.626}$ and in the women, OPP = $238.7 \times llv^{0.626}$.

6. ANCOVA (Log-linear)

6.1 Single click on Analyze in the menu bar.
6.2 Single click on General Linear Model.
6.3 Single click on Univariate …
6.4 Put lnopp in the Dependent Variable box.
6.5 Put gender into the Fixed Factor(s) box.
6.6 Put lnllv into the Covariate(s) box.
6.7 Single click on Options.
6.8 Include gender in the Display Means For box.
6.9 Single click on Continue.
7.0 Single click on OK.

Simply by taking the antilogarithms of the two adjusted means (6.775 for the men and 6.593 for the women), the difference between the men's peak power output (876 W) and women's (730 W) is obtained, adjusted for differences in lean leg volume. Note that if we divide these two adjusted means by the antilogarithm of the mean lnllv for all 81 participants – 5.97 l – raised to the power 0.626 i.e. $5.97^{0.626} = 3.060$ we obtain the mean power function ratio standards for the women, 239 $W.l^{0.626}$, and the men, 286 $W.l^{0.626}$ as derived earlier.

ACKNOWLEDGEMENT

We are grateful to Patrick Johnson and Ann Rowlands for their help with the descriptions of the statistical analyses (SPSS Version 15.0) given in Appendices A and B.

FURTHER READING

Books

Winter E. M. (2007) Scaling: adjusting physiological and performance measures for differences in body size. In: (E. M. Winter, A. M. Jones, R. C. R. Davison, P. D. Bromley and T. H. Mercer, eds) *Sport and Exercise Physiology Testing Guidelines Volume One: Sport Testing*. Oxon; Oxford.

Winter E. M., Jones A. M., Davison R. C. R., Bromley P. D. and Mercer T. H. (2007) *Sport and Exercise Physiology Testing Guidelines Volume Two: Exercise and Clinical Testing*. Routledge; Oxon.

Journal articles

Nevill A. M., Brown D., Godfrey R., Johnson P. L., Romer L., Stewart A. D. and Winter E. M. (2003) Modelling maximum oxygen uptake of elite endurance athletes. *Medicine and Science in Sports and Exercise*; 35: 488–94.

Welsman J., Armstrong N., Nevill A., Winter E. M. and Kirby B. (1996) Scaling peak O2 for differences in body size. *Medicine and Science in Sports and Exercise*; 28: 259–65.

Website

International Society for the Advancement of Kinanthropometry http://www.isakonline.com/

REFERENCES

Armstrong N., Kirby B. J., Welsman J. R., and McManus A. M. (1997) Submaximal exercise in prepubertal children. In: (N. Armstrong, B. J. Kirby and J. R. Welsman, eds) *Children and Exercise XIX: Promoting Health and Well-Being*. E. and F. N. Spon; London: pp. 221–7.

Armstrong N., Welsman J. R., Kirby B. J. and Nevill A. M. (1999) Longitudinal changes in young people's peak oxygen uptake. *Journal of Applied Physiology*; 87: 2230–6.

Åstrand P-O., Rodahl K., Dahl H. A. and Strømme S. B. (2003) *Textbook of Work Physiology*; 4th Edition. Human Kinetics; Champaign, IL.

Batterham A. M. and Jackson A. S. (2003) Validity of the allometric cascade model at submaximal and maximal metabolic rates in exercising men. *Respiratory Physiology and Neurobiology*; 135: 103–6.

Batterham A. M., Tolfrey K. and George K. P. (1997) Nevill's explanation of Kleiber's 0.75 mass exponent: an artifact of collinearity problems in least squares models? *Journal of Applied Physiology*; 82: 693–7.

Baxter-Jones A., Goldstein H. and Helms P. (1993) The development of aerobic power in young athletes. *Journal of Applied Physiology*; 75: 1160–7.

D'Arcy-Thompson W. (1917) *Growth and Form*. Cambridge University Press; Cambridge.

Darveau C. A., Suarez R.K., Andrews R. D. and Hochachka P. W. (2002) Allometric cascade as a unifying principle of body mass effects on metabolism. *Nature*; 417: 166–70.

Eston R. G., Robson S. and Winter E.M. (1993) A comparison of oxygen uptake during running in children and adults. In: (W. Duquet and J. A. P Day, eds) *Kinanthropometry IV*. E. & F. N. Spon; London: pp. 236–41.

Eston R. G., Winter E. and Baltzopoulos V. (1997) Ratio standards and allometric modelling to scale peak power output for differences in lean upper leg volume in men and women. *Journal of Sports Sciences*; 15: 29.

Goldstein H. (1995) *Multilevel Statistical Models*. 2nd Edition. Edward Arnold; London.

Huxley J. S. (1932) *Problems of Relative Growth*. Dial; New York.

Jakeman P. M., Winter E. M. and Doust J. (1994) A review of research in sports physiology. *Journal of Sports Sciences*; 12: 33–60.

Johnson P. J., Winter E. M., Paterson D. H., Koval J. Nevill A. M. and Cunningham D.A. (2000) Modelling the influence of age, body size and sex on maximum oxygen uptake in older humans. *Experimental Physiology*; 85: 219–25.

Katch V. (1973) The use of oxygen/body weight ratio in correlational analyses: spurious correlations and statistical considerations. *Medicine and Science in Sports and Exercise*; 5: 253–7.

Kermack K. A. and Haldane J. B. S. (1950) Organic correlation and allometry. *Biometrika*; 37: 30–41.

Kleiber M. (1961) *The Fire of Life*. John Wiley & Sons Inc.; New York & London.

MacDougall J. D., Wenger H. A. and Green H. J.

(eds) (1991) *Physiological Testing of the High-Performance Athlete*. 2nd Edition. Human Kinetics; Champaign, IL.

McMahon T. (1973) Size and shape in biology. *Science*; **179**: 1201–4.

Nevill A. M. (1994) The need to scale for differences in body size and mass: an explanation of Kleiber's 0·75 exponent. *Journal of Applied Physiology*; **77**: 2870–3.

Nevill A. M. and Bate S. (2005) Allometric cascade model and metabolic rate. [Letter to the Editor] *Respiratory Physiology and Neurobiology*; **146**: 1–2.

Nevill A. M. and Holder R. L. (1994) Modelling maximum oxygen uptake: a case-study in non-linear regression model formulation and comparison. *Applied Statistics*; **43**: 653–66.

Nevill A. M., Ramsbottom R. and Williams C. (1992a) Scaling physiological measurements for individuals of different body size. *European Journal of Applied Physiology*; **65**: 110–17.

Nevill A. M., Ramsbottom R., Williams C. and Winter E. M. (1992b) Scaling individuals of different body size. *Journal of Sports Sciences*; **9**: 427–8.

Nevill A. M., Stewart A. D., Olds T. and Holder R. L. (2004) Are adult physiques geometrically similar? The dangers of allometric scaling using body mass power laws. *American Journal of Physical Anthropology*; **124**: 177–82.

Nevill A. M., Holder R. L., Baxter-Jones A., Round J. and Jones D. A. (1998) Modeling developmental changes in strength and aerobic power in children. *Journal of Applied Physiology*; **84**: 963–70.

Nevill A. M., Brown D., Godfrey R., Johnson P. J., Romer L., Stewart A. D. and Winter E. M. (2003) Modeling maximum oxygen uptake of elite athletes. *Medicine and Science in Sports and Exercise*; **35**: 488–94.

Norusis M. J. (1992) *SPSS for Windows Advanced Statistics Release 5*. SPSS, Chicago.

Packard G. J. and Boardman T. J. (1987) The misuse of ratios to scale physiological data that vary allometrically with body size. In: (M. E. Feder, A. F. Bennett, W. W. Burggren and R. B. Huey, eds) *New Directions in Ecological Physiology*. Cambridge University Press; Cambridge: pp. 216–39.

Rasbash J. and Woodhouse G. (1995) *MLn Command Reference*. Multilevel Models Project, Institute of Education; London.

Rayner J. M. V. (1985) Linear relations in biomechanics: the statistics of scaling functions. *Journal of Zoology* (London) Series A. **206**: 415–39.

Ricker W. E. (1973) Linear regression in fishery research. *Journal of Fisheries Research Board Canada*; **30**: 409–34.

Round J. M., Jones D. A., Honour J. W. and Nevill A. M. (1999) Hormonal factors in the development of differences in strength between boys and girls during adolescence: a longitudinal study. *Annals of Human Biology*; **26**: 49–62.

Sarrus F. and Rameaux J. (1838) *Bulletin de l'Academie Royal de Medecine, Paris*; **3**: 1094–1100.

Schmidt-Nielsen K. (1984) *Scaling: Why is animal size so important?* Cambridge University Press; Cambridge.

Sholl D. (1948) The quantitative investigation of the vertebrate brain and the applicability of allometric formulae to its study. *Proceedings of the Royal Society Series B*; **35**: 243–57.

Snedecor G. W. and Cochran W. G. (1989) *Statistical Methods*. 8th Edition. Iowa State Press; Ames, IA.

Sokal R. R. and Rohlf F. J. (1995) *Biometry*. 3rd Edition. W.H. Freeman and Company; New York.

Tabachnick B. G. and Fidell L. S. (2007) *Using Multivariate Statistics*. 5th Edition. Allyn and Bacon; Boston, MA.

Tanner J. M. (1949) Fallacy of per-weight and per-surface area standards and their relation to spurious correlation. *Journal of Applied Physiology*; **2**: 1–15.

Tanner J. M. (1964) *The Physique of the Olympic Athlete*. George, Allen and Unwin; London.

Tanner J. M. (1989) *Foetus into Man*. 2nd Edition. Castlemead Publications; Ware, UK.

Winter E. M. (1992) Scaling: partitioning out differences in size. *Pediatric Exercise Science*; **4**: 296–301.

Winter E. M. (1996) Importance and principles of scaling for size differences. In: (O. Bar-Or, ed) *The Child and Adolescent Athlete*. Blackwell; Oxford: pp. 673–9.

Winter E. M., Brookes F. B. C. and Hamley E. J. (1991) Maximal exercise performance and lean leg volume in men and women. *Journal of Sports Sciences*; **9**: 3–13.

Winter E. M. and Brooks G. A. (2007) From Euclid to molecular biology and gene expression: where now for allometric modeling? *Exercise and Sport Science Reviews*; 35: 83–4.

Winter E. M. and Maughan R. J. (1991) Strength and cross-sectional area of the quadriceps in men and women. *Journal of Physiology*; 43 (Suppl): 175P.

INDEX